ORDNANCE SURVEY MEMOIRS OF IRELAND

Volume Thirty-Seven

PARISHES OF COUNTY ANTRIM XIV
1832, 1839–40

Published 1996.
The Institute of Irish Studies,
The Queen's University of Belfast,
Belfast.
In association with
The Royal Irish Academy,
Dawson Street,
Dublin.

Reprinted 2021 by Ulster Historical Foundation

Grateful acknowledgement is made to the Economic and Social Research Council and
the Department of Education for Northern Ireland for their financial assistance at different
stages of this publication programme.

We would also like to thank Carrickfergus Borough Council for their support of this volume.

British Library Cataloguing-in-Publication Data.
A catalogue record for this book is available from the British Library.

Paperback ISBN 13: 978-0-85389-562-6
Hardback ISBN 13: 978-0-85389-563-3

Printed in Ireland by SPRINT-print Ltd.

Ordnance Survey Memoirs of Ireland
VOLUME THIRTY-SEVEN

Parishes of County Antrim XIV
1832, 1839–40

Carrickfergus

Edited by Angélique Day and Patrick McWilliams

The Institute of Irish Studies
in association with
The Royal Irish Academy

ACKNOWLEDGEMENTS

During the course of the transcription and publication project many have advised and encouraged us in this gigantic task. Thanks must first be given to the Royal Irish Academy which has made available to us the original manuscripts. We are also greatly indebted to Librarian Siobhán O'Rafferty and her staff for their continuing help in deciphering indistinct passages of manuscript.

We should like to acknowledge the following individuals for their special contributions. Dr Brian Trainor led the way with his edition of the Antrim Memoir and provided vital help on the steering committee. Dr Ann Hamlin also provided valuable support, especially during the most trying stages of the project. Professor R.H. Buchanan's unfailing encouragement has been instrumental in the development of the project to the present. Without Dr Kieran Devine the initial stages of the transcription and the computerising work would never have been completed successfully: the project owes a great deal to his constant help and advice. Dr Kay Muhr's continuing contribution to the work of the transcription project is deeply appreciated, as is that of former editor Nóirín Dobson. Mr W.C. Kerr's interest and expertise have been invaluable. Professor Anne Crookshank and Dr Edward McParland were most generous with practical help and advice concerning the drawings amongst the Memoir manuscripts.

We would like to thank the Director of the Ordnance Survey, Dublin and the keepers of the fireproof store, among them Leonard Hines. All students of the nineteenth-century Ordnance Survey of Ireland owe a great deal to the pioneering work of Professor J.H. Andrews, and his kind help in the first days of the project is gratefully recorded. We acknowledge gratefully the help of a transcription prepared by a local group in Carrickfergus which was co-ordinated by Sean Neeson and supervised by the late Sean McMenamin, and we would like to thank Doreen Corcoran of the Carrickfergus Historical Society for her help and support.

The essential task of inputting the texts from audio tapes was done by Miss Eileen Kingan, Mrs Christine Robertson, Miss Eilis Smyth, Miss Lynn Murray and, most importantly, Miss Maureen Carr.

We are grateful to the Linen Hall Library for lending us their copies of the first edition 6" Ordnance Survey Maps: also to Ms Maura Pringle of QUB Cartography Department for the index maps showing the parish boundaries. For providing financial assistance at crucial times for the maintenance of the project, we would like to take this opportunity of thanking the trustees of the Esme Mitchell trust and The Public Record Office of Northern Ireland.

Right:
Map of parishes of County Antrim. The area described in this volume, the parish of Carrickfergus, has been shaded to highlight its location. The square grids represent the 1830s 6" Ordnance Survey maps. The encircled numbers relate to the map numbers as presented in the bound volumes of maps for the county. The parishes have been numbered in all cases and named in full where possible, except those in the following list: Aghagallon 1, Aghalee 2, Ballyclug 9, Ballycor 10, Ballylinny 11, Ballymartin 12, Ballynure 14, Ballyrashane 15, Grange of Ballyrobert 16, Grange of Ballyscullion 17, Grange of Ballywalter 18, Ballywillin 19, Blaris and Lisburn 21 & 60, Grange of Carmavy 23, Carncastle 24, Carnmoney 25, Cranfield 28, Derryaghy 30, Derrykeighan 31, Grange of Doagh 32, Donegore 33, Drumbeg 34, Grange of Drumtullagh 36, Dunaghy 37, Grange of Dundermot 38, Dunluce 40, Glynn 44, Inver 46, Island Magee 47, Kilbride 48, Killagan 49, Grange of Killyglen 51, Kilraghts 52, Kilroot 53, Kilwaughter 54, Kirkinriola 55, Lambeg 56, Larne 57, Granges of Layd and Inispollan 59 & 45, Magheragall 62, Magheramesk 63, Mallusk 64, Grange of Muckamore 65, Newtown Crommelin 67, Grange of Nilteen 68, Rashee 73, Rathlin Island 74, Grange of Shilvodan 75, Templecorran 77, Templepatrick 78, Tickmacrevan 79, Tullyrusk 81, Umgall 82.

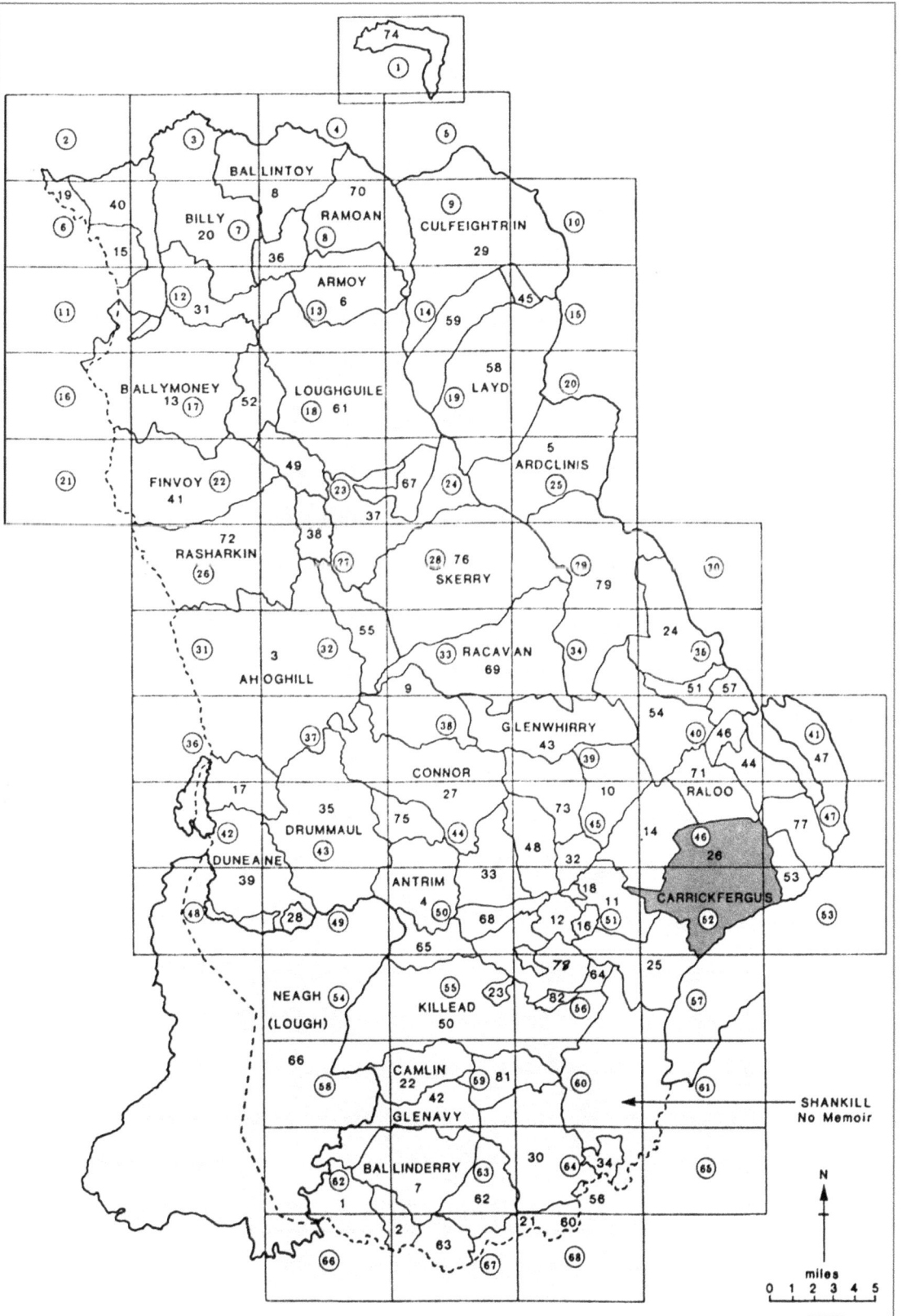

74

1

2 3 4 5

BALLINTOY

19 40 8 70

BILLY RAMOAN 9

6 20 7 8 CULFEIGHTRIN 10

15 36 29

ARMOY

11 12 31 13 6 14 59 45 15

58

BALLYMONEY LOUGHGUILE LAYD 20

16 13 17 52 18 61 19

5

21 FINVOY 22 49 ARDCLINIS

41 23 67 24 25

37

72 38

RASHARKIN 27 28 76 79

26 SKERRY 79

55 24

31 3 32 33 RACAVAN 34 35

AHOGHILL 69 51 57

9

54

36 37 38 GLENWHIRRY 40 46 41

43 39 44 47

17 CONNOR 71 47

35 75 27 73 10 RALOO

42 DRUMMAUL 44 45 14 77

43 48 32 46

DUNEANE 39 33 18 26

48 28 49 ANTRIM 50 68 11 CARRICKFERGUS 53

4 50 12 16 51 52 53

65

79 64 25

NEAGH 54 55 23 82 57

KILLEAD 82 56

(LOUGH) 50

66 CAMLIN 59 81 60 61

58 22 42 SHANKILL

GLENAVY No Memoir

30 64 34 65

BALLINDERRY 63

62 7 62 56

1

2 21 60

63 67 68

66

miles

N

0 1 2 3 4 5

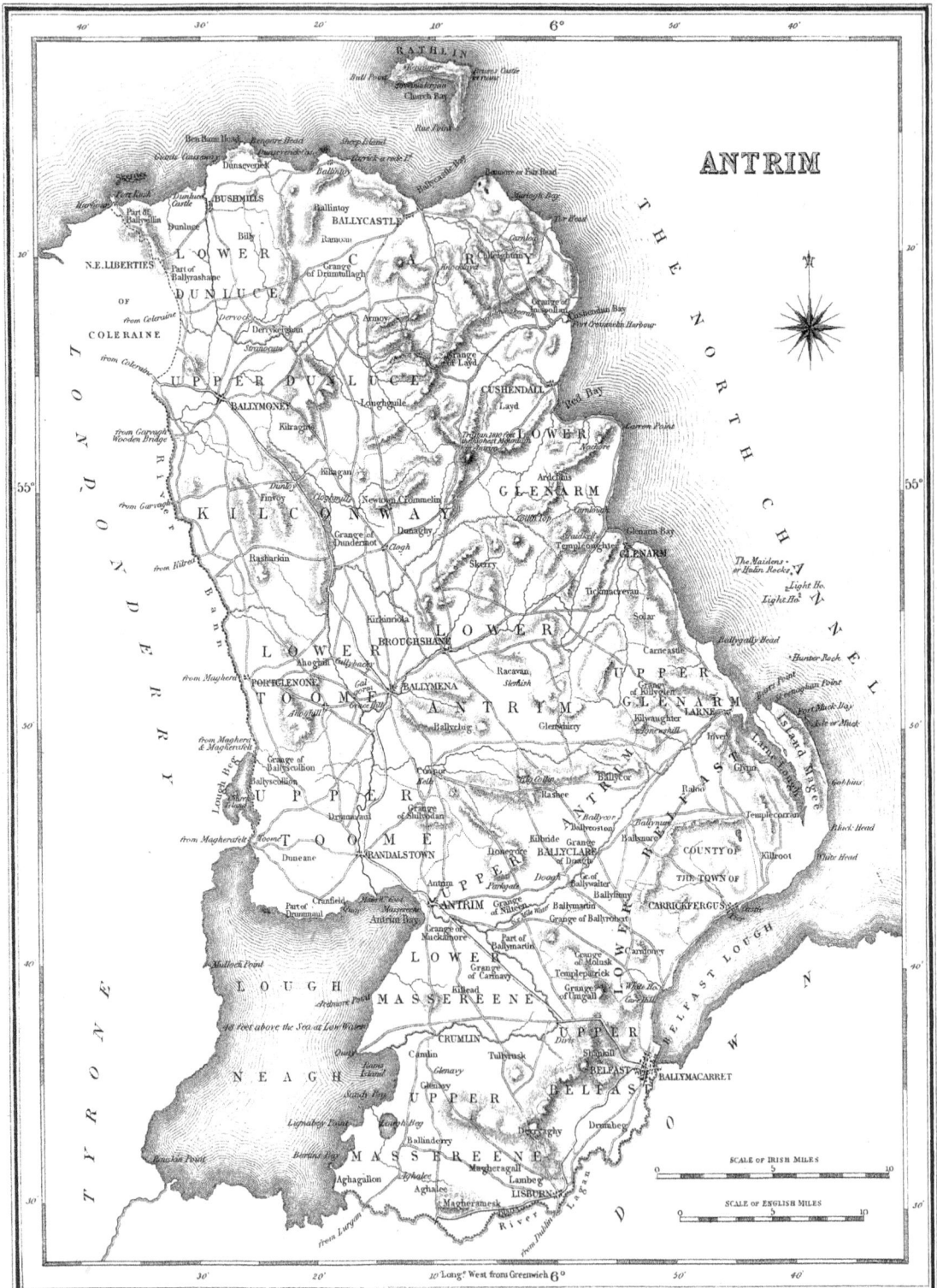

Map of County Antrim, from Samuel Lewis' *Atlas of the counties of Ireland* (London, 1837)

CONTENTS

List of selected maps and drawings

INTRODUCTION AND GUIDE TO THE PUBLICATION OF THE
ORDNANCE SURVEY MEMOIRS

The following text of the Ordnance Survey Memoirs was first transcribed by a team working in the Institute of Irish Studies at The Queen's University of Belfast, on a computerised index of the material. For this publication programme the text has been further edited: spellings have been modernised in most cases, although where the original spelling was thought to be of any interest it has been retained and is indicated by angle brackets in the text. Variant spellings for townland and lesser place-names have been preserved, although parish and major place-names have been standardised and the original spelling given in angle brackets. Names of prominent people, for instance landlords, have been standardised where possible, but original spellings of names in lists of informants, emigration tables and on tombstones have been retained. We have not altered the Memoir writers' anglicisation of names and words in Irish.

Punctuation has been modernised and is the responsibility of the editors. Editorial additions are indicated by square brackets: a question mark before and after a word indicates a queried reading and tentatively inserted information respectively. Original drawings are referred to in the text, and some have been reproduced. Manuscript page references have been omitted from this series. Because of the huge variation in size of Memoirs for different counties, the following editorial policy has been adopted: where there are numerous duplicating and overlapping accounts, the most complete and finished account, normally the Memoir proper, has been presented, with additional unique information from other accounts like the Fair Sheets entered into a separate section, clearly titled and identified; where the Memoir material is less, nothing has been omitted. To achieve standard volume size, parishes have been associated on the basis of propinquity.

There are considerable differences in the volume of information recorded for different areas: counties Antrim and Londonderry are exceptionally well covered, while the other counties do not have quite the same detail. This series is the first systematic publication of the parish Memoirs, although individual parishes have been published by pioneering local history societies. The entire transcriptions of the Memoirs made in the course of the indexing project can be consulted in the Public Record Office of Northern Ireland and the library at the Queen's University of Belfast. The manuscripts of the Ordnance Survey Memoirs are in the Royal Irish Academy, Dublin.

Brief history of the Irish Ordnance Survey in the nineteenth century and the
writing of the Ordnance Survey Memoirs.

In 1824 a House of Commons committee recommended a townland survey of Ireland with maps at the scale of 6," to facilitate a uniform valuation for local taxation. The Duke of Wellington, then prime minister, authorised this, the first Ordnance Survey of Ireland. The survey was directed by Colonel Thomas Colby, who had under his command officers of the Royal Engineers and three companies of sappers and miners. In addition to this, civil assistants were recruited to help with sketching, drawing and engraving of maps, and eventually, in the 1830s, the writing of the Memoirs.

The Memoirs were written descriptions intended to accompany the maps, containing information which could not be fitted on to them. Colonel Colby always considered additional information to be necessary to clarify place-names and other distinctive features of each parish; this was to be written up in reports by the officers. Much information about parishes resulted from research into place-names and was used in the writing of the Memoirs. The term "Memoir" comes from the abbreviation of the word "Aide-Memoire." It was also used in the 18th century to describe topographical descriptions accompanying maps. [In 1833 Colby's assistant, Lieutenant Thomas Larcom, developed the scope of the officers' reports by stipulating the headings or "Heads of Inquiry" under which information was to be reported, and including topics of social as well as economic interest. By this time civil assistants were writing some of the Memoirs under the supervision of the officers, as well as collecting information in the Fair Sheets.

The first "Memoirs" are officers' reports covering Antrim in 1830, and work continued on the Antrim parishes right through the decade, with special activity in 1838 and 1839. Counties Down and Tyrone were written up from 1833 to 1837, with both officers and civil assistants working on Memoirs. In Londonderry and Fermanagh research and writing started in 1834. Armagh was worked on in 1835, 1837 and 1838. Much labour was expended in the Londonderry parishes. The plans to publish the Memoirs commenced with the parish of Templemore, containing the city and liberties of Derry, which came out in 1837 after a great deal of expense and effort.

Between 1839 and 1840 the Memoir scheme collapsed. Sir Robert Peel's government could not countenance the expenditure of money and time on such an exercise; despite a parliamentary commission favouring the continuation of the writing of the Memoirs, the scheme was halted before the southern half of the country was covered. The manuscripts remained unpublished and most were removed to the Royal Irish Academy, Dublin from the Ordnance Survey, Phoenix Park. Other records of the Ordnance Survey, including some material from the Memoir scheme, have recently been transferred to the National Archives, Bishop Street, Dublin.

The Memoirs are a uniquely detailed source for the history of the northern half of Ireland immediately before the Great Famine. They document the landscape and situation, buildings and antiquities, land-holdings and population, employment and livelihood of the parishes. They act as a nineteenth-century Domesday book and are essential to the understanding of the cultural heritage of our communities. It is planned to produce a volume of evaluative essays to put the material in its full context, with information on other sources and on the writers of the Memoirs.

Definition of descriptive terms

Memoir (sometimes Statistical Memoir): an account of a parish written according to the prescribed form outlined in the instructions known as "Heads of Inquiry," and normally divided into three sections: Natural Features and History; Modern and Ancient Topography; Social and Productive Economy.

Fair Sheets: "information gathered for the Memoirs," an original title describing paragraphs of information following no particular order, often with marginal headings, signed and dated by the civil assistant responsible.

Statistical Remarks/Accounts: both titles are employed by the Engineer officers in their descriptions of the parish with marginal headings, often similar in layout to the Memoir.

Office Copies: these are copies of early drafts, generally officers' accounts and must have been made for office purposes.

Ordnance Survey Memoirs for County Antrim

This volume, the fourteenth and final for the county and the thirty-seventh in the series, contains the Memoir for the county of the town of Carrickfergus. The manuscript account is one of the largest Memoirs extant for any part of the country bar

Templemore, county Londonderry, which was the only Memoir published at the time of the 19th century Ordnance Survey.

During the course of proof-reading and editing this transcription, it became clear that major editorial work would be necessary to bring this volume into line with others already published. It comprises a complete account, numbering 5 volumes and an appendix of manuscript material, by the most prolific Memoir writer James Boyle, prepared in the latter part of 1839 and finished in 1840 when the Memoir scheme was drawing to a halt.

In addition, there is a complete set of Fair Sheets prepared by John Bleakly on criminal statistics and containing other Social Economy information incorporated by Boyle in his appendices, as well as Fair Sheets by the other experienced assistant Thomas Fagan, who collected source material mostly relating to Modern and Ancient Topography. This wealth of material points to the unique history of Carrickfergus with its Norman castle, its strategic position on Belfast Lough, its long urban history and influence on the surrounding countryside, and its relation to the fast-growing, industrialising town and region of Belfast.

The editors have reluctantly decided to present only material that derived directly from the observations and researches of the Memoir team when in the parish in the 1830s. While it is clear that Boyle and his colleagues met with Samuel McSkimin, and relied on his authority and his famous work *The history of Carrickfergus* for writing-up their reports, the former's close adherence to McSkimin for the history of the town and corporation has led the editors to omit this historical narrative of the town. Therefore readers interested in this are recommended to consult McSkimin. All references to Carrickfergus' development from 1800 onwards remain, though pressure of space does not allow a meteorological register to be included here.

With the above exception, the editors have chosen to preserve Boyle's account, omitting only school statistics which were covered in more lively detail by Bleakly. Despite the restrictions of space, as many extracts as possible from the Fair Sheets are presented here, both because of their unique information (for example Fagan's record of the soldier deserters in the prison) and for their incomparable style. The Fair Sheets, which have been arranged according to the subject headings of Larcom's Heads of Inquiry, also include lists of informants, which not only gives a fascinating glimpse into the methodology used by the Memoir writers but also casts light on individuals and society in Carrickfergus of the early 19th century

An enormous effort went into the preparation and writing of the Memoirs at this very late stage of the Memoir scheme, when its very future as part of the Ordnance Survey was being questioned. As well, some fine drawings illustrating the locality were accomplished, complete with a record of hours spent sketching, all of which provides a valuable record of time taken to reach such standards of excellence.

This transcription of the Memoir has its origins in that prepared by a local group from Carrickfergus organised by Sean Neeson and the late Sean McMenamin. The editorial team would like to pay tribute to all those concerned in this magnificent labour and also the support and interest shown by members of the Carrickfergus Historical Society, particularly Doreen Corcoran, who made this work available to us at a later date.

Drawings in the Memoir papers are listed below and are cross-referenced in the text; some are illustrated. The manuscript material is to be found in Boxes 7 and 8 of the Royal Irish Academy's collection of Ordnance Survey Memoirs, and section references are given beside each parish below in their printed order.

Box 8 I 5, Box 7 I 5, Box 8 I 1, Box 7 I 3, Box 8 I 2, 6, 4

The following sections have been omitted in their entirety:
Box 7 I 1, 2, 4, 6, Box 8 I 3

Drawings

(Box 7 I 3):

Plan of Carrickfergus in 1550 [illustrated]; plan of Carrickfergus within the walls, with scale.

Plan and drawing of Carrickfergus by John Dunstall, 1612, with annotations.

View of castle from Scotch Quarter [illustrated].

Castle: window on east side; entrance to sally-port; ornamental stone in east half-moon; window in magazine yard; 2 arrow-slits in tower; window in tower; stones drawn to scale, 1 inch to 4 feet.

Window in the east half-moon, with scale.

Interior of gateway of castle.

2 windows in Carrickfergus church, with scale.

Stone face in east gable of church [illustrated]; stone cross in church [illustrated].

Ancient seal of Mayor of Carrickfergus.

Common seal of Carrickfergus [illustrated].

Seal of port of Carrickfergus.

Specimens of masonry of Duncrue church, with scale.

Druidical altar.

Druidical altar with man and stick [illustrated].

Druidical altar.

Plans and sections of 3 forts, with scale.

Plans and sections of 7 forts, with scale.

Plans with section of 7 tumuli.

Plan and section of a fort and cove, with scale.

Enclosures near Friar's Glen, with scale.

Iron spear, iron instrument, iron blade from Troopers Land.

Mould from Troopers Land, with key and dimensions; stone amulet.

2 wooden methers with dimensions [illustrated].

Wooden vessel, with dimensions.

Brazen cup; stone amulet; brazen pin [illustrated]; rings of armour, iron ring, 2 brazen rings from Troopers Land.

Brazen instrument found near Great Patrick [illustrated]; cup from Troopers Land all by James Boyle].

(Box 8 I 6):

Great Patrick copied from plan in McSkimin's history.

Plan of cave in West Division, with dimensions.

Outline of steel weapon in West Division.

Stone mould with annotation.

Holestone.

Arrow or spearhead from Troopers Land.

Horn amulet, steel ring and brass ring from Troopers Land.

Brass cup found near the Knockagh.

Copper article found near Great Patrick [all by Thomas Fagan].

Parish of Carrickfergus, County Antrim

Statistical Return by Lieutenant C.H. Mallock,
April 1832

NATURAL STATE

Locality

Carrickfergus and Knockfergus in the charters of
James and of Elizabeth are indiscriminately
applied in mentioning the town, but
Carrickfergus is now the name that is always
used.

It is situated in the half-barony of Lower
Belfast, on the south east border of the county of
Carrickfergus.

It is bounded on the north by the parishes of
Ballynure and Raloo, on the south by Belfast
Lough, on the east by the parishes of Kilroot and
Templecorran or Broadisland, on the west by the
parishes of Ballynure, Ballylinny and
Carnmoney. It extends from north to south about
5 miles and from east to west about 6; it contains
16,709 acres.

It is divided into 5 [divisions], almost the whole
of which are the property of the Donegall family,
at least nominally but not in reality as, from the
leases in perpetuity under which the land is generally held by the present occupants, they may
almost be considered as the actual proprietors.
One of the divisions, named the Commons, may
be considered as belonging to the freemen of the
corporation, all of whom have the right of pas-
turing their cattle on the Commons and also the
right of turbary.

NATURAL FEATURES AND NATURAL HISTORY

Surface and Soil

From the sea-shore to the distance of about 2
miles the land rises very gradually, then for about
a mile and a half the hills become much steeper
till, coming upon the Commons, which are about
800 or 900 feet above the sea; then for about a
mile or a mile and [a] half the ground is nearly
flat and almost the whole of it is either bog or
mountain pasture; then the land slopes very gradually off to the north and from the boundary of
the Commons is all enclosed, but cultivation
appears almost in its infancy.

At the south east corner of the parish the flat
ground does not extend much more than a mile
from the shore and is terminated by the sudden
rise of a ridge of rocks called the Knocker. This
ridge rises to the height of 900 feet, in many
places almost perpendicular but in all parts,
except at the east extremity, may be said to be
inaccessible.

The Knocker ridge is one of the most remarkable features on this shore of the Belfast Lough.
It extends from the county boundary in an easterly direction for about 1 mile and [a] half, being
almost parallel to the lough shore. The general
appearance of the country, until coming to the
high ground, is that of a thriving and rich district,
there being a number of good houses, plantations
and high chimneys of manufactories appearing at
different points. All the lower part of the land is
good and well cultivated.

Produce and Turbary

Oats, potatoes, barley, wheat and flax are all cultivated, the 3 last but in small quantities.

There is a great extent of mountain and bog
ground, but only patches here and there that are
good for fuel.

Limestone and Minerals

Limestone is found in 2 or 3 places on the
Commons, but the hills from Carrickfergus to the
points where it might be obtained are so exceedingly steep that the quarries are not much worked.
The lime in the adjoining parishes is of a better
quality and obtained with less labour.

Minerals: I do not know of any having been
found. Gypsum is found in beds of considerable
extent on the lough shore, at a little depth below
the surface.

MODERN TOPOGRAPHY

Towns and Villages

The only town is that of Carrickfergus, which is
a borough and enjoys several privileges, amongst
others the third part of all customs of goods
imported or exported between Fair Head,county
Antrim and Beerlooms, county Down, but this
privilege has been sold by the corportion.

Carrickfergus returns 1 member who is elected
by the freemen, of whom there are about 1,000
or 1,200. Notwithstanding this large number,
until of late years the borough has generally been
considered as a close one, and the property of the
Donegall family. At present a strong party are
making head against the Donegall family. The

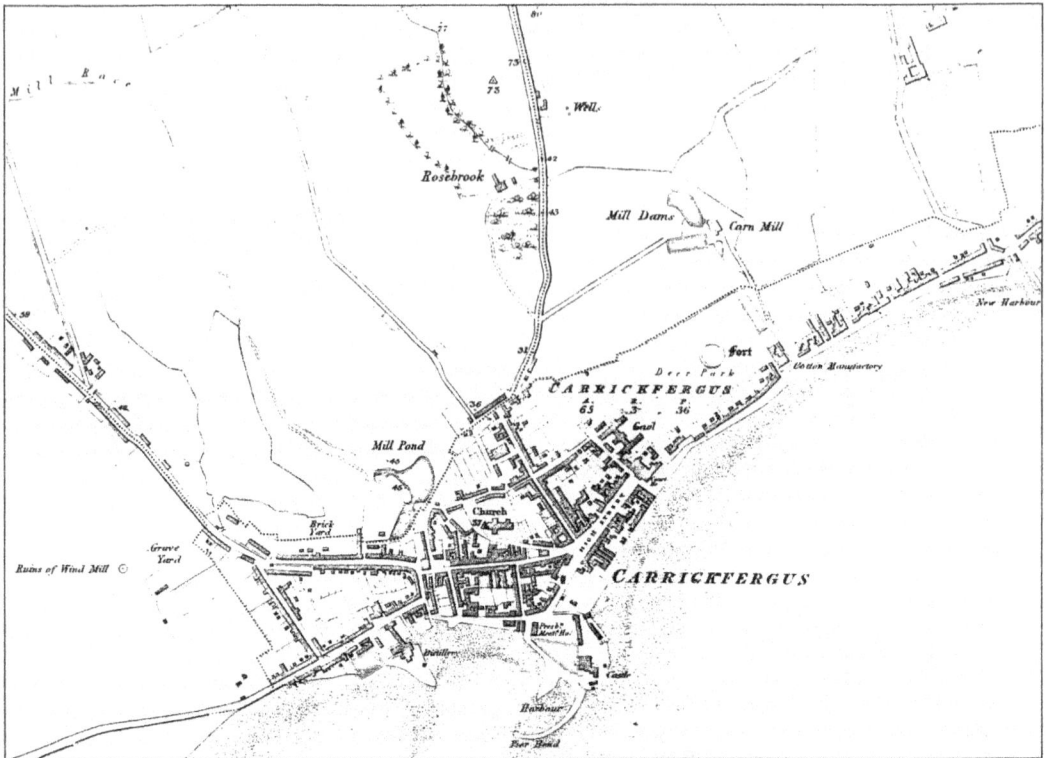

Map of Carrickfergus from the first 6″ O.S. maps, 1830s

Marquis of Downshire, who has property in Carrickfergus, is said to support this party.

The corporate body consists of a mayor and 17 aldermen. Hitherto some member of the Donegall family had generally been the mayor, executing the office by deputy, who is a magistrate in right of office and has the power of holding 2 courts weekly. By the charter of the corporation, "leave is given to the corporation to elect a town clerk as often as need shall require; coroners to be elected annually, on the same day as the mayor; the sword-bearer to be chosen by the mayor, sheriffs and aldermen; the sergeants-at-mace to be appointed from time to time by the corporation."

All wrecks between Fair Head and Beerlooms are granted to the corporation, as well as the right of ferry to the county Down.

Carrickfergus is entirely independent of the county of Antrim: but the gaol and court house of the latter county are in the town of Carrickfergus and belong to and are a part of the county of Antrim, the assizes for which are held in this town, though frequent endeavours have been, and are still making, to have the assizes held in some more central part of the county; but it is probable that no change will be made as, at all events, assizes must be held in Carrickfergus.

There is a gaol and also a court house belonging to the county of Carrickfergus, but both are so much out of repair that they are useless and the prisoners are sent to the Antrim gaol and the Carrickfergus business is transacted in the civil court of the Antrim court house.

Harbour and Castle

There is a small quay for vessels to load and unload, but the depth of water in the basin is not sufficient for vessels of considerable burthen. The only direct import into Carrickfergus is that of coals, and is proved by the return of customs, which in the year 1820 was 518 pounds, almost the whole of which sum was received from the duty on coals. The other trade of the town is carried on through Belfast.

Adjoining, and on the south of, the town stands the castle, which is a very old building and does not appear to be well calculated for defence, either on the water or on the land side. It is one of the magazines for the north and is generally garrisoned by a company from Belfast. There are also 3 or 4 invalid artillery men quartered here, to look after the ordnance and other stores.

Principal Buildings

There are 6 places of worship within the county. 4 of these, namely the church, a meeting house, a Wesleyan Methodist chapel and an Independent chapel, are in the town. The Independent chapel has been purchased by the Ordnance and will, it is supposed, be taken down. The other places of worship mentioned are a Presbyterian meeting house on the east side of the Larne mountain road, quite on the verge of the county, and a new Catholic chapel close to the town, on the right of the road to Belfast.

The Board of Ordnance have some property in the town, namely the castle, castle garden, reservoir, parade, meeting house, half the street from the meeting house to the castle gate, one half of Castle Street, about two-thirds of a house and garden immediately opposite the castle gate, also a house and garden on the right hand side of the Ballynure road. Immediately adjoining the town, on the right of the road to Belfast, is a small field and dog-kennel also belonging to the Ordnance department

General Remarks

Carrickfergus is upon the whole but a poor town; it appears gradually to decline in proportion as Belfast progresses. There are 2 inns within the town, both of which are bad ones. There is a market held on every Saturday but not well supplied as, from the vicinity of Belfast, 8 miles distant, the inhabitants generally supply themselves from thence. There is a constant communication with Belfast by means of cars every morning, and a coach from Larne which passes through the town every day; Larne is distant 9 miles.

There are 2 fairs held in the year, one on the 1st November, the other on the 12th May, but little business is done at either.

There is only 1 village within the county, that of Eden at the south east corner, a place of no importance.

Manufactories

The principal ones are those of cotton, of which there are 6 [crossed out: 3 large ones], 1 within the town and 3 others about a mile distant, on the Ballynure road, and 2 in the East Division. There are 2 distilleries also situated within the town and 1 tanyard.

Roads

There are but 3 principal roads within the county. That on the shore of Belfast Lough is a level and good road. The other roads are those called the Ballynure road and the Larne mountain road. Both of these are so very hilly after leaving the town for about 2 miles, as to render them almost impassable for loaded carts; and from the nature of the ground the northern part of the county could not be opened except at a very considerable expense. A road is now in progress running through the county in a direction parallel to the lough shore and about 1 mile and a half distant from it.

NATURAL FEATURES

Rivers

There is one small river named Woodburn, the falls on which are very considerable, all of which have been taken advantage of by the erection of manufactories.

There are several small streams throughout the county, except on the Commons where, unless in very wet weather, none can be traced. A large supply of water for the manufactories in the Eastern Division is obtained from Loughmorne, and might be made much more available. Loughmorne is a sheet of water of 106 acres, varying in depth from 18 to 50 feet. It is 3 miles from the sea-shore, its elevation 593 feet.

Bogs and Woods

There is a great extent of boggy ground in the northern part of the county; the greater part of it comes under the character rather of mountain pasture than of bog.

There are not any woods but many young plantations, all of which appear to thrive well.

SOCIAL ECONOMY

Population

The last return gave a population of 8,030; of this number, 917 were Catholics, the far greater portion of the remainder were Presbyterians. Since the period alluded to there has been a great increase in the population, more particularly amongst the Catholic.

ANCIENT TOPOGRAPHY

Antiquities

The castle and the ancient walls of the town may be considered amongst the principal antiquities.

In the West Division there is a tract of land called Abbey Land, said to have belonged to the abbey of Woodburn, the site of which is not now known.

In the East Division there is an old fort generally known as Duncrue Fort; adjoining this are some ruins, said to be those of Killyanne or Duncrue church.

In the West Division, on Slievatrue or Slieveatriar mountain, are the remains of a large cairn. Some years since, in clearing off the top, an urn was found containing ashes.

The present jail is on the site of a Franciscan monastery, from which the monks were violently ejected. There are 2 traditions current with regard to these monks, from which it would appear that, although they had not sufficient power to retain their property, yet that they were all powerful when they chose to curse.

One tradition is that where Loughmorne now is, there was formerly a large town, the people of which, having refused to give assistance to one of the holy brotherhood when in distress, he left the town and prayed that it might be a lough ere morn. Thus was the name of the lake derived. I have been gravely assured by the country people that they have occasionally seen the houses at the bottom of the lake.

The other tradition is that when the monks were turned out of their monastery, they prayed that the place might become a resting place for thieves ever after. It is considered by many that had it not been for this curse the jail, which from its situation is particularly inconvenient for the county of Antrim, would have been given up long since. [Signed] C.H. Mallock, Lieutenant Royal Engineers, Mohill, 22nd April 1832.

Memoir of the Parish and the County of the Town of Carrickfergus by James Boyle, February 1839 to February 1840

MEMOIR WRITING

Composition of Memoir

This Memoir was commenced 9th February and was completed [blank]; the time employed on it was 1,115 hours, equals 123 days. 29th December 1839.

Preface

The information contained in this Memoir, in every instance where it could be effected, has been brought down to the present date. The sources of the information, though numerous and very various, are in all instances authorities.

The records of the corporation, possessed by their officers, are few, and the information they contain is meagre, uninteresting and of no assistance to a work such as this; they merely relate to the letting of farms and tenements. But among some of the old inhabitants many old manuscripts in the writing of their forefathers who had been connected with the corporation still remain as unsupported evidences of their former transactions, which, by destructive concealment of their official records, it has been endeavoured to suppress.

The repository of these papers is known as the "town chest." There are 2 keys to this box, one possessed by the mayor, the other by the town clerk, so that it cannot be opened unless in [the] presence of both. However, on a recent occasion on lifting the chest the bottom was found to be movable, and it was also discovered that most of the important papers had been removed.

To Mr Samuel McSkimin, the ingenious author of the *History of Carrickfergus*, I have felt myself most indebted for his unwearied exertions and valuable assistance in affording me access to his manuscripts and documents, on which he has spent much money and upwards of half a century in collecting.

To Edward Bruce Esquire of Scoutbush, a gentleman of high literary and scientific attainments, I have to express my acknowledgement for the meteorological register.

Through the courtesy of the local officers of the gaol much of the information contained in the criminal returns has been obtained. It is to be regretted that, from some local regulations in their establishment, further information could not be acquired.

From the different municipal officers and local functionaries every assistance within their power has been most politely afforded.

The illustrations of this Memoir are drawings made by myself from the articles which they represent.

In no instance, where information could be ascertained by personal inquiry or observations, has the authority or assistance of individuals been made available. [Signed] James Boyle, 29th November 1839.

NATURAL FEATURES

Hills

The parish of Carrickfergus presents an exceedingly diversified and agreeably varied surface. In its bold and strongly marked features, which rise abruptly to considerable elevations from the level plains along its coast, it largely contributes to the picturesque scenery for which Belfast Lough is celebrated, while in its deep and wild ravines which rip its acclivities it possesses some almost romantic scenes.

This parish includes a considerable portion of the hilly and almost mountainous ridge which extends north eastward along the eastern coast of this county (and the western of Belfast Lough) from Divis mountain, near its southern side. This chain is, in several instances, intersected by valleys of such depth as almost to isolate the hills which they include. As they proceed northward there is an almost progressive decline in the elevations of the hills from 1,567 feet (the height of Divis) down to 600 feet above the level of the sea, which is the height of the ridge at the point where it is crossed by the northern confine of this parish, after which it becomes lost in the undulating grounds on the western shore of Larne Lough.

The hills are of basaltic formation; their eastern declivities are abrupt and frequently precipitous, while towards the north west their slopes are rather gentle and varied.

In this parish a precipitous cliff of from 20 to 150 feet high extends north eastward from the southern almost to the northern boundary of the parish, traversing it near its centre. It forms the summit of the eastern declivity of the ridge, which rises apparently abruptly from a broad plain which extends all along the western shore of Belfast Lough. On a nearer approach, the descent from the base of the cliff is found to be broken by 2 broad plateaux or terraces. The upper of these is varied by numerous little ridges and deep valleys, which are strewed with rocks fallen from impending cliffs. The lower is half a mile broad, quite flat, inclining gently towards the north. From it there is [a] gradual fall towards the lough, terminating in a trifling bank on its coast.

As it approaches the north of the parish the cliff becomes less lofty and is finally lost near its centre. Several deep gorges or valleys rip up the eastern side of this range. A somewhat broad valley separates it from Carnmoney hill in the adjoining parish of Carnmoney. Near the centre of the parish 2 deep gorges with steep banks several hundred feet high, which unite near the base of the ridge, penetrate for a considerable distance into it. There are also several minor glens and valleys which terminate at the brow of the hills.

The summit of this feature consists of a large and very varied table land, interspersed with numerous hills and knolls, and which occupies the intervening spaces between the summit of the cliffs and the north western confines of the parish. From the latter there is [a] gentle but very varied fall north westward, the support of the ridge, on that side, being formed by numerous minor features which form the south eastern side of the valley of the Six Mile Water.

From the north eastern side of the parish a feature extends to the Larne river, forming, by its eastern side, the western of the valley of Glenoe.

The highest point in the parish is Slieve True hill (1,025 feet above the level of the sea), near its south west corner. Its form is somewhat conical, rising abruptly on all sides to an elevation of about 280 feet above the adjacent ground. Near the south centre of the parish, and at the verges of the cliff, is the Knocker (the name of the mountain), 917 feet; near the north west frontier is Carn Billy, 941 feet; three-quarters of a mile north of the latter is North Carn, 892 feet; at the north centre is Slimmerow, 946 feet; a mile south of the latter is Toppin, 928 feet; and a mile to the eastward of Toppin is Carnwhissock, 745 feet above the level of the sea.

The mountains and higher ground are chiefly under wild pastures interspersed by small patches of cultivated land. The lower grounds are generally cultivated and planted.

Lakes: Belfast Lough

This well-known arm of the sea was formerly known as Carrickfergus Lough. It probably obtained its present name on the sale of the customs of Carrickfergus by the corporation in 1637 and on the transfer of the trade from that town to Belfast about the same period.

The lough extends with a trifling curvature from south west to north east along the eastern coast of this county. Its extreme length from the estuary of the River Lagan at Belfast to the Black Head (the eastern point of this county) on the seacoast is 15 miles. Its extreme width at its mouth, between Black Head and Orlock Point on the north west coast of Down, is 7 and a half miles. Its width opposite the town of Carrickfergus is 3 and three-quarter miles. Its channel is beyond half-way from the Carrickfergus shore and vessels of burthen keep along the opposite shore, under which, though further up, are good roadsteads and safe anchorages for the heavier vessels which cannot get up to Belfast.

Near the southern end of this parish, and a little offshore, is good holding ground and safe anchorages for lighter vessels, where they are protected from the northern, western and south western gales.

There are neither headlands, promontories nor bays along the coast of the lough, which mainly consists of a shingly beach occasionally alternating with a trifling cliff or bank.

The extreme length of coast in this parish is 4 and two-third miles; its direction is from south west to north east.

Lough Mourne

Lough Mourne is situated in the North East Division, near the north eastern confines of the parish, at an elevation of 592 feet above the level of the sea, from which it is distant, at its nearest point, 3 and a half miles. It includes an area of 89 acres 3 roods 22 perches. Its figure is irregular: its extreme length from south east to north west is 1,281 yards and its extreme width east to west 484 yards. Its depth is said to be very great but probably does not exceed 30 feet.

One trifling stream issues from its southern extremity. It is termed the Orland stream. It supplies a cotton mill in the vicinity of Carrickfergus. Several little rivulets flow into it, but as these would not nearly afford a sufficient supply to such a sheet of water, the belief that it is fed by a large spring near its centre is probably correct.

Its bed is clayey, its banks are low marshy and dreary, and the surrounding scenery bleak and uninteresting. The water is very clear. It has been rarely frozen in winter. It is abundantly stored with pike and eels, and is much frequented by wildfowl in winter. This lake is said to be the largest at the same elevation in Ireland.

There are several absurd and uninteresting traditions respecting the origin of this lake, among which is that applied to almost every other in Ireland, namely that it was once a city but that an old man, coming in late one evening and being refused shelter or charity, went off saying that it would be a "lough ere morn," which was verified, hence its name.

Woodburn River

Though the term of river cannot be with propriety applied to any of the numerous streams which ripple over the surface of this parish, still they are not the less deserving of notice from the incalculably valuable supply of water which they are capable of affording and to which the parish is indebted for much of [its] prosperity, in the number and extent of its manufactories.

The principal of these streams is the Woodburn river. It is formed of 2 minor streams or branches which take their rise at similar elevations, 831 feet above the level of the sea, the western in the West Division and the eastern in the Commons. After flowing for about 2 and a half miles and descending to a level of 230 feet, they unite their waters 2 miles north west of the town of Carrickfergus. The stream thus formed pursues a somewhat southerly, though irregular, course for 1 and seven-eighth miles and discharges itself into Belfast Lough within the tideway, three-quarters of a mile west of the town of Carrickfergus.

The average inclination of the western branch is 1 in 20 and of the eastern 1 in 28 feet; the average inclination of the stream from the junction of its branches to its mouth is 1 in 30 feet. The inclinations of the branches are very irregular, the courses being frequently interrupted and crossed by ledges of rock or by successive little steps which produce numerous waterfalls or rapids, many of which are not deficient in beauty.

The inclination of the stream is also, near the junction of its branches, rather irregular. Advantage is taken of several valuable falls and rapids to erect carries and turn off water for machinery. Towards its mouth its inclination gradually becomes more regular as its bed is absolutely levelled by the immense quantity of rolled stones and pebbles brought down by it in its very violent and impetuous floods.

The extreme breadth of the eastern branch of this stream is 9 feet and of the western 8 feet. Its breadth below their junction varies from 13 to 38 feet and averages 19 feet. Its depth depends of course on the proximity of the carries, but its ordinary natural depth does not exceed 2 feet. Towards its mouth, from the immense depth of the shingly gravel, its ordinary depth does not exceed 1 foot.

Its bed from its sources to its mouth is almost entirely rocky. It has eaten its way in some instances through a red ochreish rock which, in its eastern branch, it had scarped to an immense depth. In other cases trapp and the ordinary basalt appear in all deeply worn and strewed with rocks and stones.

The banks of its branches vary in height from 40 to 300 feet. Each waters a deep and narrow ravine, the ground at first falling pretty rapidly but finally precipitously on either side. It may be asserted that in Antrim there are not, for the size of the streams, such strongly marked ravines as these. The banks of the stream below the junction of its branches are much less strongly marked and are soon after lost in the almost level holmes along its margin.

The floods of this stream in heavy rain, but more particularly during a thaw, are very formidable and, from its velocity and the height of its sources, very violent and impetuous. They rise with extreme rapidity but almost as quickly naturally subside. The quantity and size of the stones rolled down by them is very great, but no deposit is made. The holmes along the banks of the stream are inundated and occasionally, but not often, during harvest crops and soil are swept off by the floods. Some few deposits of gravel have within memory been made on its holmes by the inundations of this stream.

The scenery along the banks of the branches of the Woodburn river is exceedingly wild and romantic. Their steep declivities are clothed with a low coppice or brushwood, which the fertile greensward from which it springs, and the ivy with which it is interwoven, gives them an unusual aspect of richness. Further down the stream the numerous modern plantings, the steep banks alternating with the low and fertile holmes, present no ordinary variety and in their contrast with the lonely wildness of the former seems to possess tenfold beauty.

Other Rivers

The Orland water issues from the southern extremity of Lough Mourne, 593 feet above the level of the sea and 4 miles north east of the town of Carrickfergus. It pursues a south easterly course for a short distance, but soon after changes its direction to the south west and, after an irregular run of 6 and a quarter miles, discharges itself into the sea near the Scotch Quarter, Carrickfergus.

Its average inclination is 1 in 55 feet. Its extreme length is 6 and a quarter miles. Its extreme breadth does not exceed 9 feet nor its depth more than a few inches. Its bed is gravelly and stony. Its banks, though inconsiderable, are sufficient to confine its trifling floods. It has been and is capable of being applied to machinery to a small extent. It is very advantageously situated for the purposes of drainage and irrigation, though it is but little used for either.

The Sulla Tober or Cilla Tober (properly Suil-a-thobbar) or "the well eye," issues from a limestone rock at an elevation of 416 feet above the sea and at a distance of 2 miles north of the town of Carrickfergus. From there it pursues an irregular southerly course for 2 and a quarter miles and, passing through the Scotch Quarter, Carrickfergus, discharges itself into the sea. Its average inclination is 1 in 31 feet. Its extreme breadth is 10 feet and average depth 7 feet. Its bed is gravelly and stony.

Its banks are inconsiderable. It occasionally but not frequently overflows them, committing some trifling mischief to the crops and lands along it, but it soon naturally subsides. It affords a constant and valuable supply of water power to machinery, to which it was formerly more extensively applied. It receives the contributions of numerous trifling rivulets which flow down the steep acclivity from which it issues and is very usefully situated for the purpose of drainage. To irrigation, it is also easily applicable.

The Copeland water takes its rise from several sources, at a mean elevation of 504 feet above the level of the sea, at the north eastern side of the parish. It pursues its direction to the southward and, after flowing along the eastern boundary of the county town of Carrickfergus for 3 and a half miles, it discharges itself into Belfast Lough at its south eastern corner. Its average inclination is 1 in 36 feet. Its ordinary breadth does not exceed 8 feet. Its source is in a limestone bed. Its channel is stony and rough.

Its banks are inconsiderable and sometimes inadequate to confine it in its floods, which, however, usually subside without committing any mischief. It is applied to a small extent to machinery. It is capable of affording a further supply of water power and is also very usefully situated for the purposes of irrigation and drainage, to which, however, it is to a very trifling extent applied.

The Silver stream is an inconsiderable rivulet which, at an elevation of 714 feet above the sea, issues from the brow of the hill near the south west centre of the parish and flows south east for 1 and three-quarter miles along its southern boundary. It discharges itself into the lough at the south east corner of the parish. Its average inclination is 1 in 14 feet. It is capable of being applied to drainage and irrigation, but in no other respect is of importance or worthy of further notice.

There are numerous minor streams or rivulets flowing down the declivities and irrigating the surface of the parish, which afford an abundant supply of water for every purpose. There is also a sufficient supply of spring water of an excellent quality. The streams and springs also issue from a limestone bottom and their water is therefore considered very pure and wholesome.

Mineral Springs

This district was during the last century celebrated for the number, variety and valuable properties of its mineral waters which are, even locally, almost unknown.

Near the eastern side of the town, in the bed of a stream, is a mineral spring of nitrous taste and possessing a purging property. During an epidemic [of] dysentery, which prevailed about the year 1741-42, the waters of this well, made into a posset with milk, were used with extreme success, and again in 1786, when a violent flux prevailed here, it was found to be very useful. Dr Rutty, in a work on the mineral waters of Ireland, has particularly noticed and recommended the waters of this well, of which he has given an analysis.

An arch was many years ago erected over it by a Miss Spaight, from whom it took its name. The arch has, however, long since fallen in and the well almost been destroyed.

About 1 mile east of the latter, and about the same distance from the sea, in a yellow clayey bed, is a saline spring of very strong taste and in strength said to be very nearly equal to the Lymington or Harrowgate waters. About 80 years since an unsuccessful attempt to divine rock-salt was made here.

Near the west bank of Lough Mourne is a spring of sulphureous chalybeate waters which is said to have been brought into notice in 1731. It was in former times much celebrated for its efficiency in curing several diseases, great numbers having resorted to it in summer, when tents for the purpose of entertainment were pitched. It has, however, been latterly almost unknown and it is now almost covered up with mud.

Bogs

The bogs of this parish are confined to numerous patches of trifling extent, which are only to be found in the hilly and thinly-peopled district along its northern confines. From the trifling extent of bog in the neighbourhood, these patches are gradually diminishing and in a comparatively few years will have been quite cut out. It is said that many of them are the sites of "loughans" or small lakes, which formerly abounded in the Commons and hilly districts of the parish, and that such are laid down in the old maps of the country. This is quite probable from the formation of the country and the abundance of springs which, after running a short distance, again enter the ground and are lost. These loughans may have been fed by streams or springs which had eventually disappeared in the limestone cavities, and the growth of vegetable matter on their stagnant bed may have caused their origin.

Timber of various kinds, oak, hazel, alder and sallow, have been found near their subsoil. None of the timber was large, nor could it be ascertained as to whether it has been burnt or broken down.

Bog or peat is to be found at a few inches from the surface within the low water mark, and at a distance of about 200 yards from the shore of the lough opposite the Irish Quarter. The thickness of the stratum varies from 6 inches to 3 feet. It rests on a subsoil of blue clay. When burned it has a very disagreeable and strongly sulphureous smell, with a bluish flame.

In the bog have been found embedded the trunks and leaves of alders, sallow and hazel, which lie north east and south west. On some of the trunks the common moss is still to be found and among it the shells of the common snail. Some of the timber is petrified and is very hard and white. The part that remains in its original state is frequently to be found perforated by the razorfish. Where the bog remains firm and compact, the nuts are to be found perfect but not petrified. Where it is soft or broken, most of the nuts are petrified. Some of them are transparent, strong[ly] resembling window glass, while others are brownish, like the pebbles along the beach.

Bog containing timber and nuts have been dug on the opposite coast of the lough; neither the timber nor the nuts were petrified.

The situation of the bog on this coast is accounted for by the ascertained fact that the sea has been making very serious inroads on the shore. Several lots of ground let off by the corporation have been carried away. One of these extended for nearly 200 yards from the present shore.

Woods

In the numerous and extensive patches of brushwood which are still to be found occupying the banks of the streams, the precipitous declivities and the rocky and irreclaimable districts of the parish, as also in the quantity of timber found in its bogs, there is ample evidence of the parish having at a remote period been thickly wood[ed]; but these are now the only remains of natural wood to be found [in] it, and they are rapidly disappearing before the labours of the husbandman and the intrusions of the cattle. The descriptions of wood thus found, and which seem to be indigenous to the soil, are oak, ash, hazel, holly, sallow, alder and the sloe-thorn. Ivy is abundant, but the most prevalent wood is the hazel.

Coast

4 and two-third miles of the north western coast of that area of the North Channel, known as

Belfast Lough, are formed by the south eastern side of this parish. The direction of the coast, like that of the lough, is from south west to north east. There is not any variation from the ordinary direction of the former, as it possesses neither headlands, bays nor creeks. The only promontory is the rock on which Carrickfergus Castle stands, which extends about 360 feet to seaward and rises about 30 feet above the water.

The coast of this parish is very low. It consists chiefly of a low shingly and rocky beach, which alternates occasionally with a trifling rocky cliff or clayey bank.

The tide recedes in some places to a distance of more than three-quarters of a mile, laying bare a dreary beach of sandy slob or mud. When the tide is in, the drive along the Carrickfergus shore is, as it is justly termed, delightful: on one side the lough, studded with its numerous shipping, and the opposite fertile and diversified coasts of Down; on the other hand are the rich level plains of Carrickfergus, varied with numerous gentlemen's seats and plantings, above which impend the precipitous summits of the lofty and picturesque mountains.

Climate

There is much variety of climate in this parish, its temperature, humidity, liability to frost depending of course upon the situation of its different districts, their elevations, vicinity to or distances from the sea, and their aspect.

Speaking generally, the climate of the parish is not considered moist; it is rather cold and is believed to be healthy and bracing.

From the direction of Belfast Lough, which bears south west by north east, the low eastern districts of the parish along its coast are very much exposed to the south eastern, southern and south western gales, the 2 latter of which blow for fully 9 months in the year. To the eastern, and particularly to the north eastern, gales, the latter of which sets in from the seaward, it is much exposed, but these rarely prevail.

During the months of March and April the easterly wind is more prevalent than during the remainder of the year. From the northward and westward this side of the parish is protected by the high ridge which traverses its centre parallel to the coast of the lough. The hilly districts occupying the western portion of the parish are exposed to every wind, but particularly to the western and north western.

During the continuance of the northerly or easterly wind the weather is dry and cold. Frost setting in during the prevalence of these winds is sure to continue. The weather during the prevalence of south easterly winds is wet and dirty.

The south wind in summer is generally dry and warm. In winter it is usually raining, especially if there has been a frost. The south west is the most rainy point. The west is much less so, and the north west wind is generally attended with squally and stormy weather, particularly in spring and winter.

Along the coast early frosts are unusual and frost is less felt at any season than in the interior of the parish. In its western districts, along the banks of streams and the edges of bogs and moist districts, frosts are felt in the beginning of September, but they rarely prove injurious to the crops.

Crops

The climate is not supposed to be suited to the growth of wheat, but this idea seems to be erroneous, at least so far as respects the low eastern districts of the parish. It is, however, still but little cultivated, though more frequently than formerly and is found to succeed.

In the eastern districts of the parish wheat is usually sown on the raising of the potatoes. Its being reaped depends of course on the season, but commonly takes place between the middle of August and the first week in September.

Oats and potatoes are the crops principally cultivated. The former is generally sown during the latter part of March and the early part of April. The reaping of oats commences in the latter part of August and in the eastern district of the parish is completed by the beginning of October.

Barley is sown in April and is reaped during the latter part of August. Potatoes are generally planted between the latter part of March and the beginning of June. The general raising of the crop takes place between the last week in October and the end of November.

A table containing a register of the weather from 7th of February till 30th of November 1839 will be hereafter forwarded.

MODERN TOPOGRAPHY

Carrickfergus: Situation

The seaport, borough, market and post town of Carrickfergus is situated in the parish of the same name, which is also a county of itself, locally situated in the county of Antrim, of which it is the ancient capital and county town. It extends for 1 mile along the north west shore of Belfast Lough, and is situated on the mail coach and leading road from Belfast to Larne, and to the other towns along the eastern coast of Antrim. It is in the diocese and constitutes a portion of the deanery of Connor. The assizes for the county of the town of Carrickfergus and county of Antrim, which are included in the north east circuit, are held in Carrickfergus.

It is 112 miles north of Dublin and 10 and a half miles north north east of Belfast, of which port it forms a member. Its harbour is situated in latitude 54 degrees 42 minutes and 45 seconds north and longitude 5 degrees and 47 minutes west; 9 and a half miles north west by west from the Copeland Islands' lighthouse.

The extreme length of the town and suburbs from south west to north east is 1 mile, and its extreme breadth, from the castle at its south east side to the North Gate at its north western, 484 yards. The walls include a somewhat elliptic area of 476 yards in length by 315 yards in width; the circumference of the space included by the water is 1,248 yards.

Scenery

Carrickfergus occupies a delightful situation on the extremity of a trifling projection of the coast, which terminates in a rocky tongue rising boldly from the water to a height of about 30 feet. The gently undulating surface of the almost level grounds, stretching along the shore, is under general cultivation and is exceedingly diversified by the numerous gentlemen's seats, ornamental plantings and comfortable-looking farmhouses, and contrasts finely with the bold hilly ridge which, rising abruptly from the plains, extends southwards almost as far as the eye can reach and presents in its lofty and almost precipitous promontories an exceedingly interesting variety.

Southwards the view from the town embraces Belfast Lough, with its numerous shipping, the town of Belfast and the blue mountains of Mourne; on the opposite side the coast of Down, studded with the numerous villages along its shores; while towards the north east the prospect is bounded by more distant southern coasts of Ayr and Galloway shires.

In itself Carrickfergus constitutes no trifling ornament to the scenery of the lough. From almost every point it is seen to advantage. Its ancient and lofty castle, situated on the extremity of a low promontory, presents in its dark massive walls a conspicuous and interesting appearance, standing boldly out from the other buildings and rising considerably above the adja-

cent levels. It is seen from many miles distant and from every point in the surrounding country. The spire of its church, situated on an eminence near the centre of the town rises gracefully above it and assists in breaking the almost unvaried outline of its houses. The whitened houses and cottages in the Scotch Quarter have a pretty effect from the water and, like every other distant view of the town, convey an impression which a nearer approach will quickly dissipate.

HISTORY

General History

From its importance as a military position, and its exposed situation on the Irish coast so near that of Scotland, Carrickfergus has, since a very early age, been intimately connected with the different events which have affected the province of Ulster, and has for centuries been the great object of the successive English and Scottish invasions, and has been often fiercely contended for by them and by its more legitimate claimants.

For many years, and until 1637, its consequence depended not only on its military capabilities but on its commerce. By a return of the amount of "customs of prohibited goods, and the 3d per pound for other goods due by common law" for 7 years prior to 1609, it appears to have been the third port in Ireland as to trade, Dublin and Waterford only exceeding it.

Since the sale of its customs in 1637, the trade, which was then transferred to Belfast, had gradually declined, and as the struggles to which it was for its importance as a stronghold indebted have long since terminated, it had with them ceased to enjoy any rank in the military or political affairs of the county; and but for the periodical contests of rival parties, in which its inhabitants have the privilege of recording their opinions, and of displaying some of the obstinacy (tho' with more rancorous feelings and from less disinterested motives) which animated their forefathers, Carrickfergus would have been consigned to the oblivion to which it is, from many causes, most deservedly entitled.

Pre-Norman History

Carrickfergus, which by some historian has been identified with the ancient Dun Sobarky or Dun Sobairchia of Ptolemy, in whose maps it is said to have by that name been laid down, has been known successively by the name of Crag-fergus, Carig-fergus, Caregfergus, Karregfergus, Rockfergus, Knockfergus and Carrickfergus, the former part of the name signifying "a rock" while the latter is said to have been that of its founder, a King of Scotland who flourished, as it is said, 300 years before Christ.

Crag or karreg in Welsh, and carrick in Irish, signifying "a rock," at once apply to the rocky promontory on which the castle stands, which may have been the first structure erected here and which undoubtedly was that to which the town was indebted for its origin, increase and importance.

The origin or the date of the origin of Carrickfergus, as well as the name of its founder, are, however, involved in obscurity. The first notice of it, at least so far as can be locally ascertained, is in the legendary history of the celebrated Fin MacCoul, who flourished in the 3rd century, and who is said to have selected it as the scene of some of his exploits.

In 697 a desperate engagement is said to have taken place at Lemnha near Carrickfergus, between the Island and the British Picts, who then invaded this country, and the natives; the former were commanded by Conquar MacEcha MacMaldwin and the latter by Aodh, King of Dalriada, both of whom fell in the action. [Insert footnote: I have, in vain, after a minute search, endeavoured to discover the locality of Lemnha].

In 960 Carrickfergus was plundered by the Danes from Lough Cuan or Lough Strangford. The ravages of the Danes in Ulster between the 8th and 11th centuries, during which they destroyed the records of the county, may perhaps account for the interval which takes place in the annals of the kingdom, and it is not until the year 1172 that any important event connected with Carrickfergus is noticed.

NATURAL FEATURES

Yearly Climate

1799. This year was remarkably cold and wet, and the frost and snow setting earlier than usual, the crops were in every respect defective. In the following spring oatmeal sold at 5s 8d per peck and potatoes at 2s 8d per bushel.

1800. Owing to the exceedingly dry summer of this year, the crops were equally defective. In November oatmeal sold at 5s 8d per peck and potatoes at 2s 8d ha'penny per bushel. Early in the ensuing spring Indian corn meal and rye flour were imported on a bounty, or by the government to mitigate the distress of the lower class.

1812. In April potatoes sold at 3s per bushel, and in July oatmeal advanced to 6s 10d per peck.

1813, 25th December. On the evening of this day a frost commenced, which continued hoary until the following day, when it became very hard and continued so until January, on the 8th and 9th of which month a considerable quantity of snow fell. On the 10th, 11th and 12th it snowed almost without intermission, the roads being by this time choked up to the depth of 20 feet. The frost continuing, the cold, particularly at sunrise, was very intense. On the morning of the 13th the thermometer stood at 14, the lowest point observed.

Showers of snow, sleet and rain continued to fall from the 25th to the 30th, the frost continuing. A slight thaw commenced on the 1st February, and on the 4th conveyances, for the first time since the 10th January, commenced plying to Belfast. The thaw, accompanied by heavy falls of rain, continued until the 14th February, but the low grounds were not cleared of snow until the end of March.

1814, 11th September. Between 8 and 9 at night a luminous bow, shaped like a rainbow, appeared in the horizon. It was of a whitish colour, extended north and south, and remained visible for about an hour.

1816, 24th September. Between 8 and 9 at night a bow similar to that seen in 1814 appeared, stretching east and west.

The summer and autumn of this year were cold and wet. The reaping of corn did not commence until the 16th September and very little was cut before the middle of October. In December much grain had remained uncut. Markets of course advanced, and in May following (1817) oatmeal sold at 3s 5d and wheatmeal at 4s 2d per peck. In June oatmeal had advanced to 6s 4d per peck. The ports being thrown open, a considerable quantity of rye flour was imported from America to Belfast.

Disease accompanied famine, and a typhus fever, which set in in August, continued with alarming prevalence until the February following. It was computed that 600 individuals in Carrickfergus had fever and that of them 61 died between March 1817 and June 1818.

1818. The summer of this year was very warm. The thermometer ranged as follows in the shade: May 25th, 70; June 6th, 72; 9th, 73; 11th, 78 and a half; 12th, 83; about 3 p.m. July 16th, 76.

1819, 19th February. A bow, resembling those seen in 1814 and 1816, stretching north east by south west appeared from 8 till 10 at night. The night was calm and an aurora borealis appeared to the northward. On the 15th September and following night a similar bow appeared at the same hour.

1821, 17th April. About 12 at night a beautiful lunar rainbow appeared stretching nearly east and west. From the 24th May till the 9th July only 2 slight showers fell in the parish, on the 5th June and 6th July, and about the beginning of the latter month hoar-frost was to be seen every morning on the mountains.

MODERN TOPOGRAPHY AND HISTORY

Court House

1824, 17th January. The quarter sessions for the county of the town of Carrickfergus were held for the first time in the county of Antrim court house.

1827. In April the gaol and court house of the county of the town of Carrickfergus began to be taken down. An act of parliament had been passed, directing that all prisoners belonging to Carrickfergus should be kept in the prison of the county of Antrim.

1828. In the month of June the foundation of a new court house for Carrickfergus was laid on a part of the site of the former one, but projecting more into the market place. When 2-storeys high and about to be roofed, the grand jury assembled at the summer assizes presented it as a nuisance, and on the 24th August it began to be taken down; and a few days afterwards its materials were sold for 35 pounds.

Walls

The old wall which encompassed the town of Carrickfergus has from time to time suffered so much from mutilation that it is now only to be traced at intervals. The portions of it which remain are, however, generally in such a perfect state as to convey a sufficient idea of their original strength and state; and if left unmolested they are, from their solidity of construction, likely to last for ages.

The total linear length of the wall is 1,268 yards, of which about 900 yards still remain in a more or less perfect state. They include an oblong figure 476 yards in extreme length and 315 yards in extreme breadth. Their thickness varies from 5 feet to 6 and a half feet and their height, where they are perfect, from 10 to 18 feet. They are almost exclusively constructed of rude undressed stones, most of which, from their being water-worn, have been procured from the beach. They are of a species of whin or hard trapp. They are not generally large, nor are they are closely or carefully laid.

The outer stones present a good face, while the heart of the wall is filled up with shingle and smaller stones and pebbles which are firmly cemented by a very hard but coarse grouting poured among them. The walls are very strong and very difficult of removal. Some very hard brick and pieces of sandstone occasionally occur in the walls.

The wall on the southern side of the town is washed by the sea. It protected the town on this side for a distance of 535 yards.

The wall where it retains its original height is loopholed at the top. There [are] also some embrasures in it. The loopholes are faced with brick; they are about 6 feet apart.

Bastions

The walls were protected by 7 bastions. Of these, 2 are in a perfect state, 3 somewhat mutilated and 2 entirely removed; one of the latter was taken down in 1838 to make way for some improvements.

The bastions occur at irregular intervals. That at the Water Gate, on the eastern side of the town, has been almost entirely removed. The distance from it to the north east bastion, with which it is connected by a curtain in perfect preservation, is 112 yards. This portion of the wall is 18 feet high and from 5 to 6 feet thick on the top. The north east bastion presents 2 faces; one is of 80, the other of 81 feet; its perpendicular is 27 feet. Its parapet, which is loopholed, is 5 feet high; it is formed of earth. The gorge is of masonry, the interior being filled with earth. The angles are of cut sandstone and are carefully finished.

The north east bastion is connected with the northern by a portion of the wall in a perfect state; the distance between these bastions is 103 yards. The north bastion presents 2 faces of 75 feet; its perpendicular is 27 feet. The salient angle is of cut sandstone. This bastion, which is finished like the former, is in good preservation.

The distance from the north bastion to the North Gate is 51 yards and to north west or "middle west" bastion 95 yards. The wall connecting these bastions has been much injured, as has also the latter bastion. It presents 2 faces of 75 feet each; its perpendicular is 25 feet. The distance between the last and the next bastion is 102 yards; the wall connecting them is in a very imperfect state, as is also the bastion. It presents 2 faces of 81 feet each; its perpendicular is 25 feet.

From the west bastion to the West Gate is a distance of 33 yards. The intervening wall is in tolerable preservation, but the west gateway has long since been pulled down.

40 yards south of the gateway stood the south west bastion, which was pulled down in 1838,

and about 30 yards south [of] it was Woodburn Gate, now Quay Gate, which has not existed within memory. From this gate the wall extended along the beach to the western side of the castle, a distance of 220 yards, and from the eastern side of the castle to the East or Water Gate, a distance of 313 yards. The latter portion of the wall still remains; it is from 12 to 18 feet high on the outside.

Gates

Carrickfergus was formerly entered by 4 gates, namely North Gate on its northerly side, Quay Gate and West Gate on its western side, and Water Gate at the eastern side.

Of these, the North Gate only now remains. This gate, as well as West Gate, were formerly protected by a ditch and enclosed by drawbridges. The deep ditches and drawbridges of the latter remained within memory, and a small part of the arch over the former is still to be seen. Water Gate and Quay Gate were defended by battlements.

The North Gate was formerly known as Spittal Gate, from its being on the road to Bride's hospital, and also as Glenarm Gate, it being on the former highway to that town. It is in good preservation. It consists of a circular, arched gateway 13 feet high and 11 feet wide, surmounted by a battlemented summit. Its total height is 19 and a half feet and the thickness of the wall 8 feet. The gateway is of cut sandstone. The ringcourses are sprung from projecting stones, which seem to have originally been ornamented but are now much disfigured. Inside the gateway, and between the external ringstones, its height is carried up near to its summit, where it terminates in a square roof or head; in this are some small apertures.

Of the other gates not a vestige now remains, but their sites are still termed gates. Woodburn Gate is now known as West Gate, West Gate as Irish Gate and Water Gate as East Gate.

History of Walls

The first attempt at protecting Carrickfergus by a wall was in 1574, when a wall of sods was commenced, previous to which it had been protected by a ditch. Respecting this wall of sods the following entry appears in the records: "October 10th 1574. This present day it was ordered and agreed by the maior, sheriffs and burgesses and cominalty that there should a vamour of sodds or turffs rounde aboughte the towne for the defence or better strengthening of the inhabitants of the

same, whiche should be finished by the hole corporacon, the former mounds at the fower corners of the towne excepted, which was made and compiled at the charge of the prince, whiche vamour, as aforesaid, was finished within one monthe after the decree made."

This wall does not appear to have contributed much to the security of the inhabitants, for in the following year the Scots attacked the town and the corporation entered into an agreement with the lord deputy. The following entry of it appears in the records: "October 8th 1575, at his honor being heare, we the maior and corporacon for the better furthering of the towne, take in bargaine of his honor, to wall from Her Majesty's castell on the north east unto the mount of the myle, along by the sea syde at 5s sterling the foote, every foote to be made 7 foote on the foundation, 4 foote in the topp of the wall and 16 foote in heyght, as apereth by the indentures of the bargaine, bearing date 21st October," the owners of this ground to receive 6d per running foot for their loss.

Owing to the resignation of Sir Henry Sidney in 1578 and to some minor causes, the walling of the town was laid aside, and nothing with respect to it seems to have been done until the 10th June 1594, when the corporation sent to England as a deputation, William Lyndsey, recorder, and William Johnson, alderman, to urge Her Majesty respecting the walling of the town. They rested their claim chiefly on their contact with Sir Henry Sidney, and estimated the expense of finishing the walls at 1,500 pounds. Her Majesty, however, pleading inability, declined assisting them, on which the deputation said that the corporation would wall the town within 3 years and a half, and would also in 2 years after pay Her Majesty 40 pounds per annum, if the Crown would in the meantime give the corporation 300 pounds and resign to them the third part of the customs of the port valued at 7 pounds 10s per annum, and also Her Majesty's part of the imports of this port worth 20 marks a year. But these overtures were rejected by Elizabeth, on the plea that she was ignorant of the value of the customs.

She, however, wrote to the lord deputy (Sir William Russell) and the Council in Ireland, desiring them to make every inquiry respecting the customs and imports and to inform her how Carrickfergus could be best fortified, and stating that she considered the town deserving of favour from the marked attention of the inhabitants to her interest. On the matter being thus left to the lord deputy, the agents applied to the Earl of Essex to use his interest with Sir William Russell, to whom he wrote during the ensuing year. Still, in 1596 nothing whatever seems to have been done, for on the 12th November the corporation wrote to the lord deputy complaining of their expense in "repairing the rampier or towne walles, beinge maide with soddes, everie winter the same doth fall down to our great ympoverisment."

The rebellion of Hugh O'Neill, Earl of Tyrone, and the landing of Spaniards on the southern coast of Ireland, still further protracted any assistance to the corporation. In 1607 a letter was addressed to Sir Arthur Chichester the lord deputy, complaining that much of His Majesty's grant remained unfulfilled and requesting aid in behalf of the walling of the town. This memorial proved unsuccessful, for the deputy in his answer, dated February 28th 1608, replied that His Majesty had consented to furnish 100 men to assist in walling the town, the corporation to find "a hundred good able and sufficient men, to arme, muster and keepe in readiness for the defences" of the town and every other service that might be required of them, but neither officers nor men to receive any pay. The completion of the walls seems to have been effected without further interruption.

Till of late years the walls were pulled down and mutilated with impunity, but in 1815, a complaint being made to Baron McClelland, the judge of assizes, by the mayor and sheriffs, one individual was obliged to rebuild a portion he had taken down. Since this they have remained unmolested.

Buildings

Besides the remaining portions of its walls, the public buildings of Carrickfergus consist of the castle, county gaol and court house, church, 2 meeting houses for Presbyterians and 1 for Independents, 2 chapels for Methodists and 1 for Roman Catholics, 2 piers or quays, a market house and a market place.

Castle

The castle occupies a bold and conspicuous position on the extremity of an almost insulated rocky tongue, which projects for about 120 yards from the south eastern side of the town into the water. The entire of this tongue, which includes a mean width of 40 yards and length of 120 yards, is occupied by the castle. It is at high water surrounded by it on 3 sides, but at low water the beach at its base is laid bare. The rock rises abruptly at its extremity to a height of 30 feet and declines rapidly on the opposite side towards the land. The exterior walls are adapted to the irregularities in the rugged face of the rock which has been scarped from their base.

The position of the castle is low and now by no means commanding or important. Its projecting situation renders it exposed to many points on the land side, and as the channel of the lough is quite out of its range, it could singly be of no use in defending its entrance; neither could it, on account of the trifling depth of water beneath it, be rendered available in protecting vessels of burthen.

The castle includes a massive square tower or keep situated on the eastern side of the rock. At its base is the magazine yard, a small enclosed space which, with the tower, is supposed to have originally constituted the extent of the fortress. At the northern extremity of the yard or outer ballium is the entrance, a machicolated gateway between 2 semicircular towers, connected above by a portcullis room. The gateway is approached by a narrow way 113 feet long and 8 feet wide, which forms an angle to it. It is protected on each side by a high wall closely loopholed for musketry.

A battery for 7 guns adjoins the eastern side of the northern tower. It is supported by bomb-proof vaults. A parapet wall pierced with embrasures for cannon includes the remainder of the work. On the western side the parapet wall is from 30 to 40 feet high on the outside and 16 feet high in the inside. It is here, as is also the wall encompassing the 3 sides of the magazine yard, provided with a banquette near its summit and with loopholes for musketry.

In the outer ballium, and immediately within the gateway, are 2 small ranges of barracks, one on each side. They are 2-storeys high. That on the right side is 119 feet long and contains quarters for 80 men. The range on the opposite side is 102 feet long. It contains on its upper floor, which opens upon the battery, quarters for 4 officers; the understorey, which opens into the castle yard, is, with the vaults underneath the battery, appropriated to the keeping of stores and lumber.

Near the centre of the yard is a furnace for heating shot.

There are 2 pumps in the castle, one fed by spring water, which is somewhat brackish; the other is fed by rain water, descending into a reservoir from the summit of the tower.

The castle is capable of mounting 34 guns, there being embrasures for the number. One gun (a 12-pounder) only is mounted. The others of the same calibre lie on skids, and their carriages are kept in the stores.

The castle and its works are generally in good repair. Plans of it and drawing of its architectural details will be found in the illustrations of this Memoir.

Keep

The keep is a massive structure of square form, built of stone, and in good preservation. Its extreme external height is 90 feet and its dimensions at the base 54 by 52 feet. It consists of 5 floors or storeys, exclusive of a subterranean vaulted magazine. It contains 9 apartments or rooms, 2 of which, on the third and fifth storeys, measure respectively 39 feet 6 inches by 17 feet 6 inches. The other apartments range in size from 38 feet 6 inches by 15 feet 6 inches to 20 feet by 15 feet 6 inches.

The walls diminish in thickness as they approach the top. At the base the north wall is 9 feet thick, while the others do not exceed 8 feet 4 inches in thickness. In the fifth or upper storey the walls are 7 feet thick.

The summit of the castle is almost flat. It is supported by an arch of masonry which rises a little on the top. Its floor is formed of Roman cement. On the south west and south east angles of the summit stand 2 small slated watch-houses.

The summit is enclosed by a battlemented parapet wall from 5 to 9 feet high and 2 feet 2 inches thick. It is approached by a helical stone stair which is constructed in the western wall of the keep and opened or commenced behind the doorway on the first floor, and comes out in the watch-house at the south east angle on the summit. Its lower entrance has been built up, and its first and only entrance is now on the third floor. The stair, which is beautifully constructed, and which has been very greatly used and worn, is lit from the outside by small apertures resembling arrowslits. The stair is 5 feet in diameter. It is constructed exclusively of sandstone, with very little mortar, and without either iron or wood.

The only entrance to the tower is in its east side, from the magazine yard, by a plain, circular, arched doorway 6 feet 10 inches high and 4 feet 6 inches wide. It is 12 feet above the ordinary level of the ground and is approached by a flight of stone steps of somewhat modern erection. The tower is lit by plain, circular, arched windows, which are also of modern construction, many of the original windows, which were much smaller, having been built up and the others having been enlarged to their present size. The former windows were circular-headed and very narrow, and

Carrickfergus Castle

were faced on the outside with cut sandstone. Their positions and forms may be understood by referring to the sketches of the castle.

Several small arrow-slits, also built up, occur in the building. It may be remarked that in the south side of the castle (that next the water) neither windows nor arrow-slits had originally been constructed.

Within the keep is a draw-well (now covered) which is 37 feet deep. It is now quite dry. In cleaning out about 36 years since several pieces of deeply corroded iron were found. To these may be attributed the supposed chalybeate taste and sanatory properties which it was believed to have possessed, for which it was celebrated, and connected with which are some traditions which will be found in subsequent pages.

Attached to the western side, and at the south west angle of the keep, are 2 machicolations, one outside the other. The lower aperture of the larger one is about half-way from the base; it is about 3 feet wide. It is supported by well-cut blocks of sandstone and is carried up like a buttress to nearly the summit of the tower. The outer machicolation is attached to the former, its lower aperture is about two-thirds way from the base of the tower; its width is about 18 inches and its height about 10 feet. These machicolations are neatly constructed and have cut sandstone quoins and supports. There is not the slightest appearance of their entrance in the inside.

A plain projecting fillet or cordon extends about half-way from the top, along the western and about half of the northern side of the tower. This is the only attempt at architectural ornament in it.

The masonry of the keep is remarkably hard and solid. The stones, which are large, well shaped and laid (though but little dressed or shaped) being well bedded, they are, with the exception of the yellow sandstone quoins and windows and doorway jambs and arches, of the ordinary whin of the country. They are cemented by coarse grout of the hardest description. Great difficulty was experienced a few years since in breaking out a window in the south side of the tower, it being found necessary to break the stones, which could not be detached from the grout.

Attached to the south west and north west angles are buttresses which are carried almost to the summit of the tower. In the east side of the tower is a fissure which is about 15 feet in length. It was caused by the erection of the present arched roof in 1815 when, in a niche beneath the spring-ing of the former arch, a human skeleton was discovered. The tower is well floored and in excellent order internally.

Magazine Yard

The magazine yard, as it is now termed from its containing some houses used as magazines, seems to be of similar antiquity with the tower. Their masonry is alike and the extremities of its walls are built into the angles of the tower in a manner which at once determines this circumstance. The yard includes an irregular space 88 feet in extreme depth and presenting to the outer yard or ballium a front 113 feet long. Its southern and eastern sides run along the margin of the rock. This yard is enclosed by a wall from 4 to 6 feet thick, pierced by embrasures in the rear, and with loopholes for musketry along its summit. It is also provided in the inside with a banquette 5 feet from the top.

At the eastern extremity of the front wall of the yard, and also at the extremity of the rock, is a small tower or turret 5 feet square and similar in height to the wall. It is now filled up to the banquette. It seems to have protected a sally-port and stair which descended to the water. The sally-port, now built up, can still, by its cut-stone jambs and arch, be traced in the front of the turret next the outer yard, where it is only 4 feet 2 inches high and 2 feet 10 inches wide, but is said, during some repairs, to have been found to widen towards the opposite side.

The entrance to the magazine yard was formerly by a large, circular, arched gateway in the wall, which was 8 feet wide and (is now) 8 feet high. Over this is the extraordinary aperture for defence shown in the illustrations. It consists in a circular-headed arch or niche measuring at the exterior 8 feet 2 inches in extreme height, 3 feet 10 inches in width and 5 feet 6 inches in depth. In the front face of the wall is an arrow-slit formed of cut sandstone, circular-headed and measuring 4 feet 2 inches high and 3 and a half inches wide. In each side of the niche is a circular-headed recess 5 feet 7 inches high, 3 feet wide and 18 inches deep, from which arrows might be discharged through the slit, with safety to the bowman. The masonry in this structure is excellent and in good preservation. It is now 13 feet from the ground. The wall in which it is constructed is 5 feet 6 inches thick.

The ringstones of several beautifully formed circular arches are still to be traced in the wall on the south side of the yard. They are now but a few feet above the floor of the yard. The arches have long since been built up. The stones are neatly cut and very closely jointed. More care seems to have been bestowed in the masonry in these arches than in that of any other portion of the building.

In the exterior face of the wall around the magazine yard, and also in those encompassing the remainder of the work, are numerous arches, arrow-slits and other apertures, which are easily to be traced by their ringcourses, jambs and heads of yellow sandstone, which is very conspicuous in the black stone of which the walls are formed. From exposure to the weather and the sea air the sandstone has been much worn. These apertures must be of great antiquity, as they are several feet below the present surface of the yard and but a little above that of the rock.

The masonry of the outer walls is different from that of the keep, the stones in the former being much smaller, not laid in courses, and having been but little improved in shape by the hammer. They are sharp in the edges and appear to have been quarried.

In removing some rubbish and earth in the interior of the magazine yard in 1803, a large quantity of human bones were discovered at a little distance from the surface.

The walls encompassing the outer yard or ballium are, for some distance above the level of the rock, of the same style of masonry. Arrow-slits and arches, similar to those described above, occur in them beneath the present surface of the yard and almost on a level with that of the rock. The walls have been increased in height, in some instances to double that of their original elevation. In 6 instances, where there are projections of the rock, little turrets or towers are erected. They are so small as to be useful only in flanking the approaches to the castle, and are therefore filled up level with the banquette. Their angles, as are all the angles in the exterior of the works, are carefully built with cut sandstone quoins.

Half-Moons

The 2 semicircular towers at the northern extremity of the castle yard defend its only entrance, which is by a gateway between them. They are connected in their upper storey by a portcullis room, in front of which is a machicolation, the width of the gateway. The external diameter of these towers is 37 feet. Their lower storey has been built up. The upper or second, on a level with the portcullis room, contains some apartments, and in each tower is pierced with 3 embrasures. Their summit, as also that of the curtain connecting them, is flat and is encompassed by a battlemented wall. These walls are from 5 to 6 feet thick and very firmly constructed, in a style

of masonry more modern than that in the keep. The embrasures are of course of comparatively recent date. The second floor is approached, on the side from the terre pleine of the battery and on the west, by a stair leading to it and to the banquette.

The half-moons are said to have been the residence of the constable. In the eastern one is a chamber of small dimensions lit by a handsome window consisting of 2 spacious circular-headed lights, included in a large, circular, arched space, on each side of which is an ornamented stone column with a capital somewhat in the Corinthian style. A similar column between the lights supports their arches. This is supposed to have been in one of the constable's apartments.

Gateway

The gateway, which is between the towers, is evidently of very great antiquity. From the style of its masonry, the construction of its arches and from the yellow sandstone, quoins and ringcourses and their worn appearance, its erection has probably been coeval with that of the keep, or perhaps with that of the still more ancient-looking exterior walls of the outer yard which encompass the rock. The gateway seems to be of remoter erection than the half-moons, which bear much less the stamp of antiquity.

The gateway is 9 feet 6 inches high, 23 feet in depth, 11 feet at the inside and 7 feet 6 inches at the outside.

It presents on the outside a circular-segment arch of cut stone and on the exterior of the inside front a beautifully formed circular arch, each 9 feet 6 inches high. The latter recedes about 2 feet from the ordinary line of the building. The recess is surmounted by a large circular-segment arch of great antiquity as to appearance.

Between the arches the gateway is 20 feet high. Its roof which, as also the interior of the gateway, describes a pointed arch, is supported or ornamented by cut-stone ribs springing from each side. Above the outside arch, in the inside, are 2 arches, one above the other, supported by machicolated abutments which tend to strengthen the supports of the roof. The upper of these arches forms a portion of a circle; the lower is pointed. In each side of the gateway is an arched recess (probably) for the protection of sorties, 7 feet high, 6 feet 7 inches wide and 3 feet 9 inches deep.

Immediately within the inner arch is the portcullis, which is moved by a windlass in the room above.

The architecture of this gateway, though perfectly plain, exhibits much care and neatness in the masonry; the quoins and ringstones of the exterior are all of yellow sandstone, which is rapidly decaying. The interior is also of cut stone but chiefly of a whitish sandstone. It is therefore probable that a double gateway formerly and originally only was erected, and that the inner and upper arches and roof, which are of a different style and different stone, and are also in more perfect preservation, were erected at a subsequent period.

Style of Masonry

With the exception of the window in the eastern half-moon, and a sculptured stone which was inserted in the wall of the same tower, there is no attempt at ornamental architecture in any part of the works. There seems at the same time to have been an attempt at uniformity and neatness in the masonry, which is generally of an excellent description and in perfect preservation.

The apartments in the tower and half-moons, their floors and stairs, and in fact everything connected with the work are kept in perfect repair by the Board of Ordnance.

Erection of Castle

The erection of this castle is locally attributed to Fergus, King of Scotland, who is said to have flourished about 320 before Christ. Tradition affirms that Fergus, in coming over to drink the water of the well, now within the castle, for the cure of leprosy with which he was afflicted, was lost during a storm off the rock on which the castle stands, and his body, being washed ashore, was found about 3 miles further up and interred in the church of Monkstown, of which the ruins are still to be seen (see Memoir of the parish of Carnmoney). The waters of the well in this castle are said to have in early ages been celebrated for their efficacy in the cure of several diseases.

(There was a Fergus MacEarch who flourished in the 4th century. He was a prince of Dalaradia and is said to have established an Irish colony on the opposite coast of Caledonia. To him may the circumstances just alluded to be with much more probability attributed. The mere statement of the interment in Monkstown church, before the introduction of Christianity, is of course sufficient to disprove the tradition given here).

The erection of the present keep is with more probability attributed to the early English settlers in the reign of Henry II. The square form, its style of architecture and its cordon or fascia are strik-

ingly characteristic of the Norman castles erected by the followers of Strongbow on their landing in Wexford, to which it bears a strong resemblance. There does not appear to have been any notice of it until the reign of Henry II, when his son John, Earl of Morton, Lord of Ireland, in writing to his father from his place, mentions his having taken the castle.

Another circumstance may be adduced as corroboration of the conjecture as to its erection during the reign of Henry II. The ancient seal of the mayor of this corporation (see drawing) bears a spread eagle, the crest of the DeCourcys, senior Barons of Ireland, to whom the province of Ulster was granted by Henry, of whose reign many silver coins have been found about the castle.

Constable

The castle of Carrickfergus seems from a very remote period to have been the most important post held by the English in Ulster and frequently to have been their only stronghold in it. In consequence of this, many privileges were conferred on the constable of the castle, who appeared to have formerly been a person of distinguished rank. Until the reign of Edward IV he was (save in the minority of the heir) always nominated by the Earls of Ulster, the castle being a portion of their hereditary possessions; but Edward, who was Earl of March and Ulster, having ascended the throne, the earldom and of course the patronage also devolved to the Crown.

By the charter of Queen Elizabeth he is "by reason of his office" a freeman of the corporation, and the mayors were sworn before him or his deputy. It appears from the records that he received the king's share of the customs of this port, that he and his wardens (20 Englishmen) had annually 100 cows grazed free by the corporation. He had also the best fish out of each fishing boat that arrived from time to time within the liberties, by the title of the "tythe of fish." This custom was continued by the commanding officer here until 1755, when it was discontinued.

The constable also had a "fair lodging" in the castle, it is supposed, in the second storey of the eastern tower. The castle was for a long time used as a prison for the county Antrim. It is supposed that the half-moons were appropriated to this purpose. And the assizes were also, during the reign of James I, held in the castle. In the charter given by James the castle is declared to be in the county Antrim, to which the judges of assizes are to have liberty at all times to pass, to hold assizes for the same county.

History of Castle

1814. A small tower on the south was taken down and rebuilt.

1815. The lead covering on the keep, which had been laid down in 1754-55, was removed, and the tower was arched with stone and floored on the summit with Roman cement. Exclusive of the cement, this repair cost 482 pounds. A fissure in the north wall was caused by the pressure of the new roof.

1816. The castle and tower, which had hitherto since 1792 been occupied as a barrack, and variously garrisoned by from 100 to 300 men and furnished with artillery, was converted into a magazine for the arms of the disbanded militia and volunteers of the district, and for the ammunition of the troops in the north of Ireland. The rooms were fitted up with arm-racks and stands, and at one period contained 10,000 stands of arms, besides Ordnance stores. The 2 small ranges of barracks immediately within the gateway were alone appropriated to the military, of whom a company were until 1839 quartered here.

1834. In this year the arms were removed to Charlemont Fort in the county Tyrone, as was also the ammunition. The storekeeper was also placed on a retired allowance. In 1834 the detachment quartered here was reduced to a sergeant and 12 men.

In June 1839 the detachment was wholly withdrawn and a master gunner (who resided in the house belonging to the Board of Ordnance, outside the castle) and 2 invalid artillerymen constituted the entire garrison. The stores consist of the instruments necessary for working the guns, 31 in number which, with one exception, are dismounted, and the gunpowder belonging to the different wholesale dealers in that article in the neighbouring counties.

On the 3rd September 1839, owing to an application to the government from the mayor, a detachment of a subaltern and 30 rank and file were sent here, as a protection to the gunpowder belonging to the different principal dealers in the district, of which upwards of 20 tons were then stored in the castle.

Gaol

The gaol of the county Antrim and county of the town of Carrickfergus is situated in Gaol Street, near the eastern extremity of High Street and at the northern side of the court house. This building includes a quadrangular area 273 feet in length and 176 feet in depth, presenting a front of 273 feet. Its external appearance is perfectly plain. The street in which it stands is an obscure narrow lane of which it forms one side. It is therefore only to be seen from the front. In this, however, the town does not sustain any loss, as its sombre front of blackish stone, varied only by the usual melancholy appendage of a drop, presents an aspect gloomy and uninteresting in the extreme.

The gaol consists of 2 parallel wings at right angles to the front, connected at the centre by a range similar to them in height. In front they are connected by a range containing the governor's apartments. The entrance to the prison is by a plain doorway in the latter, from which a flight of stone stairs leads to the second storey of the central range, in which is the office of the gaol.

The space in rear of the central range is for the male felons. It measures 74 by 52 feet and is enclosed in the rear by a wall 21 feet high. On the south side of the southern wing is a yard for minor offenders measuring 71 by 48 feet 6 inches. The juvenile offenders' yard is at north or outside of the northern wing; it measures 53 by 16 feet 6 inches. The female prisoners' yard is at the same side of the same wing but separated from the former yard; it measures 62 by 53 feet. The male debtors' yard is at the south or outside of the southern wing and next the minor offenders' yard; it measures 76 by 38 feet 6 inches.

A stone wall 21 feet high extends from the front, around the sides and rear of the prison and yards. Beyond this is the Sentry's Walk, an alley from 6 to 18 feet wide which extends round 3 sides of the prison. It is enclosed on the outside by a stone wall from 16 to 18 feet high. The entrance to this from the street is between the gaol and court house.

The length of the wings is 158 feet and of the central building which connects them 74 feet. On the northern side of the female yard is a brick house containing 2 apartments for females, measuring 39 by 17 feet. The chapel occupies a third floor on the front of the gaol but, with these exceptions, the building consists of but 2 floors. The understorey is 8 feet 6 inches high and the upper 10 feet 3 inches high in the clear.

The total number of cells in the gaol is 50. Of these, 30 are on the under and 20 on the upper floor. The cells vary in dimensions from 8 by 7 feet to 9 feet 10 inches by 6 feet 4 inches. They have vaulted roofs and, as are also the other apartments, are fire proof.

Prisoners' Accommodation

The prison is arranged to accommodate an indefinite number of prisoners, up to 320. They are crowded together, without respect to the nature of their crimes among the females, whether debtors or criminal. The prison and its inmates are classed under 4 wards, namely the felons' ward, the minor offenders' ward, the male debtors' ward, and the female debtor and criminal ward. The felons' ward has 2 airing yards (as before described), one for adults and one for juvenile offenders. It has 2 day rooms for the same classes; that for adults measures 18 feet 10 inches by 15 feet 10 inches and that for the juvenile class 16 feet 9 inches by 16 feet. There is also the cooking room for the gaol, which measures 24 by 9 feet 6 inches. There are 20 cells attached to this ward; of these, 10 measure 9 by 7 feet and 10, 8 by 7 feet. Each cell contains 1 bed, on which 3 persons sleep.

The minor offenders' ward has a day room 16 feet 8 inches by 15 feet 10 inches, 2 watch-rooms and 10 cells, each measuring 9 feet 6 inches by 6 feet. Each cell contains 2 beds for 3 persons each.

The male debtors' ward contains 3 day rooms and 2 work rooms, 3 bedrooms and 6 sleeping cells for debtors. The bedrooms and cells contain accommodation for 63 debtors.

In the female ward female debtors and criminal offenders are indiscriminately and improperly confined. Besides an apartment each for the matron and her assistant, this ward has a day room 29 feet 6 inches by 14 feet 3 inches, a work and schoolroom 33 feet 2 inches by 14 feet 4 inches, and 10 cells, each 9 feet 10 inches by 6 feet 6 inches. Each cell contains 2 beds, in each of which 3 persons sleep.

Besides the wards and apartments which have been described, there is a chapel, suitably fitted up, a spacious office for the governor and other local officers, and the other requisite apartments, such as store-rooms, watch-rooms etc.

The hospital, which is within the gaol wall, is 3-storeys high, tolerably spacious and well ventilated, and affords ample accommodation. It contains, besides an apartment for the matron and other necessary officers, a room for females, measuring 15 feet 4 inches by 14 feet 8 inches, fitted with 3 beds, each of which accommodates 2 persons; 4 male rooms, 2 of which measure 15 feet 2 inches by 14 feet 8 inches, and 2 15 feet 4 inches by 14 feet 8 inches; each contains 3 beds, in each of which 2 persons lie.

State of Gaol

It may have been seen by the foregoing description of this gaol that its accommodation is much too limited, that the cells are too much crowded and the number of persons allotted to a bed is much too great. But it is in the female ward that the want of accommodation is so painfully felt, for here the female debtors and the female felons are indiscriminately associated and not unfrequently occupy the same bed. For a series of 9 years the average number of persons confined in this gaol annually at a time has been 232. Of these, the average number of females was 56.

The gaol in its present state is not adequate to the confinement of one-fourth that number, were it to be estimated by the present system of prison discipline and prison accommodation. The former cannot be now preserved, nor can the silent system, so much approved of, be enforced.

With the exception of the adult male felons', the yards are much too small; that of the females is particularly so. From the height of their walls, and the total absence of any draught or thoroughfare, there is no possibility of ventilation and their air is of necessity by no means pure.

The stones are for the most part broken in the Sentry's Walk, in which there is a much purer atmosphere and a more free circulation of air.

Other Prisons

From a very early period the castle of Carrickfergus was used as a place of confinement, chiefly for state prisoners or those charged with political offences. Many persons of rank and nobility in their day have been imprisoned in it.

Carrickfergus possessed, in "wyrol tower or prison," also called "Castle Worraig" and the "old gatehouse," another prison. This structure, which was removed about 1780, stood at the eastern extremity of High Street and near the site of the present county Antrim court house and gaol. Its position will be seen by referring to the plan of the town as taken in 1550, in which it is laid down as "wyrol castle or prison." It was the prison of the county Antrim. It was also known as the Mayorality Castle, from the mayor having always been elected there, and from the assizes and courts having been held in it. It was a high square tower consisting of 3 floors, on the lowest of which the criminals were kept. The second was occupied by the gaolers' and debtors' rooms, and in the upper the mayor's courts and assizes were held. The entrance to this building was by a projecting stone stair, in front of which were the stocks.

Until the year 1827 there was a separate prison for the county of the town of Carrickfergus. This building, which was taken down in 1827, stood at the western extremity of High Street. It was erected about the year 1613 and was partly rebuilt in 1727. Prior to 1776 the latter prison belonged to the county Antrim, but it was in that year ceded to Carrickfergus, the grand jury of which gave in return Castle Worraigh, their gaol and court house to the county Antrim.

In 1817 one of the judges of assize refused, on account of its ruinous state, to hold the assizes in the county of Carrickfergus court house. They were then removed to that of the county Antrim, in which they have since been held. Debtors were confined in the old gaol until 1820, when they were removed to the county Antrim gaol.

The present gaol, which serves as a prison for the county Antrim and county of the town of Carrickfergus, was commenced in 1778 and cost, conjointly with the court house which adjoins it, 5,785 pounds 6s 4d. In November 1815 the first stone of a wing added to the western side of the gaol was laid, and soon after 2 wings were added to the rear of the building. The yards were then much enlarged, and a chapel, infirmary and several offices and rooms were added to it. These additions, which were completed on the 1st November 1819, cost nearly 16,000 pounds, of which sum 395 pounds were awarded as damages to individuals whose property had been encroached on. Since this period no alterations or additions of any consequence have been made to this gaol.

In 1827 the gaol and court house of the county of the town of Carrickfergus commenced being taken down.

Annals of Prisons

The following annals of the prisons of Carrickfergus have been extracted from the records of that town, and may not be altogether uninteresting.

1656, July. 26 Roman Catholic priests and schoolmasters were confined at Carrickfergus, prior to their being transported to Barbados.

1747. In this year there is mention made of the criminal prisoners receiving 10d ha'penny per week. If convicted, their allowance was usually reduced to 6d or 7d and sometimes so low as 3d per week. In 1757 the allowance was increased to 14d per week, at which rate it continued for many years.

1729. There were only 70 prisoners confined in this gaol. Of these, 28 were pirates. In 1748 there were but 59 prisoners confined here, and in 1760 there were not any criminals in prison. From 17th April to the 15th June 1762 there was but 1 person in prison, and from 13th October 1764 until February 1765 there was but 1 person, a female, in gaol here. At Lent assizes 1765 there

was not a prisoner for trial. There were 64 prisoners for trial in the spring of 1764. In 1783 there were in September but 19 prisoners for trial. At Lent assizes 1792 there were but 36 criminals for trial.

At the summer assizes of 1816 there were 72 prisoners for trial. 5 of these were sentenced to be hanged, 9 transported, 2 whipped and 9 imprisoned. At the spring assizes of 1817 there were 142, and at the summer assizes of the same year 176 prisoners for trial, the latter being the greatest number known in the county. There were at the same time in gaol 94 other convicted prisoners and 64 debtors. At Lent assizes 1818 there were 97, and at summer assizes 64 prisoners for trial. At Lent assizes 1819 there were 90 prisoners, of whom 44 were found guilty. At the Lent and summer assizes of 1820 there were respectively 114 and 64 persons on the criminal calendars. At Lent and summer assizes 1821 there were respectively 96 and 93 prisoners for trial. At the Lent assizes of 1823 there were 36 prisoners, of whom 26 were convicted. From this period until the present the criminal returns of this county will be found in the appendix at the end of this Memoir.

From April 1747 till August 1771 53 male and 3 female convicts were transported from this gaol, and from May 1818 until January 1823 57 persons, of whom 17 were females, were sent off for transportation.

Between March 1797 and May 1819 32 persons have been executed here. Of these, 15 were for murder, 3 for conspiracy to murder, 2 for parricide, 2 for high treason, 1 for rape, 2 for highway robbery, 5 for burglary, 1 for forgery and 1 for administering unlawful oaths. Since 1819 to the present period (1839) 4 have been executed. Of these, Hugh Loughridge and his mother were executed for murder in August 1824; William McVey was hanged for murder on the 11th April 1829; and Jane Graham was executed for a similar crime, 31st March 1830.

Prison Expenses

In 1666 an agreement was made between the county Antrim grand jury and corporation of Carrickfergus, by which the latter engaged to keep the court house and gaol in proper repair and to defray all the expenses, and find all necessaries for the safety and maintenance of the prisoners, for 70 pounds per annum.

The expense of the support of the prisoners from the 14th April till the 29th September 1711 was 11 pounds 10s 5d; from January 3rd till April

11th 1743, 4 pounds 16s 3d; from August 1716 till April 1717, 10 pounds 8s; from April 15th 1718 till April 1719, 15 pounds 7s 1d ha'penny; from April 12th till August 1762, 1 pound 11s 8d; from March 12th 1813 till March 22nd 1814, 1,086 pounds 6s 5d; from summer assizes 1819 to summer assizes 1820, 1,960 pounds 12s 8d; from summer assizes 1821 to spring assizes 1822, 1,000 pounds; from 2nd March 1822 till 19th March 1823, 1,500 pounds; in 1836 the gaol expenses amounted to 2,276 pounds 5s 2d ha'penny; in 1837 to 2,617 pounds 11s 2d; and in 1838 to 2,575 pounds 11s 8d 3 farthings.

Court House

The court house of the county of Antrim and county of the town of Carrickfergus stands at the eastern extremity of High Street, of which it forms the termination, presenting to its western or entrance front. Its southern side extends for 64 feet along the northern side of the Scotch Quarter which diverges from High Street.

It presents in its drab stone-finished front, low elevation and square-headed windows a plain old-fashioned and uninteresting appearance, which is still further increased by its high-pitched hipped roof and the heavy balustrade surmounting its parapet. The entrance is by a plain doorway with merely an architrave and frieze. There is a row of plain square windows in its entrance front. The walls are 22 feet high. The entrance or western front of the court house is 100 feet in length; its depth is 64 feet.

Immediately within the doorway is a large common hall, beyond which is the record and on the left side of which is the crown court. From this hall doors and passages lead to the courts and the different offices and apartments connected with them, and with the public officers of the county, amounting in number (including the apartments of the porter) to 31.

The hall measures 43 by 28 feet 8 inches. The criminal court, which is plainly but pretty comfortably fitted up, measures 31 by 31 feet and the record court 24 by 30 feet. Both these courts and the hall occupy the total height of the building. The grand jury room is a spacious apartment 30 by 34 feet 6 inches, suitably fitted up. A large circular table accommodating the entire grand jury occupies the centre of the room. Affixed to rollers suspended from the wall are the Ordnance maps of the county Antrim united on one sheet.

The other apartments comprise those necessary in such public buildings for the accommodation of juries and of the different public officers. They are suitably and comfortably fitted up, though their general arrangement and that of the building is by no means judicious.

The court house was founded the 1st March 1779 and cost, together with the gaol which adjoins it, and which was commenced on the preceding year, 5,785 pounds 6s. Until the year 1817 it had exclusively belonged to the county Antrim, the county of the town of Carrickfergus having a court house and prison of its own, but, owing to the ruinous state of the latter, the assizes have (since 1817) for both counties been held in the former.

Market House

The market house stands in the northern side of High Street and near the centre of the town. It is a plain but neat-looking, stone-finished building consisting of 2 floors and measuring in front 62 feet and in depth 27 feet. On the ground floor is a small weigh-house formerly opening into the street by 3 lofty arched gateways which are now built up.

On the upper floor is the corporation assembly room measuring 39 by 21 feet 8 inches. It is used for holding petty sessions, public meetings etc. The news room, which measures 16 by 11 feet, is on the same floor. The market house was erected (in 1755) by subscription.

Market Place

The new market place is conveniently situated on the western side of North Street and near the centre of the town. It consists of a quadrangular enclosure measuring internally 22 by 97 feet. Along its southern side a row of 10 shops or stalls for butchers and other dealers, neatly and uniformly constructed, extends. On the opposite side there is a spacious slated shed. The western side of the market is enclosed by a lofty stone wall, near the centre of which is a shed containing the public crane and the office of the weigh-master. The eastern side, which forms the western side of the street, is enclosed by a dwarf wall surmounted by a high iron railing. In this side is the principal entrance by a large iron gate and 2 lesser ones. There is also an entrance (but little used) in the southern side, from Lancasterian Street.

The market place is paved and kept in good order. It is both uniform and substantial in its appearance and construction, and is admirably adapted in every respect for the purpose for which it is intended. It should have been stated that there is a weighbridge near its centre.

This market place was erected in 1836. The cost of its erection amounted to 700 pounds, of which Peter Kirk Esquire (M.P. for the borough), mayor, contributed 100 pounds, 300 pounds was raised by the sale of the site of the old gaol and court house of the county of the town of Carrickfergus, and the remainder was defrayed by the corporation. Of the 700 pounds which it cost, 300 pounds was expended in purchasing the site, which had formerly been that of a tanyard.

Parish Church

The parish church of Carrickfergus, or the church of St Nicholas, stands on an eminence near the centre of the town and near the western extremity of High Street.

It is of a cruciform figure and consists of a nave and chancel standing east and west, and 2 aisles or transepts intersecting it at its centre. The length of the church from east to west, inside, is 135 feet. Its width in the west end or nave is 25 feet 2 inches, while in the chancel or east end it is only 20 feet 10 inches. The internal length of the northern or Donegall aisle is 32 feet by 20 feet 2 inches wide. The height of the church in the inside is 26 feet. At its western end is a square belfry, which supports a neat cut-stone spire. The height of the former is 75 feet and of the latter 45 feet. The tower or belfry measures externally 18 by 18 feet. It is built in rubble masonry with cut sandstone quoins, and is surmounted by a neat cornice and balustrade. It contains a well-toned bell and a good clock with 4 dials.

There are 2 entrances to the church, one by the belfry and the other by a doorway at the northern side of the church. The latter passes through a vestry room (measuring 27 feet 6 inches by 16 feet) which was built by the late Dean Dobbs in 1787. It appears to have been one of the original entrances, from its pointed arch corresponding with that of the windows. It was, however, only reopened on the erection of a vestry room, previous to which it had been built up. In its east side is a similar doorway now built up. The doorway in the belfry is square-headed.

Formerly the only entrances were on the south side, by 2 small doorways, one of which had a pointed and the other a circular arch. They were built up on the opening of the present ones.

Windows and Walls

The church is lit by 22 windows besides 2 lights in the ceiling. Of these, those in the northern and southern sides of the nave and chancel, besides the east window, are pointed; with exception of the last, they have heavy cut-stone mullions and mouldings, and, particularly that on the north side of the chancel, are of evident antiquity. They are divided by 2 mullions, which ramify near the top into trefoil-headed lights. Their dimensions are from 10 to 11 feet high and 5 to 5 and a half feet wide on the outside. The present east or chancel window is pointed but is smaller than the former, which had 2 stone mullions ramifying near the top into 6 trefoil-headed lights.

This present window, which is of stained glass, represents John baptising Christ. It was brought from the private chapel of Dangan House, county Meath, in 1800, and presented to the parish by the late George Burleigh of Burleigh Hill, Esquire. Its elevation on the outside is 18 feet and its width 7 and a half feet. In the western end are 2 small round windows of stained glass presented by the same person.

The windows in Freeman's Aisle are square and appear next in antiquity to those in the nave and chancel. There are 3 of them; that in the gable or south is divided by 4, while those on the east and west side are divided by 2 heavy stone mullions.

There are at present 4 Gothic windows in the northern or Donegall aisle. They measure 12 feet 6 inches high and 2 feet 10 inches wide on the outside. It is said that this aisle was formerly lit by square-headed windows, similar to those in Freeman's Aisle. The present windows have metal frames.

The walls of the church are 3 feet 6 inches thick and are in excellent repair. They are now roughcast, but are said to contain a considerable quantity of cut sandstone, in quoins and mouldings about the doorways and windows. Attached to these are 17 remarkable-looking buttresses, of which there are 2 at each angle of the eastern gable and at the angles of the aisles. There is also a large plain buttress 27 feet long and 2 feet 6 inches thick at the base, attached to the northern side of the nave. It reaches to the summit of the side wall. The others vary in their projection at the base from 3 feet 6 inches to 7 feet and in thickness from 2 feet 9 inches to 3 feet 9 inches. The 2 at the south east angle of the eastern gable have columns cut in their quoins or corner stones.

State of Church

The external appearance of the church is rather venerable and interesting, and seems to have suffered but little by the encroachments of modern repairs.

The internal arrangement of the church is neat and comfortable. A flagged alley, with a row of pews on each side, occupies the aisles. At the western end is a plain but neat gallery, supported by metal pillars and approached from the belfry. It contains a small but well-toned organ, besides being capable of accommodating 87 persons.

The church contains accommodation for 766 persons. It is well heated and ventilated, and kept in excellent repair. The stained glass in the east window is rich, and most of the new windows are stained or coloured and admit a clear, though sombre, light. The pulpit is at the angle formed by the nave and Donegall aisle. The chancel is under the east window and presents in its gilt characters and old-fashioned devices an interesting and characteristic appearance. The aisles are studded with numerous monuments and tablets, and the flags of the aisles serve as tombstones to several individuals of note.

Donegall Monument

The most remarkable monument is that which is erected against the gable or extremity of Donegall aisle and which is remarkable for its size, beauty and costliness. The aisle in which it stands is the private property of the Marquis of Donegall, having formerly been the family chapel. Until the year 1832 it had, from its ruinous state, been shut out from the church and been used only as the cemetery of the family. It was then, however, repaired and refitted with pews, and is now in perfect repair. Its floor is [blank] feet higher than that of the nave and is approached by stone steps. The 2 front pews looking into the body of the church are the property of Lord Donegall. Underneath the floor of this aisle lie interred the different members of the family who have died in this county since the time of Sir John Chichester, who was taken prisoner and beheaded by the MacDonnells near Ballycarry on the 4th November 1597. Near his coffin, which is broken in, is the blade of a small sword and a quantity of lime.

On the east side of the aisle is a tablet of white marble surmounted by a coronet. On the tablet is an inscription to the memory of Arthur Chichester, 3rd Earl of Donegall, who was killed in 1706 at Monjuich, an almost impregnable fort that secured the land side of Barcelona in Spain. He was interred at Barcelona. On his death, King Charles of Spain wrote a letter to Queen Anne extolling his courage and lamenting his fate.

The Donegall monument, which is erected against the extremity of the aisle, is a magnificent and costly structure. It was raised by (strange as it may appear, nothing whatever respecting it can be ascertained). It is partly and principally of a reddish marble, and partly of alabaster. Its breadth at the plinth is 15 feet and its extreme height 24 feet. The designs, arms and devices are in high relief. The figures, which are detached, are as large as life, and the workmanship is at once rich, chaste and elaborate.

On the plinth of the sarcophagus Sir John Chichester, who had been decapitated by the MacDonnells, is represented in armour, kneeling with his hands clasped as if in the act of prayer. [Insert footnote: MacDonnell, who had beheaded Sir John, having obtained his pardon and being in Carrickfergus, came to see the family monument of the Chichesters in this church. On seeing the effigy of Sir John he asked: "How the De'il he came to get his head again, for he was sure he had anes ta'en it frae him" *Lodge's Peerage*]. This figure has suffered sadly, the head having been taken off and merely set on, and the hands also having been broken.

Over the sarcophagus are 2 full-sized figures of Sir Arthur Chichester, 1st Lord Baron of Belfast, and his lady. Both are in a praying posture; they kneel face to face and are clothed in long robes with ruffs. Sir Arthur wears armour under his clothes; between them on a cushion lay the effigy of their infant son Arthur. These figures occupy 2 niches, with circular and richly ornamented tops. 2 handsome Corinthian columns on each side support a rich architrave and entablature, which are surmounted by an attic on which the family arms are sculptured in high relief, and on each side of which are 2 Corinthian columns supporting a handsome entablature. On the pediment are 2 compartments representing trophies and military devices in basso relief, and on each side are large black tablets on which are inscribed the epitaph.

The structure and style of this monument are evidently Italian. It is much to be regretted that so little care has been bestowed on it and that it is even still so little protected.

Suspended from the wall above the monument hang on one side a sort of tunic painted scarlet and ornamented with heraldic bearings and devices, and a helmet, and on the other a shield and 2 small swords. It is not known to whom they belonged or how they came there.

Erection of Church

The date of the erection of the church is wrapped in obscurity, but there are several circumstances connected with it which clearly indicates its being of considerable antiquity. A belief exists that it was founded on the site of a pagan temple; from whence this notion (which is mentioned in Gill's manuscripts) is derived is not known. It was dedicated to St Nicholas, who is probably intended to have been represented in the stone face on the outside of and near the top of the western gable.

It is supposed to have originally been the oratory or chapel of a Franciscan monastery which stood on the site of the present gaol. This conjecture is rendered more probable by the circumstance of there having been a subterranean passage leading from the one to the other, a distance of yards.

Subterranean Passage

The entrance to this passage is in the east gable of the church; it is by an arched aperture in the wall and is now not more than 2 feet above the floor of the chancel. It is impossible to explore it for more than 3 feet, from its being choked up with rubbish; but it has, in sinking sewers, foundations along its line, been discovered at intervals and to a certain extent satisfactorily explored.

About 64 years since it was opened in 4 places and found to be constructed exclusively of cut stone. It is from 4 feet 6 inches to 5 feet high, of a similar width, and has an arch roof. Its floor, which is also of cut stone, has a semicircular channel along its centre, for the purpose of carrying off any water which might get into it. About midway between its extreme points there is, on either side of the passage, a sort of chamber or recess with a stone seat. This is supposed to have been intended as a rest place for the nuns on their way to and from the chapel. No other discoveries were made in it and, as it is now quite closed up, it is impos-

sible to furnish further information respecting it.

In digging a grave under the communion table many years ago, was found a stone cross with the date 1164 inscribed very rudely on the top.

A stone vessel resembling a font, but with 2 handles and a hole in the bottom, was, with some other articles which are not now forthcoming, found about the same time.

Improvements to Church

It is probable that the present chancel, which is 1 foot 2 inches narrower than the nave, at one period constituted the extent of the chapel, as the church is said to have been. The nave, from its buttresses and from its forming a prolongation of the chancel, may have next been erected, but there is not any record as to when the aisles were built.

At the west end of the building there formerly stood a steeple with a clock and bell. The clock was first set up in 1678. The bell was given to the parish by Andrew Willoughby. On it was engraved "Androo Willouby, mayor [?h p] 84."

In 1770 the old steeple was taken down and the present belfry and tower were erected at an expense of 541 pounds 19s 7d, of which the following sums were contributed, viz. Earl of Donegall 130 pounds; Barry Yelverton Esquire 100 pounds; E.D. Wilson Esquire 37 pounds 1s 4d, also a quantity of oak timber; Conway P. Dobbs Esquire 12 pounds; Marriott Dalway Esquire 11 pounds 7s 6d; Rev. R. Dobbs (dean) 10 pounds; Rev. Isaac Haddock (curate) 5 pounds 5s 7d; Richard Fletcher Esquire 100 barrels of lime; the remainder was defrayed by the parish. At the same time a new clock was erected in it.

On the 13th April 1832, the day on which the news of the passing of the Reform Bill reached Carrickfergus, the church bell split open, to the no small surprise of the inhabitants, who looked

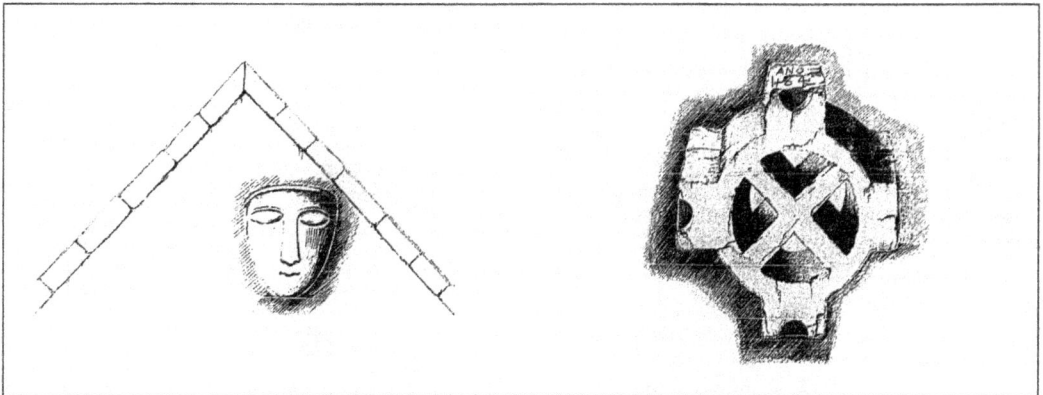

Face and cross in church

on such an event as more than ominous. The bell was taken down and recast, and restored to its original place on the 15th September following.

History of Church

1808. The assembly, on the 3rd of April, agreed to purchase an organ for the church and to pay the organist out of the rents of the common lands, then about to be let. E.D. Wilson Esquire proposed to grant a free house to the organist. The assembly, however, on the 21st May following, rescinded their resolution.

1812, 16th May. The roof of the west part of the church fell in. It was entirely, with the exception of the north aisle, newly roofed in summer. The Marquis of Downshire contributed 100 pounds towards its repairs.

1818. Owing to the ruinous state of many of the seats, the church underwent a thorough repair. All the seats were taken down and made uniform. The aisles were newly flagged and the gallery was taken down. Several of the large windows were newly fitted and repaired. The expenses of the seats were paid by the claimants, but those of a few who refused or were unable to pay were publicly sold by the churchwardens and the surplus given to their respective owners.

1820. A gallery was erected in the place of that taken down. To this E.D. Wilson Esquire contributed 100 pounds; the remainder was defrayed by the parish.

In 1830 the organ was erected by subscription and in 183[blank] the Donegall aisle was opened up and the church generally improved.

Trinitarian Meeting House

The Orthodox Presbyterian meeting house, in connexion with the Synod of Ulster, is situated in a neatly enclosed space on the western side of North Street and near the north centre of the town.

It is a plain and substantial but very neatly-finished structure of a rectangular form, built principally of stones finished and kept in excellent repair. It measures externally 77 feet 6 inches by 53 feet and is 34 feet high. It is well lit by 2 rows of windows on each side. Its internal arrangement is neat and judicious. It consists of a vestibule or hall opening by 2 doors into the body of the house, which contains 79 pews. The gallery, which is spacious, is supported by 8 metal columns and contains 38 pews, affording, with those in the aisle, accommodation for 1,000 persons.

On the gallery, which is approached from the hall by 2 flights of stairs, is a committee or session room measuring 28 feet by 10 feet 6 inches. Besides this, there is a small private [room?] for the ministers on the ground floor. This house is very comfortably and substantially fitted up. The alleys are bounded and matted, and the pews and woodwork are neatly executed.

The space on which this meeting house stands measures 108 by 78 feet. It is enclosed in front by a neat iron railing.

This house stands on the site of the former one which had been erected about a century ago. The ground on which it stands was granted in 1740, for a lease of 999 years, by Thomas Robinson to Robert Moore, James Craig, David Legg and James Cobham, in trust for the congregation, for the sum of 5 pounds in hand and 1d per annum. In 1762 an attempt was made to break the lease but the plaintiffs were nonsuited.

On Sunday the 1st April 1827 service was for the last time performed in the old meeting house, the removal of which commenced on the following day. On the 9th May following, the first stone of the present house was laid by the Rev. James Seaton Reid (now Dr Reid), then minister of the congregation, who contributed 50 pounds towards its erection. The house was opened for worship on the 8th February 1829, when 50 pounds was collected towards defraying the debt incurred by it. The total cost amounted to 2,000 pounds, which was raised by subscription.

Unitarian Meeting House

The Unitarian meeting house is situated in the Scotch Quarter, 120 yards from the eastern extremity of High Street. It is a rectangular building measuring externally 50 by 41 feet and 26 feet high. It is constructed entirely of brick but is still in quite an unfinished state, though commenced early in 1838. Its entrance front at the southern gable consists of a portico with 2 tall brick columns supporting a frieze. It is well lit by 8 circular-headed and 1 square-headed window. It is substantially fitted up with pews. The alleys are floored with timber and, when finished, it will be a neat and comfortable place for worship. It contains accommodation for 260 persons.

It is intended that it shall be stone finished externally. Its estimated cost is 1,000 pounds. Already 879 pounds 18s 9d, which has been raised by subscription, has been expended on it.

Independent Meeting House

The Independent meeting house is situated in Castle Street, near the south centre of the town.

It stands in an enclosed space within a few feet of the beach.

It is a plain rectangular structure measuring internally 40 feet 6 inches by 32 feet 6 inches. It is well lit by 4 large windows with arched heads. It is substantially and comfortably fitted up with pews and contains accommodation for 250 persons. It is as yet in rather an unfinished state, but several improvements connected with it are contemplated.

It was opened for worship on 16th September 1821. The cost of its erection, amounting to 480 pounds, was defrayed by subscriptions. The ground on which it stands was granted by Henry C. Ellis Esquire.

Wesleyan Methodist Chapel

The Wesleyan Methodist chapel is situated at the western end and on the northern side of West Street. It is a plain but neat-looking, stone-finished house of rectangular form, measuring internally 51 by 29 feet 6 inches. It stands in [a] space measuring 135 by 39 feet, enclosed in front by an iron railing. The house is well lit by 7 arched and 5 square windows. It is comfortably and neatly fitted up internally and is in excellent repair. It contains 25 simple pews, besides a portion of the house which is fitted up with forms. It is capable of accommodating 326 persons.

This house was opened for worship on the 12th May 1812. The cost of its erection, amounting to 600 pounds, was defrayed by subscriptions.

Ranters' Chapel

The Ranters' or Primitive Methodist chapel is a plain little building, built of stones and lit by 4 square windows. Its form is square measuring internally 31 by 18 feet 3 inches. It contains no pews and is merely fitted with a few forms. It is situated in the Scotch Quarter. It was erected in 1838 at an expense of 60 pounds, which was raised by subscriptions.

Roman Catholic Chapel

The Roman Catholic chapel is situated on a gentle acclivity at the western side of the town and stands in an enclosed space of half a rood. The house, which is plainly and substantially built, is of rectangular form and measures 45 by 24 feet. It is well lit by 4 spacious painted windows. There is only 1 pew, the accommodation for the congregation being confined to movable forms. It is capable, in its present state, of accommodating 350 persons.

It was erected in 1826 at a cost of 356 pounds which, together with 100 pounds, the sum paid for the ground on which it stands, was raised by subscription.

Contiguous to the chapel is the residence of the priest, which was erected at the same time at an extra expense (similarly defrayed) of 75 pounds, exclusive of the internal fitting and finishing, which was borne by the priest.

Shipping Quay

There are 2 quays or harbours at Carrickfergus, namely the Shipping Quay, which is its port and harbour, and the Fishers' Quay, which was erected as a protection to the fishing boats of the town.

The Shipping Quay or harbour of Carrickfergus is near the centre of the town and at the southern side of the castle. It consists of a small basin including an area of 41,560 feet, protected on the southern and eastern, or sea, side by a stone pier which, describing a somewhat elliptic curve, extends southward for 540 feet from the eastern extremity of the rocky tongue on which the castle stands and which forms the northern end of the harbour. The basin is confined on its western or land side by a small pier or quay extending for 186 feet, parallel to the other. The entrance to the harbour, between the southern extremities of the piers, is 160 feet wide.

A causeway or roadway 28 feet wide and 181 feet long connects the harbour with the town and encloses, between it and the castle, a triangular dam including an area of 11,616 feet. Formerly a fosse or ditch connected the waters on the south west and north east sides of the port, thereby insulating the castle.

The outer or shipping pier is 540 feet in extreme length, 36 feet in width at the base and from 9 to 12 feet high from the base to the roadway, which is from 21 to 30 feet wide, exclusive of a footway 2 feet 6 inches wide which is raised 2 feet 6 inches [above] the roadway. It is protected on the sea side by a parapet wall 5 feet high and 2 feet 6 inches thick.

This pier is firmly built of stones. The stones in the retaining walls are large, well bedded and dressed, and those along its edges are squared. The roadway is well paved and the footway is flagged with large stones.

The ballast pier, or quay, forming the western side of the basin is 186 feet long and 120 feet in extreme width. Its height from the base is from 8 to 10 feet. It is a plain solid structure of large stones which, with the exception of those forming the summit of its retaining walls, are almost entirely undressed. Its surface is formed of ballast and binding.

The bed of the harbour is of a tough sandy clay. The depth of water in the harbour at neap tides is from 7 to 8 feet and at spring tides from 8 to 11 feet. It admits vessels drawing 9 feet.

This harbour is much too confined for the trade of the port, to which 39 vessels now belong, while 10 years ago there was not more than a third of the number. It affords, however, ample protection from the prevailing winds.

It is at present in excellent repair, a considerable sum having been expended on it during the present year. The expenses connected with it are defrayed from the harbour dues, which amount to about 140 pounds per annum.

The dam alluded to is connected with the harbour with which it communicates by means of a sluice. It admits the water at high tide and this, at low water, is discharged into the harbour and assists in clearing it of mud and sand.

The date of the original erection of the quay is not precisely known. In a plan of the town, supposed to have been made in 1550, the "peare" is laid down, but it at that time was constituted of wood. In the records of Carrickfergus for 1575, the following entry appears: "Aprile [blank], in this courte was Michael Savidg for breaking downe the timber of the peer and occupying it to his owne use, figured at 20s sterling." In 1627 its construction of stone commenced and cost 1,100 pounds, besides much labour not charged by the inhabitants for their men and horses.

Since that period, upwards of 1,400 pounds have been expended on it, of which 500 pounds were granted in 1783 by the Irish parliament and 64 pounds 17s 6d in 1804 by the assembly.

In 1821, the quay being much choked with mud, a committee was, with the approbation of the mayor, formed for improving it. A sum was subscribed for the purpose and each vessel unloading at the quay was ordered to pay 2d per ton, or 1s per ton subscription, and 1d per ton for 2 years after.

With the exception of the salary of the harbour and ballast-master, 25 pounds per annum, and that of the water-bailiff, 10 pounds per annum, the dues and charges of the harbour, amounting to 140 pounds per annum, go towards the expenses of its improvement.

Fishers' Quay

The Fishers' Quay is situated at the Scotch Quarter and near the eastern extremity of the town. It consists merely of a stone pier extending towards the sea for 360 feet and slightly curved towards the south west at its extremity. The pier is 10 feet high from its base to the roadway, which is 21 feet wide, and is protected on its north eastern side by a parapet 3 feet 6 inches high and 3 feet 6 inches thick.

The entire structure is of white limestone and is firmly built, the stones being large, well dressed and well bedded. The roadway is formed of large flat stones and is firmly secured at its edges by well-dressed blocks.

The depth of water in this harbour at neap or average tides is 6 feet and at spring tides 8 feet.

This pier, or harbour, was erected in 1831, solely for the protection of the fishing craft of Carrickfergus and cost between 1,300 and 1,400 pounds, of which sum the Fishery Board contributed about two-thirds, the remainder having been subscribed by landed proprietors and others connected with the corporation.

It affords ample protection from the heavy swells setting in from the north east or mouth of the lough, but it is quite exposed to the prevailing winds and storms from the south south west and west, and is therefore of but little use. Its plan and design are therefore injudicious. It suffered considerable damage from the storm of the 7th January 1839 and has not since been repaired.

Hotels

There are 2 tolerable hotels in Carrickfergus, namely the Queen's Arms and the Corporation Arms. Their accommodation is good and reasonably extensive. Post horses, chaises and cars are kept at each of them. Both hotels are situated in High Street and within a few doors of each other.

Private Residences

The residences of the private families in Carrickfergus are exceedingly plain and unpretending in their appearance. Few of them are modern, and still fewer spacious or handsome in their appearance. They are, with 2 exceptions, small but commodious dwellings, rather antiquated than otherwise in their external aspect.

The following are the principal families residing in Carrickfergus: James Wills Esquire, Joymo[unt]; Mrs Dawson, High Street; Mrs Dobbs, High Street; Rev. Henry Carter, Governors Place; Alexander Johns, High Street; Mrs Lesly, Joymount Bank; William Burleigh Esquire, Scotch Quarter; Stephen Rice Esquire, Scotch Quarter.

Houses

Carrickfergus, including the town and suburbs, consists of 746 houses, of which 1 is 4-storeys high, 70 are 3-storeys, 302 are 2-storeys and 373 consist of but 1-storey; 491 houses are slated and 255 are thatched; 692 are occupied and 54 are unoccupied.

The greater number of the houses are built of stone. Many of the cottages, particularly those of more recent erection, as also some modern houses, are of brick; but the majority of the older houses and cottages are of stone.

With the exception of 1 house in High Street, laid down as Dobbins' in the plan of 1559, and which has already been noticed, none of the ancient or original dwelling houses remain, nor are there any which, in their appearance or structure, bear any indications of antiquity. There were, until very recently, a few old houses built in frames of oak, in a style formerly termed cadge-work. Remains of these are to be found in some of the old outhouses which have been suffered to remain in rear of one or two dwelling houses in High Street.

The best houses in Carrickfergus have been erected within the last 30 years, within which period the town has undergone much improvement as to appearance. The larger houses are situated in the principal streets. Many of them are tolerably spacious and present plain modern fronts. They, as also the better descriptions of 2-storey houses, are chiefly occupied by shopkeepers and private families. The latter are generally of a good description as to size and substance and are mostly in good repair. A few of them are stone-finished and are rather neat-looking, but the majority are roughcast and whitened.

A smaller description of 2-storey houses is inhabited by petty dealers and publicans, and a few by tradespeople and mechanics. They are deficient in neatness, though they are generally substantial and in tolerable repair.

Cottages

There is great variety in the appearance and keeping of the cottages. Those within the walls are situated in retired dirty lanes and are, with a few exceptions, dirty and comfortless habitations, very limited in size, and in very bad repair. They are mostly roofed with thatch, are built of stones, badly lit and have damp, earthen floors. They are, however, but few in number and are inhabited by a very poor class.

The cottages in the Irish Quarter, though generally substantially built and roomy, are, with but few exceptions, very dirty and comfortless, and many of them are falling into bad repair from want of a trifling but timely repair. Those in Davys Street are of good height and proportions, and are roofed with slates; but their dusky grey roughcast, added to their extreme untidiness, gives them an aspect of discomfort and misery.

But a few of the cottages in this suburb have any pretensions to comfort or cleanliness, and still fewer of them to neatness or uniformity in keeping or appearance, though they are substantially built and are dry. They are, for the most part, inhabited by the families of labourers and a few hucksters.

In the Scotch Quarter the cottages, particularly those of more recent erection, are generally of brick and, though rather limited in size, are pretty comfortable and are dry and warm. They are also more uniformly built and are somewhat more neatly and cleanly kept than those in the Irish Quarter, though they have in these respects but little to boast of. There is an untidiness of appearance about their doorways which conveys an idea of more discomfort than really exists. They are for the most part, and indeed with but a few exceptions, inhabited by fishers.

General Remarks

The want of uniformity in their structure and the irregularity in their heights and sizes, added (with the exception of High Street) to the extreme dirtiness of the streets, renders the appearance of the houses and cottages still less interesting and agreeable! The streets, with the solitary exception, are narrow and gloomy; and they are ill-paved and, in wet weather, particularly disagreeable. The narrow and ill-paved footways afford no protection to the pedestrians and they are, at any season, disagreeable for walking.

Carrickfergus is neither lit nor watched, nor does it come under the act for paving or cleansing.

New Houses

From the year 1820 till the year 1835, 20 houses were erected in Carrickfergus; 4 were 3-storeys, 11 were 2-storeys and 5 were 1-storey high. Within the same period 6 houses were rebuilt and 44 were raised a storey and improved. From the year 1835 till 1839 inclusive, 5 3-storey and 3 2-storey houses have been erected. During the same period 11 houses were raised, 3 rebuilt.

The recently erected houses are mostly situated in Governors Place, Castle Street and the Scotch Quarter; and those which have been enlarged or improved are situated in these and the other principal streets.

Those recently erected are much superior in size and appearance to the other houses of similar description. The 3 and 2-storey houses are mostly of brick. The former are rather handsome structures, particularly those built in 1839 by Mr T.D. Stewart, which are situated in Castle Street and Market Place. From their situation and appearance, they have tended much towards the improvement of the town.

High Street

Carrickfergus, like most walled towns, seems to have, in the direction of its streets, undergone but little change, any alterations which had taken place being more the result of addition and increase than of deviation from the original plan. A reference to the plan of the town made in 1550 will illustrate this, as its design at that period seems to have formed the skeleton of its present arrangement and disposition.

At the time at which this plan was made, the town had been encompassed by a ditch, the walling of the town not having been commenced until 1574. The ditch included a larger space than that included by the walls. Of this but a small portion, as now occupied by the town, was then built on. The church and castle are accurately laid down, but a few houses or "castles" named after their owners and some small huts thinly scattered along the lines of the present principal streets seem to have constituted its entire extent. It does not appear that, at this period, the streets had any names. They would seem more probably to have been given to them at a much later period.

The principal street is High Street, the great thoroughfare of the town. It extends south westwards for 134 yards from the court house, running parallel to and within a few yards of the beach. It contains the county court house, the hotels and principal houses, which present a pretty uniform and respectable appearance. Its width, including a paved footway on each side, is from 65 to 80 feet. It is paved in the centre and is neatly and cleanly kept. High Street contains 30 houses, of which 22 are 3-storeys, 7 are 2-storeys and 1 is 1-storey high. Their general appearance is modern and respectable and that of the street spacious and uniform.

High Street is said to have derived its name from its having contained the highest houses in the town. One of the original houses, shown in the plan as Dobbin, is still in perfect preservation. It is on the

east side of the street and in line with the other houses, from which it is distinguished merely by 2 small square turrets, one at each angle in front. At the western end, and at the centre of High Street, stood Great Patrick, a cross erected on a circular basement of 6 steps. It is shown in the plan, but nothing more than its name is now known respecting it. The county of Carrickfergus court house stood at the western extremity of this street.

At the western end of High Street is the old market place, formed by a trifling expansion of this street and the radiation or diverging of 4 other streets from it. It is from 50 to 100 feet wide and about 130 feet long. It contains the market house and 9 good-looking houses.

The market house and a dwelling house adjoining it stand on the site of 2 ancient houses or "castles," one of which belonged to the O'Neills and the other to the family of Davys; near it, as shown in the plan, stood a large building marked "Machne Coole," and in its vicinity were 3 other "castles" belonging to the Wylles and one belonging to Patrick Savage.

Other Streets

Castle Street forms a prolongation of High Street and leads from it to the castle and quay. It terminates at the parade near the castle gateway. It is 87 yards long and is 30 feet wide. It consists of 15 houses, of which 2 are 3-storeys and 12 2-storeys high, ranged in single row along its western side.

Governors Place or Walk extends westward from the south western end of Castle Street and terminates at the site of Quay Gate, where it joins the Irish Quarter. On its eastern side are the Independent chapel and coastguard station-house (formerly the custom house) which almost adjoins the quay. On the opposite side is a single row of 12 neat houses, either 2 or 3-storeys high, which front the lough, from which they are separated merely by a wall on the other side of the road.

The length of this street is 179 yards and its width 32 feet. It is chiefly of modern erection and was widened and opened in 1835, when it became the thoroughfare leading to High Street. Its situation is very cheerful and agreeable and its appearance modern-looking.

West Street extends westward from the western side of the Market Place and terminates at the side of the West Gate, which opened into the Irish Quarter. It is one of the original streets but seems in 1550 to have been occupied by huts. Previous to 1835 it was the thoroughfare leading through the town to High Street, but since the opening of a line through Governors Place in that year it is rarely frequented by conveyances. Its length is 228 yards and its width varies from 16 to 28 feet. It contains 53 houses, of which 18 are 3-storeys, 32 2-storeys and 2 are 1-storey high.

The Wesleyan Methodist chapel is situated in this street. Several of the houses are good-looking, spacious and of comparatively modern erection, but there is a great want of uniformity and inattention to neatness which, added to the narrowness and extremely dirty state of the street, contrives to render it in every respect gloomy and disagreeable. It is wretchedly paved.

From the same end of the street Church Street diverges westwards for 57 yards, terminating [in] a gateway opening into the churchyard. It is merely a narrow lane 17 feet wide, containing a single row of 8 pretty good and modern dwelling houses.

North Street strikes off northwards at a right angle from the market place and terminates at the North Gate, which is still in preservation. Its length is 241 yards and its width 25 feet. It contains the market place and the Orthodox Presbyterian meeting house and 50 houses, of which 3 are 3-storeys, 30 are 2-storeys and 17 are 1-storey high.

North Street is one of the original streets. In the plan a large castellated house marked Sindalls is the only building shown in it. The present houses are generally small but are of comparatively modern erection. They present little neatness or uniformity of appearance, nor is the street either clean or smooth.

From the north east end of High Street a lane known as Gaol Lane or Antrim Street strikes off northward at a right angle to it. This street derived its former name from the county Antrim gaol which formed its eastern side. From the northern end of this street Back Lane strikes westward and, extending parallel to High Street, joins North Street near its centre.

Lancasterian Street, forming a continuation of Back Lane, extends irregularly to Cork Hill, a narrow lane which connects it, by diverging eastward, with West Street at the West Gate. From West Street 2 little streets or lanes strike off eastward, connecting it with Governors Place.

The foregoing include the streets and lanes within the walls. The principal streets, or those deserving any notice, have been described. The others are but mere lanes, very narrow and apart from any thoroughfare. The houses are small and generally inhabited by tradespeople, those occupied by persons in business being almost exclusively confined to the principal streets.

From the north east extremity of High Street a road diverges along the beach. On the land side of this are 2 respectable private residences which, with the county court house, occupy a portion of the site of Joymount Castle, erected by Sir Arthur Chichester in 1610, on the sites of Castle Worraigh and the ancient abbey of St Francis. The length of this street, terminating at the Water Gate, is 83 yards.

Scotch Quarter

Carrickfergus possesses 2 extensive suburbs in the Irish and Scotch Quarters, the former on its western and the latter on its north eastern side, both lying outside its walls.

The first erection of houses in these quarters seems to have taken place in 1627, at which period they were known as the west and east suburbs. Their present names do not appear in the records until the year 1680.

The Scotch Quarter, according to tradition, derived its name from its having been occupied originally by a colony of fishermen who fled from Argyllshire during the persecutions of 1665. It has since been inhabited by their descendants, who follow the same calling.

It consists principally of a street extending north eastward (inclusive of Green Street) along the beach for 806 yards, for three-fourths of which distance it has but a single row of houses fronting the water. At its north eastern extremity, which is known as Green Street, it has a row of cottages on each side. Here its width does not exceed an average of 30 feet, but at its other end it averages 40 feet.

The Scotch Quarter contains 153 houses, of which 1 is 4-storeys, 7 are 3-storeys, 24 are 2-storeys and the remainder are 1-storey cottages and cabins. According to the *Parliamentary boundary report* of 1832, there were then in the Scotch Quarter only 13 houses worth 10 pounds and since then only 1 house above that value has been erected. A few of the larger houses are occupied by private families and are rather modern-looking, though without any pretensions to size or neatness. The majority of the 2-storey houses are small and of an inferior description. The cottages are generally indifferent in size and appearance, and as to comfort they have no visible pretensions; the latter are chiefly occupied by fishermen.

The houses at the western end of the Scotch Quarter are pretty good-looking but they gradually fall off in appearance and finally, at its eastern extremity, dwindle into small and dirty cabins.

This part of the town occupies an agreeable and cheerful situation, with a good aspect. It is irregularly built and the mixture of good houses with indifferent cottages takes from the appearance of both.

Irish Quarter

The Irish Quarter is situated on the western side of the town. It is believed to have originated about the year 1670 and probably is indebted for its increase to the proclamation issued in 1678 by the Duke of Ormond, then lord deputy, by which Roman Catholics were ordered to move without the walls of all forts, cities and corporate towns, and by whom this quarter was formerly exclusively inhabited. This suburb contains 3 streets and lanes, containing 192 houses and cabins.

The principal streets are known by the name of Irish Quarter South, extending south westward along the shore from Water Gate, and Irish Quarter West, diverging due westerly from West Gate. These 2 streets form the side of a triangle of which Davys Street, at the western side of the quarter, forms the base; and they are connected, at their eastern extremities, by a little street common to both.

Irish Quarter South consists of a double row of houses and cottages extending for 293 yards along the road to Belfast, the width of which varies from 26 to 31 feet. It contains 3 3-storey and 29 2-storey houses and 51 cabins. The larger houses are of modern erection and are rather neat-looking. The cabins are generally small and dirty. The street is rough and the whole forms an entrance by no means calculated to create a favourable impression of the town.

Irish Quarter West is a dirty irregular-looking street extending westward from West Gate along an unfrequented road (leading across the mountain to Ballynure) for 279 yards. It contains 38 small 2-storey houses of an inferior description and 71 cottages and cabins, the appearance of which is comfortless and dirty. The street, which is dirty and very rough, is 30 feet wide. Few of the houses or cottages are of modern erection and but a few of them have been lately altered or improved.

Davys Street, connecting the 2 former streets near their western extremities, is 139 yards long and 23 feet wide. It contains 27 2-storey houses and 17 cottages. The former are small and both

are, with a few exceptions, dirty and comfortless-looking.

North Gate Out is the name given to 22 houses situated immediately outside the North Gate. Of these 1 is 3, 10 are 2-storeys and 11 are 1-storey high. They stand in various directions but chiefly in a row fronting the gate. They are of an inferior description, generally in indifferent repair, and are occupied by the lower classes.

SOCIAL ECONOMY

Extent of Carrickfergus

The boundaries of the county of the town of Carrickfergus and its franchises, as determined by the charter of Elizabeth, differed from those as subsequently established by James I. The latter were again altered "at the riding of the franchise of the county of the town of Carrickfergus, on Monday the 1st August 1785, pursuant to notice given by order of William Kirk Esquire, mayor of said town, for the time being." The following limits, which still continue, were then established.

"It is found the lands subject to pay cess and other taxes to said corporation are all situated and bounded within the mares and marks following, viz.

From town north east to the Copeland water, bounded by nearly north north west up the course of said water to the Copeland bridge, bounded on the north east by the Bishop of Down and Connor, and on the south west by Ezekiel Davys Wilson Esquire.

From Copeland bridge up said river to the foot of Crossmary, bounded on north east by Conway Richard Dobbs Esquire and Mariot Dalway Esquire, and on the south west by Ezekiel Davys Wilson Esquire.

From Crossmary nearly north north west to Clubbs ford or pound, and from thence to a gate, the entrance of the Park moss, called McFerran's gate, from which through the middle of the said moss, bounded by Mariot Dalway Esquire on the south west, by Richard G. Ker Esquire on the north east to Johnson's ford, about 20 perches below the Ladies Causeway. From the upper end of said moss round John Calbraith's house, which is the farthest limit of the corporation, that way.

From John Calbraith's house about west by Craigbuy farm, to the Dead Wifes Grave, bounded on the north west by Lord Dungannon and on the south west by Mariot Dalway Esquire.

From the Dead Wifes Grave by a stone ditch over a small river, to the corner of a ditch near the Priests Cairn, and thence nearly west to the old wall of Raloo, within about 50 perches of the Standing Stone, and then between Mr Lyndon's and Mr Dobbs' land, to George Patterson's house.

From said George Patterson's going nearly south and keeping Mr Ellis and Captain Crymble's estate, which they hold from Conway Richard Dobbs Esquire, to the westward and turning westwardly along the wall that divides McCann's field from the Englishman's Mountain, at which place there had been great encroachments made on the corporation, from said place to the Standing Stone. From the Standing Stone along said mountain to 3 lying stones commonly called the Three Brothers.

From the 3 lying stones about west north west along a ditch on the north east side of Straidnahana to Bruslee Flush, or lower end of Straidnahana, which is the farthest bound of the corporation at that place.

From Bruslee Flush southerly to the Ree hill and along said hill by the march ditch between said hill and Carntall, observing the turnings of said ditch, then turning about south east along the west side of My Lord's Mountain to the head of James Anderson's farm.

From James Anderson's farm down the south west side by a rivulet called Silver stream, which runs nearly south to the sea, and bounds the corporation all the way. From the mouth of the said stream the sea is the bounds into the town."

Names of people present at aforesaid riding: William Kirk Esquire, mayor; Alexander Gunning Esquire, deputy recorder; Robert Clements Esquire [and] Thomas Kirk Esquire, sheriffs.

Disputed Areas

At a court held for the purpose by Noah Dalway Esquire, mayor, in July 1807, 426 persons were admitted to as freemen. An objection having been made to the admission of several persons residing in Straidland and Little Ballymena, which, it was alleged, were without franchises, as these lands paid no taxes to the county of the town of Carrickfergus, a suit was entered in the court of King's Bench against these persons, and soon after against all those at that time admitted, on the grounds that the mayor and freemen had no right to admit persons to their freedom, without their having first memorialled the assembly to that effect.

The suit was tried in the county Antrim court, before Baron McClelland on the 21st March 1810, when a verdict was returned (by a special jury) "that the lands of Straid and Little Ballymena were without the franchises, though still belonging to the Corporation of Carrickfergus." It is said that the circumstances of the roads and bridges in these lands being made by the county Antrim was the main cause of the verdict. In consequence of this decision, the freemen, amounting to about 80, who had been made within 7 years, were disfranchised. The suit cost the parties upwards of 4,600 pounds.

The boundary of the county, as described, is exceedingly irregular towards its south west side. With this exception it is pretty even <een>, including an area of somewhat square measuring in the mean 5 and a half miles from south west to north east and 4 and a half miles from south east to north west. It contains 16,634 acres 1 rood 38 perches and is divided into 4 portions, namely the West Division, including 6,739 acres 2 roods 14 perches; the Middle Division (with its 2 detached portions), 3,868 acres 13 perches; the North East Division, 3,296 acres 3 roods 8 perches; and the Commons, containing 2,730 acres 3 perches. The names of the ancient townlands have long since become obsolete and are now only to be found in old maps and leases, and are known only to some of the inhabitants.

The Commons are mostly under mountain pasture, as are also the northern sides of the West and North East Divisions.

The lands of Straidland and Little Ballymena are not of course included in the area given above.

No alteration of the boundaries was proposed in the Municipal Bill of 1832.

Charters

Several charters, it is not known how many, have been granted to Carrickfergus. The last, and that by which it is at present governed, was granted on 14th December 1613 by James I.

It cannot locally be ascertained as to when this district was incorporated as a county of a town, but there are several circumstances which satisfactorily determine the extreme antiquity of this event: among others, none more clearly than the ancient rent paid to the Crown, which was "the rysinge of one mann, with a bow without a stringe and an arrow without a feather."

No counties were erected in Ireland between the 12th year of the reign of John and the year 1556; and as there are records and evidence of this having been a county and having a sheriff long previous to the latter period, it is probable that this was one of the counties held by the English, and to which sheriffs were appointed by

Henry II and which were confirmed by John on his visit to Ireland in 1210.

The shrievalty of this county was formerly held conjointly with that of Antrim, as appears from the following (the most ancient) patent respecting the sheriffs. It is dated the 11th September 1325 (the 20th of Edward II): "The king, to his beloved John Deathye, greeting. Know ye that we have committed to you the office of sheriff of the counties of Carrickfergus and Antrim, to hold during your pleasure."

In the Down Survey it is termed the "county palatine of Carrickfergus."

The ancient charter, with the curious rent paid to the Crown, was retained until the 7th of Queen Elizabeth, when Sir Henry Sidney, then lord deputy, having caused the mayor to lay it before him, "delayed the charter," declaring it was not proper that any body of men should have such privileges.

4 years after (in 1569) he obtained a new charter from the queen, in which "her highnesse promised, in lieu of the former charter, the walling of the towne, the building of the peare, and allot such auncient lands as by former charter were held and injoyed." This charter also sets forth the loyalty of Carrickfergus, the suffering of the inhabitants by the rebellions of the Irish and incursions of the Scots, their gallantry exceeding that of the other cities and towns in Ireland, of the ecclesiastical obedience of the inhabitants, of their "usual repairinge to the churche and embracing God's true religion and service, a matter very acceptable to us," with an encouragement to them to "continue in their good cause and carriage."

This charter having in many places been found obscure and imperfect, the corporation in 1608 petitioned James I for a more ample explanation of their privileges, which he granted in 1613. It is more full and explicit than the former, which in every respect [it] ratifies and confirms.

By-Laws

The mayor, aldermen and burgesses constitute a council or court of common council, called the assembly, vested by charter with "full power and authority from time to time, and as often and at all times when it shall seem good or expedient unto them, to erect, constitute, ordain and make such reasonable laws, statutes, constitutions, decrees and orders in writing, as shall seem to them in their discretion, to be both good, healthful and profitable, honest and necessary for the good ruling and governing of the said town, and of all and singular, the officers, ministers,

burgesses, artificers, inhabitants and of all other residing in the said town."

Style and Officers

The style of the corporation is "the mayor, sheriffs, burgesses and commonalty of the town of Carrickfergus."

The officers of the corporation are as follows: 17 aldermen, including the mayor, 24 burgesses, 2 sheriffs, a recorder, who may be an alderman or burgess, a town clerk, a clerk of the peace (who may also hold the last office), 2 coroners, 4 sergeants-at-mace, a sword-bearer, a waterbailiff, who is one of the sergeants-at-mace. There is also a treasurer of the corporation. There is no emolument now attached to the offices, which are held by the gentleman who receives their rents.

The corporation formerly appointed a trumpeter at 2 pounds 10s, a drummer at 1 pound 5s and a fiddler at 1 pound 10s per annum.

Assembly

The common council or governing body of the corporation is termed the assembly, who, agreeably to the charter, may from time to time, as has before been mentioned, make such by-laws as they may deem necessary for its regulation.

The assembly consists of the mayor, aldermen and burgesses. Formerly the commons were represented in the assembly by 4 or sometimes by 2 members of their body, chosen annually among them. They signed every official document as "representatives of the commons." This is noticed in the records of the corporation as early as 1576. In 1701 there is an entry referring to it. It is not known as to when the freemen lost their right in this respect.

Election of Officers

The mayor and sheriffs are elected annually on the first Monday after Midsummer, and enter upon office on Michaelmas Day, when they are sworn in, in open court. They are elected or chosen by the aldermen, burgesses and commonalty. The mayor is chosen from the aldermen and sheriffs from the burgesses.

The former, on being sworn into office at the assizes, and upon all state occasions, wears a scarlet robe, and a sword and mace are carried before him, the former by the sword-bearer, the latter by a sergeant-at-mace.

The sword and mace were the gift of Colonel Robert Gardner in 1712. The first robe was given by William Hill Esquire to Solomon Faith, mayor in 1677.

The aldermen, 17 in number, elect each other. By the charter they are "to be from time to time, assisting and helping unto the mayor," and "chosen from the free burgesses or inhabitants." There have, however, been instances of a violation of this part of the charter.

The burgesses elect each other, the mayor having a vote in the election. Formerly the number was unlimited, but about 150 years ago the assembly restricted their number to 24.

The recorder, coroners and other officers are elected by the corporation for life.

The charter declares that the coroners "are to be elected yearly by the corporation on the same day as the mayor, or upon any other day when it shall seem most expedient;" but for many years past they have been elected for life. Formerly the sheriffs, on going out of office, became coroners for the following year, except when the same persons continued in the office of sheriff for 2 consecutive years, on which occasion the assize or quarter sessions grand juries appointed 2 burgesses to be coroners.

One of the coroners was formerly termed "speaker of the commons," perhaps from being their mouthpiece on public occasions.

By the charter the corporation may "from time to time, and as often as need shall require, appoint one honest and discreet man to be town clerk," and who is also clerk of the peace for the county of the town. In former times he was also the chamberlain of the corporation and was free from all levies and assessments.

The charter declares that the mayor and sheriffs and aldermen may from "time to time, as often as it shall be needful" appoint a sword-bearer. He is, however, usually appointed by the assembly. His only duty is carrying the sword before the mayor, at assizes and on his being sworn into office.

There are 4 sergeants-at-mace. By the charter, the mayor, sheriffs, burgesses and commonalty may "from time to time, name, choose and appoint" them. With exception of one who is also water-bailiff, they are usually nominated by the mayor, though occasionally by the assembly. One of the sergeants-at-mace is, by the charter, authorised to be water-bailiff. He is appointed by the assembly, who formerly let the joint offices of water-bailiff and harbour-master [at] an annual rent varying from 2 pounds 10s to 3 pounds.

The water-bailiff and harbour-master has long since ceased to pay for his office. He does not receive any salary but derives his emolument from fees on his different duties.

The treasurer is appointed by the assembly. Formerly, and until 1767, the mayor was treasurer of the corporation but since that period a person is appointed exclusively to that office.

Mayor

Emoluments, privileges and duties of officers: the annual salary of the mayor was, in ancient times, the corporation's share of the customs of the port, if it amounted to 20 pounds per annum. He had also the privilege of selling wine in his house, but from this he was in 1601 prevented, under pain of forfeiting his stipend. In 1624 the customs were taken from the mayor. In June 1659 his salary was raised to 60 pounds per annum and in 1767 increased to 100 pounds per annum, its present amount.

Many curious perquisites were formerly attached to the office of mayor. In several old houses the tenants were bound to furnish yearly a certain number of fat hens or capons, or a specified sum of money in lieu, to the mayor at Christmas. The owner of the West mills was also bound to "grind all such grain as shall be spent from time to time in the mayor's house, toll free." As clerk of the market he had also the tongues of all bullocks or cows killed on Fridays, whose flesh was sold in the market on Saturdays. When the Troopers Land was unoccupied he claimed its grass as a perquisite, and he formerly had a field near the town, free.

The mayor for the time being is one of the assembly. By the charter he may hold 2 courts of record in each week, namely on Mondays and Fridays, "to hear, examine and discuss all and all manner of actions, suits and complaints, and demands of all and all manner of debts, to what sum or sums soever they do or shall amount to."

He is also vice-admiral of the seas from Fair Head on the north east of this county to Beerlooms on the coast of Down, in either way, a distance of 40 miles; and can, on behalf of the corporation, claim "all wrecks of the sea happening, found, or to be found, within Beerlooms and Fair Head, and within the town and county of the town aforesaid forever." He may issue attachments against ships, their cargoes or persons on board them, for the recovery of debts contracted within his jurisdiction. He is also entitled to hold a court of Admiralty.

The mayor was formerly a military as well as civil officer, being captain of the company of the militia raised for the defence of the town.

Seal of Carrickfergus

In old times the last act of each mayor was going in procession to divine service and thence to the castle, where the mayor-elect was sworn into office. In the evening the mayor entertained a large party at a dinner in the town hall, termed the "mayor's feast." During the day a bull was fastened to a ring and baited by dogs. The processions and feasts have long since been discontinued and the bull-baits were put an end to about 10 years since. An ox is now killed on this day and distributed among the poor. Each claimant receives a loaf of bread.

The mayor is, by the charter, appointed clerk of the market and a magistrate for the county Antrim. He may also appoint a deputy. At quarter sessions and assizes he is entitled to preside with the recorder.

It should be stated that it is not necessary that the mayor should reside within the corporation.

Recorder

The recorder "may be elected either for his life or years." He is also appointed a magistrate and may, with the consent of the mayor and a majority of the aldermen, appoint or "depute one of the aldermen to be his deputy." He has, however, always been elected for life by the entire corporate body.

Formerly he examined [and] signed all leases previously to their being signed by the mayor, for which he received a fee of 3s 4d. He also received a similar sum from each person admitted as a freeman. His duty now consists in attending the quarter sessions as a magistrate of the county, on which occasions he explains the law and pronounces the judgement of the court.

In 1593 the salary of the recorder was 20 pounds per annum, but for many years it has not exceeded half that sum, though several attempts have been made to raise it.

Sheriffs

The first act of the new mayor is to swear in the sheriffs, who are ordered to be elected by the corporation at the same time as the mayor and to be sworn in before the aldermen at Michaelmas.

They are authorised to hold courts and have leave to account in the court of exchequer by commission and to pay only 1 pound 6s 8d. The civil bill decrees issued by the assistant barristers at quarter sessions are, so far as [they] relate to the county of the town of Carrickfergus, signed by the sheriffs.

Formerly, and so lately as 1743, one of the sheriffs was nominated by the mayor and was called "the mayor's sheriff," but when in court the sheriff elected by the corporation took the right of him.

The sheriffs formerly adhered to the practice of accounting to the court of exchequer by attorney and paying its officers 1 pound 6s 8d yearly. In 1731 it appears from the records that they swore to their accounts before the mayor, previous to their being forwarded to Dublin. For many years previous to 1787 the sheriffs are said to not have made any returns. In 1797 a writ for the amount of fines and fees was issued from the court of exchequer against the sheriffs. The settlement of this, defrayed by the assembly, cost 45 pounds 18s 2d ha'penny.

They seem, however, soon after to have fallen into disregard of the regulations of the court, for in 1814 Thomas Kirk, one of the sheriffs, was arrested by order of the court and taken to Dublin, where he remained from August until December, when he was liberated on paying 35 pounds. Several similar prosecutions took place until the year 1820, when the corporation made a resolution to grant 40 pounds per annum to the sheriffs for their trouble and expenses in going to Dublin to pass their accounts.

In 1601 the salaries of the sheriffs were fixed at 6 pounds 13s 4d "without any other fee." In 1624 the following entry was made in the records: "ordered that from henceforth the 20 nobles allowed yearly from the town to the sheriffs and the 3 pounds allowed them yearly for entertaining the attorneys at His Majesty's court at Dublin shall be resumed into the towne's hands and be no more allowed; and the sheriffs from henceforth shall rest contented and only have from the towne all such fynes as shal grow due for batteryes and bloodsheds within this towne and countye for ther stipend."

In November 1732 their salaries were raised to 10 pounds each and in March 1797 to their present amount, 20 pounds per annum.

The sheriffs still receive annually 1s from each vessel trading to this port, which due is known by the term of "chapman gill." [Insert footnote: Tradition states that this money was formerly collected by the monks of some of the religious houses in this district, as spiritual service money, hence probably "chaplain or chapel gold or gelt, money for the chaplain or chapel," "gold or gelt" being formerly substituted occasionally for money]. This is collected for the purpose of interring mariners or others who may be cast ashore within the district.

Other Officers

No annual salary is attached to the office of coroner. Their only emolument is derived from their fees after inquests. The usual fee is 1 pound 6s 8d, which is obtained by presentment at the assizes from the grand jury.

The town clerk is also clerk of the peace for the county of the town, and returns all estreats to the court of exchequer, though there are instances of his not having performed this part of his duty.

In 1606 his salary was fixed at 4 pounds per annum. In 1740 it was only 2 pounds. In 1760 it was increased to its present amount, 7 pounds 10s, though it appears to have been raised in 1772 to 10 pounds by the aldermen. At the next assembly after, it was reduced to its former and present amount, as it had been raised without the consent of the burgesses. As clerk of the peace he receives an annual salary of 24 pounds, paid by grand jury presentment at the assizes. His fees are similar to those of all clerks of the peace for counties.

The salary of the sword-bearer is 5 pounds per annum, without any fees.

There are 4 sergeants-at-mace, 3 of whom receive a salary of 4 pounds per annum from the corporation. The fourth is also water-bailiff, for which, besides fees, he has an annual salary of 10 pounds.

The joint offices of water-bailiff and harbour-master were formerly let by the corporation at from 2 pounds 10s to 3 pounds per annum. This practice has, however, long since been discontinued. The district of the water-bailiff, like that of the mayor as vice-admiral, extended from Fair Head on the northern coast of Antrim to Beerlooms [on] the coast of Down, the Pool or Roadstead of Garmoyle on the opposite coast of Belfast Lough excepted.

The usual fee for executing a writ against a vessel, its cargo, or a person on board is 11s 4d ha'penny.

The annual salary of the harbour-master is 25 pounds, beside which he receives 1s in the pound for collecting harbour dues. He also acts as ballast-master. His salary is paid from the dues and charges of the harbour.

Formerly the mayor was treasurer of the corporation, but in 1767 an individual was appointed to that office at a salary of 10 pounds, which in 1770 was changed to 1s for every pound received. This is the only emolument attached to the office and is now received only on the rents paid to the corporation through their agent, who is also their treasurer.

The weigh-master receives an annual salary of 35 pounds, paid by the corporation from the proceeds of the market charges.

Salaries

Salaries of the officers of the corporation for the year 1839: mayor 92 pounds 6s 2d; 2 sheriffs, 36 pounds 18s 4d each, 73 pounds 16s 8d; recorder 9 pounds 4s 7d ha'penny; clerk of the peace (as town clerk) 6 pounds 18s 4d; 3 sergeants-at-mace, 3 pounds 13s 10d each, 11 pounds 1s 6d; sword-bearer 4 pounds 12s 4d; keeper of the assembly room 5 pounds 5s; scavenger 1 pound 16s 1d ha'penny; sexton 1 pound 3s 2d; yarn inspector 2 pounds 2s; total 208 pounds 5s 11d.

The above salaries are paid by the corporation and includes all their payments to officers, with the exception of the percentage (5 per cent) paid to their treasurer for receiving their rents. This does not, in round numbers, exceed 20 pounds per annum.

Freemen

There is an obscurity as to the ancient and original claims as to being created a freeman, and also as to the manner of admission to the freedom of this corporation.

The records of 1657 mention birthright and serving an apprenticeship of 7 years within the franchises as legal and ancient claims, but do not allude to marriage, and declare that all "otherwise admitted free" shall pay a fine of 10 pounds.

Tradition affirms that birth, marriage and servitude were the original claims to the freedom, and that all who were admitted without such were either elected by the freemen then present or were admitted by special favour.

Freemen's sons and sons-in-law, those serving or having served an apprenticeship within the corporation, freeholders of the county and grandsons of freemen by the father's side have as right been admitted.

Birth, marriage and servitude are now considered as the legal claims. Many have been made freemen by special favour, among whom were those who had been long-resident, sons of freemen though not born in wedlock, persons born in a similar manner who had married the daughters of freemen, and others upon similar grounds.

On several occasions non-residents have been made free by merely sending them tickets to that effect. In 1741 there were 120 ticket-freemen residing in Kilultagh, in the barony of Upper Massereene. An election at which the latter voted was, in consequence of a petition to parliament against the returns, declared null and void, "as the ticket-freemen made by the Mayor of Carrickfergus only, or by the mayor and sheriffs without the concurrence of the other constituent parts of the corporation, have not any right to vote for the electing members to serve in parliament for the county of the town of Carrickfergus."

Several irregularities and abuses with respect to the admission of freemen appear in the records, and several lawsuits and disputes have in consequence occurred. At a suit tried in 1810, in the county Antrim court and which cost the parties upwards of 4,600 pounds, it was decided that "the lands of Straid and Little Ballymena were without the franchises, though still belonging to the Corporation of Carrickfergus." At the same trial it was also found that the admission of freemen was not wholly in the power of the assembly.

The corporation has the privilege of making freemen at will. The mayor can open a court on giving 14 days' public notice, for the admission of those eligible, anywhere residing within the liberties. Courts for this purpose were formerly held at the quarter sessions, which were kept open by adjournment until such as had the necessary claims were duly admitted.

In 1598 the freemen amounted to but 16; in 1669 they amounted to 139, in 1683 to 302 and 1712 to about 500, of whom 140 resided in Belfast. In 1740 the resident freemen amounted to about 60. In 1741 120 ticket-freemen residing in Kilultagh (Lord Hertford's estate in the barony of Upper Massereene) were created.

In 1742 the mayor opened a court and admitted 170 persons to the freedom. At an adjournment of this court he admitted 94 others. In 1744 a considerable number were admitted.

In 1757 45 who were informally admitted were

disfranchised. In the same year 413 others were regularly admitted by the mayor. During the years 1780, 1781, 1787 and 1788 about 1,200 freemen were admitted.

In June 1802 487 persons were informally admitted and afterwards disfranchised. In September 1803 166 persons were admitted. In July 1807 426 individuals were admitted to the freedom. In 1810 80 freemen who resided without the franchise were disfranchised. During 1809, 1810, 1811, 1812, 1813, 304 persons were admitted to the freedom.

59 were admitted in 1818 and 10 in 1819. In 1829 the number of freemen amounted to 800. Since that year 516 have been admitted to the freedom of the corporation; of these, 110 were admitted in November 1837.

Guilds of Trades

There are in Carrickfergus 8 guilds of trades, namely the Tailors and Glovers, incorporated in 1670; the Cordwainers or Shoemakers, incorporated in 1674; the Gentlemen Hammermen in 1748; the Weavers in 1751; the Fishers in 1790; the Butchers in 1809; the Trawlers and Dredgers in 1812; and the Carmen in 1812. Another trade, the Mechanical Hammermen, has for several years ceased to exist.

In the charter granted by James I in 1612 leave is given "to have guild of merchants and the incorporation of other trades and callings."

In the charter of Queen Elizabeth leave is given to have a guild of merchants, called "free merchants of the staple," which in 1593 were restricted by the corporation to 20; and no others were suffered to buy or sell here under a penalty of 10 pounds. The privileges of this guild were confirmed by that alluded to as granted by James I, in the same "manner and form" as those of Dublin, and the mayor of the corporation on going out of office became "mayor of the staple" for the following year. 2 of the burgesses were also annually chosen as "constables of the staple."

In May 1622 a new charter was granted to the "staplers," with liberties similar to those of the town of Sligo. The fee paid for admission to this guild was 10 pounds. It is believed to have existed until the sale of the customs of Carrickfergus in 1637.

In the year 1670, on the 3rd of December, and in the 22nd year of the reign of Charles II, a charter was granted giving leave to incorporate trades.

The rules and regulations of the different trades are much the same, relating chiefly to the admission of apprentices and to their respective interest, and enjoin obedience to the masters and secrecy respecting their craft. Their constitution is almost precisely the same.

The master and wardens of each for the ensuing year are sworn either before the council or before the magistrates assembled on the court day next before the feast of St Stephen, on which day the guilds dine together. The mayor for the time being dines with them. It was until lately the custom for him to present each guild with 1 pound or more, according to their numbers.

The sum paid on admission to each guild varies from 8s 3d to 1 pound. Few have any funds and the only pecuniary benefits derived by the members is 3 pounds, which is contributed for their interment. The only other expenses incurred are those attendant on their annual entertainments.

Each guild holds annual and quarterly meetings for the transaction of business.

Tailors and Glovers

It appears from the registry and regulation book of this guild that Adam Dennison, glover, and Michael Russel, tailor, made application in 1670 to the mayor, Mr Anthony Horsman, and the sheriffs, Messrs Henderson and Stubbs, to be incorporated in one body, according to the charter, as freemen of the town. Their charter bears the date of the 13th September 1670.

Since then they have met quarterly and dined together on the feast of St Stephen, when they elect a master, wardens and beadles for the ensuing year. The master is sworn to discharge faithfully the duties of his office, to attend carefully to the interests of the fraternity, and among other things not to admit an apprentice to the guild who has not served out his time. The oath of the wardens and beadles is much the same and they, as also the freemen, swear obedience to the master and secrecy respecting their craft.

There are 15 rules connected with this guild. They are pretty strict and relate principally to the discipline and conduct of the fraternity. They were made by the master and wardens on the 26th December 1692 and were amended by the master in 1812.

The fee paid on admission to the guild is 8s 3d. 127 members have belonged to it; there were 47 in 1812.

Cordwainers or Shoemakers

The Guild of Cordwainers or Shoemakers was incorporated by the charter in 1674. There are a present 100 members in connection with it. As a guild, it is stationary as to its funds and the number of its members.

Gentlemen Hammermen

The Guild of Gentlemen Hammermen was incorporated pursuant to charter in 1748; Edward Bruce, mayor, Jones and William McCartney Esquires, sheriffs. William Jamfrey was the first master and Thomas Godfrey and William Thompson were the first wardens of the guild. There are at present about 50 members in existence. Their meetings are held on the 1st January. This guild is not in a thriving state.

Weavers

The Guild of Weavers was established by charter in 1751, since which period about 570 members have been admitted to it; there are at present about 100 members. In 1756 James McIlwaine was master and John McDonald and John Black were wardens of the guild. Its funds, amounting to 2 pounds 5d ha'penny per annum, are chiefly derived from the rent of a house in Lancasterian Street, in which their warping materials are deposited. The members of the guild meet annually on St Stephen's Day.

Guild of Fishers

The Guild of Fishers was incorporated on the 28th September 1790 by Ezekiel Davys Wilson, the mayor, and Robert Clement and Thomas Legg, sheriffs. Since that period they have met quarterly for business and dined together annually on the feast of St Peter. On the incorporation of the guild, the mayor presented it with a silver oar, which the master wears suspended from his neck by a blue ribbon at their meetings.

Their oath and rules resemble those of the Guild of Tailors. Their constitution is similar also. They have not any funds and their guild is rather on the decline, chiefly owing to the want of zeal on the part of their more influential members. Freemen of this guild who do not reside within the limits of the corporation are bound by their oath to give, to those who do, information as to where fish may be found.

There are at present 20 members on the books; 224 have belonged to the guild since its incorporation.

Butchers

The Guild of Butchers was established pursuant

to charter in 1809, since which period 40 members have been admitted; there are 35 at present in existence. This guild is on the decline: it is one of the poorest and least regularly conducted of the trades.

Trawlers and Dredgers

The charter of incorporation of the Trawlers and Dredgers bears the date of the year 1812. James Campbell was the first master and James Wheeler and John Johnson were the first wardens. Since its incorporation 134 members, of whom 30 are now in existence, have been admitted. This guild is in a tolerably prosperous state.

Carmen

The Guild of Carmen was established pursuant to charter on the 27th June 1812, since which period 32 members have been admitted. John Murray was the first master and William Simon and Alexander Hamilton were the first wardens. There are not any funds connected with this guild; in other respects it is stationary.

Masters of Guilds

The following are the masters and wardens of the different trades in the year 1839.

Tailors and Glovers: master Percival Ingram, warden William Larmer.

Cordwainers or Shoemakers: master William Hay, wardens William Williamson and William Hanna.

Gentlemen Hammermen: master David Legg, wardens Robert Lockhart and Isaac Baxter.

Weavers: master John Legg, wardens James Penny and Thomas Donnell.

Fishers: master James Cowan, wardens William Jack and Charles McFerran.

Butchers: master Nathaniel Moore, warden Thomas Robinson.

Trawlers and Dredgers: master John McCaffrey, wardens William Mulholland and Robert Wills.

Carmen: master Samuel Simm, wardens James Campbell and Samuel Ingram.

Jurisdiction

The administration of justice is held in civil matters in the court of record, in criminal matters in the court of petty sessions for the county of the town. Petty sessions for the district of the county Antrim, including the county of the town, and quarter sessions for the county of the town of Carrickfergus are held before the mayor, recorder and magistrates for the county of the town, 4 times a year.

Quarter sessions for this county, as a division of the county Antrim, are held twice a year before the assistant barrister.

The mayor, as also his deputy mayor, is a justice of the peace for the county of the town. The former is also a justice of the peace for the county Antrim. He is empowered to hold courts of sessions. He is vice-admiral of the liberties extending from Fair Head on the northern coast of this county to Beerlooms on the coast of Down, a distance of about 40 miles each way. From this jurisdiction Bangor on the sea-coast of Down and the Pool or Roadstead of Garmoyle on its coast of Belfast Lough are exempted.

He may have power to issue attachments against ships, their cargoes or persons on board, within his jurisdiction, for debts, no matter where they may have been contracted. He may grant licences to ships coming into the port, to buy or forestall merchandise. He is custos rotulorum of the county of the town. He is clerk of the market, escheator, and master of the assays. He may hold 2 courts of record, one on Monday and one on Friday in each week.

He has leave to appoint a deputy with power "in all things whatsoever which doth appertain to the office of mayor of the town aforesaid." The mayor is associated with the judges of assize in the commission, and before him the assizes for the county of the town are held, next before those of Antrim. He presides with the recorder and the 2 magistrates for the county of the town at the quarter sessions for the county of the town, which court has jurisdiction over all felonies and offences committed within the county of the town, with power to inflict capital punishment. The more serious offences are, however, sent to the assizes.

The aldermen have not any jurisdiction in criminal or civil matters, by virtue of their office.

The sheriffs may hold a sheriff's or county court and are empowered by charter to account annually by attorney into the court of exchequer, on paying the officers of that court 1 pound 6s 8d annually.

The recorder is a justice of the peace for the county of the town. His duty now merely consists in attending the quarter sessions for the county of the town, at which he presides as an assistant barrister, explains the law and pronounces judgement. He is the mayor's assessor in the tholsel court, and he or his deputy is judge of the court leet and view of frank-pledge, "to be held in the town twice a year." There is also a court of pie poudre.

The assembly have power to make by-laws and also have control over the funds and revenues of the corporation, which are now limited to their rents.

Fairs and Markets

2 annual fairs, which are pretty well attended, are held by charter, one "on the feast Saints Philip and Jacob the Apostles and for 2 days next following the same," the other "on the feast of All Saints and for 2 days next following." These fairs are held on the 12th May and 12th November.

In the charter leave is also given to hold 2 markets in each week, one of the markets to be held on Saturday; no day is specified for the other. A weekly market is held on Saturdays; it is very unimportant.

This district was included in the ancient manor of Joymount, of which all trace has since been lost.

Property: Corporation

The total income of the corporation, now amounting to 319 pounds 7s 8d per annum, is derived from the chief rents paid by the several extensive landed proprietors, whose ancestors, having been members of the corporation, became possessed of its landed property.

The principal proprietors are the Marquis of Downshire, Lord Blayney and the Marquis of Donegall, besides several less extensive proprietors who hold under it in perpetuity at merely nominal rents.

The charges derivable from the new market place are expended in the salary of the weighmaster, and those of the port and harbour in that of the harbour and ballast-master. The corporation possesses no other resources, nor are they in debt, but the alienation of its property and the misappropriation of its funds in former days seems to have [been] most flagrant.

The expenditure of the corporation is of necessity very limited, as it does not exceed its income. The salaries of officers now amount to 208 pounds annually, exclusively of about 20 pounds per annum paid to their treasurer and agent. The remaining sum is expended in numerous trifling amounts of incidental expenses, such as the judges' lodgings, in repairing or improving their property and in a variety of similar ways.

The corporation formerly possessed valuable property, besides important privileges and immunities. The Commons, a tract principally under mountain pasture, including 2,730 acres 3 perches, are now let. They possessed also a third part of the customs, which in 1637 were disposed of to the Crown for 3,000 pounds, to be expended in the purchase of lands for the use of the corporation. No lands, however, were purchased. 1,300 pounds was lent on interest to John Davys of Carrickfergus, who, when called on to account for it a few years after, brought in the corporation in debt to him 1s. It is not known how the remaining sum was disposed of.

By the charter the corporation had a right to the tolls and customs of the market, but these have long since been abrogated. They had also by charter a right to the "ferry or passage over the river, part of arm of the sea of the river of Knockfergus." This ferry has not been maintained within memory.

All trace of their more valuable privileges, immunities and sources of revenue have long since been lost, and their sole income, 319 pounds 7s 8d, is now derived from the chief rents paid by their tenants, for lands of which they should never have disposed.

Parliamentary Representation

The constituency was vested in the mayor, aldermen, burgesses and freemen of the town, and in freeholders of 40s per annum and upwards in the county of the town. By the act of William IV chapter 88, the non-resident freemen, except those within 7 miles, have been disfranchised, and 10 pounds householders and 20 and 10 pounds leaseholders for the respective terms of 14 and 20 years have been enfranchised. Pursuant to this act the 40s franchise terminates with the present freeholders of that description.

The gross constituency at the present time (August 1839), as entered in the books of the clerk of the peace, amounts to 1,623, but this includes re-registries and many who have died since their registration. The probable constituency does not exceed 864.

There are at present within the corporation 60 freeholders, 2 rent chargers and 20 leaseholders. The gross number of freemen on the books is 1,045; the probable number is 782. The number that voted at the contested election of 1837 was 864 and this, it is believed, may be taken as the strength of the constituency.

The following statement is extracted from the *Parliamentary boundary report* of 1832. The following particulars concerning this borough are taken from the *Parliamentary boundary report*.

"The boundary of the county as it now is does not agree with that given in the charter of Queen Elizabeth: Straid and Little Ballymena have since then been disfranchised. Neither of these townlands pay county cess.

There are only 170 houses of the value of 10 pounds. In the Scotch Quarter there are only 13 worth 10 pounds.

Under the Reform Bill, the constituency would be as follows: qualified occupiers of 10 pounds tenements 522; freeholders not occupiers 16; freemen whose right may be reserved 174; 40s freeholders whose right may be reserved 10; probable number of 20 pounds leaseholders 10; total constituency 732.

The constituency is now (1832) as follows: aldermen resident 1, non-resident 11, total 12; burgesses resident 4, non-resident 14, total 18; freemen resident 678, non-resident 104, total 782; freeholders, 50 pounds, 6; 20 pounds, 20; 40s, 13; total 39; total constituency 851."

Parliamentary Representatives

Since the period of its being enfranchised until the Union, Carrickfergus sent 2 burgesses to the Irish parliament. In the imperial parliament it has but 1 representative.

From the early date of its charter and incorporation, it is probable that Carrickfergus possessed its privilege from the commencement of such assemblies being held in this country by the English.

From its exposed situation and importance as a garrison, it was necessarily the scene of perpetual warfare and, from this cause, it is believed to have for many years been retarded from sending members to parliament, as none are entered on the rolls previous to 1559.

The custom of remunerating members of parliament and defraying expenses is known to have existed in former times. In the reign of Henry II, in the "tenendi parliamenta" signed by him, it is ordered that the expenses of 2 burgesses do not exceed half a mark a day.

In the reign of Edward II knights of the shire had 5s per day and citizens and burgesses 2s. In 1614 knights of the shire had 13s 4d per day, citizens 10s and burgesses 6s 8d.

In the parliament of 1613 Thomas Hibbots and Humphrey Johnston, citizens, represented Carrickfergus and attended, between 18th May 1613 and 14th October 1615, 147 days. Their

wages amounted to 98 pounds. This custom is believed to have been discontinued about 1662.

Contested Elections

1802. Lord Spencer S. Chichester 381, Ezekiel Davys Wilson 270.

1807. James Craig 359, Edward May Junior 318.

1807. James Craig 363, Edward May Junior 321.

1812. Arthur Chichester 460, Ezekiel Davys Wilson 406. This election was remarkable for the extent to which corruption and bribery were carried. 3 persons died during it from the effects of drunkenness.

1830. Lord George A. Hill 311, Lord Marcus Hill 241, Charles Adair 198, Sir Arthur Chichester 46. A petition against Lord George Hill's return was preferred, on the grounds of bribery and corruption, and also that he was not a burgess of the corporation. It was, however, thrown out by the parliamentary committee, owing to some informality in its preamble.

1832. Conway Richard Dobbs 495, Sir Arthur Chichester 447, James Wills 6. A petition against the return of Mr Dobbs was preferred. After an investigation of several days Mr Dobbs resigned and the election was declared null and void. To such an extent was bribery carried at this election that the committee recommended that no writ should be issued for a new election for 1 month, and that in the meantime measures might be taken either to alter the constituency of the borough or towards its disenfranchisement. No writ was issued until the general election of 1834, when the borough was contested by Peter Kirk and Thomas Verner. The latter having resigned the contest, Mr Kirk was returned.

The next election took place in July 1837, when a severe contest took place. The candidates were Peter Kirk, who polled 446, and Mathew Bolton Rennie, 418 votes, giving a majority of 28 to Mr Kirk, the present member. A petition against Mr Kirk's return was commenced but was soon after abandoned.

It is supposed that almost the entire constituency was polled at the last election. The total number of registries, as entered in the clerk of the peace's books, is 1,623; but this included duplicate and re-registries, besides those who have died off since their registration.

Governors

The governorship of Carrickfergus Castle was, in

ancient times, held conjointly with that of the town and the Clandeboys. The salary, stated to have been then attached to it, was 182 pounds 10s. It now amounts to 180 pounds. The situation is of course a sinecure.

The first governor of whom there is any notice was Captain William Piers in 1568. He was a gallant and distinguished officer. The present governor is Lieutenant-General Sir William Hutchinson K.C.H.

Constables

Considerable importance was formerly attached to the office of Constable of Carrickfergus Castle. Many important privileges were attached to it, and much care was bestowed in the selection of the individual. The constable was always a person of high rank and trust, as would appear from the names of those who held the office. Until the reign of Edward IV he was, except during the minority of the heir to the Crown, always nominated by the Earls of Ulster, the castle being a portion of their hereditary possessions. Edward, Earl of March and Ulster, son and heir of Richard Plantagenet, Duke of York, having ascended the throne by the title of Edward IV, the earldom of Ulster devolved to the Crown.

By the charter of Queen Elizabeth in 1568 the constable is "by reason of his office" declared to be a freeman. The mayors were sworn into office before him or his deputy. He also received the king's share of the customs of the port; he had the best fish out of each boat that arrived from time to time within the liberties; and his wardens, 20 Englishmen, had 100 cows annually grazed free by the corporation.

In 1327 the salary of the constable, John Deathye, was 100 marks; in 1343 it was 40 pounds per annum; in 1400 the salary of Peter Dobyn, the constable, for the first year was the profits of the water mills of Carrickfergus.

An Irish parliament which sat in Drogheda in 1494, before Sir Edward Poynings Knight, declared that none but an Englishman could hold the office of constable.

Sir Roger Langford <Landford> Knight and Sir Faithful Fortescue were appointed joint constables by James I, each having a fee of 3s 4d per day and 20 wardens under their command, at 8d each.

In 1661, 14th March, Sir Thomas Fortescue was made constable, with a salary of 6s 8d per day and 8d each for 20 wardens. In 1672 the constable's salary was 2s 6d per day. There was also a clerk of stores at 1s 8d per day and a matross at 8d per day.

The first constable of whom there is any notice was Thomas Smocke in 1326. The last was Stewart Banks Esquire in the reign of Elizabeth.

Government

2 magistrates for the county of the town reside in Carrickfergus. A chief officer and 7 coastguards are stationed in Carrickfergus, which is also the residence of the inspecting commander of the district. A detachment of infantry consisting of a subaltern, 2 sergeants and 30 rank [and] file are quartered here. A master gunner and 2 invalid artillery men are quartered in the castle. Further information under this head will be found under the heads of Crime and Local Government.

Present State of the People: Customs

There are not in Carrickfergus any ancient families nor any possessing any peculiar privileges; the jurisdiction of the corporation does not now retain any peculiar power or immunity.

Among the ancient customs which have been abrogated was that called "breynebalaf's erick," supposed to have been a portion of the Brehon Law, and by which a murder could be compromised by payment of a recompense. This custom was abolished in 1581 by the lord deputy, Sir A. Grey, who, at the same time, abolished the exaction of "loughe ympies," a fine by an erenagh to the bishop, on the marriage of any of his daughters. The letter from the lord deputy forbidding these customs is entered in the records of Carrickfergus.

A ducking-stool for scolds was formerly kept here, as appears from the following notices in the records of the town: "October 1574, ordered and agreede by the hole court that all manners of skoldes, which shall be openly detected of skolding of evill wordes in manner of skolding, and for the same shal be condemned, before Mr maior and his brethren, shal be drawne at the sterne of a boate in the water from the rude of the peare rounde abought the queene's majesties castell in manner of ducking, and after, when a cage shal be made, the party so condemned for a skold, shall be therein punished at the discretion of the maior." The cage or ducking-stool stood upon the quay, as appears from an entry in a deed granted 7th July 1671 to John Davys.

"Riding the stang" (or sting) was a punishment or infliction by the neighbours, unconnected with law, which, it is said, continued within memory of some of the old inhabitants. The custom consisted in carrying astride a pole some low character who represented the offender. The procession accompanying him frequently halted and proclaimed the alleged offence. They finally halted at the offender's house, where [h]is delinquency was formally announced and the ceremony terminated.

Several other less important customs, quite devoid of interest, have long since fallen into disuse.

Population

In 1813 the population of the town of Carrickfergus amounted to 2,650 individuals, in 1821 to 3,371 and in 1831 to 673 families, consisting of 3,516 individuals, of whom 1,562 were included within the walls, 1,196 in the Irish Quarter and 756 in the Scotch Quarter.

Of the families, 361 were employed chiefly in trade, manufacture or handicraft, 77 were chiefly employed in agriculture and 192 in various other occupations. Almost the entire population are dependent, either wholly or partly, on their exertions, in some way, for their support, there being but a few families who have fixed incomes.

Trades

Of the 361 families engaged in trade, manufacture or handicraft, about 126 are engaged in some description of dealing, such as shopkeepers, innkeepers and merchants. These naturally include the wealthier and more respectable portion of the community, though there are but few in Carrickfergus to whom the former term can strictly be applied. There are many who are comfortable and independent in their circumstances, but few possessed of capital of any amount.

The dealers, with a few exceptions, are to a certain extent engaged in farming, but more for the purpose of providing for domestic consumption than for the market. Their farms are limited in size, they are situated in the vicinity of the town and within such distance as to enable them to devote their time almost exclusively to their trade.

With 3 or 4 exceptions, the business of each individual does not exceed the limited extent of a moderate retail trade, on a scale suited to the circumstances of the people of the town and its vicinity. There is but 1 individual who can be termed a general merchant, or who imports to an extent of any consequence, and his stores, besides a grocery and hardware shop, are principally for the sale of timber, iron and slates.

There are several good shops. One in particular, just erected by Mr S.D. Stewart, is on an extensive scale, in the grocery and [?] ironmongery business. All the necessaries and most of luxuries of life are to be had here on terms but little above those in Belfast.

The tradespeople constitute rather a small proportion of the population. They principally inhabit the town and the Irish Quarter, and are, with few exceptions, engaged in occupations of ordinary mechanics.

Fishermen

The fishers colonise a large portion of the Scotch Quarter, in which their Scottish ancestors, engaged in the same callings, settled about 2 centuries ago. 57 families are at present engaged in fishing. They possess 16 boats, of which 9 or 10 are engaged fishing during the winter, while from 16 to 20 are employed during the summer. Each boat is manned during the winter by from 7 to 8 men and during the summer by from 4 to 6.

The boats, which measure from 17 to 21 in keel and 6 to 8 feet beam, and from 2 to 3 tons burthen, cost from 20 to 70 pounds. They are very deep and in their build somewhat resemble yawls. Each has 2 lug sails and 6 "booled" oars (2 on each beam), 4 of which are used summer and 6 in winter. The nets and tacklings of each boat cost 30 pounds.

They are generally well formed, in good order, and much superior to the ordinary description of Irish fishing boats. The fishermen are generally in good circumstances and live in a manner more comfortable than those of the same calling, but they are at the same time improvident and are apathetic and indolent in everything not connected with their ordinary occupation.

Labourers

The labouring class constitute a large proportion of the population. They are to be found almost exclusively in the Irish Quarter. The flax spinning mills, distillery and the manufactories in the town in its immediate vicinity afford employment to a considerable proportion of their class, of whom 200 are employed in the flax and cotton spinning mills, and the remainder of the adult employment either in agriculture or in the repair of highways.

Libraries and Societies

There is very little taste for reading or for literature in Carrickfergus. There is a reading society among the upper class. The books are transferred when read from one member [to another] and are sold at the end of the year.

A lending library in connection with the Orthodox Presbyterian congregation was established here in 1834. It consists of 300 volumes, chiefly on religious subjects, and is supported by 80 members, each of whom pays 1s per annum. A sum of 1 pound was subscribed by a few at its establishment.

There is a small library of a similar description in connection with the Sunday school of the same congregation. It consists of about 300 volumes of useful and religious works suited to the teachers and pupils. It was established in 1836.

A public circulating library containing about 500 volumes, chiefly novels, had been kept by an individual in Carrickfergus for about 20 years. It has received but little support.

A news room was established here in 1835 and is held in a room on the upper floor of the market house. There are 30 subscribers, each of whom pays 1 pound per annum. 15 newspapers, besides the *Army* and *Navy lists*, and several magazines, are taken at it.

590 copies of the public journals are circulated within the limits of the county of the town of Carrickfergus.

An amateur band termed the Harmonic Society was originally established here in 1803 and, after several dissolutions and revivals, was lastly reorganised in 1838. It consists of 16 ordinary and 3 honorary members, who meet to practise twice a week. Each member, on his admission, pays 5s and a weekly subscription of 1s 3d to 1s, which is expended in the purchase of instruments and in defraying the incidental expenses of the society.

These are the only indications of a refinement of taste or of a desire for intellectual recreation among the inhabitants. There is a branch each of the Hibernian Bible Society and Church Missionary Society in Carrickfergus. A temperance society was established here in 1829 but, from want of support on the part of individuals, it gradually declined and finally terminated its existence in 1837.

PRODUCTIVE ECONOMY

Commerce

Carrickfergus cannot now be termed commercial. Previous to the year 1637, when one-third of its customs, which were the property of the corporation, were sold to the government, the annual

amount of its revenues were inferior only to Dublin and Waterford; but since that period they gradually declined as the trade was soon after transferred to Belfast, with which it has since continued.

In 1824 the ballast office was established here, and 1825 the port of Carrickfergus was annexed to that of Belfast, and the office of port surveyor was then here abolished.

The vessels belonging to this port, 39 in number, and its revenues are now registered and included in the returns of the port of Belfast.

The 39 vessels belonging to this port include about 3,000 tons register tonnage. 3 of them are employed in foreign trade and 36 in the coasting trade; they are chiefly schooners. The dues of the port, which in 1816 amounted to 629 pounds 10s 4d, in 1838 amounted to 150 pounds.

Exports and Imports

The exports principally consist in grain, potatoes, hay, bricks, beans and black cattle. The imports consist in coals, salt, slates, oak-bark, fire-brick, tiles, grains and sandstone.

The trade of the port is on the increase and would greatly increase but for the extreme inconvenience in the situation of the harbour.

Manufactures

The manufactories and machinery of the town of Carrickfergus consist of a distillery, 2 flax spinning mills, a flour and corn mill, a corn mill, 2 tanyards and 2 brickyards, at which about 200 individuals are at present (1839) employed.

Port or Harbour

Carrickfergus is now a member of the port of Belfast, to which it was, as such, transferred in 1824. As a place of commerce it is of great antiquity and, at one time, was of considerable consequence, possessing extraordinary privileges, the principal of which were, through the exertions of Sir Arthur Chichester, then lord deputy, confirmed by James I.

Among others, the corporation possessed the third part of all customs of goods imported or exported between Fair Head on the north coast of Antrim and Beerlooms, near Portaferry, on the coast of Down, a distance of 40 miles each way.

All persons were prohibited from importing any commodities within this space, except at the quays of Carrickfergus, Belfast, Bangor and Larne. These towns, however, paid one-third of the customs to Carrickfergus. In the records there is an entry, dated 12th March 1634, by which it appears that the corporation let off one-third the customs of Bangor and Donaghadee to Thomas Whitager, alderman, for 21 years, at 20 pounds per annum. It also possessed the privilege of importing goods at lower rates than were paid throughout the country. With such advantages as these, Carrickfergus increased its commerce to a great extent and the returns of its port were among the largest in Ireland.

Carrickfergus soon, however, lost its important commercial advantages, by the sale of its part of the customs to the government in 1637. They were purchased at the instance of Lord Strafford, then chief governor of Ireland, for 3,000 pounds, which was to have been laid out in the purchase of land for the use of the corporation but which never took place. 1,300 pounds of this sum was lent in interest to Mr John Davys of Carrickfergus, but neither it nor the remaining 1,700 pounds were ever after satisfactorily accounted for. The trade was immediately transferred to Belfast, with which it has continued.

The original customs house was erected here in 1639. In 1797 a new one, now occupied by the coastguards, was erected on its site. In 1740 the revenues of the port of Larne were separated from those of Carrickfergus.

In 1824 the ballast office was established, and on the 5th January 1825 the port was annexed to that of Belfast and the office of port surveyor was abolished. In 1827 the custom house was given up to the coastguards.

Port Charges

The rates of ballast are 8d per ton: "All vessels coming into this harbour to pay 2d per ton register tonnage and 2s anchorage; vessels coming in light or taking ballast either in harbour or inside the buoys to pay 1d per ton register tonnage only. All vessels taking in a cargo to pay 1d per ton register tonnage, in addition to the 1d per ton coming in light and 2s anchorage. Vessels taking in cattle, only to pay 1d ha'penny per ton register tonnage (if coming in light); but vessels that have discharged their last cargo at this harbour to pay 1d per ton register tonnage."

Among the rules and regulations of the port it is ordered "that all moneys received be applied, under the direction of the harbour committee, for the improvement and well-being of the port and harbour, after deducting the necessary salaries and incidental expenses, and that the committee to account with the assembly once in every year

on foot of all moneys received and expended."

"The harbour committee and committee of superintendence for improvement of the port and harbour of Carrickfergus" consist of the mayor for the time being and 13 others, who have power to make by-laws and rules and appoint officers, as they may think necessary. This committee was formed on 21st January 1839 and have since attended vigilantly to the interests of the harbour.

The salary of the harbour-master and ballast-master is 25 pounds per annum, beside 1s in the pound for collecting harbour dues. The salary of the water-bailiff is 10 pounds per annum, besides fees on the execution of writs.

Pilots

There are not any licensed pilots attached to the port: jobbing pilots or boatmen from the harbour are employed.

Imports and Exports

The principal imports are coal, of which 9,000 tons, salt 200 tons, oak-bark 150 tons, slates 200 tons, fire-brick 10,000, tiles 6,000, grain 140 tons, sandstone 200 tons were imported in 1838.

The principal exports are grain, of which between 200 and 300 tons, potatoes 200 tons, hay 100 tons, bricks 250,000, beans 150 tons, black cattle about 2,000 head, and about 20 horses were shipped for exportation in 1838. Between the 16th April and 30th June 1839, 1,114 head of black cattle and 13 horses were exported.

Plan for New Harbour

The trade of the port is increasing and the present harbour is much too small, and from its extreme inconvenience greatly obstructs the trade. A survey was made in 1832 by Sir John Rennie, and a plan and report were drawn up by him for the construction of a new harbour outside the present one, by which a depth of 15 feet of water, at low water of spring tides, would be ensured and protection be formed against the accumulation of mud and sand. The total estimate for this undertaking was 55,150 pounds. No further step in this important task has since been made.

Harbour Dues

The dues of the port amount to between 140 and 150 pounds per annum. In 1803 the customs amounted to 308 pounds 5s 10d, in 1805 to 401 pounds 12s 9d, in 1807 to 472 pounds 1s 5d, in 1810 to 307 pounds 7s 10d, in 1812 to 413 pounds

18s 10d ha'penny, in 1816 to 629 pounds 10s 4d, in 1819 to 409 pounds 17s 5d ha'penny, in 1820 to 518 pounds 11s 6d per annum.

Manufactories and Machinery

The manufactories and machinery of the town of Carrickfergus consist of a distillery, 2 flax spinning mills, a flour and corn mill, 1 corn mill, 2 tanyards and 2 brickyards.

Distillery

The distillery, the property of Mr James Barnet, is situated in the Irish Quarter and immediately adjoining the beach. It consists of a still-house 40 by 40 feet and 15 feet high; a cooler 40 by 30 feet and 15 feet high; a malt-house 88 by 33 feet 6 inches and 3-storeys high; a kiln 33 by 33 feet and 2-storeys high; a mash-house 35 by 30 feet and 20 feet high; cistern and couch 33 by 19 feet and 2-storeys high; besides a back-house, copper's house and the usual offices and apartments.

This concern is built partly of brick and partly of stone, and is in excellent repair. The machinery is propelled by a steam engine of 2 horsepower and a breast water wheel 12 feet in diameter and 5 feet broad, having a fall of water of 6 feet. The supply of water power is regular.

Attached to the distillery is a steam-mill measuring 44 feet 6 inches by 21 feet 6 inches and consisting of 3 floors. The chimney is 80 feet high. Its machinery is propelled by a steam engine of 8 horsepower.

This distillery was originally established by a Mr Thompson, a Scotsman, in 1824. It continued idle during 1826 and 1827, and was re-established by its present proprietor in 1828. The total cost of its erection amounted to 10,000 pounds.

Flax Mills

Joymount Bank flax spinning mill, the property of Mr Samuel Walker, is situated on a small stream called the Cilly Tober, a little to the north of the Scotch Quarter.

The machinery, consisting of 2,500 spindles, is contained in a 1-storey house measuring externally 121 by 40 feet 6 inches and is propelled by an iron breast water wheel 28 feet in diameter and 8 feet broad, having a fall of water of 26 feet. The supply of water is constant. This concern is in perfect repair. 130 hands, of whom 75 are females and 65 are males, are employed in it. It was established in 1834.

A flax spinning mill situated a little to the north of the Scotch Quarter, and near the eastern extremity of the town, is now being erected by Mr James Cowan. It is being built of stone and will be completed during the present year (1839).

Corn and Flour Mills

Millmount corn and flour mill, the property of Mr James Wilson, is situated on a branch of the Woodburn stream in Irish Quarter West. The house containing the machinery is in bad repair. It is built of stone, thatched, consists of 2 floors and measures externally 90 by 38 feet 6 inches. The machinery, which is double-geared, is propelled by 2 breast water wheels, each propelling 2 pairs of stones. The wheel of the flour [mill] measures 17 feet 6 inches by 4 feet 6 inches broad; that of the corn mill is 17 feet 6 inches in diameter by 1 foot 6 inches broad. The fall of water on each is 17 feet. The supply of water is regular.

A mill, the property of Mr James Barnet, for grinding oats and barley, is situated on a branch of the Woodburn stream and in the Irish Quarter. Its machinery, which is double-geared, is contained in a substantial house consisting of 3 floors and which, including the kiln, measures 76 by 26 feet. It is propelled by a breast water wheel 14 feet in diameter and 7 feet broad, having a fall of water of 17 feet. The supply of water is regular. This mill was erected about 25 years ago.

Tanyards

Of the 2 tanyards in Carrickfergus, 1 only is at present occupied. It is the property of Mr John Legg and is situated in the Scotch Quarter. This manufactory consists of 64 tan-holes and 4 lime-holes, besides 4 houses. One of the latter consists of 2 floors and measures externally 130 by 22 feet. A second is 1-storey high and measures 56 by 22 feet. A third consists of 1 floor and measures 77 by 28 feet, and the fourth is also 1-storey; it measures 69 by 18 feet. 15 men are daily employed at this concern, which is in full work and in good repair. It was established about the year 1776.

The second tanyard, which is on a smaller scale, is situated off West Street. It has been unoccupied since 1838. There are 3 tan-houses connected with it. One of these measures 50 by 25 feet and consists of 2 floors; a second measures 50 by 25 feet and consists of 1 floor; and the third is similar to the latter.

Brickyards

The brickyard at the western side of the town,

near the Roman Catholic chapel, is the property of Mr James Wilson. It includes about an acre and a half and affords at present employment to 10 men, 2 women and 4 boys. It can burn from 5 to 6 kilns per annum but burns only 1 at a time. It was established about the year 1814.

SOCIAL AND PRODUCTIVE ECONOMY

Bank

The Northern Banking Company established a branch of their bank here in 1832. This has been a great convenience to the inhabitants of Carrickfergus and particularly to those engaged in trade. The late panic in the commercial world has produced a salutary effect on the management of provincial and branch banks, by checking the almost unlimited credit given by them in the north of Ireland for 3 or 4 years previous to 1837 which, instead of being a source of benefit to the country, produced most injurious effects by placing individuals without capital, resources or character on a level with the respectable capitalist.

The system has since then undergone a complete change, and branch banks have here, as elsewhere, been useful and convenient establishments. The fair trader or agriculturalist is enabled by them to await revival in trade or in market prices, instead of being obliged, in order to meet some pressing demand, to dispose of his property at a sacrifice while trade continues dull.

To the contractors for roads and other public works, and to the individuals who receive at the assizes the sums due them by the county, the bank here has proved a matter of extreme convenience.

Friendly Society

There are 3 benefit societies in Carrickfergus: they are designated as the Friendly Society, the Union Society and the Wreath Club.

The Friendly Society was established pursuant to act of parliament in 1817. The object and intention of this society was to raise by subscriptions from its ordinary members, and by donations and contributions from its honorary members and others, a fund for the support of the former when suffering from sickness or infirmity, and to provide decent interment for themselves, their wives and children.

Their quarterly meetings are held in the assembly room in March, June, September and October. Their affairs are managed by a president, vice-president, treasurer and secretary, with a committee of 12 members elected annually. 4 visitors are also elected annually for the purpose of visiting the sick. The treasurer is bound (according to the act) with 2 sureties for the faithful discharge of his duty.

The number of members at present amounts to 70. On his admission, a member must be over 16 and under 34 years of age, of good character and resident within 1 mile of Carrickfergus; but should he remove to any distance within 20 miles, he will, on forwarding a certificate from his clergyman and medical attendant, be entitled to assistance.

Each member pays 7s on admission and 1d per week subscription, exclusive of such other calls as may be made on him. He is obliged to pay 1d per week for each sick member, provided their number does not exceed 10 at a time.

No member will be entitled to receive any assistance until he shall have been 3 months admitted. He will then, in case of sickness, be entitled to receive 6s per week for the first 3 months, 4s per week for the next and, should he continue longer infirm, 2s 6d per week, always provided that his sickness shall not have been caused by his own imprudence.

1 pound 5s is given towards the interment of the wife and 10s towards that of the child of a member, provided he does not exceed 20 years of age; 2 pounds 10s (to be collected by 6d from each member) to be paid to the relations of a member towards his interment. The annual collections of the society amount to about 30 pounds. Only 4 members have died since the society was formed, but several have left the country.

The only expense connected with its management is 7s per quarter to the member who collects the subscriptions and gives notice of meetings to the members.

Ladies or gentlemen desirous of becoming members are admitted upon payment of 1 guinea, but they are exempt from fines or benefits. The rules and regulations of the society are pretty strict. Their non-observance is punished by fines which are paid into the fund. It is necessary that any change in their rules should be submitted to the counsel appointed by the attorney-general to certify the rules of benefit societies.

Union Society

The Union Society is founded on principles precisely similar to those of the Friendly Society. It was established in 1817 and consists at present of 70 members, whose subscriptions and contributions resemble those of the Friendly Society. Its funds at present amount to 76 pounds 19s 1d.

5s per week is paid to each sick and 2s 6d per

week to each superannuated member. Of the former, there is at present but 1 and of the latter, 2; 1 pound 10s is granted towards the funeral of members and 20s towards those of their wives.

Wreath Club

The Wreath or Weaving Club is composed of 30 weavers who would not consent to take the oath of the Guild of Weavers, who are sworn not to lend or assist those who are not members of their guild. It was established in 1813.

The objects of this society are very limited and unimportant, being merely to furnish themselves with wreaths or beaming-rails, towards which each member pays 1s 8d on his admission. Chequering only is woven by the members of this club. There are not funds or benefits connected with it.

Markets and Fairs: Charter

By the charter of James I leave is given to hold 2 annual fairs or "chief markets" in Carrickfergus, to be held "on the feast of St Philip and St Jacob the Apostles and for the 2 days next following," the second to be held "on the feast of All Saints and for 2 days next following." Leave is given to hold a pie poudre court, together with these fairs, as also "to the mayor, sheriffs, burgesses and commonalty to have all the liberties, free customs as also all profits, revenues, advantages."

Leave is given in the same charter to "hold 2 markets in every week," that "they may have and hold 1 the said 2 markets on Saturday, there to be held forever." No day is specified for the other market.

Fairs

The 2 annual fairs are held, one on the 12 May, the other on the 1st November. That held in November is by much the most considerable but both are unimportant, as will be more clearly understood by referring to the appendix and Fair Sheets, in which a correct statement of the commodities and cattle exposed in the May fair of 1839 will be found. These fairs are, and have for some years been, declining.

Markets

One weekly market is held in Carrickfergus on Saturdays. This market is very inconsiderable, neither grain nor manufactures being exposed for sale in it. Butter and pork are sold merely by retail and in small quantities. Butcher's meat, poultry, butter and potatoes are exposed for sale in the new market place and constitute the principal commodities. The few other miscellaneous articles are exposed in the old market place near the centre of the town.

The supply of each particular article depends on the period of the season, the quantities of each being so trifling at every period as never to cause a glut or a scarcity by comparison. A table showing the quantity of each article exposed in these markets, in 6 successive months during the year 1839, will be found in the appendix and will convey a more clear idea of their importance.

The quantities of eggs and poultry brought to market here are on the increase. The quantity of fish exposed for sale here is on the decrease, as they are chiefly bought up for the Belfast markets. Rather more butcher's meat than formerly is now exposed for sale, but of the other commodities, the quantities have undergone but little change for several years. The erection of the new market place in North Street has tended somewhat to the improvement of the market, by the excellent accommodation which it affords to buyers and sellers.

The commodities brought to this market are conveyed in the carts of their owners. The carriage of goods to or from Belfast (per carts) costs 5d per cwt.

No tolls or customs are paid in these markets. The only charges or dues are for the stalls and other accommodation in the new market place. They are very reasonable, as will be found by referring to the appendix.

Provisions

The supply of provisions in Carrickfergus is pretty regular and their prices are comparatively moderate. In the appendix, a statement of the average prices of commodities in common use, for the year 1839, will be found in detail.

The supply of butcher's meat except on Saturday (the market day) is very scanty. Beef cattle are purchased by the butchers at the neighbouring fairs, or from farmers and others in the neighbourhood. There is not any stall-feeding in the town or its immediate vicinity, and there is but little grazing of beef cattle. Mutton is less plentiful than beef. Sheep are gradually becoming more scarce, owing to the cultivation of the hilly districts and the consequent diminution in the size of farms.

Poultry are abundantly supplied, particularly on market days when they are exposed in considerable numbers. During the week they are occasionally brought in from the country. Though their prices are still comparatively moderate, they have, since the introduction of steam communication, been increased, owing to the great demand for them in the English market. The same may be said of eggs, which are collected by individuals for exportation.

Milk and butter are abundantly supplied from the hilly districts in this parish and from Island Magee. Fresh butter of excellent quality sells at from 8d to 1s per lb., according to its quality and the season. The best butter averages 10d per lb. throughout the year. Milk, both new and buttermilk, is sent to town in large casks. New milk sells at 2d per quart. Buttermilk is sold in summer at 3 quarts for 1d and in winter at 2 quarts for 1d.

Carrickfergus was formerly celebrated for its cheese, which to the present day bears a respectable character and is in considerable estimation. New-milk cheese is made in large quantities, but not so much so as formerly in the town and in its vicinity. It sells at from 4d ha'penny to 7d per lb.

The supply of fish is very plentiful at all seasons and embraces almost all the finer descriptions. The Carrickfergus oysters are celebrated for their use and flavour, and are usually sold at from 6s to 10s per 100. Turbot, haddock, plaice, soles, cod and herrings are taken in their seasons in great quantity and afford the principal supply for the Belfast market.

There are not any market gardens. The supply of fruit and vegetables is limited, both in quantity and variety. Apples, pears, plums, cherries and gooseberries are sold to hucksters by private individuals. Cabbages, leeks, onions and occasionally turnips and carrots are sold by hucksters and at private gardens.

Water

Carrickfergus is amply supplied with soft or river water for domestic purposes. It is conducted by metal mains to several pumps and cisterns conveniently situated in the streets for the use of the inhabitants.

The supply of spring water is limited: there is an excellent spring, known as Brides Well, which is situated 500 yards north of the town. A large reservoir adjoins the well, and from this a pipe conveys its water to the gaol. There are numerous private pumps in the town. Spring water is usually obtained at depths of from 20 to 40 feet.

Grazing and Potato Ground

Grazing for the milch cows of the inhabitants is abundant and is conveniently situated. It lets at from 4 pounds to 4 pounds 4s per head for the summer 6 months.

Ground for planting potatoes lets about the town at from 10d to 1s 6d per square perch.

Building Materials

Timber is procured from Belfast, from where its carriage costs 5d per ton. Pine is the description most commonly used in buildings and for roofing. Bricks of excellent quality are manufactured at the 2 brick-kilns in Carrickfergus. They cost, per 1,000, 18s at the kilns and 20s laid down. Stones, mainly whin and the harder kinds of basalt, are procured at the quarries in the vicinity of the town and cost, laid down, from 1s to 1s 3d per ton. Slates are landed at the quay from Wales. The description commonly used are countesses, which sell at from 96s to 98s per 1,000.

Lime is abundant throughout the neighbourhood. There is a quarry at Duff's hill, about 1 mile north east of the town, from whence it costs, laid down, 1s per barrel; but that from the kilns in the adjoining parish of Carnmoney, 5 miles distant, is preferred. It costs, at the kilns, 1s per barrel or 1s 4d laid down. Sand for building, from the sea-shore or from the sand-pits near the town, cost, laid down, 8d per ton.

There are 2 extensive timber and slate-yards, the property of Mr Samuel D. Stewart, from whence the inhabitants are supplied. There is also in Carrickfergus a stoneyard where sandstone, from Scotland and from Scrabo in county Down, is cut for sale.

Fuel

Coal is the fuel chiefly used. It is landed at the quay, where it costs, for English coal, from 11s to 16s per ton, and for Scotch, 9s 6d to 14s per ton. Turf is brought for sale from the Commons of Carrickfergus, a distance of from 3 to 4 miles, and is exposed in carts in the streets. In the town it is never used except for kindling coal fires. It sells at from 1s 8d to 2s 2d per load, which contains little more than a gauge or cubic yard.

Insurances

The custom of insuring machinery and the better description of houses is pretty general, but none of the smaller or less valuable houses are insured from fire. There are but very few life insurances.

Combination

During the last 7 years combination has not existed. It had previously for nearly 30 years existed among the tradespeople, but particularly among the bakers and shoemakers, but never had assumed a serious aspect.

Employment

Tradespeople and labourers are in pretty regular employment throughout the year and can earn comparatively good wages. Shoemakers and tailors occasionally, during the early part of summer, are almost unemployed for about 6 weeks or 2 months and suffer considerable privations consequent on their improvident habits.

The demand for workmen and the wages given have, during the last 20 years, declined, owing to the stoppage of several cotton print-works and factories, tanyards and a brewery which were formerly carried on here, and which not only gave employment to all the working class in this parish but attracted many from the surrounding country. A table showing the rates of wages given at several periods in this parish will be found in the appendix.

There are 5 regular carriers or carmen who ply between Carrickfergus and Belfast, performing the journey to and from in a day. The usual charge per cwt for the carriage of goods to and from Belfast is 5d per cwt.

Conveyances

Carrickfergus possesses in its public conveyances much facility for communication with the neighbouring towns, but particularly with Belfast, Larne and the towns along the coast of the county Antrim, as will be found below.

The Belfast and Larne Royal Mail Coach (which passes through Carrickfergus) was established in 1833; leaves Belfast at 9 a.m., arrives in Carrickfergus at 10.30 a.m. and at Larne at 12.15 noon. It leaves Larne at 3 p.m., arrives in Carrickfergus at 4.40 p.m. and at Belfast at 6.15 p.m. in summer. In winter it leaves Larne at 2.30 p.m. and arrives in Belfast at 6 p.m.

The Belfast and Larne Day Coach was established in 1811 and travels between those towns daily, Sundays excepted. It leaves Belfast at 4 p.m., arrives in Carrickfergus at 5.30 p.m. and at Larne at 7 p.m. It leaves Larne at 6 a.m., arrives in Carrickfergus at 8 a.m. and in Belfast at 9.30 a.m. The fares by the mail and stage-coaches are similar, viz. from Carrickfergus to Belfast, inside 2s 6d, outside 1s; from Carrickfergus to Larne, inside 2s 6d, outside 1s 3d.

By the mail coach and main road Carrickfergus is 11 and a quarter miles south of Larne and 10 and a quarter miles north north east of Belfast. By a nearer road, not usually travelled by conveyances, Larne is only 9 miles 5 furlongs distant.

On the arrival of the mail in Larne a car, one of a chain of conveyances leading round the coast, starts for Glenarm. It is drawn by a pair of horses and carries 10 passengers.

A pair-horse car carrying 10 passengers plies daily, Sundays excepted, between Carrickfergus and Belfast during the summer. It leaves Carrickfergus at 9 a.m. and arrives in Belfast at 10.30 a.m. It leaves Belfast at 4.30 p.m. and arrives in Carrickfergus at 6 p.m. The fare for each passenger is 1s.

There are 7 jaunting cars, each drawn by 1 horse and capable of carrying 4 passengers, which ply daily between Carrickfergus and Belfast, performing the journey usually in 1 hour and a half. The fare for each passenger is 1s.

There are in Carrickfergus 5 post chaises, 6 post cars and 42 post horses for hire. The charge for a chaise and a pair, or for a pair of horses, is 1s per mile; and for a car, 8d per mile Irish, for each person. The usual rate of travelling is 6 and a half miles English per hour.

Schools

There are in the town of Carrickfergus 4 schools, of which 1 derives its support entirely and the others partially from benevolence. The annual sum contributed thus amounts to 72 pounds. That paid by the pupils attending these schools is 25 pounds per annum. The number of pupils annually educated at them is 186.

The school which is wholly supported by benevolence is indebted for its existence to the late Ezekiel Davys Wilson Esquire, who died in 1821. He bequeathed the rector for the time being the annual sum of 42 pounds, chargeable on his estate forever, for education in reading, writing and arithmetic of 40 boys and 20 girls. A further sum of 4 pounds per annum is contributed by some ladies towards defraying the salary of a female teacher for this school. The remaining sum, 26 pounds, is annually granted by the Board of National Education to the 3 other schools.

Bequests

The proceeds of 9 bequests (exclusive of that just alluded to), amounting annually to 318 pounds

2s 9d ha'penny, are at present payable to different charities in the county of the town of Carrickfergus, by the trustees or heirs of the testators.

Dispensary

A dispensary for the relief of the poor residing within the limits of the county of the town of Carrickfergus was established here in 1833, since which period it has been supported partly by local contributions and partly by the sum advanced by the county grand jury. For the first 4 years this institution was properly supported, but since then the sums annually subscribed for its support have gradually been diminished until 1838, when subscriptions towards it were withheld.

In 1836 and 1837 it did not receive any assistance from the grand jury, and in 1838 the only funds for its support were 15 pounds 13s presented by the grand jury. The relief it now affords is of course very limited and its effects cannot be either perceptible or important. The great decline in the amount of the subscriptions is attributed to the angry feelings created by electioneering contests.

Mendicity Society

The Carrickfergus Mendicity Society, for the suppression of street-begging by supporting the aged, helpless and infirm and affording employment and partial assistance to the industrious poor, was established in the year 1827, since which period it has been supported chiefly by local subscription, with the aid of occasional fines from petty sessions, and the proceeds of charity sermons in its behalf. A slight decline in the annual amount of its funds has appeared since 1831, when they amounted to 670 pounds 3s 10d ha'penny. In 1838 they amounted to 501 pounds 17s 5d.

This institution is most judiciously managed. Flax is purchased by the committee, who give it out for its manufacture into yarn by the poor, whom they pay for their work and dispose of the yarn. The relief given consists in rations of oatmeal and coal, besides which about 20 individuals are lodged in houses rented by the committee. A detailed statement of the funds of this institution and of the relief afforded by it will be found in the appendix. Its objects in suppressing street-begging has, without the employment of a beadle or any other compulsory step, been quite realised.

Clothing Society

This society was instituted in 1819. Its object is to purchase clothing and blankets for the indigent and aged poor. It has been supported solely by local subscriptions and the proceeds of charity sermons. Its funds, which have not declined, have on an average of 8 years amounted annually to 23 pounds 8s 6d ha'penny and the annual number relieved during the same period has averaged 90.

General Character of Inhabitants

In most respects the inhabitants of Carrickfergus bear pretty much the same stamp of character, and in many respects their character and habits may be attributable to local circumstances which have tended towards distinguishing them from the population of any other town in the county, and which must, so long as they exist, tend materially to retard their general improvement. The circumstances alluded to are the enfranchisement of the town and still more particularly the nature of the franchise and description of the constituency.

Parliamentary Elections

Under the head of Parliamentary Representation and Representatives, it may have [been] seen that this borough has been frequently, and indeed almost invariably, at each election bitterly contested, as it ever will be under the present state of the constituency. The minds of all classes have not only been distracted by, and their thoughts directed to, these contests, which have created incalculable animosity and strife, but a far worse effect has been produced by them in the general and iniquitous system of bribery and corruption, with their attendant consequences, perjury and debauchery, which invariably characterise the elections for Carrickfergus.

Much, if not most, of this may be attributed to the power vested by charter in the mayor, as respects the admission of freemen. He may, by giving 14 days' notice, open a court and admit almost any claimant to the franchise. The consequence of this has been that, out of a gross constituency of 864, 678 are resident freemen, almost all of whom must be purchased; and therefore money alone must, as it ever for years has, decide the contests for Carrickfergus.

The highest bidder is sure to succeed, and so customary has the practice become that persons who might be supposed to look on such an action as disreputable now not only hold out for terms, but unhesitatingly assert the "right of everyone to dispose of his vote as he would of his property." This custom is not confined to the freemen. There are of course more exceptions to it among the freeholders, but still there are not 100 individuals of the entire constituency whose votes are not to be purchased.

The effects of such a system are of course to be imagined. An election nowhere exhibits more disgraceful scenes than in Carrickfergus, and the venality of its constituency is now become proverbial. The biddings of an election are hailed with the greatest anxiety because it [is] of course to be accompanied by a contest, and so distracted are the minds of the inhabitants by it that for a long time previous and subsequent little else is attended to.

Local Government

The circumstances of its incorporation and its being the county town have, at least during the last 2 centuries, done but little for Carrickfergus. Previous to the sale of the third part of its customs in 1637, the corporation and inhabitants possessed many valuable immunities granted by charter, on account of their steady attachment to the English government; but with the sale of the customs the prosperity of Carrickfergus seems to have terminated. The sum (3,000 pounds) received for the customs does not seem to have [been] satisfactorily accounted for and, as it does not seem to have been placed to the general benefit of the corporation, it most probably was appropriated to that of a few individuals.

A large extent of the lands of the corporation, held in trust by them for the benefit of the commonalty, has been alienated and become the property of individuals, several of whom, otherwise unconnected with the county even by residence, at the present moment derive large revenues from it. On the whole, the transactions of the corporation during the last 2 centuries appear to have been anything but creditable or fair; the trust which they have held being, instead of exercised for the benefit of the community, made a source of private emolument and aggrandisement. Such portions of their records as would corroborate this statement have of course been carefully destroyed, but there are many private documents which have as truly preserved for posterity many extraordinary facts connected with the proceedings. The present corporation have little in their power, but still that little renders their dissolution an event which might be desirable.

In the circumstances of its being a county town, Carrickfergus, strange as it may appear, is not indebted for any real benefit. The assizes, quarter sessions, elections and such periodical occurrences bring to the town a large influx of strangers, who, during their short stay, circulate some capital. To these occasions the majority of the people in business look forward for a large amount of their emolument, as hotels, public houses and every private house which can let a bedroom and a sitting-room is then occupied, and so great is the demand for lodgings, and so high is the rate at which they then let, that a tenant who may have taken lodgings for the year is obliged on these occasions to vacate them.

To these occasions, and to exacting the highest price for everything in demand during their continuance, do the majority of the inhabitants depend for their support; and, but for them, their condition might have been much better, and the prosperity of their town increased, by a more industrious direction of their energies either to trade or agriculture.

Character of the People

There is among the inhabitants a general want of energy of mind, to which there are but few exceptions, and there is also a want of enterprise and exertion which, even in the aspect of the town, is at once apparent. Some 3 or 4 merchants or traders have recently expended some capital in enlarging and improving their premises, and thereby improved the appearance of the town, but their example is by no means likely to be imitated.

The inhabitants seem to prefer continuing in their usual narrow and limited habits and extent of business to increasing it or their means by any unusual energy or exertion. There is a dullness and listlessness pervading the aspect of the town which is quite characteristic of its population. The assizes are looked forward to with anxiety and their every energy is put forth to seize on everyone and to exact for everything and from every stranger the utmost price, but once they are over they again relax into their supine habits, from which they are roused only on their next approach.

Many, from habit, are hard-working and, so far as regards bodily exertions while engaged at their accustomed vocations, are really industrious; this remark especially applies to the fishermen, who lead laborious lives. But take them or almost any of the other classes from their ordinary employment, and when applied to any other, particularly where mental energy or activity is required, and they will be found dull, apathetic and inert.

The general character of all classes is that of being punctual in their engagements, fair in their transactions and remarkably honest, theft being almost unknown.

Drink

Though actual intoxication is not usual, still there is, particularly among the tradespeople, fishers and working class generally, a great proneness to tippling which equally applies to both sexes and which has been productive of many bad consequences. Even among a better description (as to circumstances), the observance of conjugal fidelity is by no means strict. To the humbler ranks this more strongly applies. Instances of this kind are so frequent as to be slightly noticed, and but little approbated or discountenanced. Illegitimacy is of rather frequent occurrence and there is in the town and neighbourhood a general laxity of morals.

In the year 1821 there were but 25 houses licensed to sell spirits in the town of Carrickfergus. In 1826 there were 24 and now in 1839 there are 51.

Pawnbrokers

In the year 1828 there was only 1 pawnbroker in Carrickfergus. The sum advanced by him on pledges during that year was 291 pounds 10s, while in 1838 there were 3 pawnbrokers, who jointly advanced 2,731 pounds 4s 7d farthing. A reference to the statement of the pawn-offices in Carrickfergus shown in the appendix will perhaps prove astonishing.

It is not to be imagined that the increased resort to pawnbrokers has been caused by increased poverty, for such is not the case; for it would appear that pawnbroking has progressed as the number of spirit shops has increased and as the consumption of spirits and the more general prevalence of tippling has advanced.

Amusements and Customs

The taste for amusement has among all classes within a few years greatly declined, and many of their ancient and favourite games have fallen into disuse.

There is little sociality or society among the upper class residing in the town, but there is a very good neighbourhood consisting of several influential and hospitable families in its immediate vicinity, who are social among themselves and are very attentive to strangers.

The middle classes are rather more social. Their chief recreation is, however, confined to meeting occasionally in small numbers, either at each other's houses or, though less frequently, at an inn. There are no places for public amusements, nor would such if established be supported here.

The lower class is by no means of a gregarious disposition, nor have they almost any particular amusement. Frequenting ale houses, attending an occasional dance and fighting cocks on Easter Monday are now their only recreations.

An ancient custom of blocking up the West Gate on Christmas Eve with carts and cars is still kept up. This is said to have originated in precautions which were formerly adopted to prevent the Roman Catholics, who were assembled at worship on Christmas Eve and on other festivals, from entering the town by surprise.

General Character

All classes are civil and obliging to strangers, very peaceable towards each other and quite free from party spirit. Quarrels and assaults are unusual and feuds consequent on elections are confined to the upper class, the others caring little, if at all, as to the success of any particular individual, so as that they receive the accustomed price of their vote.

They are in general humane and charitable, and are liberal in their contributions to the support of the indigent.

Horses

There are not more than 5 saddle horses. There is a subscription pack of harriers in the neighbourhood which occasionally meet here, but there are very few horses kept exclusively for the field.

Improvements

Carrickfergus is improving in appearance and has during the last 10 years improved, though it has not increased in size nor on any side extended its limits. Between the years 1820 and 1835, 20 houses, of which 4 were 3-storeys, 11 2-storeys and 5 were 1-storey, were erected in the town and suburbs, and 50 were rebuilt or improved; of these 44 were each raised a storey. Between 1835 and 1839, 5 3-storey and 3 2-storey houses were erected and 14 rebuilt or improved. Of the latter, 11 were raised a storey.

These houses are situated in the principal streets and in the more frequented parts of the town. They are generally of a tolerable description and in their appearance and style of construction present an improvement on those of older date. They are generally suited for persons in business, families of moderate means, or for a better description of tradespeople.

The prices of building ground vary from 1s 6d to 10s per foot, according to the situation; the average price is about 6s per foot. The leases given are for 61 to 91 years or in perpetuity, according to the ability of the purchaser. The usual tenure is the last.

Progress of Improvement

The demand for houses and, with it, the rate of house rent has during the last 20 years declined considerably, and the erection of new or the improvement of old houses cannot therefore be taken as a criterion as to the prosperity of the town. Those alluded to above have been erected on their sites by the proprietors of old tenements, and those improved are generally situated in the more valuable positions for places of business. Of the 746 houses in Carrickfergus, 54 are at present (1839) unoccupied and of these many are falling into decay.

House rent of course depends upon the situation of the tenement, but it is in Carrickfergus generally very low. Formerly this town was much frequented in summer by families who came here from Belfast for the benefit of sea bathing; but for several years, in consequence of the growth of Holywood (on the opposite side of the lough), which is within 4 miles of Belfast, the erection of lodgings in Glenarm and Cushendall and the other towns along the coast of Antrim, and also along that of Down, and the great facility of communication with these, Carrickfergus has latterly been utterly forsaken as a bathing place. To this circumstance the decline in house rent is mainly to be attributed.

The amount of capital circulated in Carrickfergus is much less than it was 20 years since. The withdrawal of the military has been felt by the dealers, but they have sustained a much more severe loss in the stopping of several cotton mills and print-works in the neighbourhood which, together with the brewing, gave constant employment not merely to the natives of the town but to many strangers who came from a distance in quest of employment.

The increased facility of communication with Belfast affords an easier opportunity to many of the more independent private individuals to obtain from thence many of the necessaries of life, which they had previously procured from Carrickfergus.

There has been an increase in the shipping trade, so far as the imports and exports of grain, coal, salt, black cattle, salt and beans are concerned; and were the harbour more convenient, as to extent, approach and depth of water, the trade would increase considerably.

There is a great want of energy on the part of the corporation and of unanimity and activity on the part of the landlords and principal persons engaged in trade, nor is there anyone of rank, influence or situation to make any effort or any exertion towards improving the condition of the town or its inhabitants.

Carrickfergus is little likely to increase in importance, and should the assizes for the county Antrim be, as it has been sometimes threatened, removed to a more central town, it will, after having so long depended mainly upon them, sink much lower.

MODERN TOPOGRAPHY

Hamlet of Eden

The hamlet of Eden is situated near the coast of Belfast Lough, on the mail coach road from Carrickfergus to Larne, and 1 mile north east of the former town. Its situation is cheerful, the surrounding country being highly cultivated and diversified, and from its situation it may perhaps have derived its original name, Eaden Greena or "the sunny bank."

Eden cannot, however, boast of any antiquity, at least so far as regards its existence as a hamlet, for the first edifice erected on its site was a small thatched cabin by a cotton weaver named David Craig in 1807. Since then it has gradually increased.

It now consists of 7 2-storey houses and 36 cottages, all of which are built of stone and lime. 23 are thatched and 20 slated, and almost all are substantial and comfortable, and are generally in good repair and rather neat-looking. 6 of the cottages are unoccupied. The last addition to the village took place in 1838, when a tolerably good 2-storey house was erected. The ground is the property of the Wilson family, who let it out on leases of forever and on moderate terms for building.

Eden extends for 281 yards along each side of the main road, which forms a street 170 feet wide. There is neither trade nor manufacture in the hamlet. The inhabitants, who are quiet and industrious, are of the humbler class, as will be seen from the annexed table: carpenters 2, cooper 1, fiddler 1, flowerers 3, grocers 2, hucksters 1, labourers

15, pensioner 1, schoolmaster 1, spirit dealers 3, shoemakers 2, blacksmiths 1, total 33.

Public Buildings: Meeting House

The only public building in the county of the town of Carrickfergus, besides those described under the head of Towns, is a Covenanting meeting house which is situated on the northern confines of the county and near the old road leading from Carrickfergus to Larne.

It is a plain, substantial, rectangular structure without any pretensions to neatness in its appearance. It measures internally 40 by 26 feet. Its floor is of earth. It is filled up with pews and is capable of accommodating 186 persons. It was erected by subscription in 1805.

Gentlemen's Seats

To give a detailed description of each of the many gentlemen's residences in this parish would be almost impossible and would certainly prove uninteresting, for though many of them are handsome, spacious edifices surrounded by tastefully-wooded grounds, still there is not one of them which possesses the slightest pretensions to architectural style, or to which is attached what could, with propriety, be termed (unless by comparison) a demesne or a park ornamented with the timber of another century or traversed by drives or walks.

Most of them are of very recent erection. Many of them are spacious and respectable family mansions, constructed with considerable taste, both as to appearance and situation. Their grounds, though not extensive, are generally well laid out and are kept in good order. From their number and propinquity they tend greatly towards giving to this coast the delightful and varied effect which it has when viewed from the water.

Scoutbush, the residence of Edward Bruce Esquire, J.P., occupies a cheerful situation near the coast, 1 and a half miles south of Carrickfergus, and commands a delightful prospect of the lough and the surrounding scenery. The house is a plain but handsome and spacious edifice 2-storeys high, situated in the midst of a tastefully-planted lawn of 5 acres. The gardens and offices are of suitable extent.

Scoutbush was originally erected about 33 years since but was rebuilt by the present proprietor. It derived its name from its having, in the 17th century, been the residence of the scout-major or provost-marshal of Carrickfergus garrison. It was also for some time, from 1642 till 1648, the residence of General Robert Munroe, who commanded the Scotch auxiliary forces in Carrickfergus.

Sea Park, the residence of the Very Rev. John Chaine, Dean of Connor and Rector of Carrickfergus, is separated from Scoutbush by the main road from Carrickfergus to Belfast. It occupies a delightful situation on the shore of the lough, along which its prettily-ornamented grounds, consisting of about 16 acres, extend for about three-quarters of a mile. The house is a very neat-looking and comfortable residence. The garden and offices are suitable as to extent. Sea Park was originally erected in 1804.

Thornfield, the residence of Peter Kirk Esquire, J.P., D.L., M.P. for the borough of Carrickfergus, is agreeably situated on a gentle declivity half a mile north of the town of Carrickfergus. The house is [a] plain but neat and modern-looking mansion of tolerable dimensions. It is surrounded by about 3 acres of ornamental ground, which is thickly planted. The house was erected about 4 to 5 years since by the late Sir William Kirk.

Burleigh Hill, the residence of John Robinson Esquire, is delightfully situated on a declivity about 2 miles north of Carrickfergus. The house is a spacious and modern-looking residence 2-storeys high and having a wing at each side. It is situated in a handsome lawn of about 36 acres, most of which is under planting. There is a good garden and the offices are of suitable extent. Burleigh Hill was erected about the year 1793 by the late George Burleigh Esquire.

St Catherine's, the residence of the late Colonel Walsh, is pleasantly situated near the north or Glenarm Road, about 1 and two-third miles north of Carrickfergus. The house is a plain but neat residence. The planted and ornamental grounds, which include about 12 acres, are well laid out. There is an excellent garden and good offices. St Catherine's was erected in 1805 by the late William Burleigh Esquire.

Prospect (now unoccupied), the property of C.W. Nicolay Esquire, is a handsome and modern-looking residence agreeably situated near the Glenarm Road, about 1 mile north west of Carrickfergus. There is an excellent garden and extensive offices. The planted and ornamental grounds include about 14 acres and are judiciously disposed. Prospect was erected about the year 1800 by the late Henry Clements Ellis Esquire.

Oakfield (now uninhabited), a plain but neat 2-storey house of tolerable extent, [is] pleasantly situated near the north or Glenarm Road, about 1 and a third miles north east of Carrickfergus. The plantings and ornamental grounds, though not extensive, are rather prettily laid out, and the garden and offices are of ample accommodation. Oakfield was erected about the year 1805 by the late William Dobbs Esquire, since which period it has had several occupiers.

The Mount Cottage, the residence of Richard Thompson Esquire, is a very pretty residence situated near the coast and about 1 mile south of Carrickfergus. There is some glass attached to the cottage and about 3 acres of tastefully laid out ornamental grounds, including a good garden. The Mount Cottage was erected about 20 years since by the late Thomas Millar Esquire.

Glynn Park, the residence of John Legg Esquire, occupies a pretty and retired situation about three-quarters of a mile north of Carrickfergus. The house is a small but neat-looking edifice. There are 4 acres of planting which surround it. Glynn Park was erected about 40 years since by the late James Craig Esquire.

Silverstream House, the residence of Captain Manly, is situated on the Silver stream, about 3 miles south of Carrickfergus and adjoining the road to Belfast. It is a plain substantial residence.

Ravenhill Lodge, situated on the coast about 2 and a third miles south of Carrickfergus, is the residence of [blank] Jebb Esquire. [It] is a small but neat-looking house occupying an agreeable situation.

Farm Hill, the residence of Stewart Dunn Esquire, is pleasantly situated on the Woodburn Road, about 2 miles north west of Carrickfergus. It is a small but neat residence situated in a lawn of about 6 acres which is thickly planted.

Barn Cottage, the residence of James Cowan Esquire, almost adjoins the Scotch Quarter. It is a neat cottage with a neat little lawn of about 2 acres in front.

Mills and Manufactories

The manufactories and mills in the county of the town, and which have not been included among those described under of Towns, consist of 1 corn mill, 2 flax spinning mills and 2 cotton spinning mills. There is not any obstruction, arising from disputes as to rights of water, to the erection of machinery.

Corn Mills

The corn mill, the property of Mr James Berry, is situated on a small stream about 1 mile north of the town of Carrickfergus. The machinery, which is single-geared, is contained in a small 1-storey house, slated and built of stone, measuring 30 by 15 feet. It is propelled by a breast water wheel 18 feet 6 inches in diameter by 3 feet broad, having a fall of water of 15 feet. This wheel also works a threshing machine. The mill was erected in 1812.

Flax Mills

The flax spinning mill commonly known as Woodburn print-works is situated on the Woodburn stream, 1 mile north west of the town of Carrickfergus.

This establishment was erected in 1805 by Stewart Dunn Esquire, by whom it was occupied as a cotton-printing establishment until the year 1834 when it ceased work. In 1836 it was fitted up as a flax spinning mill and thread-dyeing establishment by Brown, Warnock and Company, and was by them occupied as such until the year 1838, when they resigned the business. Since that period it has been idle.

The machinery and apparatus of the flax spinning mill is contained in a house consisting of 2 floors and an underground storey, including 2 spinning rooms, one of which measures 40 feet 6 inches by 24 feet, the other 44 feet 9 inches by 24 feet, a preparation room 40 feet 6 inches by 24 feet, a twisting room of similar dimensions, the engine house 34 feet 6 inches by 10 feet, and a boiling house 34 feet 6 inches by 16 feet. The mechanics' shop, which is underground, measures 24 by 12 feet 9 inches.

The machinery is propelled by an overshot water wheel 30 feet in diameter and 4 feet 6 inches broad, having a fall of water of 15 feet. The water for the machinery is collected in a dam 280 by 60 feet and 12 feet deep, and the supply thereby rendered regular. It was constructed by Warnock and Company.

Besides the house which has been described, there are 6 others, viz. the original print-shop 52 by 28 feet, 4-storeys high; the lapping-house 32 by 26 feet, 2-storeys high; reeling-house 20 and a half by 28 feet, 2-storeys high; blue-house 27 by 26 feet, 1-storey high; dye-house 41 and a half by 16 and a half feet, 1-storey high; and a press-room 11 by 30 feet 6 inches, all of which are substantially built and in excellent repair.

On the Woodburn stream, and about 1 and a quarter miles north west of Carrickfergus, are 8 houses which are, with 1 exception, now in a dilapidated state.

These houses were erected by Lindon and Company, in connection with a bleach green and beetling mills which they established here about 50 years ago, and were by them occupied as such until about the year 1810, when they were converted into a cotton-printing establishment by Mr Samuel Hay, who carried on the printing business until the year 1830, since which time they have been unoccupied. Having become the property of Mr James Wilson, who unroofed some of the houses, he, in the year 1835, erected a flax mill on the ruins of one of them.

The machinery of this mill is contained in a 1-storey house measuring 26 by 23 feet and is propelled by a breast water wheel 13 feet in diameter and 6 feet broad, having a fall of water of 10 feet. The supply of water is constant.

The other houses which constitute this establishment measure as follows: a 3-storey house, dilapidated, 72 by 24 feet; a second 3-storey house in tolerable repair, 77 by 25 feet; bluehouse, 1-storey, in good repair, 64 by 22 feet; a 2-storey house in ruins, 120 by 21 feet; a second 2-storey house in ruins, 42 by 18 feet; a 1-storey house in bad repair, 33 by 21 feet; a second 1-storey house in ruins, 57 by 18 feet. The chimney is 40 feet high.

Cotton Mills

Woodburn cotton spinning mill is situated on the Woodburn stream, 1 mile north west of the town of Carrickfergus. The machinery, which consists of 2,666 mule spindles and 2,520 thistle spindles, is, with the carding, scutching and preparing rooms, contained in a 5-floor house measuring externally 110 by 40 feet. The chimney is 80 feet high. The machinery is propelled by a steam engine of 24 horsepower and an overshot water wheel 34 feet in diameter and 5 feet 6 inches broad, having a fall of water of 34 feet. Steam power is required owing to the scarcity of water in summer.

106 hands, of whom 24 are males and 82 females, are at present employed at this manufactory. It was established in the year 1804 by Dr Hanna of Belfast. It subsequently became the property of Mr Thomas Howe, and in 1835 that of John Vance of Belfast, Esquire, its present proprietor.

Duncrue cotton spinning mill is situated on the Woodburn stream, a short distance further up than the last-described mill. The machinery consists of 18,000 mule spindles, besides 24 cards, 8 drawing-frames, 3 fly-frames, 2 roving-frames, 15 reels, scutchers etc. It is contained in a 5-floor house measuring externally 164 by 41 feet and is propelled by an iron breast water wheel 50 feet in diameter and 4 feet 6 inches broad, having a fall of water of 50 feet. The supply of water is rendered regular throughout the year by being collected in dams. 159 hands, of whom 55 are males and 104 females, are at present employed at this mill. It was established in 1823 by its present proprietor, Mr James Cowan.

About three-quarters of a mile north east of the town of Carrickfergus, and on the Cilly Tober stream, are the ruins of 3 houses formerly occupied as a cotton-printing establishment. 2 of the houses are 2-storeys and 1 of them 1-storey high. They measure respectively 46 by 24 feet, 60 by 24 feet and 33 by 24 feet. The machinery has been removed but the water wheel which propelled it, though in a decayed state, still remains. It is overshot and measures 13 feet in diameter and 2 feet 4 inches broad, having a fall of water of 13 feet.

This concern was originally established as a linen bleach green and beetling engines about 50 years since. About 30 years ago it was converted to the purpose of printing cotton, and continued as such until 1833 when, from depression in trade, it became unoccupied. It was known as the Glenfield print-works.

The ruins of an old cotton factory and of a beetling mill are situated on the same stream with, and at a short distance from, the Glenfield print-works.

Communications

The eastern and southern districts of this parish, particularly those including the lower grounds along its coast, are amply supplied with the means of communication, while its western and northern, including its more remote hilly and uncultivated portions, are very deficient in this respect, though the construction of 1 or 2 judiciously laid out crossroads through them would be attended with great advantage to the country. The latter districts of the parish are chiefly under wild pasture and are susceptible of much improvement, but, from the circuitous and hilly state of the roads, the means of transporting farm produce to market are little short of obstructions to their improvement.

With the exception of the new line of road from Carrickfergus to Antrim, which has not been more than a year open and which is very judiciously constructed, the roads in this parish are generally very old and all of them would admit of more or less improvement, both as to direction and in obtaining more equality of surface.

There are only 2 main roads in the parish, namely that alluded to and the main road from Larne to Belfast through Carrickfergus. So far [as] this parish is concerned, the latter road is sufficient, but a line of road from Carrickfergus to Larne, whereby the distance between these towns would be reduced 1 and five-eighth miles and by which the very dangerous hills on the present road in the adjoining parishes would be avoided, is very much wanting. Such a road in an almost right line might, at a comparatively trifling expense, be made, as much of the old direct line between these towns, which is now rarely frequented, might be rendered available, and a valuable tract of country would be much improved by possessing an easier means of communication.

The by or crossroads are chiefly confined to the lower districts of the parish along the coast. They lead almost in parallel lines from the coast to the base of the hills, where most of them terminate or are connected by a crossroad which, running parallel to the latter, intersects them near their extremities. But a few of them are judiciously laid out and more of them would be useful in other districts of the parish

The bridges are generally small but they are sufficiently convenient and commodious in every respect and are generally in good repair.

Roads

There are in this parish 7 miles of main and 9 miles 3 furlongs of by and crossroads, which were made and are kept in repair at the expense of the county of the town of Carrickfergus.

The main roads are: the mail coach road from Belfast to Larne through Carrickfergus, of which there are 4 miles 6 furlongs in this parish. Its breadth is 30 feet besides a footway 5 feet broad. It enters the parish at its south east corner and, running along the shore, quits it at its north eastern corner. With a few trifling exceptions it is almost level and is kept in pretty good repair by contract.

The new line of main road from Carrickfergus to Antrim was opened in 1838. It strikes off in a north western direction from the latter road about 1 mile south of Carrickfergus and soon after pursues a south westerly direction for 5 and three-quarter miles, until it unites with the turnpike road from Belfast to Antrim. There are 2 miles 2 furlongs of this road in the parish; its breadth is 22 feet. It is judiciously laid out and has proved of great convenience to the country. It is sufficiently level, preserves a good direction and is well constructed.

These are the only roads which can be with propriety termed main roads. The following roads, though directly connecting Carrickfergus with some of the neighbouring villages, are rarely travelled by conveyances, their extremely hilly state rendering them little short of impassable to vehicles.

The principal of these roads is the North Road leading from the town of Carrickfergus in a northerly direction, and almost right line, through the parish to the town of Larne and village of Glenarm. Near the northern confines of the parish the road diverges to Larne, while to Glenarm its direction is straight. The total length of this road in this parish is 5 miles 1 furlong; its breadth is 22 feet. It runs in a right line over the ridge at a point where its elevation is 723 feet above the sea. It is therefore necessarily hilly. In ascending the ridge there is an unbroken rise of 311 feet in a distance of 3,234 feet, giving an average inclination of 1 in 10 and a half feet, but which in some parts is not less than 1 in 18 and a half feet. With this exception it is tolerably level, but is not generally kept in good repair.

The Woodburn Road leads north west through the centre of the parish, from Carrickfergus to the villages of Straid and Ballynure. Its length in this parish is 4 miles 7 furlongs; its breadth is 24 feet, besides a footway 4 feet 6 inches wide. Its direction is almost straight. As it runs over the ridge at an elevation of 893 feet it is very steep, its inclinations in some instances attaining 1 in 6 feet. The hilly parts of the road are much worn by the rains which rush down them, acquiring increased velocity and power as they proceed. The more level parts are in tolerable repair.

The by-roads are generally in tolerable repair, except in the remote districts of the parish where they are very much neglected.

A new line of road, which was intended to open a communication between the retired north central districts of this parish and the western and central districts of Antrim, was commenced about 9 years since but has never been completed. It led from the northern end of the Woodburn Road (in this parish) in a westerly direction to the direct road from Larne to Belfast, a distance of 2 miles. There is but 1 mile 2 furlongs of it in this parish. It seems to have been inadvisedly designed, nor could it ever prove of utility to the country.

Scenery

The eastern and western districts of this parish present in their scenery, their natural and artificial state, and in their general appearance, striking contrasts.

The western or north western district, occupying two-thirds of the entire extent of the parish, embraces its higher grounds, extending over a high and almost mountainous table-land, from 600 to 1,025 feet above the sea, almost entirely under wild mountain pasture, very thinly inhabited and presenting a dreary monotonous and uninteresting aspect, which is but little relieved by the dry stone fences which occasionally intersect its tamely-varied surface.

The eastern district of the parish includes a fertile plain stretching between the coast of Belfast Lough and the base of a lofty chain of eminences extending south westward almost as far as the eye can reach, their declivities crowned by a precipitous wall of basalt and their bold features occasionally presenting, in some of the more southern parishes, magnificent profiles standing out from the ordinary line of the range. In this parish there are but few deviations from the line, the summit of which, in some instances rising precipitously to an altitude of 90 feet, impends over the rich and almost level plain at its base.

The low grounds along the coast present extreme diversity, their almost level surface being thickly studded with gentlemen's seats an[d] ornamental plantings, snug farmhouses and cottages, manufactories and hamlets. Here the ground presents an appearance of extreme fertility and here its surface is altogether under cultivation or planting.

From every point of view the town of Carrickfergus is seen to advantage and constitutes to no small [extent?] variety in and ornament to the landscape. The graceful spire of its church, seated on a gentle eminence, at once points out its site from the interior of the country, while its dark frowning castle, standing boldly out on an abrupt rock, presents, in its sombre aspect and striking profile, an object conspicuous from a distance of many miles.

Viewed from the water the shores of Carrickfergus appear to tenfold advantage. Its lower districts appear clothed with plantings to the base of the precipices which tower above them, while the mountain chain, broken into several almost isolated features, presents a succession, almost as far as the eye can reach, of majestic promontories, the precipitous summits of which contrast strongly with the rich plains beneath.

Towards every point the views from every part of the eastern side of the parish are delightful.

Belfast Lough, so often a place of refuge, is frequently studded and at all times enlivened by the numerous shipping of its thriving port. At its southern extremity the town of Belfast, its forest of masts and numerous chimneys of its manufactories vary the outline of the low grounds beyond it. At its other extremity it gradually expands as it approaches the North Channel, beyond which the low coasts of Ayr and Galloway bound the view.

Looking eastward the fertile shores of Down, with their numerous watering places and villages scattered along the coast of the lough, occupy the low base of [a] trifling ridge, beyond which the blue mountains of Mourne present, in their varied and jagged outlines, a magnificent boundary to the prospect.

SOCIAL ECONOMY

Early Improvements

The different social and political events, which have from time to time borne upon the condition of the inhabitants of this district, have, with but few exceptions, been recapitulated in its annals; and as most of the information usually embraced in this section has already been arranged under the heads of Municipality, Education, Benevolence, Justice and Community, but little remains now to be considered.

Under these heads, as referring to the form the information usually classed in this section has been given, as in most instances it has been impossible to distinguish it from the rural district with which it is connected. And therefore it now remains but to notice such circumstances as have not already been brought forward, and, where a distinction can be drawn, to refer to the rural position of the county only, omitting the information which, under the several headings, has already been afforded while treating the town.

Of the aboriginal inhabitants, it may be inferred from the catalogue of names given in the appendix, not a descendant is now to be found in the district. Even of the earliest English settlers (who came over in 1182), the Sendalls, Bensons, Jordans, Copelands, Russels, Whites and Savages, their names have never been perpetuated and they are remembered only in the farms or tracts to which they gave them.

This district furnishes ample evidence of its having, from the earliest ages (even in the most remote and retired portions), been generally inhabited. By referring to the Ancient Topography of these Memoirs, it will be seen that

Plan of Carrickfergus in 1550.

its pagan remains, consisting in rude altars, graves, cairns and coves (besides a great variety of brazen and stone articles of the same remote age), are numerous in its less cultivated parts. Remains of ancient enclosures, habitations and even traces of enclosures of fields are still to be found in its wildest and now most unfrequented districts, affording abundant proof of their having, at an early period and by a rude people, been inhabited.

From the earliest ages Carrickfergus, and the lough to which, until within a comparatively recent period, it gave its name, seems to have been generally known to the Scots and English, but particularly to the island Picts by whom it is said to have frequently been ravaged. During the 7th and 8th centuries the Culdees, who had gone to Northumberland, were obliged to fly from thence to escape the persecution which they endured from Egfrid, king of that country. They returned to Ireland and, having landed at Carrickfergus, fled into the mountain fastnesses of the country, where they were pursued by Bertfrid (a general of Egfrid's), whom, however they succeeded in defeating with great slaughter.

Many townlands and localities in the neighbouring parishes of Templepatrick and Shankill still bear, in the etymology of their names, sufficient proofs of the authenticity of this event. As some of the fugitives may in all probability have crossed the mountains in this parish to those of the neighbouring ones, by the ancient paths and roads (still at intervals to be traced), they may in some instances have settled in the wilder portions of this district which now bear evidence of having once been peopled.

From its exposed position, its propinquity to Scotland and its importance as a fortress, Carrickfergus was from an early period subject to continued attacks from the Scots and (after the taking of it by the English in 1182) to frequent and bloody contests between the English, the Scots and the Irish, to each of whom, but particularly the English, its possession was an object of the utmost importance. The security of life or property must, under such a state of affairs, have been very slight and it is therefore strange that Carrickfergus should, even with all its commercial privileges, have attained such importance as it did as a place of trade.

The great event to which Carrickfergus, in common with the surrounding northern districts, is indebted for its present state in almost every respect is the colonization of Ulster, which commenced during the reign of Elizabeth but was more fully carried out in that of James I.

During the latter part of the 16th century, commencing about the year 1584, several colonists, under the auspices of the Earl of Essex, had come over from England. In 1610 and 1611 large bodies of Scottish troops, who brought their mistresses with them, landed here and many of them settled in this and the adjacent districts, establishing the first Presbyterian congregations in this country. In 1641 and 1642 upwards of 10,000 Scottish auxiliaries landed here; and by these and the other settlers of this century was the greater portion of county Antrim (including the northern and central districts) colonized.

Of the various races and families who had inhabited the parish up to this period, no trace is now to be found, except in their names which were conferred upon the tracts or farms which they had occupied, the present inhabitants being, with but [few] exceptions, the descendants of the settlers of the 16th century. Their names, their dialect or accent, their idioms, customs and habits, and the prevailing religion are all indicative of their extraction, and in few respects do they differ from the people of the country of their forefathers.

The consequences of the events just alluded to are so well known and have been so general throughout the county that they need merely be here recapitulated; for instance, the establishment of a Presbyterian congregation in 1611 and the subsequent establishment of schools. The quiet and tranquillity which now succeeded enabled the inhabitants to turn their attention to peaceful and domestic pursuits, and gave a security to property which had hitherto been unknown. Agriculture had previously been neglected, as its success was not only uncertain but the produce of the parish (except that immediately about the town) was calculated to attract the attention of some neighbouring marauders and to render the security of the county still more precarious.

Local Government

This district constitutes in itself a county corporate, distinct from the county Antrim, and as such is first mentioned in the judges' commission, the assizes for both being opened on the same day. The date of its incorporation is unknown, but from many circumstances it probably took place in the reign of John. There are records of sheriffs having been appointed by Henry II and of mayors so early as 1523. As no counties were erected in Ireland between the 12th year of the reign of John (when, on his visit to Ireland, he confirmed those erected by the first settlers in 1182) and the year 1556, and as it is quite certain that it was known as a county previous to the latter period, its erection as a county by John is more than probable.

The privileges and immunities conferred upon the Corporation of Carrickfergus were very important, and had they been retained and used for the benefit of the inhabitants they would have realized many advantages to them. But they have in some instances been sold or surrendered, and [in] most others been alienated for the benefit of individuals; so much so, that at present the corporation possesses but a nominal interest in the county of the town. Its profit rents do not now exceed 319 pounds 7s 8d per annum. The other less valuable revenues are expended in supporting the establishments from whence they derive their income, and it has not now any fund or resource which it can devote to any public improvement or benefit.

The principal landed proprietors (who hold under the corporation), for instance the Marquis of Downshire, Marquis of Donegall and Lord Blayney, derive a considerable sum from the district but, being non-resident and having no interest to serve, pay no attention to their tenantry.

Linen and Cotton

In the early part of the 17th century the manufacture of linen yarn and of linen cloth was introduced here, and until within a comparatively few years gave employment to a large proportion of the population. In 1790 the first cotton cloth was manufactured in the parish; the yarn was procured [from] Mr Grimshaw's establishment at Whitehouse in the adjoining parish of Carnmoney and webs were manufactured here on commission. In May 1796 Mr Robert Hanly first established the cotton trade on a permanent footing here, by giving out cotton to be woven on his own account. Cotton-printing was established here in 1804.

In 1807 there were in the town and suburbs 15 linen, 15 muslin, 3 cord and 124 cotton weavers. In 1809 there were 190 looms at work in the town and suburbs; in 1811 their number was reduced to 160. In 1821 there were in the town and county of the town 144 linen, 2 woollen, 1 draper and 273 cotton weavers. There is now (1839) one-half that number of any, and very few cotton weavers.

The yarn manufactured here was spun from flax grown on the land, by the females of the family, and was usually woven by the males, otherwise it was taken to Carrickfergus market, where a good price was easily obtained for it. The linen was taken to Belfast market on Fridays, where it was easily disposed of. Until the year 1826-27 the spinners and weavers generally received excellent remuneration, but since that period there has been a gradual decline in prices; and finally, in 1834, the introduction of mill-spun yarn and the subsequent erection of spinning machinery reduced the price so very low that spinning is now resorted to by the females either as an alternative to being idle or for domestic consumption.

The wages of the linen weaver have also been so much lowered that he now prefers being employed as an agricultural labourer to pursuing the trade in which he had hitherto been employed. The manufacture of linen, except for domestic purposes, has therefore been almost entirely abandoned in this district.

In 1790 the manufacture of cotton was first introduced into this district and for many years afforded a profitable employment to a large number of both sexes. Cotton-printing (which had first been introduced into the north of Ireland by Mr Grimshaw of Whitehouse in the adjoining parish of Carnmoney) was established in this parish in the year 1804. For many years the cotton trade in its different branches flourished; the first shock it received in this county was in the introduction of steam communications with England about the year 1825. Previous to this period there had been an extensive and an important market in Ireland which, as it turned out, was owing to the uncertainty of the communication by sailing vessels.

The establishment of steam communication led to an intercourse with the English which proved fatal to the Irish market. English capital, and the improvements so much more easily effected in English machinery, proved too powerful for the Irish spinners. Irish buyers, finding amusement in the excursion and calculating the certainty of a more advantageous purchase or speculation [in] England, gave the preference to the English and finally decided the fate of the Irish market.

The cotton-printing trade was similarly affected, with this addition: that the continual combination of the printers, who, from their facility in reaching Liverpool or Glasgow by steamers, gave an increased insecurity to the trade and mainly tended towards its abandonment. About 5 years since, the manufacture of linen yarn by machinery was first introduced into this neighbourhood. Since then its success has led to the erection of several extensive mills, at which a considerable number of both sexes are now employed.

Agriculture

With the exception of its manufactories, which are neither numerous nor extensive, this district is now almost exclusively agricultural. Agriculture still continues in a backward state in this parish, but particularly in the vicinity of the hills, which are chiefly under wild pasture.

In the lower grounds along the coast, which are chiefly occupied by gentlemen's demesnes, the state of husbandry is respectable and partakes of most of the modern improvements on the Scottish system; but at a trifling distance from the coast farming is in a very early state and is much inferior to that in the south western and southern districts of Antrim.

There is no attempt at system management, drainage, manuring, rotation of crops, or the introduction of green crops, while for all there is every facility. The crops are chosen from some old usage; their selection as to rotation or their adaptation to the soil is never thought of. The undulations and inequalities of its surface easily admit of its drainage by the numerous rivulets; and the latter, with the assistance of springs, might in opposite instances be as easily converted to its irrigation. As to manuring, in few instances is limestone more than 2 miles distant; to those on the coast, the sea-wrack or weed which is thrown up in such quantities along the shore furnishes (when mixed with other manures) a valuable compost.

The use of the latter in this manner was introduced in 1740, but still manuring is not practised systematically. The rotation of crops is not understood; it has been partially tried by one or two but, because they have not been "used" to it, the county farmers will not have anything whatever to do with it. The green crop system, so far as the cultivation of turnips and vetches, has, by a few, been tried and approved of, but the plundering of the farmer has offered no trifling obstacle to their more general cultivation.

However, agriculture is said to have progressed greatly within memory. 90 years ago there were only 2 wheel carts within the parish. At that time there was neither chaise nor gig, and then, goods or farm produce and manures were conveyed in panniers on horse-back, or on the old slide car, which has only disappeared within 3 or 4 years. A good description of the Scotch farm-cart is now in general use, but there are also many old "wheel cars" with solid wheels. The Scotch cart was first introduced about the year 1816, at which period the Scotch plough also came into use here. The old Irish wooden plough is, however, frequently to be met with in the more retired districts.

The sowing of hay seeds and clover seeds has of late years become more general; the taste for planting and enclosures is becoming more common. Within the last 20 years the appearance of the country has been improved by planting clumps and hedgerows. There is still much room for improvement in the fences; in the lower grounds they chiefly consist of a sod parapet occasionally thinly grown with furze. In but few instances are they furnished with a hawthorn hedgerow.

In the mountainous and more retired districts, the enclosures are chiefly formed by dry stone walls very loosely built. A ditch partly choked up and overgrown with weeds, and fringed by a tolerably broad border of wasteland which serves as a nursery for weeds, extends along at least 1 side of the fence. From this it may be inferred that farming is here conducted in a slovenly manner.

Farms and Leases

The size of the arable farms varies from 5 to 50 Irish acres; the average size is about 25 acres. Anciently many farms were let in rundale; one of these, in the Middle Division, existed until within 2 years since; but such tenures are now abolished.

The leases commonly granted are: by the Marquis of Donegall 61 years; Lord Blayney 99 years; the Marquis of Downshire 31 years and 3 lives. The other less extensive proprietors usually grant leases for 21 or 31 years without lives. The corporation have latterly given new leases of 61 years.

In 1800 a farming society was established here, but after a short existence it was dissolved or abandoned.

Natural Resources

The construction of roads through some of its retired districts, and the excellent means of com-munication with Belfast and the port of Carrickfergus, are important advantages to the agriculturalist. A few more crossroads judiciously constructed through the western side of the parish would tend materially towards its improvement, by affording greater facility of communication with Carrickfergus, Belfast and Larne.

The natural resources of the district are very valuable. Lime is abundant and easy of access. Its coast affords a large supply of seaweed for manure. The falls of water on the Woodburn stream alone are capable of furnishing a supply of water power for machinery to almost any extent. The soil is naturally good, and where unreclaimed the means of cultivating it are within reach. The fishery in the bay affords employment to many and furnishes, in seasons when provisions are low, a tolerable supply of excellent fish. In the western districts of the parish turf is abundant; in those along the coast, where bog is scarce, the means of obtaining coal landed at Carrickfergus quay are within reach of all.

The labouring class are not more numerous than is necessary. They are therefore in regular employment, either in husbandry, in repairing the highways or at the different manufactories which afford constant employment to a large proportion of them. The means of obtaining instruction and knowledge are now easily within reach of all, and in no district is there at present more care bestowed on the moral and spiritual education of the people than in this.

Obstructions to Improvement

There are several circumstances connected with the social state of the parish which, to a considerable extent, affect the conditions of its population. Of these, the principal is the state of its franchise which, as it is at present, is one of the chief incentives to perjury and general demoralization of character. It is merely necessary to refer to [Parliamentary Elections] to corroborate this assertion. So long as the constituency of Carrickfergus continues in its present state, so long will the efforts of the instructors of the people be ineffectual.

The facility with which spirit licences are obtained, and of course the facility with which whiskey is procured by the lower class, is another evil of no small amount. The increase in the number of public houses has only been equalled by the increase in the business done at the pawnbrokers. To poverty this cannot be, as it usually is, ascribed: for many years the circumstances of the lower class have not been better, and still the amount of sums advanced or pledged is actually double what it was 10 years ago. The magistrates now exert a proper discretion in refusing to grant new licences, but their endeavours are paralysed by the grantings of spirit licences by the Excise Board. The latter cost 10 pounds, while the former cost but 6 pounds.

[Crossed out: Hitherto by the clergy of the Church of England little or no attention was paid to their flock, but until the arrival of the present estimable dean, immorality and licentiousness were openly countenanced by his predecessor. By those whose rank and station in society would point them out as examples for the humbler grades, no encouragement is given to the well conducted, nor does their own character warrant their reprehending that of their inferiors in rank].

Local Government

Assizes for the county of the town of Carrickfergus and also for the county of Antrim are held in Carrickfergus. A statement of the criminal returns as extracted from the books of the county Antrim gaol will be found in the appendix.

Quarter sessions for the county of the town of Carrickfergus and also for the divisions of Carrickfergus, as a portion of the county Antrim, are held here, the former 4 times a year, at periods determined by the magistrates at January sessions in each year, pursuant to the 1st and 2nd William IV chapter 31. At these the mayor, recorder and magistrates for the county of the town preside. Criminal business only is brought before these sessions, which include in their district only the county of the town of Carrickfergus.

The quarter sessions held before the assistant barrister for the county Antrim include in their district portions of the neighbouring baronies, and are held half yearly, in April and October. At these sessions civil bills and criminal business for the division are disposed of. A statement of the criminal returns from these sessions will be found in the appendix.

According to the charter of James I granted in 1612, and which was a confirmation of the previous charters granted to Carrickfergus, the mayor may hold 2 courts of record weekly on [crossed out: Tuesdays] Monday and Friday, at which any sum may be recovered, when the causes of action has arisen within the county of the town, or, in the words of the charter, "to hear, examine and discuss all and all manner of actions, suits, complaints and demands, of all and all manner of debts, to what sum or sums soever they shall amount unto." The mode of proceeding is by attachment, judgement and executions, but courts are only held when there is business to be disposed of.

The mayor is also supposed to issue attachments against ships or their cargoes, or against persons onboard ships, for the recovery of debts contracted even without his jurisdiction. Being vice-admiral of the seas from Fair Head to Beerlooms, he is entitled to hold a court of Admiralty. This authority is occasionally exercised but not in conformity with maritime laws, and its judgements, though according to common law, are executed by the water-bailiff instead of by the sergeants-at-mace.

Petty sessions for the county of the town of Carrickfergus were established in 1827 and are held on Wednesdays. The 2 magistrates for the county of the town, namely James Wills and William Burleigh of the Scotch Quarter, Esquires, preside at these sessions.

Petty sessions for the district, including portions of the neighbouring baronies, were established here in 1837 and are held on the first Saturday in each month. 2 magistrates always preside; one of these is the Mayor of Carrickfergus who, by nature of his office, is a magistrate for the county Antrim.

Crime

It will be seen by referring to the criminal returns from the quarter and petty sessions for the county of the town of Carrickfergus that the district is quite free from outrages, whether agrarian or political, and that the character of the trifling extent of crime known in it is very mild.

Combination formerly existed among some of the trades in Carrickfergus, but during the last 7 years it has not been known. The Carrickfergus assizes not unusually have proved maidens, and on several occasions have the sheriffs been put to the expense of a pair of gloves for the judge. In almost every description of crime there has during the last 7 years been an almost gradual decrease, and from the decrease in the number of summonses issued, it would appear that there is less taste than formerly for litigation.

With respect to the criminal returns as extracted from the records of the county Antrim gaol, they bear so little reference to this county that to allude to them as connected with its social state would be inappropriate; but from the circumstances of that establishment being situated within its limits, they are necessarily included in this article without being immediately exclusively connected with it.

A court for the relief of insolvent debtors is held in Carrickfergus once in 6 weeks.

Smuggling has, since the establishment of the coastguards, been seldom attempted or detected here. Illicit distillation has not within memory been practised.

The insurance of machinery and manufactories, and also of dwelling houses, is pretty general. Farm produce is seldom if ever insured. The tranquillity of the neighbourhood, and the rare occurrences of fires, rendered, in the ideas of the inhabitants, such a step quite superfluous. There is every facility for effecting insurance, nor has there been any instances in the litigation of the payment of a policy which could have tended to deter persons from insuring. There are but a few instances of life insurance in this district.

Dispensary

The Carrickfergus dispensary, which now exists in name only, was originally established on the 1st January 1832, for the purpose of affording medicines and medical advice to those within the county of the town who were unable to pay for it. For the first year it was properly supported, the annual subscriptions being 32 pounds 5s and the grand jury grant amounting to a similar sum; but during each successive year the subscription gradually diminished, until in 1835 they amounted only to 15 pounds 12s and in 1836, 11 pounds 18s. In 1836 and 1837 no grant was made by the grand jury. In 1838 they granted 15 pounds 13s, but during this year all subscriptions were withheld.

The total sum which the dispensary has had to depend on for its sole support has not, during the last 3 years, amounted to half that expended on medicines alone during the first year of its existence. Since 1835 the surgeon has not received any salary, and as there has not since been any sum to expend upon house rent, the dispensary must have been abandoned had not the surgeon humanely used his shop and afforded his services gratuitously in giving advice and dispensing the small quantity of medicines which the funds now afford.

To the animosities produced by electioneering contests the decline of funds in this institution may solely be attributed, nor is there at present any prospect of their being increased.

During the last 7 years the number who have annually received assistance at the dispensary has fluctuated from 179 to 494, and averaged 486. Under the circumstances in which it has, as to its funds, been placed it would be useless, as the number of patients has not proportionately diminished, to make any average cost of patients, neither house rent, surgeon's salary nor the usual incidental expenses being defrayed. A table showing its funds and the number usually relieved by it will be found in appendix.

The parish is comparatively and perhaps more than commonly free from disease or sickness. The inhabitants, particularly those in the more mountainous districts, attain a good old age and are generally exempt from many of the common diseases of the county, such as fevers, dysentery and consumption. By referring to appendix, it will be found that the number of such cases have rather an inferior proportion to that of the population.

Schools

There are in the town and county of the town of Carrickfergus 18 day schools and 7 Sunday schools. Of the former, 13 are situated in the town and 5 in the country; of the latter, 6 are situated in the town and 1 in the country. The total number of scholars attending the day schools is 644; that of those attending Sunday schools is 686, of which 251 are exclusively Sunday scholars. Of the day schools, 9 are partly or entirely supported by benevolent individuals or societies; the remainder are private schools. 361 children are now (1839) attending the former and 283 the latter.

The sum annually contributed by benevolence towards education amounts to 113 pounds, that paid by the parents of the children to 1,783 pounds. The proportion of the pupils to the gross population is 1 to 13 and a half.

The public schools in this parish afford a description of education suitable to the lower class, for whom they are intended, and at a rate which places the benefit of education within the reach of all. At one of the schools (that is supported by the bequest of the late Ezekiel Wilson) 40 boys and 35 girls are instructed gratuitously in reading and arithmetic. At the other schools the nature of the instruction afforded is similar; in some instances it embraces also mensuration, geography and book-keeping. English grammar is now generally taught, but mensuration is learned by but a few.

There has, within a few years, been a great change for the better in the description of schoolmasters and also in the selection of the elementary works taught by them. The supervision of the schools, either by local patrons or qualified inspectors, is much more strict than formerly.

The private schools in the parish include 2 boarding schools, one for boys and the other for girls. These are of a very respectable character and afford an education embracing the different branches of a useful and accomplished course of instruction. At all these schools the education is elementary. At the male boarding school boys are prepared for Trinity College; at the female school the assistance of teachers of the usual accomplishments is secured and a system of instruction similar to that of the higher orders of this description of school is afforded.

There are 2 day schools for females which afford all requisites for a useful, and most of those of an accomplished, education. They are very respectably conducted and pretty well supported. There is a good day school for boys at which an excellent mathematical, classical and mercantile education may be obtained.

The other day schools are of various grades, as to the extent of the instruction which they afford and as to the terms on which it may be obtained. The usual course of instruction embraces spelling, reading, writing, arithmetic and English grammar. Book-keeping and geography is learned by some, and mensuration and algebra by a few who are intended for some particular trade. At the female schools plain and fancy needlework is taught.

Education

The system of education and the description of schoolmasters, particularly among the humbler schools, has within a few years undergone much improvement. The course of education is more extended than formerly and the character and qualifications of the schoolmasters are now more particularly inquired into.

The remuneration of the teachers is very trifling and does not exceed an average of 17 pounds per annum. In a few instances they are boarded, day about, by the families of the pupils. This custom, which is more prevalent in the retired rural districts, is less general than formerly. At the more humble description of schools the rate of payment for the junior scholars varies from 2s 2d to 2s 8d

ha'penny per quarter; for the more advanced it seldom exceeds 2s 6d.

Very few of the inhabitants are unable to read and the majority of them can also write. The entire of the rising generation either have received or are receiving education to a greater or less extent. There is a desire on the part of the parents to have their children instructed in reading and writing, and to a trifling extent in arithmetic, but further than this there is little anxiety for the benefits of education.

Among the rising generation there is much less taste for acquiring knowledge or information than among the inhabitants of the more western districts of Antrim. Though an inquisitive race, their curiosity does not extend to possessing themselves of any useful knowledge or information. They are by no means quick of apprehension or bright in their faculties; they are considered very difficult of education and very slow of comprehension.

There are not any book clubs as in the neighbouring parishes, nor any indications of a taste for literature or for acquiring knowledge.

Sunday schools are considered as having been the means of much improvement in the morals of the rising generation. The sabbath is much more strictly observed by them, and many who would otherwise be debarred from it derive by them the rudiments of education. There are at present 686 children, of whom 251 are exclusively Sunday scholars, attending the Sunday schools in this parish; see Tables of Schools in the appendix.

Intellectual Instruction

Auxiliaries to intellectual instruction: a reading society, consisting of the majority of the families of the upper class, has existed for a few years in Carrickfergus. The books are ordered at the commencement of the year and, after having been transferred from one member to another, are disposed of among the members at its expiration.

There is a library, consisting of 300 volumes, connected with the Orthodox Presbyterian congregation. The works are chiefly on religious or moral subjects. There 80 subscribers, who pay 1s per annum. A sum of 1 pound each was paid by several as entrance. This library was established in 1834.

There is a small circulating library in connection with the Sunday school of this congregation. It is intended for the use of the pupils and teachers, and consists principally of works on useful and moral subjects, which are adapted to the tastes and capacities of the middle and lower classes. It was established (by subscription) in 1836 and consists of about 300 volumes.

The Carrickfergus news room, which is situated in the second storey of the market house, was established in 1835. Its affairs are managed by a committee consisting of a chairman, a secretary and a treasurer. There are 30 subscribers to it, each of whom pays 1 pound per annum. The newspapers are sold by auction, or at half-price, to be taken away the day after their arrival.

15 newspapers including 6 London, 2 Scotch, 3 Dublin and 4 Belfast journals, are taken in. The periodicals taken are the *Dublin University, New monthly* and *Edinburgh Magazines, The quarterly review, Bentley's Miscellany* and the *Army* and *Navy lists*.

Newspapers: 590 copies of the public journals are circulated within the limits of the county of the town of Carrickfergus.

The Carrickfergus Harmonic Society holds its meetings on each Monday and Thursday, in a room in the market house. It was originally established in 1803, but has since then been several times dissolved and revived. Its last revival took place in 1838. It consists of 16 ordinary and 3 honorary members. Its instruments include most of those used in military bands. It is supported by a weekly contribution of from 1s to 1s 3d and a sum of 5s entrance paid by each member. These sums are expended in the purchase of instruments and in defraying the incidental expenses of the society.

Moral Instruction

A branch of the Hibernian Bible Society was established here in 1810. It is managed by a local committee of 6, of which the Very Rev. the Dean of Connor is the patron. Since the establishment of the society till the 23rd April 1839, 582 bibles and 453 testaments have been issued here. The society, under the auspices of the present dean, is now in prosperous state.

A branch of the Church Missionary Society was established in Carrickfergus in 1820, since which period it has been liberally supported. Its annual subscriptions have averaged 8 pounds 17s 6d. There has, however, during the last 7 years been a slight decrease in its funds.

A temperance society was established in Carrickfergus in 1829 and continued in existence till 1837 when, from want of encouragement or support from the influential, it ceased to exist. At its dissolution it consisted of 120 members.

Poor

The local institutions, the Mendicity Society and Clothing Society, for relieving the poor are creditable to the humanity and benevolence of the inhabitants of Carrickfergus, there being few places where more anxiety in ministering to the necessities of the aged, helpless and infirm is manifested. There is not any destitution, nor has there ever been any instance of any individual in distress being neglected.

The bequests have been numerous, but 9 only of a much greater number are now forthcoming. The sum annually accruing from them amounts to 318 pounds 2s 9d ha'penny. A description of them will be found in the appendix.

The weekly collection at places of worship amount to 15s or 39 pounds per annum. The average annual income of the Mendicity Society for 7 years has been 528 pounds 17s 4d and of the Clothing Society 23 pounds 8s 6d ha'penny.

Mendicity Society

The Carrickfergus Mendicity Society was established on the 1st May 1827 and has since been supported partly by voluntary subscriptions and donations, the collections at the parish church and Trinitarian meeting house, the proceeds of charity sermons preached at the different places of worship in the town and county of the town, the interest on bequests left for the support of the poor of the parish, and partly by fines paid to the magistrates at the Carrickfergus petty sessions. The society is managed by a committee varying in number and elected annually. The object is to prevent street-begging by supporting the aged, helpless and infirm, and extending relief to the labouring poor in seasons and cases of distress.

The assistance afforded consists either in a weekly pecuniary allowance, a weekly supply of oatmeal or coals, or in cases where the individuals are able to work, flax, which is purchased for the purpose, is given out by the society to be manufactured into yarn, the spinners being paid and the yarn disposed of by the committee. Besides, a small number, averaging 20 annually, are lodged in a house erected by the society.

The average annual number relieved by the society is 162. The average number who receive rations or gratuities of money, with in some instances occasional work, is 134, and the number supplied with work is 29. The average annual [crossed out: cost] amount of subscriptions and donations is 226 pounds 10s 10d, of receipts generally 528 pounds 17s 4d, of cost of management

21 pounds 2s 4d ha'penny, and of disbursements in money and for relief in various ways 473 pounds 18s 7d. The quantity of yarn annually manufactured averages 5,160 hanks. 2 years' residence within the parish is necessary for applicants to the Mendicity.

By referring to tables of the funds of this institution and of the relief afforded by it, an idea may perhaps be more easily formed of its present state as compared with former years. The maximum income of the Mendicity was, in 1831, 670 pounds 3s 10d ha'penny. From that time there has been an almost gradual decline, fluctuating from 468 pounds to 501 pounds 17s 5d, the amount of its income for the year ending May 1838. The number relieved has declined from (in 1831) 181 to, in 1838, 148.

Street-begging has certainly to a certain extent been prevented and the objects of the society almost realised. There are not, however, any beadles for the purpose, as the society rely more on the granting or withholding of assistance than to any compulsory step to effect their object.

It is much to be regretted that the efforts of the committee are not more generally aided than they are, for the support of the funds devolves on a comparatively small number, while there are many among the dealers and shopkeepers upon whom there are strong claims, but who are the least liberal in their contributions. Of this the committee almost invariably, in their annual reports, complain, but still without having produced any effect; and now, though it continues in a comparatively prosperous state, it is perhaps in great measure owing to the immediate prospect, entertained by many, of a compulsory provision being made for the support of the poor.

Clothing Society

The Clothing Society, for the purpose of purchasing blankets and wearing apparel for the poor of the county of the town of Carrickfergus, was originally established in 1819 and has since been supported by voluntary contributions and subscriptions, with occasionally the proceeds of charity sermons in its aid. Its funds, which during the last 8 years have fluctuated from 12 pounds 2s 3d to 57 pounds 1s 3d, and averaged 23 pounds 8s 6d ha'penny per annum, have not declined. The subscriptions are usually 1d per week. Each subscriber of 4s 4d per annum can recommend 1 individual, and of 1 pound, 5 individuals for relief. The number annually receiving clothing or blankets has for the last 8 years averaged 90.

The articles are distributed usually about Christmas. The affairs of the society are managed by a committee composed of a manager, secretary, treasurer and 4 collectors.

Economical return for 8 years: 1831, 12 pounds 2s 2d; 1832, 17 pounds 14s 4d ha'penny; 1833, 17 pounds 19s 10d; 1834, 20 pounds 6s 8d; 1835, 38 pounds 2s 6d ha'penny; 1836, 57 pounds 1s 3d; 1837, 17 pounds 12s 2d; 1838, 16 pounds 9s 6d. The number who annually receive clothing cannot be ascertained.

Religion

In 1765 the population of the county of the town amounted to 3,052 individuals, of whom 809 were members of the Established Church, 2,004 Dissenters, 30 Methodists and 209 Roman Catholics.

In 1813 the population amounted to 6,225 individuals, of whom 915 were members of the Established Church, 4,667 Dissenters and 554 Roman Catholics.

In 1821 the population amounted to 7,684 individuals, of whom 6,767 were members of the Established Church or Dissenters and 917 Roman Catholics.

In 1831 the population amounted to 8,700, of whom 1,353 were members of the Established Church, 5,995 were Protestant Dissenters, 345 were Dissenters (Protestant) of other denominations, 950 were Roman Catholics and 63 were of creeds which could not be accurately ascertained.

Established Church

In the Established Church the county forms one parish in the diocese of Connor, and in ancient records is always called "Sancti Nicholas." The church is still known as the church of St Nicholas. It constitutes a portion of the deanery of Connor, which formerly, and until the 20th July 1609, when James I united it to the deanery of Connor, was a rectory in the gift of the corporation. It is now in the gift of the Crown, and is united to the parishes of Raloo and Inver and the grange of Mallusk.

In a terrier in the archives of the Bishop of Down and Connor, dated 1604, it is called "ecclesia de Carrickfergus" and is represented as having "no glebe but some orchards." In a return in the registry of the prerogative court of the sees of Down and Connor, dated 1633, the living is valued at 120 pounds per annum.

Carrickfergus is a rectory, the rent charge of which amounts to 300 pounds per annum. There is no glebe house. The glebe is let at annual rent of 22 pound 7s. The annual amount of the rent charge of the deanery is 400 pounds. The present dean, the Rev. John Chaine A.M., was inducted on 24th March 1839. He resides at Sea Park, near the south western side of the parish.

The only church in the deanery is that in Carrickfergus, which affords ample accommodation to the congregation of the parish. The dean keeps 1 curate, who resides in Carrickfergus and to whom he pays an annual salary of 100 pounds. The curate is also one of the chaplains of the gaol, from which he derives a further sum of 36 pounds 18s 6d per annum.

In no congregation are the spiritual wants of its members more carefully attended to or more anxiously watched than in that which has just been alluded to.

Orthodox Presbyterians

The Orthodox or Trinitarian congregation of Presbyterians worship at the meeting house in North Street. This congregation, which amounts to 1,200 families or about 6,000 individuals, is in connection with the Synod of Ulster and belongs to the presbytery of Templepatrick. The congregation is a second class one.

The income of the minister amounts to 147 pounds per annum, viz. 75 pounds regium donum, 60 pounds stipend and 12 pounds the annual rent of a house belonging to the congregation and intended as a residence for the minister but, not being a suitable one, is let by him.

The ground on which this house stands was let in 1770 forever by the corporation to this congregation, for the purpose of building a house for their minister, at the yearly rent of 15s. They at the same time granted 20 pounds towards the erection of a house and in 1776 contributed 22 pounds 15s for the same purpose. On the 24th September 1789 a surrender was made of this lease, and a new one was granted forever on paying a peppercorn annually, and 8 pounds on the former lease was remitted.

In 1611 Mr Hubbard, the first Presbyterian minister of Carrickfergus, settled here, and since that period there has (excepting about the year 1639 when the "Non-conformists suffered such persecutions on account of their faith") been an uninterrupted succession of ministers, several of whom have been ornaments to their body.

For several years after their first settlement here they met for worship in the West mills in the Irish Quarter, but soon after erected a small meeting house a little to the south east of the site of the present one. In 1740 they obtained a lease of the ground on which the present house stands and erected that which was pulled down in April 1827; and on the 8th February 1829 the present commodious and spacious house was first opened for divine service.

For several years the Presbyterian clergy of this, like those of many other congregations, appear to have enjoyed the tithes of the parish. In the records of Carrickfergus for 1648 there is an entry in the expenses of the corporation of 4 pounds for "Mr John Gregg's chamber for one yeare" (Mr John Gregg was then minister of the congregation here). A few years previous to this there is an entry in the records of 6 pounds rent paid annually by the corporation for the house held by the rector of the parish.

Unitarian Congregation

The Unitarian Presbyterians, in connection with the Remonstrant Synod, worship at the meeting house on Joymount Bank in the Scotch Quarter. The congregation amounts to 30 families or about 150 individuals. The income of their minister, the Rev. James Nixon Porter, amounts to 105 pounds per annum, viz. 75 pounds regium donum and 30 pounds stipend. This congregation was established in 1835.

Covenanters

The members of this respectable body of Presbyterians worship at their meeting house at Loughmourne near the north eastern confines of the county. The congregation, amounting to 300 individuals, separated in 1805 from the Kells Water congregation and soon after erected their present meeting house. The income of their minister, the Rev. Dr Paul, amounting to 52 pounds per annum, is paid by the congregation.

Independent Congregation

The Independent congregation, which consists of about 100 individuals, worship at the Independent chapel in Castle Street. The income of their minister, the Rev. John McAssey, amounts to 70 pounds per annum. Of this sum, 40 pounds per annum is collected from among the congregation and forwarded to the Irish Evangelical Society, who remit it with a donation of 30 pounds to the minister. This congregation was established here in 1816 and in 1820-21 they erected their present chapel.

Methodists

Methodism is indebted for its origin in Carrickfergus to some soldiers of the 42nd Highlanders who established a class meeting in 1752. In 1765 the number of Methodists in this county was 30 and in 1823 about 80. There are at present these sects or congregations of Methodists in Carrickfergus, namely the Wesleyan Methodists, the Primitive Wesleyan Methodists, the Primitive or Church Methodists and the Wesleyan Association Methodists.

Wesleyan Methodists

The Wesleyan Methodists seem to be one of the original, if not the original, of these sects. They worship at the chapel in West Street. The congregation consists of 60 individuals. The income of their preacher, the Rev. Robert Beauchamp, is paid from the conference. It amounts for this year (1839) to 60 pounds but it fluctuates. The chapel of the sect was erected in 1811.

Primitive Wesleyan Methodists

The Primitive Wesleyan Methodist congregation was established about the year 1820. It consists of about 20 members, who worship once a fortnight at the Lancasterian schoolhouse in Lancasterian Street. There is no stationed preacher of this sect residing here but they are visited by one from Antrim.

Primitive Methodists

The Primitive or Church Methodists, who are also known as the Ranters, worship at their chapel in the Scotch Quarter. This congregation, which consists of about 20 members, was established about the year 1821. Being a branch mission connected with Belfast, it is from thence supplied with a preacher.

Wesleyan Association Methodists

The Wesleyan Association Methodists established their sect here in 1835 and in 1838 had a preacher permanently appointed here. Their number amounts to about 70. They worship in the upper floor of a 2-storey house, in which they have a room suitably fitted up and for which they pay 4 guineas per annum. The income of their minister, the Rev. Joseph Thompson, amounts to 60 pounds per annum, which is paid by the association.

Roman Catholics

In the Roman Catholic Church the county of Carrickfergus constitutes a parish in the diocese of Down and Connor and is united to the parishes of Larne, Glynn, Inver, Raloo, Kilwaughter, Templecorran, Kilroot and Island Magee and the grange of Mallusk. The Roman Catholic flock in Carrickfergus consists of about 950 individuals who, with a few exceptions, are of the humbler class. They worship at the Roman Catholic chapel at the western side of the town.

The income of the parish priest, the Rev. Arthur O'Neill, derived from his congregation in the parish, is 20 pounds which, besides board and lodging, he pays to his curate. He has a free residence under the same roof with the chapel. Besides this, he receives 36 pounds 18s 6d per annum from the county as a chaplain to the gaol.

A list of the original clergy of the various congregations in this parish will be found in the appendix, and a table showing the attendance at the respective places of worship will also be found in the appendix.

Habits of the People: Population

Under this head will more particularly be treated the inhabitants of the rural districts of the parish, the habits of those residing in the town of Carrickfergus having been already described.

The population of this district, including the town of Carrickfergus, has during the last 20 years increased but slightly, while during the 48 years previous to 1813 it had been rather more than doubled. In 1765 the total population of the parish amounted to 3,052 persons. In 1793 there were 408 persons between the ages of 16 and 45, eligible to serve in the militia. In 1800 the population amounted to 4,414, in 1813 to 6,225, of whom 3,486 inhabited the rural districts; in 1821 to 8,030, of whom 4,313 resided in the country; and in 1831 to 8,700, of whom 5,186 were without the town.

The increase in the population of the rural part of the parish, though it has been rather slow, has been gradually progressive, while in the town during a period of nearly 30 years, the increase has been almost imperceptible. The state of the population has been considerably affected by the fluctuation in the number of those employed in the cotton and print mills, which were formerly very extensively carried on here but which have during the last 20 years been gradually given up. Many families, who had been attracted here by the inducement of constant employment, in the abandonment of the trade left this district for that of Carnmoney and for Belfast, where it continues to be extensively carried on.

In the rural districts the increase in the population might, from the reclaimable and arable state of the land, be naturally expected to have attracted settlers from the densely inhabited districts in the west and south of the county. There are vast tracts of almost wasteland in the thinly inhabited and remote western districts of the parish which, without expense and with but little labour, might be brought into a state of comparative fertility; but there is unfortunately not the slightest effort on the part of any of the landed proprietors in the parish to improve either their own interests or that of their tenantry. No encouragement of any kind is held out, either for the reclamation of the land, the erection of houses or the improvement of farms.

Occupations

According to the census of 1831, the population of the rural districts of this parish amounted to 966 families, consisting [of] 5,181 individuals, of whom 2,447 were males and 2,734 females. Of the families, 221 were employed in trade, manufacture or handicraft, 485 in agriculture and the remainder, 160 families, in various other occupations. The first classification, including less than a fourth of the population, is chiefly made up of those employed at the flax spinning and other manufactories in the parish, the remainder being for the most part made up of a few linen weavers, tradespeople and petty dealers.

The people employed at the factories are now in regular employment and receive fair wages. The linen yarn trade has for so far been free from fluctuation, and its prosperity has led to the erection of several new mills, and conversion of those which had been used for cotton, for the manufacture of linen yarn, not only in this but in the neighbouring parish of Carnmoney.

Workers' Houses

Attached to several of the mills are houses in which a considerable proportion of the workpeople reside. These are substantial, dry and warm, and are neatly kept. Their rent is in most instances paid weekly. The others reside in cabins or cottages for which, with a small garden, the rent is generally, indeed almost invariably, 4 pounds per annum.

The cottages are generally dry and warm, but rather small and kept without any regard to neatness or cleanliness. They are in almost all instances built of stone and lime and are thatched, consisting of 2 small and partially separated apartments with earthen floors, one used as a kitchen, occupied during the day by the family, the other furnished with a couple of scantily furnished beds.

Their furniture is but trifling and indifferent. They are lit by a small lattice or lead window in each. Most of the families employed at the mills keep a few poultry, generally 3 or 4 hens. Each of them keeps a pig, but few of them keep a cow.

The mechanics or tradespeople are rather better off, more regular in their habits, more comfortable in their mode of living and inhabit better houses than the former. They constitute, however, but a small proportion of the population.

Agricultural Workers

Of the 485 families chiefly employed in agriculture, a small proportion are agricultural labourers or cottiers, residing generally on the farm of their employer. A few of these families hold large tracts of pasture or mountain farms and live by grazing cattle sent from the lowlands. The remainder, constituting the bulk of this class, are farmers, holding tracts of from 5 to 60 (Irish) acres of arable land. The average size of the farms is about 25 acres.

Their farms, particularly as they recede from coast, exhibit much slovenliness, particularly in their enclosures and in the quantity of weeds which they bear. Gaps partially built up are not unfrequently substituted for gates, and the broad margin of wasteground round each field exhibits a want of taste, industry and energy which almost serves as an index to the dispositions and habits of its owner.

A good fence or a neat hawthorn hedgerow is very rarely to be met with. The farm lanes and by-roads are almost impassable to a pedestrian. The stackyard is merely the garden from which the potatoes have been recently dug, and on a few brambles laid on the ground are the stacks erected. There are but few cart-sheds. The manure heap occupies a deep hollow, generally in front of the dwelling house, or in front of the stable or cow-house, which forms a prolongation of it. The out-offices are unfrequently in good repair and, still more so, kept with neatness or cleanliness.

Farmers' Houses

The dwelling house, which is usually 1-storey high, is substantially built of stone, generally slated and is of tolerable extent, depending on the size of the farm. Almost all the dwelling houses are roughcast and many of them are whitened every second year. They consist of 3 or more apartments, according to the size of the farm and of course the means of the farmer. The better description is lit by sash-frame windows of tolerable size, the others by the common leaden or lattice window.

A kitchen with an earthen floor, occupied during the day by the family, a neat parlour with a boarded floor and nicely furnished, and 2 bedrooms for the family occupy the ground floor of the better description of farmhouses. Over the rooms is a loft or garret in which the domestics sleep.

The houses of the less extensive farmers are of more humble extent. They generally consist of a kitchen and 2 sleeping apartments with earthen floors, all of which are furnished in a homely and old-fashioned style, not altogether deficient in comfort. The farmhouses in this parish are generally deficient in neatness or cleanliness of appearance and in taste and comfort as to their fitting and keeping. This particularly applies to those in the northern and western districts of the parish.

Labourers' Houses

The cottages and cabins of the cottiers or agricultural labourers are dry and warm, but dirtily and untidily kept. Their earthen floors are generally moist and their approach and entrance is almost invariably muddy and dirty, and between a range of cesspools or manure heaps. They are all built of stone, many are slated but the majority are thatched. A few are roughcast and whitened. They usually consist of 2 small apartments. In many instances they possess but 1. They usually receive light by 2 small lattice windows.

Their furniture is commonly rather scanty and of an indifferent quality. Attached to each cottage is a small garden, seldom exceeding half a rood, and a small pigsty. Each labourer keeps a pig and a few hens.

The rent of a cottage and garden is in most instances 4 pounds per annum. Towards the north western side of the parish it is sometimes a little less, but here the houses are of an inferior description and land is less valuable.

Character of the People

All classes are civil and obliging, very peaceful and amenable to the laws and authorities, friendly towards each other, humane and charitable. They cannot be termed hospitable or generous, nor are they candid or communicative; on the contrary they are suspicious and doubtful, and very cautious and shrewd. They are particularly honest and, though hard and close in their bargains, are generally punctual in fulfilling their engagements. In general civilisation and information they are rather backward and are perhaps nearly a century behind the inhabitants of the neighbouring western districts of Doagh, Ballyclare and Templepatrick in these respects.

There is not a book club in the parish, very few newspapers are taken by the farmers, nor is there among any class a taste for acquiring knowledge or information. In their capacities they are rather dull: they possess little or no mental energy, while at the same time they are really hard-working and industrious at their various occupations.

Morality

In the scale of morality they hold in many respects rather a low rank, but as they have, particularly in the Established Church, until within a very recent date been almost utterly left to themselves, and as from habitude and neglect, and from a want of example on the part of some from whom they naturally would be expected to regulate their habits, they cannot be so much condemned as they might otherwise be. It is a fact that there is a general laxity of morals throughout the district and it is equally notorious that it is not confined to any particular grade or class.

It is to be regretted that immorality, if not countenanced, is not discountenanced, that illegitimacy is rather common, that conjugal ties are not properly observed and that the marriage ceremony is frequently too long deferred. These remarks especially apply to the town and its vicinity, but to the rural districts they are also, though scarcely so strictly, applicable.

Drink

Among the lower class, particularly in and around the town, there is a great proneness to tippling, which [is] common to both sexes. This of course leads to a variety of other vices. The women, to obtain the means of procuring whiskey unknown to their husbands, must either dispose of some portion of his property or of their own apparel, or pledge it at the pawnbrokers. A habit of thus indulging increases and soon becomes so common that it cannot be laid aside, and the article which had once been a luxury now becomes a necessity. The facility for obtaining whiskey, and for obtaining the means of purchasing it, is too great.

In 1828 there were but 33 houses licensed for the sale of spirits in the parish. There are now (1839) 59. In 1828 there was but 1 pawnbroker in Carrickfergus; there are now 3. In 1828 the total sum advanced upon pledges was 291 pounds 10s; in 1838 it was 2,731 pounds 4s 7d ha'penny. In the former year the number of sums below 2s 6d advanced was 2,831; in the latter year it was 17,510.

It is not to be imagined that the increased resort to the pawn-office has been consequent on any increase of poverty, or on a diminution in the resources of the lower class. Such has not been the case: during the last 10 years their circumstances have been as good as during the previous 8, and during the last 5 years, owing to the increased demand for workers at the newly erected flax spinning mills, and owing to the increased demand for poultry and eggs for exportation, the circumstances of the humbler class have been more independent than they have been during the 10 years previous.

The pawn-offices have in Carrickfergus been the chief auxiliaries to vice. (Their management cannot be, with propriety, here detailed; but there are some facts connected with them and their profits which, if elicited, would prove rather startling).

The sabbath is so far observed here that all labour is suspended and the streets and roads are but little frequented, but on the other hand on the way home from meetings "between sermons" a visit is, by most, paid to the public house.

General Circumstances

In their circumstances the farmers may be termed as independent, so far as being generally unencumbered and free from arrears, but there is little or no capital among them. They are enabled by frugality and living in a homely manner to meet their engagements without being able to save anything. There are but a few who could be with propriety included in the class termed yeomanry. They want the substance and intelligence of that denomination, not merely in themselves but in their dwellings, farms and cattle.

The labouring class, being not more numerous than is necessary for the cultivation of the land, are in constant employment, as are also the families employed at the factories. They are therefore comparatively comfortable in their circumstances, and with a little more providence and taste for domestic economy they might be termed independent. In both these respects they are very deficient. They are improvident and are very bad managers, so that when visited by sickness or misfortune they are reduced to indigence.

An agricultural labourer can earn 7s per week without food, or 5s per week with food during the different seasons. The wages of a female to work on the farm or about a farmhouse during the spring or winter seasons is 8d per day without food and 4d per day with food. During harvest females earn as high wages as the men. The ordinary wages of a farm servant who lives with a family is 4 pounds per annum and of a female servant 3 pounds per annum. The charge per day for a horse, cart and man is 3s and for a horse, common car and man 2s 6d. For rates of wages in former years see appendix.

Food

The food of all classes (of the farmers, labourers and workpeople) is plain and homely, and admits of but little variety. Potatoes constitute the great basis of food for all and, with oatmeal, milk, salt herrings and the coarser descriptions of fish taken in the lough, form their principal food.

The farmers live very frugally and homely. During winter their breakfast chiefly consists of potatoes and milk, and during spring and summer, when potatoes are beginning to become scarce and bad, of porridge and milk. Tea is now generally used once a day by the better class of farmers, but less frequently by the more humble. Their dinner consists of fried meat, generally bacon or hung beef, fried eggs, broth made of meal and vegetables boiled with a little salt beef, potatoes and fish. Oaten bread is still much used among them, but has to a certain extent been supplanted by baker's bread.

Cheese of a coarse description is much used by the farmers; the better description of cheese, of which a considerable quantity is made during summer, is sold in Belfast or Carrickfergus and is much prized. Less animal food than formerly is now consumed by all classes.

The workpeople and agricultural labourers resemble each other in their mode of living; the former consume more tea and less solid food than the latter. Potatoes are the chief food of all. But little oatmeal is now used by either; this is chiefly owing to the quantity of raw corn now sent to market. In the neighbourhood of the coast the coarser description of fish taken afford a cheap supply of food to this class. In the remote parts of the parish milk is abundant, owing to the extent of pasture.

Potatoes, oatmeal, milk, salt herrings and fresh fish constitute almost the exclusive diet of the labouring class. Tea is becoming more generally used. Eggs are now, from the increased [demand] for them and for poultry for exportation, seldom used at home. Milk is generally plentiful and cheap: new milk sells at 2d per quart, buttermilk at a ha'penny per quart in winter and 1d for 3 quarts in summer.

There is not among any class a taste for gardening or raising vegetables. Cabbages, leeks and onions are the only vegetables cultivated. The latter are now more generally purchased by the lower class.

The food of all classes, though homely and plain, is rather more substantial in this than in most of the neighbouring districts to the westward; but it is prepared and provided with less comfort. Among no class does there seem to be any taste for neatness nor any idea of management or economy.

Fuel

In the eastern district of the parish coal is almost the only fuel, turf, which is brought from the mountains in the western side, being rarely used except for kindling coal fires. Scotch coal is sold in Carrickfergus at from 9s 6d to 14s per ton and English coal at from 11s to 16s. The former of course is commonly used. Several of the petty dealers in the parish retail coal in small quantities. Turf costs, in the vicinity of the town, about 1s 9d per gauge or cubic yard. In the immediate vicinity of the town English coal is preferred.

The bogs in the western and south western districts of the parish afford a sufficient supply of fuel to the inhabitants of those districts. In the north west of the parish turf is less plentiful and sods are not unfrequently pared and dried for fuel.

Dress

The attire of all classes, though comfortable and suitable, is much inferior to that of the people even of the adjoining western and southern districts. The inhabitants of this parish are more than half a century behind those in the western and southern parts of Antrim in their style of dressing, which, however, is quite in character with their general habits.

Their clothes are warm and comfortable, but plain and rather coarse. Their appearance on Sundays and on public occasions is decent and respectable, but there is a homeliness in the attire of the men and a want of neatness and taste in that of the females which easily distinguishes them from their western neighbours.

Dark blue coats and trousers, beaver hats and coloured waistcoats are worn by the men when from home; their ordinary daily dress is very plain. The women when from home always wear shoes and stockings, and either shawls or tartan or cloth cloaks. Stuff, or more frequently cotton, gowns of rather gay colours and bright ribbons and gloves complete their costume. Their dress, however, is not put on with taste nor made with neatness. There is a great partiality for tartan shawls and cloaks and for gay-coloured gowns and ribbons.

During the week the females are very slovenly in their appearance and persons, seldom wearing shoes and stockings and bestowing little attention on their persons.

Watches are much less common among the men, and umbrellas are less generally used by either sex than in the western and southern districts of Antrim.

Longevity

The instances of extreme longevity are not at present numerous: still there have been many which have been either recorded or remembered. The number of individuals who attain the ages of from 80 to 90 seems to be much greater in this than in any of the neighbouring districts. Of this, the tombstones in the different burial grounds furnish ample evidence, but the most remarkable and most frequent instances of advanced age are to be met with in the cottages of the less extensive farmers. The inhabitants are generally a robust and hardy race, and are more than usually exempt from the incidental complaints and prevalent diseases of the country.

Robert Hall of Carrickfergus died in 1836 at the age of 104 years. A farmer named John Herdman, residing in the West Division of the county, is now in his 99th year and in full possession of his faculties. His brother Thomas, who is in [his] 86th year, as yet exhibits no symptoms of decline. Jane Black, a mendicant, died in 1837 at the age of 104 years. In 1823 Edward McQuillan died at the age of 102. In 1819 Jane Deavy died at the age of 92 and Margaret Jamfrey at the age of 97.

In 1816 died Andrew McDowell aged 96 and Sarah Millar aged 101. In 1814 died Samuel Davison aged 91 and James Millar aged 95. In

1813 died Jane Deavy aged 100 and Hugh Hanna aged 97. In 1811 Catherine McGill died aged 98. In 1810, and on the same day, died Mary McGill aged 98 and John Connor aged 101. In 1809 John Tennant died aged 94. In 1798 William Lappin died aged 91; in 1796 Felix Hanna died aged 92; and in 1795 Margaret Mellan died aged 100.

In 1794 died Mary Campbell aged 94 and Thomas Gadfrey aged 98. In 1792 died John McGowan aged 93 and Anne King aged 91. In 1791 James Addison died aged 94. In 1790 died Richard McComb and William Semple, both aged 96, and Margaret Quinn aged 99. In 1789 Widow McGowan died aged 94. In 1788 Andrew McDowall died aged 95. In 1787 James Penny died aged 93. In 1786 died Thomas Barry aged 94 and James McGill aged 93. In 1780 Samuel Davison died aged 95.

In 1779 Catherine Wilson died aged 94. In 1763 Elizabeth Bell died aged 105 and in 1753 Margaret Fitzpatrick died aged 100. In 1742 John Logan, who had been in Londonderry during the siege by James II, died aged 100. In 1732 John Morrison died aged 94 and in 1715 Jane Carnaghan died at the age of 106; when at the age of 100 years she got a new set of teeth.

Early Marriage

The inhabitants of Carrickfergus do not generally marry early. The cautious and prudent notions so characteristic of their extraction interpose a barrier to their gratifications in most instances in which self-interest is concerned. The few instances of extremely early marriage which have occurred cannot therefore be taken as a criterion in this respect. Among the farmers and middle class men seldom marry before the age of 28 or women before that of 18 or 19, the latter more commonly about the age of 20 or 21 years.

The following instances of early marriage have occurred within memory: in 1819 Mrs Anne Lattimore of Carrickfergus was married at the age of 14 years; she has had 5 children, who are all alive. In 1826 Mrs McClure of Carrickfergus was married at the age of 13 years; she has 8 children alive. In 1831 Mrs Thompson of North Street was married at the age of 14 years; she has 4 children alive. In 1837 Mary Montgomery of the Irish Quarter was married at the age of between 15 and 16; she has 1 child alive.

Amusements

In this parish, as in throughout the surrounding country, the taste for amusement and recreation has diminished as the time for enjoying it, and a means of indulging in it, has been found wanting. Every increased exertion on the part of all has been found necessary to meet the pressure of the times, and the money, formerly earned by the produce of the wheel or the loom, being no longer forthcoming, the means of indulging are found wanting, though the latter is not so strong a reason as the former.

The people do not seem to be either gregarious or social. They are by no means a lighthearted or merry race; on the contrary, they partake more of the staid, steady character of their Scottish ancestors, to whom in their amusements they bear a strong resemblance. Many customs and amusements have been given up within memory, and those still retained are but imperfectly kept up.

Easter Monday is now almost their only day for recreation. On it cocks a[re] fought, though not so generally as formerly. Dyed eggs are rolled by children, and in the afternoon the young men and women resort to a green called the Ranbuy (Rachinbuy), a little south of the town, where they have some rustic games; they conclude the day by playing "Thread the Needle" into the town.

Shooting at geese or turkeys is still practised on Christmas Day. Each person pays a certain sum to the owner of the fowl for a shot at him. Later on Christmas Eve young men and boys assemble and, having collected carts, cars, gates, boats, barrels etc., with them block up the West Gate. There is a tradition, supposed to be erroneous, that this custom originated in the precautions taken on the eve of festivals, to secure the town from surprise by the Roman Catholics who were assembled at prayers.

Halloweve now passes almost unnoticed. By a few, nuts and apples are eaten and nuts are burned, but these customs, as also that of knocking at the doors, have been almost totally given up.

Until the last 2 years flowers were gathered on May Eve and strewed about the doors, and until within years May Day was kept up here with considerable pomp. A new maypole was erected on each May Day. A king and queen, who reigned during the ensuing year, were elected. The May boys danced around the pole and paraded the streets, fantastically dressed, and receiving from each house a contribution, it is said, of seldom less than 5s. The day terminated by adjoining to some public house.

Pancakes are eaten on Shrove Tuesday.

Until about the year 1794 the barbarous custom of throwing at a cock fastened to a stake with sticks was practised. Cocks are fought at Loughmorne on the northern confines of the parish on May Eve.

Within a few years the game of common or shinny, which was formerly very energetically kept up among the men at Christmas, has almost disappeared, being now confined to the children. Horse-races, bull-baiting and bullet-throwing, which were in former times carried [on] to a great extent here, were finally abandoned about 20 years since. The races were held on the sea-shore about 1 mile south of the town until the year 1760, when they were removed to the Commons. It is said that from 15,000 to 20,000 persons have frequently attended these races. Horse-races were held until about 15 years since on Kirk's Fall in the Commons. They had been established about 40 years ago and were held on the 2nd July, from 2 to 4 days each time.

Fairs

A horse and cattle fair was held here at the same time. The numbers of persons who attended and of cattle of different kinds brought to this fair was very considerable. Tents for the sale of refreshments were pitched and sports of great variety were got up. Subscriptions from the spirits sellers, for the purchase of bridles, saddles and other prizes for the competitors, were purchased, and these fairs continued until the deaths of their principal supporters.

The amusements consisted of horse-races, shaving and soaping a pig's tail and letting the animal run until it became the property of whoever could hold it. Races between men, and between women, jumping in sacks and a variety of similar sports were practised at these fairs.

For upwards of a century previous to the year 1641, 2 annual fairs, one on the 2nd October, the other on the 4th September, were held near the southern side of the Commons, for the sale of cattle of every description. They are now said to have been the largest held in the neighbourhood. They both continued to be held here until about the end of the 18th century when, through the instrumentality of some of the Dobbs family, they were removed to Straid hill, where they were held on the same days.

A horse fair, to which cattle of all kinds were brought in great numbers, was until about 9 years since held on the Reagh hill in the West Division. Horse-races for bridles and saddles, and some other sports, were kept up at these fairs, which were numerously attended on Christmas Day.

Their origin is unknown, but their termination was owing to the frequency of riots and drunken quarrels.

Burning fires on St John's Eve was formerly practised but has been for many years discontinued.

Superstitions

The lower class are very superstitious, in fact more so than in any other part of Antrim. The fishers are particularly superstitious and observant of omens. There is an implicit belief in witchcraft and charms, in fairies and in banshees. Many will swear that they have seen the Devil: he usually appears here in the form of a black dog, and on very dark nights.

Fairies are frequently seen about old forts and thorns. A spirit named Button Cap, from a button on the front of his cap, formerly haunted the castle, where, previous to some event, he was seen astride a cannon.

It is believed that cows are deprived of their milk either by being "elfshot" by the fairies or by being blinked. The "evil eye" is confidently believed in here.

Saturdays, or the day on which Christmas falls in that year, are deemed unlucky either for changing service or residence.

There are many other similar and vulgar superstitions of even less interest. To meet a barefooted women in the morning is by the fishermen deemed unlucky, and to name a dog, cat, rat or pig while baiting their hooks forebodes ill luck for that day's fishing. They always spit on the first and last hook they bait, and into the first fish they take off the line. The wood of hawthorn, being deemed unlucky, is never used in their boats.

Speech, Music and Appearance

The inhabitants of this district cannot be said to possess any peculiar trait or character which would distinguish them from those in the immediately adjoining parishes. Perhaps they retain more strongly the characteristics of the country of their extraction. Their dialect, accent, idioms and phraseology are strictly and disagreeably Scottish. They have many old saws and proverbs and are very cautious, inquisitive and suspicious of strangers.

They have not much taste for music. There are among the lower class few performers on any instrument. The violin is the most common, but the Highland bagpipe is the favourite one. Their airs are Scottish but merely include those common throughout the country. Their dancing is rather light and active. The figures are generally either Scotch reels and country dances. There is some taste for singing. There is usually in some part of the parish a singing school for learning sacred music.

In their stature the men are not often found to exceed the middle size, but they are well made and are hardy and robust. The females are also of rather low stature and are strongly and firmly built. In their features the men have a good expression of countenance, darkish eyes.

Emigration

Emigration, as will be found by referring to the table (appendix), prevails to a very limited extent in this district and has annually decreased. During the years 1836, 1837 and 1838 only 69 individuals emigrated; of these, 42 were included in the year 1836. The total amount of capital taken by them is supposed not to have exceeded 200 pounds. With 4 exceptions they were of the humbler rank of life, such as labourers or tradespeople; none have returned. The majority sailed for Quebec, almost all the others for New York.

The inducements to emigrate are much less strong than formerly. It is only when a peculiar opportunity, such as encouragements from friends or members of the family who have gone out, offers, that emigration now occurs. There is also a considerable degree of contentment in the minds of the people, which will ever tend against their taking any very unusual step.

Migration does not prevail in this district.

Remarkable Events

The more remarkable events which have occurred in this district have, with the following trifling exceptions, been noticed in its annals and history.

About 50 years since a calf was dropped in the Scotch Quarter which had 2 heads, 2 tails and 8 legs attached to 1 body.

About the year 1815 a lamb was yeanned in the West Division, having 1 very large eye in the centre of its forehead, and 4 others, 2 on each side near the usual places.

There is at present in the possession of Archibald McDonnell of Carrickfergus a cow, 9 years old, and of the ordinary mixed breed. When in her 7th year, at the full of the moon, her horns dropped off without having exhibited any symptoms of looseness. They were rather curved, 15 inches long and 6 inches in circumference at the root. New horns have since grown nearly to the length of the former ones, but they are still rather tender. This cow has on several occasions cast her hoofs, which grow to an unusual length.

Remarkable Person: Richard Tenison

The only remarkable person of whose birth in this parish any record has been preserved was Richard Tenison, who died Bishop of Meath. He was the son of Thomas Tenison, a burgess of the corporation, who served the office of sheriff in 1645 and resided in Cheston's Lane. He received the rudiments of his education in Carrickfergus and in 1659 entered Trinity College, Dublin. After taking his degree he for some time kept a school at Trim.

Soon afterwards he took priest's orders and was preferred to the rectory and vicarage of Laracor. He was also appointed rector and vicar of Augher Palace in the diocese of Meath. Having been appointed chaplain to the Earl of Essex, then lord lieutenant, he obtained through his interest in 1675 the livings of the deanery of Clogher, rectory of Louth and vicarage of St Patrick's, Drogheda, and the vicarage of Donoghmore near Navan.

In February 1681 he was promoted to the see of Killala and Achonry. In February 1690 he was promoted to the see of Clogher and in June 1697 was translated from thence to that of Meath. He was made a privy councillor about the same time. He died on the 24th August 1705. Dr Tenison is stated to have been an eminent divine and a powerful preacher. He is said to have converted many Dissenters to the Established Church.

Remarkable Family: Whitelocks

In the North Eastern Division, about 1 mile north of the town, is a labourer's family, of which the fourth generation now inhabit the same house, namely mother, daughter, grand-daughter and great-grandson. The daughter, Martha Bones, has a lock of snow white hair in the centre of her forehead; the rest of her hair is black. She is 47 years of age. Inside of her left arm, and a little below the elbow, she has a snow-white mark on her skin, in form resembling a heart, 1 inch in length and three-quarters of an inch broad.

Her daughter, Mary McAtamney, 24 years of age, has a longer lock of pure white hair on her forehead; the rest of her hair is red or sandy. Inside her left arm, and near the elbow, she has an oval shaped mark of [a] pure white colour, about 2 inches long and 1 and a half inches broad.

Solomon Apsely, son to the latter, aged 6 years, has, below the left knee, a white mark resembling the letter "L," 4 inches broad and 3 inches long.

The father of Martha Bones had his legs curiously marked, the skin from the calf downwards being much whiter than that above. One of her aunts, besides the usual white lock, had the figure of a heart a pure white colour on her breast. Many others of their family and ancestors now dead were similarly marked in their hair and on different parts of their body.

The curiously-marked family known as the Whitelocks allege that their ancestor, a female, came from the Isle of Wight to this country in the following manner. Their ancestor who first came to this country was a Miss Armstrong, the daughter of a gentleman of large possessions in the Isle of Wight. She, her father and all her ancestors are said to have had in their foreheads the distinguishing lock of white hair. She eloped to this country about a century and half since with a tailor and settled in the neighbourhood of Ballyclare near Carrickfergus, but subsequently removed to the latter place, where her posterity still continue to reside. To escape detection from her home (her father having offered a large reward for her discovery and his apprehension), she wore a black silk handkerchief on her head and eventually succeeded in eluding the vigilance of her friends.

It is said that in right of her, such of her descendants as are born in wedlock, and bear the white lock of hair on their forehead, are entitled to the estates of their ancestors of the island, in proof [of] which most of these particulars have been advertised by the trustees of the property who have advertised for legal claimants. The family now residing in Carrickfergus are too poor to take any steps for recovery of the properties, but independent of this there are other legal objections to them.

ANCIENT TOPOGRAPHY

Ecclesiastical Remains

In the Established Church the county of the town of Carrickfergus forms one parish in the diocese of Connor and constitutes a portion of the deanery of Connor. In ancient records it is called "The Sancti Nicholas." The parish church, situated in the town of Carrickfergus, is still known as the church of St Nicholas. In a terrier preserved in the archives of the Bishops of Down and Connor, dated 1604, it is called "ecclesia de Carrickfergus" and is represented as having "no

glebe but some orchards." In a return in the registry of the prerogative court of the sees of Down and Connor, dated 1632, the living is valued at 120 pounds per annum.

Of the numerous religious establishments in this parish, scarce a vestige now remains. Their sites alone are locally known and their histories are but imperfectly preserved in some modern writings. The religious edifices and institutions in the parish consist of an abbey, a Franciscan monastery, a hospital, 2 churches and the remains of a friar cell, and a burial ground.

Woodburn Abbey

The Premonstratensian priory of Woodburn or Goodburn occupied a retired and delightful situation on the western banks of the Woodburn stream, about 1 mile west of the town of Carrickfergus and within half a mile of the coast of Belfast Lough.

Of this abbey nothing whatever now remains except 3 old hawthorns; but within memory a small fragment of a wall and very extensive foundations of extreme strength and thickness have been dug up and removed. It is stated that the houses in the Irish Quarter were built of the stone from its ruins. Quantities of human bones, silver and copper coins, numerous pieces of sculptured and squared freestones and portions of headstones, some of which bore inscriptions, have from time to time been discovered about the foundations and in the burial ground in which they stood.

Under the foundations of one of the walls, which were about 4 feet thick, a human skeleton was found. Within the last 12 months several pieces of moulded freestone, and one on which the figure of a bird, probably a dove, was sculptured, were dug up. These remains, and the imperfect traditions of the country, are all that now serve even to indicate its site.

Woodburn Priory is believed to have been founded in 1242 by one of the family of Bissets, who had fled from Scotland in consequence of his having murdered the Duke of Atholl.

Woodburn Abbey is said to have formally been known by the name of [blank], and by tradition as Mary's Abbey. It was dedicated to the Holy Cross and was a daughter of the celebrated abbey of Dryburgh in Scotland.

In 1226, during the reign of Henry III, Allan deGolvia, Duncan deCarrig and the Bissets were granted lands here and were probably the founders, but by many [it] is alleged that the erection of Woodburn took place on the removal to it of the monks and their establishment from the celebrated abbey of Whiteabbey in the adjoining parish of Carnmoney.

In 1326 Friar Roger Outlaw, prior of Kilmainham and Lord Chancellor of Ireland, granted a lease of certain lands to Longadel Manster and dates the grant "apud abbatiam de Woodebornes." By a report made of this abbey in 1540 its annual value, besides reprises, was 10s.

Spittal House

At the northern extremity of Green Street, in suburbs and North Eastern Division of the town, is the site of an ancient religious house, the foundations of which were dug out about 50 years since, up to which period strangers and children had been interred in it. The burial ground is now partly under cultivation and partly occupied by the high road to the Glens. Extensive foundations, coffins of oak in tolerable preservation and quantities of human bones have within memory been dug up on the site of this house and burial ground.

It is said that a hospital dedicated to St Bride or more probably St Bridget stood here, and hence its present name. The Spittal House was granted to Richard Harding at the same time as St Bridget's hospital and for a like term of years, and in the deed it is termed "parcell antique hereditament," and consisted chiefly of a small plot called the Friar's Garden.

St Bride's Well

On the site of the Spittal House is a remarkably fine spring well known as St Bride's Well, from which the town derives its chief supply of water. It is about 2 and a half feet square and of similar depth. It is neatly faced with cut stones. The foundations of a wall which once enclosed it, and which was cemented with grouting, are still to be discerned. No tradition or legend whatever is connected with it.

Franciscan Monastery

A Franciscan monastery, or monastery of Grey Friars, formerly stood on the site of the present gaol, near the eastern extremity of High Street. There is not the slightest vestige of it now remaining, but the discoveries which have been made on and about its site not only serve to place its existence beyond doubt, but indicate its having been of considerable extent.

It was connected with the present parish church by means of an arched subterranean passage constructed of cut stones. This passage is said to have been used by the nuns in passing to and fro between the convent attached to the monastery and the church, which is said to have served as an oratory or chapel to the former. Its entrance is still discernible in the eastern gables of the church, and it has on several instances been opened along the line.

Among the remains found were several oak coffins of square form and of enormous thickness, resting on massive beams of the same kind of wood. In 1776, in sinking the foundations of the gaol, quantities of human bones, a brass bell and several gold rings were found. 2 of the coffins were square and very massive, and rested on heavy beams of oak. It is supposed that one of them had contained the body of Hugh deLacy, Earl of Ulster, who founded the monastery in 1232 and was interred in it, and that the other contained either that of Gerald Fitzmaurice or Richard deBurgo, who in 1242 were interred in it.

In 1805 a small brazen crucifix was dug up near the gaol. On its centre was a circular frame of space, which had probably contained some precious stones, as 2 pins, which might have served to fasten it, remained. It was carved with considerable skill. Several oak coffins were discovered in 1810 and at the same time a small and neatly sculptured stone cross and a large quantity of human bones were found. In 1815 a large gold ring was found in an adjoining garden. On the outside it bore the inscription "Amat dici pater atque princeps" (he loves to be called father and king).

Tradition states that when the monks were dismissed from this monastery, they prayed that the place might everafter be the habitation of thieves, a prayer which has indeed, and to the fullest extent, been granted, as on its site stands the present county Antrim gaol.

In 1610 Sir Arthur Chichester commenced on the site a magnificent edifice which he named Joymount, after his patron Lord Mountjoy. It is said that it was executed by Inigo Jones and that it was known as the King's Palace. It had a governorship distinct from that of the castle. During the reign of James I John Dalway was appointed governor, with a salary of 4s per day, and had under him 20 warders at 8d per day each. The last constable was George Woods, who in the same reign was granted a compensation from the loss of his office, which was then abolished.

Killyann Church

In the Middle Division, and occupying an elevated and delightful situation about 2 miles north north west of the town of Carrickfergus, are the imperfect ruins of Killyann or as it is, from an almost contiguous mound, by some termed Duncrue church. Its situation, near the summit of the steep acclivity which rises from the plain along the coast of Belfast Lough, commands a very varied and extensive prospect. A few yards west of the ruins a large circular mound or tumulus known as Duncrue Fort impends over a little ravine, watered by a rivulet which intervenes and above which it rises to a height of about 60 feet.

Of the church, which stood east and west, nothing now remains but about 15 feet in height by 12 feet in length of the west gable, which is 3 feet 7 inches thick, built of rather small and undressed fieldstones cemented by a very hard and coarse grout. The stones are round at the edges and appear to have been somewhat waterworn. They do not bear the slightest indications of having been subjected to the use of the hammer. They are openly and loosely laid in irregular courses. There are not any thorough or bond stones, nor any more than 12 inches thickness or depth. The heartings of the wall and crevices and spaces are filled up with small fieldstones. A specimen of the only remaining portion of the masonry in a perfect state will be found in the illustrations.

This church, which formerly measured 41 by 16 feet in the interior, was in a much more perfect state of preservation in 1800, when a large portion of it was thrown down. There had previously been a burial ground attached to its eastern side, in reclaiming which large quantities of human bones and portions of coffins were discovered. Near the northern side of the foundations stands an aged hawthorn.

Carnrawsie Church

The foundations of the ancient church of Carnrawsie (the carn of roses) are situated on a gentle eminence commanding a most delightful and extensive prospect about 1 and a half miles north of Carrickfergus and about three-quarters of a mile south east of the ruins of the Killyann church, which has just been described.

Of this church, which stood east and west and measured 62 feet long, only a small portion of the eastern gable about 1 foot high and 3 feet thick now remains. The stones, which do not appear to have been dressed, are of good size and are cemented by hand grouting, but as they are over-

grown with ivy no idea of the style of the masonry can be formed, nor can the width of the church now be ascertained. Previous to the year 1827 a considerable portion of the walls were standing. The burial ground, which is now under turf and tastefully planted, is no longer used as such. In reclaiming it or levelling it, a large quantity of human bones was discovered.

In an adjoining field in 1830, at some depth beneath the surface, a grave containing a human skeleton was discovered. The grave was paved at the bottom with small stones; leading from it was a narrow pipe, probably for the purpose of carrying off water. Within a few yards of the church, and in the graveyard, there was a spring well, now covered up, furnished with a pipe for taking off the superabundant water. On the west side of the burial ground there is still an aged hawthorn.

Extensive orchards once flourished about this church. From these its name may perhaps have been taken. There is no tradition which tends to throw any light on its history, further than that it was dedicated to St Nicholas, from whom the parish takes its name and to whom the church of Carrickfergus, known as the church of St Nicholas, is said to have been dedicated.

Craignabrahir

On the summit of a rocky knoll in the hilly district of the Middle Division of the county, known as Craignabrahir or the Friar's Rock, are the imperfect foundations of several small structures which seem to have been erected without the assistance of mortar or any other cement. It is probable that they may have been monastic cells, but nothing concerning them is locally known. By some it is believed that, for some time prior to the repeal of the Penal Laws, Roman Catholic worship had been celebrated here.

Burial Ground

Near the base of the precipitous cliffs which form the southern declivity of the hills in the Western Division of the county, and occupying a retired situation commanding a most extensive prospect, is a district or tract of about 50 acres commonly known as Troopers Land, which must from the earliest years have been a place of some celebrity; and in it numerous remains, not only of ecclesiastical but pagan structures have frequently, and even within a few weeks, been discovered.

In this tract there had formerly been a very singular and extensive burial ground, which appeared to have been used for the same purpose by different races. A few years since the foundations of a square building built of stones and lime, which had probably been a church, were dug up in it.

Most of the graves found in this burial ground were paved at the bottom and occasionally paved on the surfaces, and faced at the sides with stones. The stones were firmly laid and the pavement difficult to be broken up. At the head of one grave an upright stone resembling a headstone, 6 feet high 5 feet long and about 18 inches thick, stood with about half its height above the ground. It was a plain undressed slab.

In the graves, which were recklessly broken in and destroyed, quantities of urns containing decayed bones and teeth, and in some instances steel spearheads and flint arrowheads, were discovered. Many of the urns were beautifully carved on the outsides. One had a handle, and another contained a lesser urn without a bottom. Several of the urns were highly glazed on the outside. Their colour was an ochrous <ochreish> yellow, but unfortunately all have been broken and fragments of them only have been obtained. Iron and broken rings and stone and earthen amulets have been found in some of the graves. Most of these discoveries were made during the months of May and June 1839.

Cinders of wood; stone rings and amulets; moulds for the casting of celts; rings of iron and brass; fragments of urns, some of which are plain and some glazed, but all of a lightish-coloured yellow earth; decayed human bones; a few iron and broken weapons; flint arrowheads; cups of brass and of stone; and many similar remains have, from time to time, within memory been discovered, not merely within the small space which might naturally be supposed to be included in the limits of an ordinary burial ground, but over a tract of at least 100 acres.

The greater portion is covered with enormous piles of stones and masses of rocks rolled down at some remote period from the impending cliffs and precipices, and with which almost half the space alluded to is covered, and rendering its cultivation impracticable. It is merely in a few small tracts in the lower parts of this extraordinary district that cultivation has (and within a few years) been attempted, the broken and uneven surface of the ground presenting a formidable obstacle to the labours of the farmers, the discoveries which have been made among the rocky and more elevated portions being [made] while in search of rabbits or badgers which abound here, or in the removal of well-shaped stones for building.

Troopers Land: Antiquities

There are 4 structures, 3 of which have evidently been intended as altars or cromlechs. The fourth is perhaps a grave but resembles one of the former structures.

There are several extensive and curious caves in this burial ground. The most remarkable of these are circular in form, precisely resembling that of a beehive, having at the bottom a square entrance through which a man can with difficulty creep. They were from 4 to 5 feet high, about 4 feet in diameter at the bottom, gradually converging towards the summit, which was formed by a single slab from 15 to 18 inches square. They were constructed of dry stones, which were quite undressed and without any cement. Caves similar in style of construction and in form to those commonly found throughout the neighbouring district are very numerous, particularly in the more rocky parts of this tract, but from their mutilated state they cannot now be entered but merely traced externally.

The stones used in their construction, particularly in forming their roofs, are of enormous size but quite undressed. Caves of this description are to be found in the immediate vicinity of the cromlechs or graves before alluded to.

There are at least 6 little tumuli or mounds, in a more or less perfect state, scattered over the surfaces of the burial ground and in the lower grounds at a short distance from it. Their usual form is circular and their dimensions from 10 to 15 feet in diameter and from 2 to 5 feet high. No remains have been found about any of them.

A circular earthen rạth 120 feet in diameter and from 5 to 11 feet high stands on the brow of a steep declivity adjoining the burial ground and occupies a conspicuous and commanding position.

Numerous traces of paved and formed roads and paths traversing this tract in almost every direction are at intervals to be met with, and furnish ample proof of its having once been much frequented.

Several little rivulets ripple over the surface of the ground, and there are also several small springs here. There are a few stunted hawthorns and some trifling remains of hazel brushwood.

Friar's Glen

A deep and romantic valley, known generally as the Friar's Glen and occasionally as the Crooked Rig, winds a serpentine course in a north westerly direction from the almost precipitous eastern declivity of the Knocker range of hills, in the face of which its deep, narrow entrance appears. Its sides, though almost precipitous, are covered with a smooth sward and rise at their extreme height to an elevation of 130 feet above the bottom of the valley, which is but a few feet wide. They diminish a little in elevation towards the inner extremity of the glen, which suddenly terminates in a retired and lovely dell, almost shut out by the windings of the valley, and above which, on 3 sides, the ground rises abruptly, encompassing a somewhat circular recess.

Immediately at its entrance or mouth the valley expands a little, admitting suddenly a magnificent and extensive prospect of the lough, the North Channel, the coast of Down and the more distant one of Scotland. Beneath lie the rich and diversified low grounds of Carrickfergus and its town and castle, above which the valley is elevated about 500 feet. It is difficult to imagine a more magnificent or beautiful prospect than that from the mouth of the glen, or a more peaceful and retired spot than it is in itself, so shut out from the world and so perfectly adapted for the purpose to which it was devoted.

Friary

Almost at the entrance of the glen, and near the range of the steep declivity of the Knockagh, there formerly stood a religious house said to have been a friary, the foundations of which were dug up about 30 years since. Of the extent of the building, no accurate information can now be obtained, further than that it was not inconsiderable and that the walls were 4 feet thick. They were exceedingly low and were cemented by grout. About the foundations some pieces of dressed and shaped sandstone were discovered.

A few years since 2 large rings of pure gold, several silver coins of the reign of Edward IV and VII, and Louis XIV, were discovered. On the inside of one of the rings was inscribed "I love God" in ill-shaped Roman capitals, now almost obliterated. A wooden drinking vessel, somewhat resembling a modern tumbler in form and size but having a handle, and a large quantity of human bones were also discovered in the rich mould about the foundations.

Friar's Well

Within 12 feet north west of the site of the foundations is a very fine spring well about 2 feet deep and 2 feet in diameter. It seems to have formerly been faced with stones. It is locally known as the Friar's Well. A few old stunted hawthorns grow around it.

Mound

Almost contiguous to, and on the northern side of, the site of the foundations is a semicircular earthen mound 15 feet in diameter and 3 feet high. It contains a trifling hollow on its summit and is paved on the sides with stones which seem to have been somewhat carefully laid, but which are now almost quite covered with herbage.

At the extremity of the glen is a fine old hawthorn, and near it, during the enforcement of the Penal Code, it is said that the Roman Catholic worship was celebrated. There are several old hawthorns growing along the sides of the glen.

Enclosures

On the summit of a knoll almost overhanging the north eastern extremity of the glen are the faint traces of several enclosures, some of which are of circular and some of square form. They are formed of earth, with the exception of one, in the low parapet of which 45 undressed stones, none of which exceed 2 feet in height, appear almost at regular intervals, but their appearance seems to have been owing to the demolition of the parapet, which at present does not exceed 18 inches in height. The other parapets and enclosures are still less discernible. No discoveries have been made about them.

Great Patrick

The [manuscript] plan of this structure is copied from that shown in the plan of Carrickfergus as taken in 1550 and which is preserved in the Lambeth Library.

Great Patrick stood at the centre of the town, near the east end of High Street and the southern end of North Street, thus occupying a position in the principal and most frequented part. Not a vestige of it now remains, nor is anything whatsoever locally known or remembered, further than that when removing some of the monument from the spot where it is said to have stood in 1818, a foundation of dressed stones, solid and about 6 feet square, was discovered and removed. From the plan given, it seems to have consisted of a cross erected on a circular base formed of 6 steps. It is believed to have been connected with the several religious establishments of which in early ages Carrickfergus was the seat.

Castles

There were formerly 3 castles of some importance in the county of the town of Carrickfergus, namely the castle of Carrickfergus, Castle Lugg and a castle situated in the Middle Division said to have belonged to the family of Russell, who have now for 2 and a half centuries in this district been extinct. Of the first, and by far the most interesting and important of these, a detailed description has been given under the head of Towns. The others, the only remaining military edifices in the parish, will be found described hereafter.

Castle Lugg

Castle Lugg is said to have in ancient times been known by the name of Cloughnahearty. Its present name, according to tradition, was derived from the family of Lugg (now Legge), by whom it was built or inhabited.

The ruins are situated in the West Division, about 3 miles west of the town of Carrickfergus and on the summit of a trifling bank about 10 feet above the shores of the lough, from which it is separated by the main road from Carrickfergus to Belfast. Of the castle, which seems to have solely consisted in a square tower similar to those in the counties of Wexford and Kilkenny, nothing now remains but a portion of the northern wall 27 feet long and 25 feet high, with a very small portion of the eastern side attached to it.

The walls, which are 3 feet 6 inches in thickness, are built of sharp, undressed quarrystones, well laid and closely and firmly cemented by grouting made from sea sand. The stones, which are generally small, are larger towards the base. Those at the corners have been removed for modern purposes. Several pieces of sandstone occur in the walls; they are, however, undressed.

A chasm from 4 feet 6 inches to 5 feet wide reaches from the base to the summit of the wall. It is, except for a short distance about half-way up, faced at each side with jambs expanding inwards. The upper portion of the aperture may have been a window and the lower a doorway, the intervening wall having been removed. It is now almost entirely built up. No cut or dressed stone is to be found in any part of the walls.

In digging about the castle, a considerable quantity of human bones and several large iron keys were some years since discovered.

There is no tradition or local record to throw any light on the origin, history or destruction of this castle. The Luggs, by whom it was inhabited, held some extensive tracts of the adjoining land.

Castle

In the Middle Division about 2 miles north west of the town of Carrickfergus, and occupying a conspicuous and elevated position 80 yards west of Duncrue Fort, are the foundations of an ancient castle surrounded by a moat. The ground on which the castle stands is almost flat, but immediately from western and southern sides it descends rapidly. Its situation is retired and in no respect commanding or important.

The foundations, which are now but faintly discernible, include a square measuring 34 by 26 feet, and stand north and south near the centre of a platform of somewhat oval form, measuring in the extreme 330 by 150 feet and encompassed by a moat or ditch 15 feet wide and about 6 feet deep. The moat is crossed at the eastern side by an earthen approach 12 feet wide.

Of the thickness of the foundations no accurate idea can now be formed. They seem to have been very massive and were cemented by a very coarse and hard grout. A large whinstone 5 feet long and 2 feet thick, which formed one of the quoins, now appears about a foot above the ground at one corner of the buildings. No foundations now appear in the interior.

A few years ago a circular floor of sandstone flags about 18 feet in diameter was discovered near the centre of the castle. The flags are said to have been very closely jointed and fitted. 3 steps of cut sandstone led to this floor. On being exposed to the atmosphere the flags crumbled away.

This castle is said to have been founded by, or to have belonged to, the family of Russell, who became extinct here about 2 and a half centuries ago.

Scoutbush

About 1 and a half miles west of the town of Carrickfergus, and about one-third of a mile from the shore of the lough, were, until within a recent date, the remains of an ancient military position formerly known by the names of the Scout Guard and Lettice Land. The former is derived from its having been the station of the scout-major, and the latter was given it from Lettice, daughter of Francis Knolles and wife of Walter Devereux, Earl of Essex, Governor of Ulster. The deep trench which encompassed it included a quadrangular area of about 2 acres. It was entered by drawbridges on the eastern and northern sides, and [said] to have been flanked by bastions at the angles.

Tradition states that this was the favourite residence of Robert Monroe, who commanded the Scottish auxiliary forces here from April 1642 till 1648. In the former year it is said that it was the residence of a respectable Protestant family named Crymble, who were massacred one night through the treachery of a Roman Catholic nurse who let down a drawbridge and admitted the rebels. The elder Crymble is said to have made a desperate resistance, having killed several of his assailants and driven others over the drawbridge after his bowels had fallen out.

Pagan: Cromlechs and Cave

In the ancient burial ground in Troopers Land is a structure which may be either a cromlech or a grave, but more probably the latter. It consists of a large rude slab 6 by 5 feet and 18 inches thick, supported by 3 other stones which elevate it but a few inches above the ground, beneath which, as also that around it, is strewed with enormous masses of rock and smaller stones, some of which had been used in the construction of a large cover which ran almost under it, but which has been partly destroyed. The cromlech does not, however, appear to have been covered. Its upper stone is almost horizontal and lies east and west.

About 500 yards north of the altar just described, and 100 yards north of the burial ground, stands a large square stone 5 feet 10 inches high by 4 feet and 3 feet 6 inches thick, and about 3 feet 6 inches square on the summit, which is nearly flat. It is firmly set upon a pavement of other stones and about its base are several others firmly laid about it. This stone is quite rude and undressed, though pretty smooth on the sides. It occupies the summit of a rocky knoll on the steep declivity under the precipices of the Knockagh and is seen from a considerable distance.

The third structure of this kind merely consists of a large undressed slab 5 feet 6 inches by 3 feet 8 inches and 13 inches thick, lying horizontally east and west and in the midst of a large heap of fragments of rock, which have been recently removed from about it by persons searching under it for badgers. It seems to be supported by several other stones.

A cave, now almost demolished, runs close by it and seems to have originally been of considerable extent, but from the displacement of the stones it cannot be accurately traced or laid down, and an unsatisfactory sketch of the stones is all that can be obtained.

Cairns

There are in this county 4 cairns, all of which have suffered considerably by mutilation.

The most remarkable is that on Slieve True mountain, 1,025 feet above the level of the sea. Its situation, on the summit of the mountain, is the most elevated in the county and is very conspicuous. It commands a most extensive prospect on all sides, but particularly towards the south and east, the view including the North Channel and the Scottish coast as far as the eye can reach. The cairn is rendered more conspicuous by the ruins of a schoolhouse which was erected on it many years ago but which, from its exposed situation in an almost uninhabited district, was unfrequented and soon fell into ruins. The cairn occupies the summit of a hemispherical knoll which is rocky and interspersed with looser stones.

The cairn, which has been sadly mutilated by the removal of some of the stones and the erection of the schoolhouse, seems to have originally been of circular form. It now is more nearly elliptic. Its exterior diameter is 80 feet and its extreme height (at the centre) about 5 and a half feet. It is formed of loose stones of every variety of size, the longest, which lies near the centre of the cairn, measuring 5 and a half by 3 and a half feet and 2 feet thick. It is a rude undressed slab of whin and may probably have formed the covering of the grave which occupied the centre of the cairn. The stones would average about 40 lbs each.

At the centre of the cairn was the grave in which, about 50 years since, 2 cinerary urns containing bones and ashes were discovered. This grave had been covered by the large slab before mentioned and its discovery was in consequence of a man having dreamed that money was concealed under the stone. Nothing, however, was found but the urns and a badger, which had concealed itself in it at this time, which was prior to the erection of the schoolhouse. The height of the cairn is said to have been 20 feet. The slab which covered the grave is vulgarly believed to have formed part of a druidical altar.

About half a mile south west of the cairn are 3 rocks or large stones, now forming part of the fence which bounds the north west side of the county. These stones, which are rude masses, are locally known as The Three Brothers. They are in line, the central one being 7 feet from the southern and 12 feet from the northern. They are from 6 to 8 feet long, 3 feet high and about 4 and a half feet in breadth; they have probably originally stood upright. This cairn was originally known as the White Cairn, probably from the grey lichen which grew on the stones.

The mountain is vulgarly supposed to have derived the name Slieve Trian, locally given to it and which signifies "the mountain of three," from the 3 stones alluded to. It is, however, much more probable from the circumstance of its having been a place of sepulture that its original and correct name was Sliebh-a-thirui or "the mountain of wailing or lamentation," a name much more in character and much more appropriate to such a structure.

About 1 mile south west of Slieve True, and on the summit of a somewhat conspicuous hill called the Reagh hill (the king's hill), a cairn 60 feet in diameter formerly stood. This structure, which was exclusively constructed of stones, has been almost entirely demolished. It is not known if any remains were found in it. A horse fair and horse-race have from time immemorial been annually on Christmas Day held on this hill.

In the West Division, and occupying a situation by no means conspicuous on the eastern declivity of the Knockagh hill, the remains of a cairn of stones which has been 30 feet in diameter are to be seen. Many of the stones are very large. That which covered the grave in the centre of the cairn is a large slab of whin measuring 6 by 4 feet and 18 inches thick.

On the summit of a conspicuous hill called Carn-na-neade, in the Middle Division, a large cairn formerly stood. It has, however, been several years destroyed and a large wall built of the stones of which it was constructed.

Standing Stones

There are several upright stones in the county which have evidently been set in their present position for some particular purpose. Their positions are laid down in the 6 inch maps, but they do not seem to bear any relation to each other, or to any of the standing stones in the neighbouring districts.

3 stone columns of considerable height stood within memory in the Commons. They were at a considerable distance from each other, but they have long since been removed.

A stone 3 feet high and about 18 inches square occupies a somewhat conspicuous position on the eastern declivity of the Knockagh hill.

On a hill near the western side of the West Division there is a standing stone 4 feet high and 2 by 1 and a half feet thick. All these stones are rude and quite undressed.

Caves

There are several caves in this county, some of which are partly and others quite artificial in their construction. The most remarkable are those in the precipitous cliff along the southern brow of the Knockagh range of hills. There are 4 of them. The most western, locally known as Hangman's Cave, is about 50 feet from the base of the cliff and 150 feet from its summit. It has been explored and is said to be capable of accommodating 20 men. Its height is about 6 feet. It is supposed to be artificial.

The second is about 20 feet east of this and almost on a level with it. It is said to be much larger than the former and also to be artificial, but a long time has elapsed since it was explored.

About a mile east of these, and about half-way from the base of the cliff, which here is about 100 feet high, is a large artificial cave which might contain 10 or 12 persons.

About half a mile from the last is an artificial cave. It is about 30 feet from the base and 50 feet from the summit of the cliff. It consists of 2 apartments, one of which would contain 10 and the other 5 persons. This cave was formerly approached by hewn steps which have long since been destroyed.

In the face of a precipitous cliff about 50 feet high, overhanging a waterfall on the Woodburn river, and about 2 miles west of Carrickfergus, are the entrances to 2 caves which are hewn out of the solid rock. They are 8 feet apart and are 30 feet above the bed of the stream, but neither can now entered from their being choked up with rubbish.

Their situation renders their approach very difficult and dangerous. One is said to be of considerable size, the other is of but trifling capacity. The former is known as Peter's Cave, it is said, from its having been at some remote period inhabited by a simpleton named Peter McGuckian.

Coves

Coves have occasionally, but not frequently, been found in this county. Those which have been discovered have been, with one exception, totally destroyed, from their having obstructed the labours of the farmer. From the description given of them they seem to have been precisely similar in their style of construction to those in the adjoining parish of Carnmoney and in the districts along the Six Mile Water, namely being constructed of large dry stones, their sides inclining inwards towards their summit, which was formed by large slabs laid transversely and consisting of several apartments communicating by means of narrow pipes. Their width at the bottom varied from 3 and a half to 5 feet and their height from 5 to 5 and half.

The only cove of which any satisfactory information can be afforded is that of which a plan is given in the appendix. It is situated in a gentle declivity in the low grounds in the West Division. It occupies the interior of a fort 70 feet in diameter and about 6 feet in height above the bottom of the ditch, which is 15 feet wide. An eastern rampart which encompassed it is now destroyed.

The cove consists of 3 chambers at right angles to each other and forming 3 sides of a square; the western chamber is 33 feet long and the northern and southern are each 21 feet. The entrance to them was in the western side of the fort, by a narrow pipe which has been destroyed. A portion of the southern chamber about 13 feet long only remains in a perfect state. It is constructed in the manner before described. It is from 3 and a half to 4 feet high and 3 feet wide.

Tumuli

There are now in this parish 6 structures which may perhaps correctly be classed under this term, though their only claim to it, so far as can be ascertained, is their form and dimensions. Several very small mounds or tumuli, from 10 to 15 feet in diameter and from 2 to 5 feet high, of convex form, have been removed or partially demolished in the burial ground in Troopers Land, but without any discovery resulting from their demolition. They were found to consist merely of earth and stones. That at the friary or Friar's Glen seem to have been intended for a purpose different from the former. It is of convex form, 15 feet in diameter and 3 feet high. It is paved around with stones and contains a trifling hollow on its summit.

The forms and dimensions of the 6 other tumuli will be best understood by referring to the plan in the illustrations. Their usual form is that of a truncated cone. Occasionally they are convex on the summit. Their diameters vary from 30 to 90 feet and their altitudes from 6 to 30 feet.

They are constructed almost exclusively of earth, the stones which appear having casually been used. It is impossible to attribute to them any particular intention or purpose, as they occur in every variety of position. 3 are in the immediate vicinity of streams. 2 of these stand within 80

yards of each other, on the steep acclivity of [a] bank on the eastern side of the Woodburn stream.

Duncrue Fort is situated on the brink of a rivulet, as is also that known as the Fairy Mount. Some of the mounds were encircled by a ditch and parapet. The traces of both are still to be seen round the last mentioned and a ditch is to be found encircling each of the others.

Within memory 4 of these structures have been demolished: in 2 of them human bones and skulls were discovered; near the base of another an earthen urn was found; and near the summit of the fourth a brazen pin and some other articles, which cannot now be remembered, were found.

Forts

There are at present but 13 forts or raths in this parish. Within memory upwards of 60 have been destroyed, from their having interfered with the progress of agriculture. They were nearly all situated along the more gentle declivities in the eastern district of the parish and in that portion of it now most generally cultivated and inhabited. Of those which remain, all have suffered to a greater or less extent from mutilation, either in the destruction of their parapets or the filling up of their ditches.

In their style of construction there is but little variety. They are formed almost exclusively of earth. Their form is, with 2 exceptions, circular or nearly so; one is square and one oval. The only diversity therefore consists in the number of their parapets and ditches, of each of which there is most frequently but one. Their proximity to a stream or rivulet seems to have been the only consideration in the selection of their site, as they are more frequently to be found in low and exposed, than in commanding, situations.

In their demolition many discoveries have been made, such as human skulls and bones, bones of cattle, wood cinders and ashes, querns, brazen and iron weapons and instruments, stones hatchets and flint arrowheads.

Enclosures

For a considerable distance underneath the cliff on the southern side of the Knockagh mountain, the surface of the ground bears the marks of former habitations and enclosures. The latter are very numerous. They resemble those described in the Memoirs of the parish of Donegore. They consist merely of a low parapet, in no instance exceeding 3 feet in height, from 6 to 9 feet thick and built of earth and very large stones. The latter in some instances appear between 2 and 3 feet above the parapet. They are not carefully laid and in but [blank] cases are contiguous.

The usual dimensions of these enclosures is 13 by 10 feet, but in some instances they measure 16 by 23 feet; each has an entrance. No remains of any kind have been found about them, nor is there any circumstance or tradition to throw any light on their use or intention.

In the same division (the West), and about half a mile north east of the ancient burial ground in Troopers Land, the surface of the ground bears the indication of its having been formerly much frequented. Numerous enclosures of various forms, but mostly rectangular, constructed in a manner precisely similar to those described above, lie scattered over a considerable extent of ground; but all are so mutilated and obliterated that the dimensions only of some of the enclosures can be ascertained. The largest of these measures internally 23 feet square. The ruins of a cairn are also to be seen here.

In digging about these foundations during the last 20 years, immense quantities of human bones and many earthen urns have been discovered. It has evidently been an ancient burial ground, perhaps during the ages of paganism, and had probably been used as such after the introduction of Christianity, when a place of worship may have been erected in it.

The most remarkable of these enclosures, though now nearly demolished, is that near the Friar's Glen, and which has already been described.

There is every probability that the Commons and other internal and less frequented districts of the county were at some remote period pretty thickly inhabited and generally cultivated. The Commons are now to a great extent under pasture. The traces of ancient sod fences, of thick walls of dry stones and of habitations of the aboriginal [inhabitants] are still easily discernible. The latter are very small and seem to have been constructed chiefly of sods. Ditches now nearly filled up are also to be traced, and the former divisions or boundaries of gardens and fields are perfectly traceable. No remains of any kind have been found, nor are there any other evidences in support of this supposition.

Old Mills

600 yards west of the centre of the town, and within a few yards of the Roman Catholic chapel, is a gentle swell, on the summit of which are the ruins of a very old windmill 13 feet in diameter in the inside. The walls, which are 3 feet thick, are very strong, built of well laid, but undressed, stones and cemented by very hard grouting.

On this swell Duke Schomberg planted one of his batteries when he attacked Carrickfergus. The position is not more than [blank] feet elevated above the centre of the town, but its situation is commanding. The remains of the works thrown up by the duke were demolished so recently as 1837, when a small brass cannon (since disposed of) and some silver coins were found about it.

At the distance of about 1 furlong west of the site of Woodburn Abbey are the traces of an old corn mill and mill-dam which had belonged to the abbey.

Gallows

About half a mile west of the town, on the seashore and within a few feet of the Belfast road, the ancient gallows, a place of execution, stood until 1819, when they were taken down and sold by auction for 5s 10d. They were constructed of wood and set upon a platform of mason work. They are said to have been of great antiquity.

Urns

Urns, in great variety of form and design as to ornament, and also in their composition, have from time to time been, and are still being, found in this county; but unfortunately not more than a fragment of any of them can now be obtained, from their having been broken in their removal or by accident on their being discovered.

The most remarkable urn was found in the month of June 1838, in the district known as Troopers Land, in the West Division. It was found at a depth of 2 feet beneath the paved bed of a grave in the old burial ground which has already been described. This urn contained a lesser one without a bottom. Both were of a pale yellowish clay, well burned and glazed. The larger urn had one handle and was tastefully ornamented on the outside. Both contained ashes or pulverised bones. They were unfortunately broken in the removal of the pavement and earth which covered them.

At a depth of about 3 feet beneath the paved bottom of a grave in the same burial ground a large, well-burned and glazed urn, without any ornament, and of a pale yellowish colour, was found on the 1st June 1839. It contained partially decayed jaw-bones with very large teeth, with small fragments and ashes of bones, besides a solid iron spearhead. The spear is greatly cor-roded and encrusted. Instead of having a socket, its extremity is solid.

Urns have been found in different parts of the Middle Division. An earthen urn, not glazed, was found in May 1839 at a depth of about 3 feet from the surface. It contained some calcined or decayed bones and dust.

In removing a portion of the town wall of Carrickfergus in 1838, to make way for a new line of road, a human skeleton, an earthen urn, about 20 Dane's pipes, a small gold and several silver coins were discovered beneath the foun-dations of the wall, and at a depth of 3 feet from the surface of the adjacent ground. The urn was of earth, slightly ornamented, but not glazed. It contained some pulverized or decayed bones.

About [?16] years since, in opening a mound or fort in the Middle Division, a place resembling a lime-kiln was discovered in its north west side. It was constructed of stones, without any cement. At the bottom of this some charcoal or charred wood and ashes and human bones were discov-ered. At a few yards distance was a circle of stones about [blank] feet in diameter.

Within this, and [at] a depth of about 2 feet from the surface, [were] several earthen urns con-taining ashes, charcoal and bones. A flat stone bearing marks of fire covered each urn, and near them lay the skulls and bones of animals and a deer's horn. The urns were broken probably by the superincumbent pressure. Each was capable of containing about 6 quarts. They were rather coarser in the grain, of a light reddish colour on the outside, but dark inside, as if some substance had been burnt in them. Their mouths were straight. Round the outside of each was a raised and ornamented circle.

In the cairn on Slieve True mountain an earthen urn with some blackish substance adhering to its inside was discovered about 45 years since.

Weapons

Weapons of metal and stone have been found in considerable numbers and in great variety throughout the county. Iron knives of rude work-manship, though of somewhat modern form, an iron spear and iron blades, evidently the extrem-ities of swords, have been picked up in the old burial grounds. The spear shown in appendix was found in an urn, with some bones and ashes, in the old burial ground in Troopers Land. Instead of having a socket, it is solid. The knife shown in [appendix] was found in the same place.

Iron may have been in use in this district at an earlier period than many of the neighbouring ones, as its ore was brought here from England, it is said, previous to the 6th century.

The brazen weapons include celts in great vari-ety of form and size, and of different degrees of workmanship; some of them are beautifully cast and quite perfect; spears varying in length from 5 to 16 inches and of several forms; skenes, some of which are quite perfect; and brazen swords and axes. The moulds for casting celts have been found.

Stone hatchets are occasionally, but not fre-quently, found. Flint arrowheads are frequently picked up; some have been found in graves and, it is said, also in cinerary urns.

Wooden Vessels

The wooden vessels, of which drawings will be found [below], were found beneath the surface of the bogs in the Middle Division. They seem to be

Methers.

made from the bog sallow. The methers, with the exception of the bottom, are hollowed out of a single piece. The dish is smoothly finished and is also of a single piece of wood. They are in tolerable preservation.

In a bog in the Middle Division, and [at] a depth of from 5 to 6 feet from the surface, 3 wooden vessels, resembling in size and shape the common noggin of the country, but bound by copper hoops and ornamented curiously by being inlaid along the lip and handles with the same metal, were found a few years since.

At a depth of several feet beneath the surface of a bog in the same division a large wooden box, resembling a coffin in shape but greatly decayed, was found several years ago. It contained some old silver coins which have long since been disposed of.

Coins

Silver coins in large quantities have from time to time been, and are daily being, found in the town of Carrickfergus and throughout the county, even in its now less frequented districts. They embrace the coinage of every reign of English sovereigns since that of Henry II. Those of the Alexanders, Robert and David Bruce, John Baliol and several other Scottish kings have been picked up, as have also several of those of Louis XIII of France. Almost all the silver coins have found their way into the hands of the Belfast silversmiths.

A few gold coins, perhaps 4 or 5, have been found in the county, one of them beneath the foundations of the town wall. The inscriptions on them are said to have been illegible.

Copper tokens issued by merchants in this and many of the neighbouring towns have been found here. They bear on one side the name of the person by whom they were issued and the name of the town; on the other is their nominal value, generally 1d; some which passed for 2d have also been found. Their dates are usually from 16[blank] to 16[blank]. The tokens found which have been issued from Carrickfergus bear the names of William Stubbs, Henry Burns, John Davadys, John Wodman, Anthony Hall, Andrew Willoughby.

Rings and Pins

On the site of the friary or religious house in the Friar's Glen 2 large rings of gold were a few years since dug up. In one of them was a plain cross, with the inscription "I love God." They were otherwise, it is said, quite plain.

In sinking the foundations of the present gaol in 1776, several large gold rings, a bell and some human bones were dug up. Near the same place (which had been the site of a Franciscan friary, a large gold ring was dug up a few years ago.

Several iron rings, similar in size to that shown in appendix, were found together in the ancient burial ground in Troopers Land. They are supposed to have belonged to a coat of mail or armour.

Brazen pins, such as that shown in [appendix] (which was found in the burial ground in Troopers Land), have not infrequently been found in this county. Some are much larger than that represented, which seem to have been much in use. To one, a small brass chain about 3 inches long was attached.

Hammer

A hammer, made of some very hard description of stone, and precisely resembling an ordinary-sized sledgehammer in form and size, was found, together with 2 brazen hatchets, at a considerable depth from the surface of a bog in the North East Division. It has found its way into some private cabinet.

Miscellaneous Discoveries

At a depth of 4 feet from the surface of a bog in the Middle Division in 1836, the leathern sole of an ancient channelled boot was discovered. The heel, which is said to have been of very neat shape and finish, was studded with wooden pegs. To it was affixed a very handsome and modern-shaped brass spur, on which were inscribed the letters R.L.

In the ancient burial ground in Troopers Land 2 brazen brooches or rings. They are castings and are slightly moulded. There is a cut or separation in each, to admit of their being linked together. 2 similar brooches, but without any cut and having a small ring attached to each, were found in the same burial ground.

[An] iron instrument was discovered beneath the surface of the ground, near the grave or altar in Troopers Land. It is very much encrusted and eaten by rust. It may perhaps have been the handle of a censer or crucible.

2 amulets found in the ancient burial ground in Troopers Land: the larger is merely a common fieldstone of a reddish porphyry, worn very smooth and through which a hole, countersunk on each side, has been smoothly drilled. The other, which was found within a few feet of it, is

of bone and is very neatly moulded and finished on both sides.

Clay pipes, usually known as "Danish pipes," have been found in considerable numbers throughout the county. In removing a portion of the town wall a few years since, about 20 of these pipes were found beneath its foundations.

[A] brazen instrument was some years since found beneath the surface of the ground, at a depth of 6 feet, in the boggy soil and near the foundations of Great Patrick. It is in tolerable preservation and the carving or workmanship is easily to be traced on it. It was heavily gilt but much of the gilding has been worn away. No other articles were found near it, nor is there any conjecture as to what it may have been.

Arrows

Flint arrowheads, exhibiting the workmanship of various ages, from the rudest to the most perfect, and in great variety as to size, are very frequently picked up in the fields. They are, however, more numerous in the vicinity of forts.

Hatchets

Stone hatchets are not so frequently found in this parish as in most of the districts of Antrim, nor are those which have been picked up of so perfect a finish, as to smoothness of form, as they usually are. This perhaps may be owing to the early age at which iron was introduced here.

Cups and Pot

[A] brazen cup was lately found in the ancient burial ground in Troopers Land. It is a perfect casting and is smoothly finished, and in excellent preservation. It is one-twelfth of an inch in thickness.

A stone cup or ladle was found in 1836, near a stone supposed to be part of a cromlech, in the ancient burial ground near Troopers Land. It was formed of whinstone. The cup or bowl was circular, about 5 inches in diameter and 2 inches deep. At one side was a handle 2 inches long with [a] small hole drilled through its extremity. It was smoothly and rather neatly finished, and was ornamented with some rude carving on the outside. This article has unfortunately been mislaid.

A brazen pot, still in common use, was found about [blank] years ago, at a depth of 6 feet from the surface of a bog in the North East Division. Its diameter at the bottom is 9 inches and at the top 5 and a half inches. It is 7 inches in depth. It has a flat lip 1 and a half inches wide and stands

on 3 legs each 1 and a half inches high and 1 and a half broad. It has 2 handles or ears, each 1 and a half inches long. There are 3 raised beads or mouldings round the middle of the pot and 3 round each of the legs. It is an excellent casting and it is in pretty good preservation.

Appendix to Memoir by James Boyle

SOCIAL AND PRODUCTIVE ECONOMY

Census of 1813

County of the town of Carrickfergus.

Carrickfergus town: 213 inhabited houses, occupied by 249 families, 18 uninhabited, 30 families employed in agriculture, 118 families in trades and manufactures, 101 other families, 510 males, 673 females, total 1,183, 305 Protestants, 759 Protestant Dissenters, 119 Roman Catholics.

Irish Quarter: 173 inhabited houses, occupied by 189 families, 4 houses building, 13 uninhabited, families employed in agriculture, 132 families in trades and manufactures, 28 other families, 390 males, 447 females, total 837, 268 Protestants, 524 Protestant Dissenters, 524 Roman Catholics.

Scotch Quarter: 131 inhabited houses, occupied by 141 families, 3 houses building, 2 uninhabited, 7 families employed in agriculture, 120 families in trades and manufactures, 14 other families, 205 males, 345 females, total 630, 84 Protestants, 516 Protestant Dissenters, 30 Roman Catholics.

West Division: 216 inhabited houses, occupied by 222 families, 5 houses building, 7 uninhabited, 150 families employed in agriculture, 63 families in trades and manufactures, 9 other families, 535 males, 609 females, total 1,144, 103 Protestants, 862 Protestant Dissenters, 174 Roman Catholics.

Middle Division: 235 inhabited houses, occupied by 236 families, 12 houses building, 15 uninhabited, 132 families employed in agriculture, 93 families in trades and manufactures, 10 other families, 593 males, 657 females, total 1,250, 86 Protestants, 1,070 Protestant Dissenters, 144 Roman Catholics.

North East Division: 208 inhabited houses, occupied by 217 families, 9 houses building, 6 uninhabited, 127 families employed in agriculture, 87 families in trades and manufactures, 3 other families, 499 males, 593 females, total 1,092, 64 Protestants, 986 Protestant Dissenters, 42 Roman Catholics.

County Antrim gaol and court house: 71 males, 18 females, total 89.

Total: 1,166 inhabited houses, occupied by 1,253 families, 33 houses building, 61 uninhabited, 475 families employed in agriculture, 613 families in trades and manufactures, 165 other families, 2,083 males, 3,342 females, total 6,225, 915 Protestants, 4,667 Protestant Dissenters, 554 Roman Catholics.

Census of 1821

Carrickfergus town: 237 inhabited houses, 13 uninhabited, 2 4-storeys, 48 3-storeys, 103 2-storeys, 104 1-storey, total inhabitants 1,515, 688 males, 927 females, 1,296 Protestants, 225 Roman Catholics.

Irish Quarter: 216 inhabited houses, 3 uninhabited, 2 3-storeys, 52 2-storeys, 162 1-storey, total inhabitants 1,125, 543 males, 582 females, 950 Protestants, 175 Roman Catholics.

Scotch Quarter: 142 inhabited houses, 2 uninhabited, 1 4-storeys, 1 3-storeys, 13 2-storeys, 127 1-storey, total inhabitants 731, 339 males, 392 females, 705 Protestants, 26 Roman Catholics.

North East Division: 249 inhabited houses, 2 ruinous, 14 uninhabited, 15 2-storeys, 234 1-storey, total inhabitants 1,300, 638 males, 662 females, 1,241 Protestants, 59 Roman Catholics.

Middle Division: 291 inhabited houses, 18 uninhabited, 4 3-storeys, 23 2-storeys, 264 1-storey, total inhabitants 1,538, 760 males, 798 females, 1,390 Protestants, 148 Roman Catholics.

West Division: 289 inhabited houses, 2 building, 1 ruinous, 14 uninhabited, 1 3-storeys, 18 2-storeys, 270 1-storey, total inhabitants 1,675, 702 males, 773 females, 1,191 Protestants, 284 Roman Catholics.

County Antrim gaol and court house: 1 house, total inhabitants 211, 162 males, 49 females.

Castle and barrack: 2 houses, 1 4-storeys, total inhabitants 135, 103 males, 32 females.

[Total]: 1,467 houses, 2 building, 3 ruinous, 64 uninhabited, 4 4-storeys, 56 3-storeys, 224 2-storeys, 1,161 1-storey, total inhabitants 8,030, 3,915 males, 4,115 females, 6,767 Protestants, 917 Roman Catholics.

Population in 1831

West Division: 328 inhabited houses, occupied by 351 families, 7 building, 20 uninhabited, 96 families employed in trades and manufactures, 189 families in agriculture, 66 other families, 872

males, 976 females, total 1,848, 438 males 20 years and upwards.

Middle Division: 330 inhabited houses, occupied by 358 families, 5 building, 23 uninhabited, 154 families employed in trades and manufacture, 161 families in agriculture, 43 other families, 951 males, 1,050 females, total 2,001, 446 males 20 years and upwards.

North East Division: 230 inhabited houses, occupied by 257 families, 5 building, 13 uninhabited, 71 families employed in trades and manufacture, 135 families in agriculture, 51 other families, 629 males, 708 females, total 1,337, 310 males 20 years and upwards.

Town within the walls: 269 inhabited houses, occupied by 304 families, 1 building, 24 uninhabited, 655 families employed in trades and manufacture, 28 families in agriculture, 121 other families, 750 males, 812 females, total 1,562, 304 males 20 years and upwards.

Irish Quarter: 218 inhabited houses, occupied by 267 families, 7 building, 19 uninhabited, 151 families employed in trades and manufacture, 38 families in agriculture, 78 other families, 542 males, 654 females, total 1,196, 252 males 20 years and upwards.

Joymount Bank: 35 inhabited houses, occupied by 38 families, 1 uninhabited, 19 families employed in trades and manufactures, 5 families in agriculture, 40 other families, 126 males, 163 females, total 289, 61 males 20 years and upwards.

Scotch Quarter: 50 inhabited houses, occupied by 64 families, 2 building, 1 uninhabited, 19 families employed in trades and manufacture, 5 families in agriculture, 40 other families, 126 males, 163 females, total 289, 61 males 20 years and upwards.

The Green: 48 inhabited houses, occupied by 57 families, 2 building, 3 uninhabited, 17 families employed in trades and manufacture, 3 families in agriculture, 37 other families, 141 males, 156 females, total 297, 60 males 20 years and upwards.

Total: 1,497 inhabited houses, occupied by 1,696 families, 29 building, 104 uninhabited, 682 families employed in trades and manufactures, 562 families in agriculture, 452 other families, 4,092 males, 4,608 females, total 8,700, 1,911 males 20 years and upwards.

Names in Church and Churchyard

Names of persons interred in the parish church and churchyard.

In the church: Catherwood, Chichester, Clements, Couper, Davys, Dobbin, Dobbs, Gardner, Gill, Hill, Lang, MacDonnell, O'Brien, Openshaw, Williamson.

In the churchyard: Addison, Alexander, Anderson, Ansell, Barkly, Baxter, Bashford, Benn, Bigger, Blair, Booth, Bowden, Bowman, Breaden, Brown, Burleigh, Campbell, Caters, Cattens, Chaplin, Carnaghan, Clarke, Cox, Cranmer, Crooks, Crig, Creight, Cunningham, Davey, Davis, Dobbs, Doyle, Drenning, Eccleston, Fairfoot, Ferrell, Flinter, Gilliland, Glass, Grant, Gunning, Hanly, Hanna, Hay, Hamilton, Haggan, Hendren, Higginson, Hill, Hillditch, Holms, Howard, Hudson, Irwin, Jack, Jaffrey, Jamison, Johnson, Jordan, Junkin, Kair, Kerr, Keilty, Kennedy, Kinkaid, Kirkpatrick, Larmour, Laverty, Lockhart, Logan, Lee, Lewis, Lynch, Lynchy, Mackay, MacBride, MacBrin, MacCarn, MacCann, MacClevery, MacConnell, MacCullough, MacDowell, MacFerran, MacGill, MacGown, MacIlherron, MacIlwrath, MacKeen, MacMaster, MacSkimmin, Martin, Mathews, Mayne, Mean, Miller, Millikin, Montgomery, Moore, Morrison, Mulholland, Murray, Murphy, Murnay, Nelson, Nisbet, O'Donnell, Parks, Parkhill, Parsons, Picken, Poagher, Reid, Robinson, Rowan, Sanderson, Seeds, Shearer, Singleton, Sheilds, Stephenson, Stewart, Strain, Talbot, Thompson, Veacock, Wales, Weatherup, Wheeler, Williamson, Wisoncraft, Wood, Wright.

Townland Names

Etymology of the names of the ancient townlands, districts and other localities in the county of the town of Carrickfergus.

Aldoo "the black valley or point;" Ardboley "the summit of the lofty milking-place;" Altivaddy "the dog's point or valley;" Aughnaskeigh, from the ancient hawthorns growing along the banks of the stream.

Ballylaggan "the town of flats or low valleys;" Ballynascreen "the town in the shelter," from its sheltered situation under a bank or perhaps from the shelter afforded by a wood which is said to have formerly flourished here; Brianlagne, from the union of 2 branches of the Woodburn stream, including a tongue of high land with steep banks.

Cairnarosie "the cairn of roses;" Cairnconlan, from an ancient cairn, now destroyed, erected over one of the family of Conlan who are now extinct; Cairnarock or Cairnabrock "the badgers' cairn;" Cairnakecla, unknown; Cauldhame "the cold home," from the cold springy nature of the land; Craigboy, from the yellow surface of the rocks; Crossgreen, from some old cross now unknown; Clipperstown, so called from an inhabitant who, from his craft and cunning, was nicknamed Clipper; Cilla Tobar, properly Suill-a-thobbar; the original and correct name was applied to the source of this stream, which issues from a limestone rock signifying "the well eye;" Crossmary [blank]; Cloughey Land, from the rocky and stony surface of the ground.

Duncrue "the fort of the (in the shape of the) horseshoe." This fort and townland were in former times known as Duinn Cruin or "the stooped or impending fort." The name is appropriate, as the fort impends over a rivulet above which it is elevated about 60 feet. Duff's hill (Dhu hill) "the black hill," from the black boggy surface of the land. Drumrammer "the fertile ridge or eminence."

Eden or Eaden, a village; Eaden signifies "a face or aspect;" Eadengranna "the sunny brae or face of a declivity;" from this the former derives its name; Glenside, from its situation along a glen or valley; Hogg's Park, from a pig-walk or place in which swine were fed or let loose; Isle of Glass, from the green and verdant surface of the land.

Killycroft, from the existence of a burial [ground?]; Knocker, properly Knockagh "a ridge or a chain of contiguous hills" or "a number of neighbouring hills;" Lagna Tomach "the valley of the small hills or tufts;" Lough Mourne, from a small lake of that name; Morne or Mourne signifies [blank]; Luberlady [blank]; Ree hill, probably from the dark grey colour of the hill; it might originally have been Rhi hill or "the king's hill;" Rachinboy or Rath-buy "the yellow fort."

Seskin or Shaskin signifies "a swamp or marsh;" Slievetrue, properly Sliebh-thirue "the mountain of wailing or lamentation," which name it has probably derived from the large cairn or place of sepulture on its summit; Slimmerow, a corruption of Slieve Roe (or Sliebh Ruagh), derived from the reddish colour of the bare and barren summit of the mountain; Straidnahana, properly Straidnahania, a plain or flat abounding with the wild plant commonly termed coltsfoot; Scoutbush, the name of a gentleman's seat, derived from an ancient strength which, during the latter part of the 17th century, had been the residence of the scout-major or provost-marshal of the garrison of Carrickfergus.

Troopers Land, a district under the Knocker mountain formerly appropriated to grazing the troop horses in the garrison and supplying them with hay; Wolf's Moss, a bog which is said to have derived its name from its having been the haunt of a wolf which had, for several years, committed great devastations among the flocks in the neighbourhood.

The names of the remaining localities and districts have been derived either from those of their earliest possessions or from some obviously local circumstance. The names of many tend to throw considerable light on the extraction of the families to whom they were in all probability granted, many of whom are now quite extinct.

The following are the names which have been thus derived: Gormalsland, Marshaltown, Downshiresland, Kingsland, Tollsland, Jordansland, Barrysland, Portersland, Peggsland, Bellsfarm, Bashfordsland, Kaneshill, Youngers, Lyndons Park, Whitesland, Hagansland, Pennysland, Byrttsland, Merrionstown, Horsmansland, Englishman's Mountain, My Lord's Mountain, Shanksland, Dorisland and Nairnstown.

The derivation of the others, or rather the circumstances from which they have been derived, are obvious, for instance Ninescoreacres, Fourscoreacres, Demesne Lands, Prospect, Sea Park, Oakfield, Barrackfield, Windmill Hill, Woodburn.

Trades and Occupations

Apothecaries 2, architects 1, armourers 1, attornies 1, auctioneers 1; bakers 6, bank manager 1, barber 1, bellowmakers 1, bonnetmakers 8, boot and shoemakers 6, brewer 1, butchers 11; cabinetmaker 1, house carpenters 14, hedge carpenters 2, mill carpenters 2, ship carpenters 3, carriers or carmen 4, cartmakers 2, chandler and soap-boiler 1, proprietor of circulating library 1, clergy of all denominations 9, various clerks 6, sellers of old clothes 1, proprietor of coal stores 2, coastguards 8, coopers 5, copper and tinsmith 1, crane-master 1, curriers 5; proprietors of dairies 2, delf and glass shops 5, proprietor of distillery 1, dressmakers 13, dyers 2; excise officers or gaugers 2.

Farmers 6, proprietor of yarn factory 1, fishermen 57, flax dressers or hecklers 12, proprietor of flax stores 1; gardeners 2, private gentlemen 2, grocery, wine and spirit dealers 5, grocers and publicans 10, grocers and woollen drapers 2, greengrocer 1, grocers 14, gunnery-master 1; hotel keepers 3, haberdashers and grocers 6, haberdashers 2, harbour-master 1, huntsman 1, huxters 23; ironmongers 1, dealer in old iron 1;

lamp-lighter for the gaol 1, agricultural labourers 93, letter carrier 1; magistrates 2, malster 1, masons and bricklayers 12, masters of ships 6, coal and salt merchants, slate and timber merchants 2, flowerers of muslin 55, timber merchants 2, corn millers, flour millers 1, milliners 3; nailers 8.

Painters and glaziers 2, pawnbrokers 4, pensioners 5, police constabulary 7, postmaster 1, physicians 5, manufacturer of pop 1, plasterers 1, calico printers 3, process servers 1, prostitutes 10, poor [blank], publicans and spirit-sellers 33; saddlers 4, sawyers 2, schoolmasters 7, schoolmistresses 8, secretary of the grand jury 1, seamsters 6, scriveners 1, town sergeant 1, slaters 2, blacksmiths 6, tinsmiths 2, tinsmith and plumber 1, stonecutter 2, surgeons 2, sailors 45; tailors 8, tanners 1, thatchers 2, tide-waiters [blank], turnkeys (gaol) 8; upholsterers (female) 1; watch and clockmakers 3, washerwomen 14, calico weavers 35, wheelwrights and turners 2; [total] 718.

Houses: 4-storey houses 1, 3-storey 70, 2-storey 302, cottages 373, total 746; public buildings [blank], inhabited houses 692, uninhabited 54, thatched 255, slated 491.

Petty Sessions

Table of cases for 8 years.

Number of cases of assault: 30 in 1828, 26 in 1832, 24 in 1833, 26 in 1834, 20 in 1835, 20 in 1836, 16 in 1837, 10 in 1838.

Injury to the person: 4 in 1828, 2 in 1832, 4 in 1834, 4 in 1835, 2 in 1836, 3 in 1837, 4 in 1838.

Housebreaking: 1 in 1828.

Theft: 6 in 1828, 5 in 1832, 10 in 1833, 6 in 1834, 6 in 1835, 9 in 1836, 4 in 1837, 2 in 1838.

Trespass: 20 in 1828, 19 in 1832, 10 in 1833, 16 in 1834, 14 in 1835, 10 in 1836, 13 in 1837, 9 in 1838.

Injury to property: 6 in 1838, 4 in 1832, 3 in 1833, 6 in 1834, 6 in 1835, 4 in 1836, 6 in 1837, 2 in 1838.

Disputes about wages: 18 in 1828, 15 in 1832, 20 in 1833, 26 in 1834, 24 in 1835, 20 in 1836, 14 in 1837, 16 in 1838.

Riot: 3 in 1838, 1 in 1832, 3 in 1833, 3 in 1834, 1 in 1838.

Rescue: 1 in 1828, 3 in 1833, 2 in 1834, 2 in 1835.

Breaches of game laws: 2 in 1828, 1 in 1832, 1 in 1835, 1 in 1836, 3 in 1837.

Breaches of excise laws: 2 in 1828, 2 in 1832, 3 in 1833, 2 in 1834, 3 in 1834.

Nuisances on roads and streets: 19 in 1832, 19 in 1833, 15 in 1835, 6 in 1836, 16 in 1837, 20 in 1838.

Drunkenness: 6 in 1837, 2 in 1838.

Miscellaneous cases: 20 in 1828, 10 in 1832, 10 in 1833, 9 in 1834, 26 in 1836, 9 in 1837, 15 in 1838.

Number of summonses issued: 366 in 1828, 312 in 1832, 263 in 1833, 246 in 1834, 270 in 1835, 272 in 1836, 330 in 1837, 260 in 1838.

Number of cases sent to assizes: 5 in 1837, 4 in 1838.

Number of cases sent to quarter sessions: 15 in 1837, 10 in 1838.

Fines for 8 years: 4 pounds 13s in 1828, 5 pounds 9s in 1832, 6 pounds 1s 7d in 1833, 6 pounds 19s 9d in 1834, 6 pounds 18s 11d in 1835, 14 pounds 12s 3d in 1836, 20 pounds 8d in 1837, 5 pounds 6s 1d in 1838.

NB No record for the years 1829, 1830 or 1831 was preserved.

Statement of cases for 2 years. Assault: 14 in 1837, 22 in 1838; injury to the person: 3 in 1837; trespass: 8 in 1837, 5 in 1838; murder: 1 in 1837; injury to property: 2 in 1837; housebreaking: 1 in 1838; theft: 7 in 1837, 3 in 1838; breaches of game laws: 2 in 1837; felony: 2 in 1837; riot and assault: 2 in 1837, 1 in 1838; rescue: 1 in 1837; drunkenness: 4 in 1837; nuisances on roads: 2 in 1837, 1 in 1838; disputes about wages: 6 in 1837, 4 in 1838; miscellaneous cases: 3 in 1837, 2 in 1838; [total] 57 in 1837, 39 in 1838.

Number of summonses issued: 109 in 1837, 100 in 1838; number of cases sent to assizes: 1 in 1837, 2 in 1838; number of cases sent to quarter sessions: 1 in 1837, 2 in 1838; amount of ines levied: 1 pound 11s in 1837, 1 pound 1s in 1838.

Quarter Sessions

County of the town of Carrickfergus: criminal return for 8 years. Larceny: 1 in 1831, 6 in 1832, 4 in 1833, 1 in 1834, 1 in 1835, 5 in 1836, 9 in 1837, 1 in 1838; assaults: 1 in 1831, 18 in 1832, 10 in 1833, 4 in 1834, 1 in 1835, 16 in 1836, 3 in 1837, 6 in 1837; receiving stolen goods: 1 in 1838; misdemeanours: 1 in 1838.

Dispensary

Return for 7 years.

1832: 390 patients cured, 26 relieved, 19 died, total 435; surgeon's salary 21 pounds, house rent 4 pounds, cost of medicine 30 pounds 18s 3d, other expenses 5 pounds 3s 3d, total 61 pounds 1s 6d; income from subscriptions 32 pounds 5s, grand jury 32 pounds 5s, total 64 pounds 10s.

1833: 487 patients cured, 68 relieved, 24 died, total 579; surgeon's salary 21 pounds, house rent 4 pounds, cost of medicine 22 pounds 18s 5d, other expenses 1 pound 8s 5d, total 59 pounds 6s 10s; income from subscriptions 31 pounds 8s 6d, grand jury 31 pounds 8s 6d, total 62 pounds 17s.

1834: 443 patients cured, 80 relieved, 20 died, total 548; surgeon's salary 21 pounds, house rent 4 pounds, cost of medicine 20 pounds 15s 2s, other expenses 1 pound 3s 7d, total 46 pounds 18s 9d; income from subscriptions 17 pounds 8s, grand jury 17 pounds 8s, total 34 pounds 16s.

1835: 496 patients cured, 78 relieved, 32 died, total 604; surgeon's salary 16 pounds, house rent 4 pounds, cost of medicine 18 pounds 16s 5d, other expenses 4s 4d, total 39 pounds 11d; income from subscriptions 15 pounds 12s, from grand jury 15 pounds 12s, total 31 pounds 4s.

1836: 372 patients cured, 65 relieved, 22 died, total 459; house rent 1 pound, cost of medicine 8 pounds 4s 3d, other expenses 2 pounds 4s 11d, total 11 pounds 9s 2d; income from subscriptions 11 pounds 18s, total 11 pounds 18s.

1837: 279 patients cured, 55 relieved, 16 died, total 350; cost of medicine 9 pounds 9s 9d, total 9 pounds 9s 9d; income from subscriptions 15 pounds 13s, total 15 pounds 13s.

1838: 378 patients cured, 32 relieved, 17 died, total 427; cost of medicine 10 pounds 7s, other expenses 4s, total 10s 11d; income from grand jury 15 pounds 13s, total 15 pounds 13s.

Dispensary

Table of cases for 7 years.

Abcess, 2 in 1835; amenorrhoea, 6 in 1835, 2 in 1836; anasarca, 4 in 1832, 4 in 1834, 9 in 1835, 5 in 1836, 2 in 1837, 2 in 1838; amaurosis, 2 in 1838; ascites, 6 in 1832, 2 in 1833, 6 in 1834, 9 in 1835; asthma, 16 in 1832, 8 in 1833, 10 in 1834, 9 in 1835, 24 in 1836, 12 in 1837, 110 [insert alternative]: 14 in 1838; burns, 2 in 1836.

Cardiolgia, 2 in 1836; catarrh, 36 in 1832, 30 in 1833, 20 in 1834, 22 in 1835, 38 in 1836, 12 in 1837, 15 in 1838; cephalgia, 5 in 1832, 6 in 1833, 4 in 1834, 4 in 1836, 2 in 1838; colica, 5 in 1832, 6 in 1833, 4 in 1834, 3 in 1835, 1 in 1837, 2 in 1838; constipation, 4 in 1836, 3 in 1837, 13 in 1838; cynanche tonsillaris, 17 in 1832, 12 in 1833, 14 in 1834, 10 in 1835, 6 in 1836, 2 in 1837, 12 in 1838.

Debilitas, 15 in 1832, 13 in 1833, 10 in 1834, 9 in 1835, 17 in 1836, 4 in 1837, 9 in 1838; dentitis, 11 in 1832, 12 in 1833, 13 in 1834, 16 in 1835, 20 in 1836, 16 in 1837, 12 in 1838; diarrhoea, 13 in 1832, 10 in 1833, 12 in 1834, 16 in 1835, 20 in 1836, 16 in 1837, 12 in 1838; dolor temoris, 2 in 1834, 2 in 1837; dolor venticuli, 2 in 1836; dolor patoris, 2 in 1836, 10 in 1838; dyspepsia, 15 in 1832, 7 in 1833, 9 in 1834, 8 in 1835, 16 in 1836, 6 in 1837, 5 in 1838; dysenteria, 2 in 1832, 3 in 1833, 4 in 1834, 2 in 1835, 1 in 1836, 2 in 1837.

Epilepsy, 2 in 1836, 1 in 1838; epistaxis, 2 in 1832, 3 in 1833, 1 in 1838; erysipelas, 1 in 1832, 2 in 1833, 2 in 1834, 2 in 1835, 2 in 1836, 2 in 1837; febris, 3 in 1832, 26 in 1833, 20 in 1834, 17 in 1835, 12 in 1836, 81 in 1837, 81 in 1837, 140 in 1838; fistula, 2 in 1836; fractures, 1 in 1832, 2 in 1833, 12 in 1834, 14 in 1835, 2 in 1836, 2 in 1838; gastrodina, 8 in 1832, 2 in 1833, 6 in 1834, 14 in 1835, 6 in 1836, 4 in 1837, 2 in 1838; gonorrhoea, 1 in 1832, 4 in 1833, 12 in 1835.

Haemorrhagia, 2 in 1832, 2 in 1838; haemoptisis, 2 in 1832, 3 in 1833, 2 in 1834, 11 in 1835, 2 in 1836; haemorrhoids, 2 in 1832, 2 in 1833, 3 in 1834, 12 in 1835, 2 in 1836, 3 in 1837; haematemesis, 4 in 1832, 2 in 1836, 2 in 1837; herpes, 2 in 1832, 13 in 1833, 1 in 1834, 11 in 1835, 12 in 1836, 1 in 1837, 4 in 1838; hepatitis, 4 in 1832, 5 in 1833, 4 in 1834, 13 in 1835, 2 in 1836, 3 in 1837; hydrocele, 1 in 1832, 2 in 1833, 1 in 1836, 1 in 1838; hysteria, 2 in 1832, 3 in 1833, 2 in 1834, 11 in 1835, 2 in 1836.

Impetigo, 16 in 1832, 12 in 1833, 11 in 1834, 10 in 1835, 2 in 1836; inflammations, 21 in 1832, 36 in 1834, 14 in 1836, 12 in 1838; influenza, 43 in 1833, 33 in 1834, 24 in 1835, 102 in 1837; leucorrhoea, 2 in 1832, 4 in 1833, 6 in 1834, 11 in 1835, 10 in 1836, 2 in 1837; lithasis, 1 in 1832, 2 in 1833, 1 in 1837; lumbago, 2 in 1833, 14 in 1834; menorrhagia, 16 in 1833, 12 in 1834, 13 in 1835, 2 [insert alternative: 12] in 1836; morbilla, 33 in 1832, 20 in 1833, 36 in 1836.

Odontolgia, 20 in 1832, 6 in 1833, 39 in 1834, 26 in 1835, 20 in 1836, 13 in 1837, 12 in 1838; ophthalmia, 6 in 1832, 9 in 1833, 16 in 1834, 14 in 1835, 2 in 1837, 12 in 1838; otitis, 4 in 1833, 2 in 1834, 11 in 1835; palpitations, 4 in 1832, 6 in 1833, 8 in 1834, 12 in 1835, 3 in 1836; paralysis, 2 in 1836, 2 in 1838; phthysis, 4 in 1832, 6 in 1833, 3 in 1834, 12 in 1835, 3 in 1837; pleuritis, 12 in 1832, 25 in 1833, 14 in 1834, 16 in 1835, 12 in 1836, 9 in 1838; pneumonia, 7 in 1832, 10 in 1833, 8 in 1834, 16 in 1835, 2 in 1836, 4 in 1838; prolapsus uteri, 2 in 1838; psora, 5 in 1832, 6 in 1833, 4 in 1834, 13 in 1835, 21 in 1836, 20 in 1837, 12 in 1838; pyrosis, 4 in 1833, 4 in 1836.

Rheumatism, 39 in 1832, 50 in 1833, 46 in 1834, 56 in 1835, 35 in 1836, 20 in 1837, 20 in 1838; synorhas, 3 in 1832, 20 in 1833, 10 in 1834, 1 in 1835; syphilis, 8 in 1832, 10 in 1833, 2 in 1834, 14 in 1835, 2 in 1836, 2 in 1838; scabies, 2 in 1832, 10 in 1833, 6 in 1836, 12 in 1837, 11 in 1838; scarlatina, 16 in 1832, 29 in 1833, 23 in 1834, 12 in 1835, 15 in 1836, 1 in 1838; scrofula, 12 in 1832, 26 in 1833, 14 in 1834, 16 in 1835, 14 in 1836, 4 in 1837; tetanus, 2 in 1836; tinea capitis, 12 in 1836, 2 in 1838; tupis senetis, 3 in 1836; tumours, 12 in 1832, 13 in 1833, 16 in 1834, 12 in 1835, 4 in 1836, 10 in 1838; typhus, 3 in 1832.

Ulcer, 26 in 1833, 26 in 1834, 26 in 1835, 23 in 1836, 12 in 1837, 6 in 1838; variola, 2 in 1837, 7 in 1838; vermes, 36 in 1832, 46 in 1834, 30 in 1835, 29 in 1836, 34 in 1837, 4 in 1838, 27 in 1838; vertigo, 12 in 1833, 4 in 1834, 2 in 1837, 7 in 1838; vulnus arteria radicalis, 1 in 1838; vulnus genie, 1 in 1838.

[Total]: 433 in 1832, 581 in 1833, 538 in 1834, 616 in 1835, 460 in 1836, 354 in 1837, 426 in 1838.

Pawnbrokers

A statement of the sums advanced upon pledges at the pawn-offices in Carrickfergus since 1828.

1828, William Hendron, 4,341 tickets issued, annual amount advanced 291 pounds 10s 2d, 2,831 sums under 2s 6d, 1,400 between 2s 6d and 5s, 110 between 5s and 10s.

1829, William Hendron, 2,564 tickets, amount 216 pounds 5s ha'penny, 1,760 sums under 2s 6d, 730 between 2s 6d and 5s, 54 between 5s and 10s.

1830, William Hendron, 1,818 tickets, amount 129 pounds 1s 3d ha'penny, 1,675 sums under 2s 6d, 98 between 2s 6d and 5s, 46 between 5s and 10s, 5 between 10s and 30s.

1831, William Hendron, 1,880 tickets, amount 133 pounds 13s 8d ha'penny, 1,690 sums under 2s 6d, 100 between 2s 6d and 5s, 9 between 5s and 10s.

1832, William Hendron, 1,457 tickets, amount 109 pounds 7s 5d ha'penny, 1,202 sums under 2s 6d, 240 between 2s 6d and 5s, 9 between 5s and 10s, 6 between 10s and 30s.

1833, William Hendron, 1,718 tickets, amount 131 pounds 3s 2d, 1,602 sums under 2s 6d, 100 between 2s 6d and 5s, 16 between 5s and 10s.

1834, William Hendron, 927 tickets, amount 81 pounds 1s 2d, 842 sums under 2s 6d, 70 between 2s 6d and 5s, 15 between 5s and 10s.

1835, William Hendron, 1,372 tickets, amount

79 pounds 3s 2d, 1,200 sums under 2s 6d, 106 between 2s 6d and 5s, 66 between 5s and 10s.

Arthur McCurley, 12,600 tickets, amount 1,390 pounds, 6,000 sums under 2s 6d, 3,050 between 5s and 10s, 2,400 between 10s and 30s, 1,140 between 10s and 30s, 10 above 30s.

1836, William Hendron, 2,661 tickets, amount 214 pounds 10s 3d ha'penny, 2,538 sums under 2s 6d, 113 between 5s and 10s, 66 between 10s and 30s.

Arthur McCurley, 13,700 tickets, amount 1,420 pounds, 6,350 sums under 2s 6d, 3,500 between 2s 6d and 5s, 2,600 between 5s and 10s, 1,230 between 10s and 30s, 20 above 30s.

1837, William Hendron, 1,771 tickets, amount 147 pounds 13s 10d ha'penny, 1,560 sums under 2s 6d, 155 between 2s 6d and 5s, 56 between 5s and 10s.

Arthur McCurley, 14,800 tickets, amount 1,480 pounds, 7,400 sums under 2s 6d, 5,210 between 2s 6d and 5s, 2,120 between 5s and 10s, 60 between 10s and 30s, 10 above 30s.

1838, William Hendron, 1,000 tickets, amount 75 pounds 4s 11d, 860 sums under 2s 6d, 100 between 2s 6d and 5s, 25 between 5s and 10s, 15 between 10s and 30s.

Arthur McCurley, 14,860 tickets, amount 1,500 pounds, 10,350 sums under 2s 6d, 3,260 between 2s 6d and 5s, 162 between 5s and 10s, 72 between 10s and 30s, 16 above 30s.

Hugh Stuart, 12,583 tickets, amount 1,155 pounds 19s 8d ha'penny, 6,300 sums under 2s 6d, 3,500 between 2s 6d and 5s, 2,000 between 5s and 10s, 653 between 10s and 30s, 100 above 30s.

[Totals]: 90,022 tickets, amount 8,554 pounds 13s 11d ha'penny, 54,160 sums under 2s 6d, 21,752 between 2s 6d and 5s, 9,748 between 5s and 10s, 3,161 between 10s and 30s, 156 above 30s.

Mendicity Society

Carrickfergus Mendicity Society: economical return for 7 years.

1831: income from subscriptions 263 pounds 7s 10d, interest of bequests 31 pounds 15s 5d, collections at places of worship 117 pounds 9s 9d ha'penny, fines from magistrates 8 pounds 5s 11d, total 423 pounds 18s 11d, yarn 241 pounds 18s, balance 4 pounds 6s 10d, total 670 pounds 3s 10d ha'penny; expenditure: oatmeal 233 pounds 17s 3d ha'penny, coals 38 pounds 16s 3d, flax 110 pounds 1s 6d, wages for spinning 149 pounds 13s 9d ha'penny, lodgings for the poor 8

pounds, weekly distribution 52 pounds 6s 2d, total 513 pounds 18s 2d, house rent 10 pounds 10s, salaries 15 pounds 2s 6d, miscellaneous 8 pounds 11d; balance in treasurer's hands 623 pounds 9s 10d ha'penny, total 46 pounds 14s.

1832: income from subscriptions 232 pounds 12s 6d, interest 34 pounds 13s 1d, collections 87 pounds 10s, fines 13 pounds 6s 10d, total 367 pounds 12s 4d, yarn, 190 pounds 11d, total 561 pounds 16s 3d; expenditure: oatmeal 181 pounds 12s 10d, coals 39 pounds 1s 10d, flax 104 pounds 3s ha'penny, wages for spinning 128 pounds 14s ha'penny, lodgings for the poor 8 pounds, weekly distribution 52 pounds 6s 2d, total 513 pounds 18s 2d, house rent 10 pounds 10s, salaries 15 pounds 2s 6d, miscellaneous 8 pounds 10s 1d ha'penny; balance 548 pounds 8d ha'penny, total 13 pounds 18s 4d.

1833: income from subscriptions 211 pounds 11s, interest 20 pounds 18s 6d, collections 79 pounds 6s, fines 19 pounds 10s 7d, total 331 pounds 6s 1d, yarn 127 pounds 8s 2d, balance 9 pounds 6s 6d, total 468 pounds 9d ha'penny; expenditure: oatmeal 132 pounds 8s 10d ha'penny, coals 34 pounds 19s 9d, flax 75 pounds 10s 2d, wages for spinning 114 pounds 5s 4d, lodgings for the poor 3 pounds 16s, weekly distribution 57 pounds 19s 8d, total 419 pounds 2s 9d ha'penny, house rent 10 pounds 10s, salaries 14 pounds 10s, miscellaneous 7 pounds 11s 11d ha'penny; balance 451 pounds 14s 9d ha'penny, total 11 pounds 11s ha'penny.

1835: income from subscriptions 214 pounds 10s, interest 34 pounds 18s 2d 3 farthings, fines 13 pounds 4s 7d ha'penny, total 338 pounds 8s 6d 3 farthings, yarn 163 pounds 5s 11d ha'penny, balance 34 pounds 14s 3d, total 536 pounds 8s 3d; expenditure: oatmeal 173 pounds 18s 10d, coals 40 pounds 16s 5d, flax 95 pounds 14s 9d, wages for spinning 101 pounds 19s 9d, lodgings for the poor 4 pounds 15s 4d, weekly distribution 71 pounds 4s 1d, total 488 pounds 9s 2d, house rent 10 pounds 10s, salaries 14 pounds 11s 3d, miscellaneous 9 pounds 11d ha'penny; balance 522 pounds 10s 9d, total 13 pounds 17s 5d 3 farthings.

1836: income from subscriptions 210 pounds 11s 4d, interest 39 pounds 1s 10d, collections 75 pounds 5s 1d, fines 17 pounds 4s 4d, total 342 pounds 2s 7d ha'penny, yarn 131 pounds 2s 4d, balance 16 pounds 18s 7d, total 490 pounds 3s 6d; expenditure: oatmeal 187 pounds 7s 7d, coals 46 pounds 16s 9d, flax 67 pounds 4s 4d, wages for spinning 75 pounds 6s 10d, lodgings for the poor 4 pounds 15s 4d, weekly distribution 75 pounds 14s 8d, total 457 pounds 5s 6d, house rent 10 pounds 10s, salaries 14 pounds 7s 6d, miscellaneous 8 pounds 6d; balance 490 pounds 3s 6d.

1837: income from subscriptions 202 pounds 1s 8d, interest 25 pounds 16s 3d, collections 149 pounds 15s 6d, fines 16 pounds 12s 2d, total 394 pounds 5s 7d, yarn 79 pounds 7s 8d, total 473 pounds 13s 3d; expenditure: oatmeal 193 pounds 4s 11d, coals 33 pounds 8s, flax 47 pounds 5s 6d, wages for spinning 19 pounds 1s 7d, lodgings for the poor 7 pounds 8s 8d, weekly distribution 54 pounds 12s 6d, total 385 pounds 1s 2d, house rent 10 pounds 10s, salaries 14 pounds 7s 6d, miscellaneous 6 pounds 9s 11d; balance 473 pounds 11s 5d, total 57 pounds 16s 8d 3 farthings.

1838: income from subscriptions 251 pounds 1s 6d ha'penny, interest 39 pounds 19s 6d, collections 82 pounds 1s 6d ha'penny, fines 10 pounds 9s 5d ha'penny, total 383 pounds 12s ha'penny, yarn 64 pounds 1s 9d, balance 54 pounds 3s 7d ha'penny, total 501 pounds 17s 5d; expenditure: oatmeal 215 pounds 15s 6d, coals 43 pounds 9s 9d, flax 52 pounds 3s 10d, wages for spinning 70 pounds 5s ha'penny, lodgings 10 pounds 2s, weekly distribution 73 pounds 9d, total 464 pounds 16s 10d ha'penny, house rent 10 pounds 10s, salaries 14 pounds 7s 6d, miscellaneous 6 pounds 19s 4d; balance 497 pounds 11s 5d, total 4 pounds 6s.

Mendicity: Poverty Relief

1831: 159 on the books, 59 admitted, total 218, 23 struck off, 14 died, 135 receiving rations, 46 receiving work only, total 181; the quantities of meal, coals and flax for this year could not be ascertained.

1832: 181 on the books, 29 admitted, 210 total, 29 struck off, 12 died, 130 receiving rations, 39 receiving work only, total 169; 14 tons 15 cwt 1 qr oatmeal, 54 tons coals, 72 cwt 2 qrs flax, 8,000 hanks of yarn spun.

1833: 169 on the books, 25 admitted, total 194, 21 struck off, 13 died, 128 receiving rations, 32 receiving work only, total 160; 14 tons 1 cwt oatmeal, 61 tons coals, 10 cwt 6 qrs 13 lbs flax, 7,003 hanks of yarn.

1835: 158 on the books, 42 admitted during the year, total 200, 17 struck off, 13 died, 142 receiving rations, 28 receiving work only, total 170; 15 tons 18 cwt oatmeal, 67 tons 15 cwt coals, 11 cwt 10 qrs flax, 7,352 hanks of yarn.

1836: 170 on the books, 25 admitted during the year, total 195, 19 struck off, 18 died, 130 receiving rations, 28 receiving work only, total 158; 16

tons 3 cwt 3 qrs oatmeal, 67 tons coal, 8 cwt 1 qr 2 lbs flax, 6,280 hanks of yarn.

1837: 158 on the books, 39 admitted during the year, total 197, 34 struck off, 12 died, 132 receiving rations, 19 receiving work only, total 148; 17 tons 2 cwt oatmeal, 53 tons 15 cwt coals, 7 cwt flax, 3,848 hanks of yarn.

Benevolence: Bequests

[Table contains the following headings: name, object, funds, management and source, expenditure, relief afforded, money, numbers relieved].

1782, the interest of 2,000 pounds invested in 3 per cent government interest, to be annually distributed among 19 poor freemen; management: bequeathed to the owners of the Ballymena estate in trust; the bequest is managed by John Forsyth Esquire, the agent of the estate; funds: 64 pounds per annum, being the interest of 2,000 pounds vested in 3 per cent consols bequeathed in trust to the owners of the Ballymena estate by William Adair Esquire; relief afforded: 64 pounds per annum, the interest of 1,000 [sic] pounds; 2 pounds each is annually given to 32 poor freemen; number relieved: formerly 19, at present 32 receive 2 pounds per annum.

23rd March 1761, the bequest of Henry Gill Esquire, of 10 pounds per annum, with a free house and garden, to such as might not have residences to "14 aged men in decayed circumstances" who "were remarkable for their inoffensiveness and good behaviour" that have been either born in or inhabitants of the town and parish of Carrickfergus; management: bequeathed in trust to 6 trustees, 3 trustees to be continued in charge of it; the present are Rev. R.V. Wilson, C.E. Dobbs, Richard Dobbs, J.B. Adair and William Burleigh; funds: 201 pounds 12s, the bequest of the late Henry Gill Esquire, left by him chargeable on his estate, to be paid by his heirs to the trustees appointed; relief afforded: free house and garden to each of 14 aged and poor persons, 14 pounds 8s per annum to be paid to 14 poor men; number relieved: 14.

1792, the bequest of Mr Craig who, in or about the year 1792, purchased from Mr John Chaplin a property encumbered with a debt of 300 pounds (late currency) to the parish; management: the interest of the sum paid by the trustees to the treasurer of the Mendicity Society; funds: the bequest of Mr Craig of 9 pounds 11s per annum, being the interest of 3 and half per cent government stock of 300 pounds, late Irish currency; relief afforded: 9 pounds 2s 11d per annum, the interest of 300 pounds late currency paid to the Mendicity Society; number relieved: uncertain.

1792, for the poor of Carrickfergus; management: in trust of the rector and churchwardens, paid by them to the treasurer of the Mendicity Society; funds: 8 pounds 6s 2d, the interest of 150 pounds late Irish currency bequeathed by Hercules Ellis Esquire and paid by his heirs; relief afforded: 8 pounds 6s 2d per annum, the interest of 550 pounds late currency paid to the Mendicity Society; number relieved: fluctuating.

1813 and 1828, the bequest of Martha Thompson of 100 pounds late [currency] and of 300 pounds late currency from Miss Margaret Spaight for the poor of the parish; management: these sums, jointly amounting to 400 pounds late currency, are vested in 3 and a half per cent government stock in the name of the rector and churchwardens for the time being; funds: 13 pounds 18s 4s per annum, the interest on 100 pounds, the bequest of Mrs Martha Thompson, and 300 pounds, the bequest of Miss Margaret Spaight, which are vested in 3 per cent government stock; relief afforded: 13 pounds 18s 6d per annum, the interest of 400 pounds late currency paid to the Mendicity Society; number relieved: fluctuating.

1821, the bequest of Ezekiel Davys Wilson, to be paid by Dr Duncan Wilson, his heir, and to be expended in bread to be distributed at Easter, Christmas and Whitsuntide to September among the most regular attendants at church; management: the sum is annually expended and is given at the stated times to most regular attendants at church by the rector for the time being; funds: 8 pounds 8s per annum, being the annual interest sum charged on and paid by the proprietors of the estate of the late E.D. Wilson Esquire, the testator; diet: the bequest is expended in bread, which is distributed among the most regular attendants at church; number relieved: fluctuating.

1821, the bequest of 50 pounds by the late Ezekiel Davys Wilson, the interest to be paid by the proprietor of his estate for the use of the Mendicity Society; management: chargeable on Ezekiel Davys Wilson, the interest to be paid to the rector and churchwardens for the time being; funds: 2 pounds 15s 4d ha'penny per annum, being the annual interest of 50 pounds bequeathed by the late Ezekiel Davys Wilson Esquire; relief afforded: 2 pounds 15s 4d ha'penny per annum, paid for the support of the Mendicity Society; number relieved: fluctuating.

1822, the bequest of 200 pounds from the late Mrs Anne Wilson, for the Mendicity Society and for the poor of the parish; management: the interest is paid monthly by the executor to the testator, to the treasurer of the Mendicity, the principal being vested in houses and lands; funds: 10 pounds per annum, being the annual interest of 200 pounds, the bequest of the late Mrs Anne Wilson, arising from houses and lands; relief afforded: 10 pounds per annum, paid monthly to the Mendicity Society; number relieved: fluctuating.

Establishments for instruction: 9 schools wholly or partly supported by benevolence; object: the removal of ignorance; when established: at sundry periods; management: by sundry committees and societies; funds: 62 pounds from public sources, 51 pounds from private sources; expenditure: house rent 7 pounds, salaries 97 pounds, incidental expenses 9 pounds; number relieved: 361.

Establishments for the Indigent

Mendicity Society; object: to remove and prevent street-begging by assisting the aged, helpless and infirm, and employing the labouring poor; established 1827; management: a committee, secretary and treasurer; funds: subscriptions and donations, interest of bequests for the poor, proceeds of charity sermons, collections at the parish church and Trinitarian meeting house; fines, average of 7 years, 528 pounds 11s 7d; expenditure: house rent 10 pounds 10s, incidental expenses 7 pounds 10s 6d, total 18 pounds 6d; relief afforded: 134 weekly receive rations of oatmeal and coals; the sum distributed in weekly gratuities is 61 pounds 13s 11d; the average weekly distribution of gratuities amounts to 61 pounds 13s 11d; flax is given out to be manufactured into yarn and the poor are paid for their work; number relieved: the average annual number for 7 years is 204.

Clothing Society; object: to provide the poor with blankets and clothing in winter; when established: 1819; management: by a committee of ladies, a manager, secretary, treasurer and 4 collectors; funds: subscriptions and donations and the proceeds of charity sermons for the purpose; average of 7 years, 25 pounds 10d ha'penny; relief afforded: blankets, petticoats, cloaks, coats and shoes; number relieved: the average annual number for 7 years is 90.

Establishment for the relief of mental and bodily diseases: dispensary; object: to relieve the sick residing within the limits of the county of the town of Carrickfergus; established 1832; management: a secretary, treasurer and the medical officer, on whom the trouble of management almost entirely devolves; funds: average annual sum granted by the county for the 3 years ending December 1835, 21 pounds 9s 6d, and for the 3 years ending December 1838, 5 pounds 4s 4d; from private sources: average annual amount of local subscriptions for the 3 years ending December 1835, 21 pounds 9s 6d, for the 3 years ending December 1838, 9 pounds 3s 8d; expenditure: house rent, average annual sum paid for the 3 years ending December 1835, 4 pounds, for the 3 years ending December 1838, 6s 8d; average annual salary paid for the 3 years ending December 1835, 19 pounds 6s 8d; the surgeon has received no salary since 1835; number relieved: average of the 3 years ending December 1835, 577, 3 years ending December 1838, 409; relief afforded: medical advice and medicine; annual average cost of each patient for the 3 years ending December 1835, 1s 6d ha'penny; for the 3 years ending December 1838, 6d 3 farthings.

Public Worship

The following table exhibits the state of public worship, as ascertained from the most authentic sources.

Established Church, exclusive of the Methodists: date of establishment uncertain; extent of accommodation 760, average attendance 500 at morning and 200 at evening service; place of worship: the parish church of St Nicholas in the town of Carrickfergus; service: twice every sabbath and on the principal holy days; congregation increasing; 2 clergy: the dean, who is by office rector of the parish, and 1 curate; the former as Dean of Connor is also rector of the parishes of Raloo and Inver and of the grange of Mallusk; both clergymen reside in this parish.

Wesleyan Methodists: date of establishment 1780; population 60, extent of accommodation 336, average attendance 50; place of worship: Wesleyan chapel in West Street, Carrickfergus; service: twice each sabbath and once each on Tuesdays and Thursdays; congregation stationary; 1 clergyman.

Primitive Wesleyan Methodists: date of establishment 1820; population 20, extent of accommodation 50, average attendance 20; place of worship: the Lancasterian schoolhouse in Lancasterian Street, Carrickfergus; service: once on every alternative sabbath; congregation stationary; no stationed minister in Carrickfergus, visited by one from Antrim.

Primitive Methodists: date of establishment 1837; population 20, extent of accommodation 80, average attendance 20; place of worship: chapel in the Scotch Quarter of Carrickfergus; service: twice on each sabbath and occasionally on Thursdays; congregation decreasing; being a church mission, there is no stationed preacher, visited by one from Belfast.

Wesleyan Association Methodists: date of establishment 1835; population 70, extent of accommodation 50, average attendance 20; place of worship: in a room rented for the purpose in [Blank] Street, Carrickfergus; service: twice each sabbath; congregation increasing slightly; 1 clergyman.

Trinitarian congregation: date of establishment 1611; population 6,000, extent of accommodation 1,000, average attendance 600; place of worship: meeting house in North Street, Carrickfergus; service: twice on each Sunday in the summer, once in winter; congregation increasing; 1 clergyman.

Reformed Presbyterians or Covenanters: date of establishment 1805; population 300, extent of accommodation 186, average attendance 160; place of worship: Covenanting meeting house in Loughmorne; service: once on each sabbath; congregation increasing; 1 clergyman.

Unitarian congregation: date of establishment 1835; population 150, extent of accommodation 260, average attendance 150; place of worship: Unitarian meeting house in the Scotch Quarter, Carrickfergus; service: twice each sabbath during summer, once during winter; congregation increasing; 1 clergyman.

Independents: date of establishment 1816; population 100, extent of accommodation 250, average attendance 60; place of worship: Independent chapel in Castle Street, Carrickfergus; service: twice each sabbath; congregation increasing; 1 clergyman.

Roman Catholics: date of establishment uncertain; population 950, extent of accommodation 300, average attendance 250; place of worship: Roman Catholic chapel, Carrickfergus; service: once each sabbath and once on each Monday; congregation increasing; 2 clergymen, the parish priest and 1 curate; the former is also the parish priest of Larne, Glynn, Inver, Raloo, Kilwaughter, Templecorran, Donegore, Kilroot and Mallusk.

Emigration Table

1836: 8 over 50 years, 1 between 40 and 50, 5 between 30 and 40, 10 between 20 and 30, 14 between 20 and 10, 4 under 10; 1 with between 10 and 20 pounds capital, 41 with under 10 pounds; 2 farmers, 7 tradesmen, 7 labourers, 26 others, 1 Established Church, 37 Presbyterians, 4 Roman Catholics, 20 males, 22 females, total 42.

1837: 1 between 40 and 50 years, 6 between 20 and 30, 2 between 20 and 10, 1 under 10; 1 with between 20 and 40 pounds, 9 with under 10 pounds; 1 tradesman, 3 labourers, 6 others, 10 Presbyterians, 4 males, 6 females, total 10.

1838: 3 over 50 years, 1 between 40 and 50, 2 between 30 and 40, 5 between 20 and 30, 3 between 20 and 10, 3 under 10; 2 with between 20 and 40 pounds capital, 15 with under 10 pounds; 2 farmers, 9 tradesmen, 4 labourers, 2 others, 17 Presbyterians, 7 males, 10 females, total 17.

Wages

Rates of wages in Carrickfergus in the years 1755, 1811, 1822 and 1839.

1755: men's wages per year with diet 3 pounds 8s 3d; mowing per day with diet 9d, without diet 1s 1d; cutting turf with diet 4d, without diet 1s; reaping with diet 4d, without diet 6d ha'penny; setting or raising potatoes with diet 4d, without diet 6d ha'penny.

1811: menservants' wages with diet 12 pounds to 13 pounds, womenservants' wages from 3 pounds to 6 pounds; mowing per day with diet 2s, without diet 2s 8d ha'penny, per acre 7s 7d; cutting turf with diet 1s 1d to 1s 3d, without diet 2s 1d; reaping with diet 1s 1d, without diet 1s 8d; setting or raising potatoes with diet from 1s 1d to 1s 7d, without diet 1s 8d to 2s.

1822: menservants' wages with diet from 6 pounds to 9 pounds; mowing with diet per day 1s 3d to 1s 8d, without diet 2s 1d to 2s 6d; reaping with diet 10d, without diet 1s 3d; setting or raising potatoes with diet from 10d to 1s, without diet 1s 3d.

1839: masons and bricklayers per day 2s 9d, slaters 3s, stucco plasterers 3s 4d, house carpenters 3s, labourers 1s 2d, stone cutters per week 18s to 21s, saddlers 15s to 21s, curriers 20s to 25s, tanners (foremen) 10s to 13s, tanners common 7s, flax dressers (foremen) 25s to 30s, flax dressers common 10s, watch and clockmakers 20s, coopers 15s, boot and shoemakers 15s, bakers with diet 7s.

Provisions and Commodities

Table showing the prices of provisions and commodities in Carrickfergus in the year 1839.

Bacon 6d to 7d per lb.; barley 9s to 10s 6d per 112 lbs; beans 9s to 9s 6d per 112 lbs; beef 4d to 6d per lb.; bran 8s to 10s per 112 lbs; fire-bricks 10s per 100; common bricks 18s to 20s per 1,000; fresh butter 8d to 1s per lb.; Carrickfergus cheese 4d ha'penny to 7d per lb.

Eggs: duck 4d to 6d per dozen; hen 4d to 6d per dozen; turkey 10d to 1s per dozen.

Fruit: apples 2s 6d to 3s 6d per bushel; cherries 5d to 8d per lb.; currants 2d farthing per quart; gooseberries a ha'penny per quart; pears 1s 3d to 5s per 100; plums 1s 8d to 3s 4d per 100.

Fish: cod, 8 to 25 lbs each, 4s to 18s per dozen; clams 6d per dozen; crabs 5d to 7d per dozen; flukes 15s per 120; jenny monnoes 2s per dozen; greylords 5s per dozen; haddock 6s to 18s per dozen; halibut 3s per lb.; hake 3s 6d to 4s 6d per dozen; fresh herrings 4s to 10s per 120; salt herrings a ha'penny each; lithes 5s to 6s per dozen; ling 1s per stone; lobsters 10s to 12s per dozen; mackerel 3s to 5s per dozen; oysters 4s to 8s per 120; plaice 12s to 15s per 120; soles 1s 3d to 1s 8d per pair; scallops 4s per dozen; skates or ray 4s to 6s per dozen; turbot 3s 6d to 8s each; whiting 6d to 9d per dozen.

Fuel: English coals 11s to 16s per ton; Scotch coals 10s to 14s per ton; turf 1s 6d to 2s per gauge.

Lamb 3s 6d to 5s per quarter; lime laid down 1s to 1s 4d per barrel; hay 2s 6d to 4s per cwt; milk: butter 1d to 1d ha'penny per 3 quarts; sweet and new 2d per quart; mutton 4d ha'penny to 6d ha'penny per lb.; oats 7s to 10s per cwt; oatmeal 15s to 18s per cwt.

Fresh pork 4d to 5d per lb.; potatoes 2s 2d to 3s per cwt; poultry: chickens 1s 3d to 2s per pair; ducks, 10d to 1s each; geese 1s 8d to 2s 6d each; hens 8d to 1s each; turkeys 2s 6d to 4s 6d each.

Sand laid down 8d per ton; stone, quarried and laid down, 1s to 1s 3d per ton; straw 2s to 2s 3d per cwt; slates: countesses 97s 6d per 1,000; princes and queen tons 55s per 1,000; ladys 50s per 1,000; ridge tiles 5d each; timber: American red pine 80s per ton; American white pine 66s 8d per ton; 12-feet deals 20 pounds per 120.

Veal: fed 6d per lb.; slink 1s to 1s 3d per quarter.

Commodities at Market

A table of the commodities exposed for sale in Carrickfergus weekly market in the following months in 1839.

Potato baskets, stalls for the sale of: 1 in February, 1 in March.

Beef and mutton, stalls: 5 in February, 7 in

March, 6 in April, 8 in May, 5 in June, 7 in July.

Fresh butter, parcels: 63 in February, 94 in March, 76 in April, 91 in May, 83 in June, 81 in July.

Stable brooms, stalls: 2 in March, 2 in April, 3 in May, 4 in June, 8 in July.

Cabbage plants, stalls: 2 in April.

Dairy utensils, stalls: 1 in February.

Delf and earthenware, stalls: 1 in April, 1 in May, 2 in June.

Ducks, parcels: 11 in March, 8 in June.

Eggs, parcels: 31 in February, 134 in March, 86 in April, 78 in May, 67 in June, 61 in July.

Fish, stalls: 9 in May, 13 in June.

Forest trees, loads of quicks: 1 in February.

Hardware, stalls: 1 in February, 3 in March, 2 in April, 2 in May, 2 in June, 5 in July.

White hampers, stalls: 1 in February.

Hens, parcels: 9 in February, 16 in March, 8 in April, 5 in May, 18 in June, 23 in July.

Hosiery, stalls: 1 in April.

Oats, loads: 1 in February.

Potatoes, loads: 45 in February, 33 in March, 31 in April, 39 in May, 47 in June, 14 in July.

Pigs: live, 18 in February, 13 in March; sucking, load or litters: 1 in April, 1 in May, 2 in June.

Pedlars, stalls: 1 in March, 1 in May, 2 in June, 4 in July.

Farming riddles, stalls: 1 in February, 2 in April.

Live sheep: 2 in March, 2 in April.

Turkeys, parcels: 2 in February, 2 in March, 1 in June.

Thorn quicks, loads: 1 in March.

Fed veal, carcases: 1 in March, 1 in May, 2 in June; slink veal: 2 in March.

Vegetables, stalls: 3 in February, 2 in March, 2 in April, 3 in May, 2 in June, 19 in July.

Turf, loads: 17 in July.

Fruit, stalls: 12 in July.

Corporate and Municipal Officers

1839. Mayor: Marriott Dalway Esquire, Bellahill; aldermen: Marquis of Donegall, David Gordon, Sir Arthur Chichester, Cortland M. Skinner, Thomas B. Adair, Rev. Lord Edward Chichester, Thomas L. Stewart, Joseph McCartney, Thomas Verner, (x) Peter Kirk M.P., Rev. Samuel Smyth, Henry Adair, Lord Belfast, Marriott Dalway, Sir Stephen May, (x) James Cowan.

Burgesses: Richard Dobbs, (x) William Duncan, John Campbell, Charles E. Kirk, Hugh Kennedy, William Stewart, Daniel Gunning,

Foster Coulson, Rev. A. Macartney, R.S. Bradshaw, James Owens, Lord Arthur Chichester, George Joy, (x) John Robinson, (x) Stewart Dunn, Rev. Dean Chaine, (x) Daniel Blair, C. Nicolay, (x) George Forsyth, (x) William Burleigh, (x) John Legg, (x) Stephen R. Rice, Conway E. Dobbs, (x) Valentine Boyd.

NB Those only marked thus (x) are resident within the liberties; the names are placed according to seniority.

Recorder: Conway Edward Dobbs Esquire; sheriffs: George Forsyth M.D. and John Legg; coroner: George Portis Price; town clerk: David Legg; sword-bearer: John Smyth; water-bailiff: James Burns; town serjeants: John Mulholland, James Burns, Andrew Stewart.

Established Clergy

1802, Thomas Graves; in 1811 he exchanged livings with the Rev. Theophilus Blakely; 1811, Theophilus Blakely; in 1824 he removed to Achonry, having exchanged deaneries with the Very Rev. William Green, dean of that place; 1825, Henry Lesley, formerly Rector of Ahoghill, having exchanged livings with the Rev. William Green, late Dean of Achonry, inducted January 29th; 1839, John Chaine, on the resignation of Dean Lesley, inducted 24th March 1839 and read assent and consent on the following day.

Unitarian, Covenanting and Independent Ministers

The first minister ordained to the Unitarian congregation was the Rev. William Malcolm in 1835; he continued in the congregation but 1 year. The present minister, the Rev. James Nixon Porter, was ordained in 1838.

The Rev. John Paul, the present minister, has had charge of the Covenanting congregation since its formation in 1805.

Independent ministers: the first was the Rev. George Hamilton, ordained in 1816; he was succeeded by the Rev. William Flinter in 1817; the Rev. John McAssey, the present minister, in 1838.

Catholic Clergy

The following are the only Roman Catholic clergy who have been known to officiate here since the Reformation: 1717, James Sheil, 1729, Bonr. Boylane, Franciscan friars; 1732, [blank] Moore; 1739, [blank] Cairns; 1757, Edward McIlea; 1761, Felix Scullion; 1788, James McCarey; 1802, Thomas Cassidy; 1813,

Constantine Boyle; 1814, Daniel McMullan; 1820, Arthur O'Neill.

Corporation: Income and Expenditure

Income and expenditure in 1820: amount of rents 335 pounds 19s 5d; expenses: mayor 100 pounds, recorder 10 pounds, sheriffs 40 pounds, extra to the sheriffs 40 pounds, town clerk 7 pounds 10s, sword-bearer 5 pounds, 3 serjeants-at-mace 12 pounds, judge's lodgings 21 pounds 13s 9d, weigh-master 5 pounds 13s 9d, yarn-gauger 1 pound 2s 9d, ringing bells 1 pound 5s, attending sluice 3 pounds 8s 3d, law agent 4 pounds 10s, scavenger 2 pounds, [total] 254 pounds 3s 6d.

Report on County Antrim Gaol by James Boyle, May 1839 to February 1840

SOCIAL ECONOMY

Notes on Criminal Returns

These returns were commenced 9th May 1839 and were completed 22nd February 1840; the time employed with them 207 hours. 22nd February 1840.

In the classification of crime for 1839 there are a few instances in which the numbers convicted and acquitted, when added, will not amount to that of those committed. This difference is to be made up of those untried, as will be found by referring to the detailed extracts from the gaol books.

In the extracts for the same year there are several vacancies in the information as to the education of the committed, and their numbers in the sheet of classification will therefore not be found to correspond. In these instances the prisoners have been transferred from the gaol to the House of Correction in Belfast before they could be examined in the former place.

Unless at periods when there may not be accommodation in the House of Correction for those sentenced to "hard labour," prisoners are not kept to hard labour in the county gaol; and on the other hand, all prisoners sentenced to be or confined in the House of Correction are, except when specified to the contrary, to be considered as being sentenced to imprisonment with hard labour.

The returns for the year 1832 cannot now be obtained. The number of recommittals farther back than 1836 cannot be accurately ascertained. A number of them is given in the returns for 1835,

but it is not quoted in the Memoir, being probably incorrect; or at least, its accuracy cannot by me be vouched for. [Signed] James Boyle, 22nd February 1840.

County Antrim Gaol

The county Antrim gaol has, since the year 1827, been the place of confinement for offenders from the county at large and from the county of the town of Carrickfergus.

The criminal returns appended to this Memoir have been extracted from the gaol records. They embrace (with the exception of the year 1832) a period of 12 years, from the year 1827 to 1839 inclusive, and include the crime of the county for that period, embracing those cases sent to the House of Correction at Belfast, which is principally allotted for the confinement of such prisoners as have been sentenced to hard labour.

In the returns alluded to it will be found that the greatest numbers confined in gaol at one period ranged between 155 in 1835 and 327 in 1838. From these numbers, as also from the returns, soldiers have been excluded. Their numbers, and the expenses incurred by them for a series of years, will be found under a separate form.

Prison Accommodation

By comparing the numbers confined in this prison with the accommodation it should properly afford, as given in its topographical description, it will be found that it is quite impossible to effect a proper classification of prisoners, or to enforce some of the most essential prison regulations; and that, instead of being what it should be, a place for improving their morals and habits of its inmates, it is in fact more calculated to produce a contrary effect.

The limited extent of accommodation quite precludes the [?] commonly necessary classification, let alone that of a more minute and detailed description now generally adopted. Felons hardened in crime, and who in many instances have more than once before been confined here, are associated with those who have committed their first petty offences against the laws, or who are at most but young in iniquity.

The female ward admits of no classification whatever, for in it both debtor and felons are indiscriminately confined and have, on more than one occasion, occupied the same bed.

The following summary of the extent of accommodation in this prison may now fully convey an idea of the foregoing statements: the male felons' ward contains 20 cells, with a bed in each for 3 persons; the minor offenders' ward contains 10 cells, with a bed in each for 3 persons; the female ward, for debtors and criminals, contains 10 cells, with 2 beds in each; 3 persons sleep in each bed. The male debtors' ward contains 3 bedrooms for master debtors; there are 5 beds, for 3 persons each, in each bedroom. The 6 cells in the same ward contain a bed each, for 3 persons.

Extent of Crime

It is fortunate that, in this county, crime is of so mild a nature and so comparatively rare, the crime of murder, though the committals would indicate otherwise, being almost unknown. From the varied manner in which the gaol returns, for the period for which they have quoted, have been kept, uniformity of comparison under their heads cannot be deduced further back than 1835, since which year information as to the state of the prisoners as to education can only be afforded.

During the years 1835, 1836, 1837, 1838 and 1839 the proportion of those who were ignorant to those who were to a greater or less extent educated averaged 1:5 and a third. This may at first seem surprising, and almost at variance with the prevailing impression as to crime being confined to the less civilised and enlightened; but when the proportions of those merely attending the schools in the different parishes of the county to their population, varying from 1:5 to 1:17 and averaging about 1:13, is borne in mind, the proportions will still be found in favour of the educated. Besides, the ignorant are chiefly included among those committed for larceny.

A large proportion of these are females and are under the age of 21, and nearly seven-eighths of them belong [to] those arrested in Belfast. There is but little of what can be termed crime among the educated, most of whom have been committed for assault or riots, and but few of them for felonies. The proportions of female offenders were: 1835, 1:5; 1836, 1:3 and five-eighths; 1837, 1:1 and three-quarters; 1838, 1:2 and seven-eighths; and in 1839, 1:2.

In 1836 the number of recommittals were 191; in 1837, 241; in 1838, 207; and in 1839, 482. In the first year 90 of these were females, in the next 124, [in the next] 88 and in 1839, 222, some of whom had been recommitted 8 times. The re committals were principally confined to those under 30 years of age and to committals for larcenies.

Retributive Justice

By 7th George IV chapter 74, all prisoners supported at the public expense, debtors included, are obliged to work. In this prison the males are employed in breaking stones for the highways, in picking oakum, or in exercising the trades to which they have been brought up. A number are employed in prison duties, such as cleansing the gaol and assisting in the preparation of food. The females are employed at needlework, knitting [and] spinning, or in prison duties. A table showing the number of each employed at each description of work, and the quantity, value and expense of the work performed by the male and female prisoners, will be found appended to this Memoir.

The quantity of stones annually broken averages about 2,200 tons. They either are taken in at 1s per ton unbroken and are sold broken at 1s 2d per ton, or they are brought in by roadmakers, who pay 4d per ton for breaking them. About 6 tons of oakum are annually picked; it is brought in at 12 pounds and is sold picked at 18 pounds per ton.

The prison dresses and bedding are all made and repaired by the prisoners. The female work is performed at similarly low prices. A large quantity of a finer description of work is now done by them, and at present several are employed in making shirts and quilts for exportation to the United States. The low rate of the work performed in the gaol obtains for its inmates a constant supply. The wages seem exceedingly and unnecessarily low, but the intention is more to keep the prisoners employed and to make their residences a place of punishment, than to derive any profit or emolument from it. Pursuant to the same act, each prisoner receives one-third of his earnings, which is handed to him on his discharge from gaol.

The only punishments which have been found necessary in enforcing discipline are solitary confinement and the withdrawal of supper. The want of sufficient accommodation precludes the enforcement of the silent system.

Notwithstanding its crowded state, the gaol has been comparatively free from sickness and quite so from contagious or infectious complaints. The utmost attention is paid to cleanliness and to ventilation. The following numbers of sick cases have annually occurred since 1832, viz. 1832, 47; 1833, 40; 1834, 50; 1835, 54; 1836, 104; 1837, 120; and in 1839, 136.

Diet

The diet is what is termed "mixed diet." From June till October each prisoner receives 4 lbs of potatoes and 1 pint of buttermilk for dinner; during the remainder of the year he receives 4 lbs of potatoes and 1 pint of sweet milk for dinner. For breakfast the allowance is half a lb. of oatmeal stirabout and 1 pint of new milk. The average daily expense of each prisoner's diet (in 1839) was 3 pounds 7s 8d; in 1836, '37 and '38 it was 3 pounds 5s 8d.

Dress

There is not any regular prison costume. Those only who require clothes are clad in those supplied by the gaol. The suit consists of a brown fustian jacket and trousers, upon which their number is stamped in large white letters. The prison shoes have thick wooden soles shod with iron. The females wear a petticoat, bed-gown and cap supplied by the gaol. The cost of a male dress is 14s 4d ha'penny and of a female dress 8s 2d.

Education

Very great attention is paid towards both the moral and intellectual instruction of the prisoners. The instruction of those confined in it was first introduced into the gaol in 1828 and has since been carefully attended to. There are at present (August 1839) 185 prisoners, of whom 147 are receiving instruction. Of the pupils, 44 are females and 103 males.

The males are divided into 3 classes, namely the adult and juvenile felons, and the minor offenders' classes. The first consists of 39, the second of 24 and the third of 40 pupils. They are taught by the same master in their respective wards. Their intellectual education consists in spelling, reading and writing. The books of the Board of National Education are used. Their moral education is confined to reading the Scriptures (of both versions), no catechism being taught. The prisoners are also regularly visited by their respective chaplains.

The instruction of the female prisoners was commenced in 1823. It consists in spelling and reading the books of the Board of National Education. They are also taught knitting, plain needlework, flowering and quilting. The females are included in 1 class. Their instruction is conducted by the matron and deputy matron. Their moral education is similar to that of the males. A statement of the gaol schools in a tabular form will be found later.

Prison Management

Though the prison is so very limited in its accommodation, still as to cleanliness and neatness, in its internal keeping and regularity in its system of management it is perhaps by few excelled. Every attention, consistent with its regulations, seems to be paid to the wants of the prisoners; and its arrangements as to discipline and management seem to be conducted systematically.

The Board of Superintendence appointed for its supervision consists of 12 members, who mostly reside in the neighbourhood of Carrickfergus. They should meet once a month at least, but their meetings are few and far between and seldom occur, except when some unavoidable business calls them together.

The following extracts from the reports of the Inspector-General of Prisons will perhaps more fully and satisfactorily describe the state of this institution and account for its very imperfect state, as respects accommodation.

1836: "It is gratifying to state that, so far as the officers are concerned, every duty is attended to: cleanliness, economy, regularity at meals, school instruction, work at stone-breaking, and as much good order as practicable in the absence of classification and single cells at night. The arrangements made by the local inspector and governor are very creditable to them. A boy class has been established which promises well, and the female classes are enlarged and attended to by a qualified matron and assistant. The books are regularly kept, and the sick carefully attended to by the medical officer."

The report for 1837 states: "At the last assizes for Carrickfergus, in consequence of a communication made by the judge to the county grand jury, a committee was appointed, consisting of 3 grand jurors, to communicate with the inspector-general and to report upon the best means of providing adequate prison accommodation for the county Antrim.

I had in consequence the satisfaction of meeting the members of that committee on the day of my inspecting the House of Correction, and I trust from the view they seemed to take with me on the subject, they may recommend the grand jury to leave the county gaol as it now is, but to be confined to the safe custody of untried criminals and debtors, and to build a house of correction at Belfast to contain all convicted criminals.

At present an average of half of the convicted cases undergo imprisonment at the House of Correction. The average number within the present year has been 25, the maximum 150 prisoners. It would therefore appear that to make the House of Correction to provide separate cells for the whole of the convicted, 300 would be necessary. There are but 36 cells in the present House of Correction and it would be vain any new and expensive building, as an addition to the present one or new site would be necessary."

Another cause is assigned for the apparent apathy respecting the enlargement of the prison accommodation of this county: by the municipal bill at present under the consideration of the legislature, it is proposed to give Belfast a separate jurisdiction of its own, whereby the gaol of the county Antrim would relieved of half the annual number of its inmates and be quite equal to the proper accommodation of the prisoners from the county at large.

Officers' Salaries

Salaries of the officers connected with the county Antrim gaol: governor 276 pounds 18s 6d, clergyman of the Established Church 36 pounds 18s 6d, clergyman of the Presbyterian Church 36 pounds 18s 6d, clergyman of the Roman Catholic Church 36 pounds 18s 6d, local inspector 96 pounds 6s 2d, physician and surgeon 74 pounds, deputy governor and clerk 45 pounds, matron 18 pounds, deputy matron 27 pounds 13s 10d, schoolmaster 22 pounds, hospital nurse 35 pounds, 8 turnkeys 30 pounds each, lamp-lighter 13 pounds 17s, [total] 989 pounds 11s.

The governor, deputy governor, matron, deputy matron, hospital nurse and the turnkeys reside in the gaol and, with the exception of the governor, receive rations.

Number of Prisoners

Statement of the greatest number confined at one time in the following years, viz. 1831, 283; 1832, 220; 1833, 182; 1834, 184; 1835, 155; 1836, 231; 1837, 306; 1838, 327; and in 1839, 324; the least number in the last year was 112.

A statement of the number of soldiers confined in the country Antrim gaol, and of the sums drawn for their subsistence: 1830, 2 soldiers, 13s 6d; 1831, 10 soldiers, 4 pounds 18s 6d; 1832, 12 soldiers, 5 pounds 7s 6d; 1833, 16 soldiers, 12 pounds 4s; 1834, 24 soldiers, 16 pounds 4s; 1835, 17 soldiers, 7 pounds 5s 9d; 1836, 10 soldiers, 4 pounds 7s 9d; 1837, 21 soldiers, 6 pounds 14s 6d; 1838, 23 soldiers, 10 pounds 1s 3d; 1839, 15 soldiers, 6 pounds 10s 6d; total: 150 soldiers, 74 pounds 7s 3d.

Gaol: Economical Return

[Table contains the following headings: year, average number confined, expenditure subdivided by different items, cost of male and female work, total annual cost, profits on male and female work].

1836, 213 confined; officers' salaries 637 pounds 18s 8d, diet 359 pounds 5s 2d 3 farthings, fuel 90 pounds 10s, soap and candles 24 pounds 8s, straw 12 pounds 3s 10d, medicine 56 pounds 9s 7d, stationery and furniture 66 pounds 13s 1d ha'penny, male clothing 60 pounds 8s 9d, female clothing 17 pounds 3s 8d, repairs 54 pounds 2s 3d ha'penny, sundries 54 pounds 4s 7d, cost of male work 98 pounds 13s 11d, female work 17 pounds 19s 6d ha'penny, total annual cost 2,276 pounds 5s 9d ha'penny; profit on male work 47 pounds 19s 10d, on female work 32 pounds 18s 1d ha'penny.

1837, 205 confined; officers' salaries 960 pounds 11s 1d, diet 1,104 pounds 11s 9d, fuel 110 pounds, soap and candles 30 pounds 14s 2d, straw 18 pounds 9s 9d, medicine 70 pounds, stationery and furniture 104 pounds 10s 2d ha'penny, male clothing 54 pounds 2s 8d, female clothing 16 pounds 18s 1d ha'penny, repairs 68 pounds 14s 6d ha'penny, sundries 77 pounds 17s 9d ha'penny, cost of male work 145 pounds 11s 3d ha'penny, female work 32 pounds 9s 3d ha'penny, total annual cost 2,617 pounds 11s 2d; profit on male work 40 pounds 8s 8d, on female work 35 pounds 8s 2s.

1838, [blank] confined; officers' salaries 960 pounds 11s 1d, total annual cost 2,575 pounds 11s 8d 3 farthings.

1839, 226 confined; officers' salaries 961 pounds 4s 2d, diet 1,042 pounds 3d, fuel 90 pounds, soap and candles 36 pounds 11s 6d, straw 10 pounds, medicine 77 pounds 19s 8d, stationery and furniture 74 pounds 12s 11d ha'penny, male clothing 60 pounds 18s 8d, female clothing 22 pounds 5s 4d ha'penny, repairs 66 pounds 2d ha'penny, sundries 59 pounds 16s 6d, cost of male work 167 pounds 12s 11d, female work 38 pounds 13s 10d ha'penny, total annual cost 2,798 pounds 6s 9d ha'penny; profit on male work 252 pounds 5s 2d, on female work 88 pounds 19s 7d ha'penny.

Table of Hard Work

1836, males: 1 carpenter, 7 other trades, 78 stone breakers, 14 prison duties, 64 unemployed or sick, total 166; females: 23 needlework, 12 knitting and spinning, 3 other prison duties, 9 unemployed or sick, total 47; total number of prisoners 213.

1837, males: 2 carpenters, 2 tailors, 2 shoemakers, 5 other trades, 50 stone breakers, 15 prison duties, 68 unemployed or sick, total 164; females: 8 needlework, 16 knitting and spinning, 4 other prison duties, 13 unemployed or sick, total 41; total number of prisoners 205.

1838: [blank].

1839, males: 2 carpenters, 2 tailors, 3 shoemakers, 9 other trades, 106 stone breakers, 30 unemployed or sick, total 152; females: 44 needlework, 24 knitting and spinning, 4 washing, 5 other prison duties, 9 unemployed or sick, total 86; total number of prisoners 238.

Gaol: Schools

[Table contains the following headings: name of class, intellectual and moral education, number of pupils subdivided by age, sex and religion, name and religion of teachers, when established].

Adult felons: intellectual education: spelling, reading and writing; the books of the Board of National Education, only 8 learn writing; moral education: the prisons are visited by their respective chaplains, Authorised and Douai Versions of Scriptures taught daily; pupils: 39 above 15 years, total 39, all male, 4 Established Church, 6 Presbyterians, 29 Roman Catholics; teacher John Larmour, Presbyterian; established 1820.

Juvenile felons: intellectual education: same as above and also *Thompson's Arithmetic*; 7 learn arithmetic and 10 learn writing; moral education: same as above; pupils: 12 under 10 years, 2 between 10 and 15, 10 above 15, total 24, all male, 8 Established Church, 3 Presbyterians, 13 Roman Catholics; same teacher; established 1820.

Minor offenders: intellectual education: same as above; 10 learn arithmetic and 9 learn writing; moral education: same as above; pupils: 40 above 15 years, total 40, all male, 10 Established Church, 8 Presbyterians, 22 Roman Catholics; same teacher; established 1820.

Female: intellectual education: spelling and reading books of the Board of National Education, plain needlework, flowering, quilting and knitting; moral education: same as above; pupils: 10 under 10 years, 34 above 15, total 44, all female, 11 Established Church, 7 Presbyterians, 26 Roman Catholics; teacher Mrs Orr, Presbyterian (the matron), assisted by Miss Margaret Morgan and some ladies of Carrickfergus; established 1823.

[Total pupils]: males, 12 under 10 years, 2 between 10 and 15, 89 above 15, total 103; females, 10 under 10 years, 34 above 15, total 44; total number of pupils 147, 33 Established Church, 24 Presbyterians, 90 Roman Catholics.

Criminal Return in 1839

Records of Prisoners

[Table contains the following headings: number, name, age, religion, crime, number of times recommitted, sentence or acquittal, commutation of punishment, state of education, date of committal].

1, John Armstrong, 27, Presbyterian, murder, acquitted, can read, 1st January.

2, Mary Armstrong, 33, Presbyterian, murder, no prosecution, can read, 1st January.

3, William Ross, 28, Presbyterian, arson, acquitted, can read and write, 1st January.

4, Skeffington Robinson, 17, Presbyterian, assault, recommitted twice, imprisoned 1 month or pay 2 pounds, can read, write and cipher, 1st January.

5, Thomas Thompson, 26, Presbyterian, assault, imprisoned 4 months, can read, write and cipher, 4th January.

6, Archibald Morrison, 35, Presbyterian, assault, imprisoned 3 months, can read and write, 4th January.

7, James Craig, 22, Presbyterian, assault, imprisoned 1 month, can read, 12th January.

8, William Bleake, 28, Roman Catholic, assault, imprisoned 6 weeks on bail to keep peace, can read and write, 12th January.

9, Edward Forfey, 24, Roman Catholic, assault, imprisoned 6 weeks on bail to keep peace, can read, 12th January.

10, David Gilliland, 20, Presbyterian, assault, imprisoned 6 weeks on bail to keep peace, can read, 12th January.

11, Francis Gilliland, 23, Presbyterian, assault, imprisoned 6 weeks on bail to keep peace, can read, 12th January.

12, Joseph Shanks, 15, Presbyterian, assault, imprisoned 2 weeks, can read, 12th January.

13, Joseph McErlane, 25, Presbyterian, assault, imprisoned 1 year in House of Correction, can spell, 14th February.

14, George Kerr, 18, Established Church, assault, imprisoned 1 month in gaol or pay 1 pound 2s 6d, can read, 14th February.

15, James McGarrell, 32, Roman Catholic, assault, imprisoned 1 month in gaol or pay 1 pound 5s, can read and write, 14th February.

16, John McCaigny, 48, Roman Catholic, assault, acquitted, can spell, 23rd February.

17, Francis O'Neill, 40, Roman Catholic, assault, recommitted twice, transported for 7 years, can read, 1st March.

18, Adam McGarry, 27, Roman Catholic, assault, acquitted, can read, 1st March.

19, James Kennedy, 21, Presbyterian, assault, imprisoned 3 months and fined 2 pounds, can read, 14th March.

20, James Magee, 70, Roman Catholic, assault, acquitted, can read, 21st March.

21, Robert Lindsay, 30, Presbyterian, assault, no prosecution, can read and write, 22nd March.

22, Hamilton Morrell, 26, Presbyterian, assault, imprisoned 1 month or pay 2 pounds 12s, can read and write, 27th March.

23, Robert Morrell, 21, Presbyterian, assault, imprisoned 1 month or pay 2 pounds 12s, can read, write and cipher, 27th March.

24, James Kennedy, 22, Roman Catholic, assault, imprisoned 12 months and bail to keep peace, can read, write and cipher, 5th April.

25, James Dillon, 27, Roman Catholic, assault, imprisoned 2 months and bailed to keep pace, can read, write and cipher, 5th April.

26, James McDade, 21, Roman Catholic, assault, imprisoned 6 weeks in House of Correction, can read, write and cipher, 5th April.

27, Hugh McCann, 37, Roman Catholic, assault, imprisoned 1 fortnight in gaol, can read and write, 5th April.

28, Daniel Mooney, 25, Roman Catholic, assault, imprisoned 3 months, can read, write and cipher, 5th April.

29, James Sloan, 57, Presbyterian, assault, acquitted, can read and write, 5th April.

30, Francis McNaghten, 18, Roman Catholic, assault, imprisoned 6 weeks and pay 1 pound 12s, can read, 5th April.

31, James Mitchell, 18, Roman Catholic, assault, imprisoned 6 weeks and pay 1 pound 12s, can read, 5th April.

32, William Goodall, 17, Established Church, assault, no bill found, can read, write, do arithmetic, 13th May.

33, John Galbraith, 44, Established Church, assault, find bail to keep peace, can read, write, do arithmetic, 14th May.

34, Sarah Pinkerton, 25, Roman Catholic, assault, no bill found, can read, 16th May.

35, John Slevin, 26, Roman Catholic, assault, imprisoned 6 months in House of Correction, can read and write, 3rd June.

36, John Henry Matear, 60, Established Church, assault, detained as insane, can read and write, 11th June.

37, Robert Johnson, 23, Roman Catholic, assault, imprisoned 1 month, can read and write, 25th June.

38, Patrick Loughrey, 22, Presbyterian, assault, 4 months in House of Correction, can read, 28th June.

39, John McKillen, 28, Presbyterian, assault, 3 months in House of Correction, can read, 28th June.

40, James Stewart, 27, Presbyterian, assault, imprisoned 1 fortnight in goal, can read and write, 11th July.

41, Robert Henderson, 27, Presbyterian, assault, recommitted once, no bill found, can read and write, 20th July.

42, John Etherton, 30, assault, imprisoned 10 days, can read and write, 22nd July.

43, James Ferris, 28, Established Church, assault, pay 1 pound 2s or imprisoned 1 month, can read, 2nd August.

44, William Thompson, 14, Established Church, assault, imprisoned 1 fortnight, can read, 3rd August.

45, William McKeever, 19, Roman Catholic, assault, acquitted, can read, 15th August.

46, James McAuley, 19, Roman Catholic, assault, acquitted, can read, 15th August.

47, Archibald McAuley, 30, Roman Catholic, assault, acquitted, can read, 15th August.

48, Mary McDermott, 24, Roman Catholic, assault, recommitted once, transmitted to lunatic asylum, can read, 19th August.

49, John McAllister, 19, Established Church, assault, recommitted once, imprisoned 3 months, can read and write, 2nd September.

50, John Ryan, 70, Roman Catholic, assault, not tried, can read and write, 2nd September.

51, Margaret Drummond, 22, Roman Catholic, assault, no bill found, can read, 7th September.

52, Neal Hilland, 56, Roman Catholic, assault, not tried, can read, 10th September.

53, Patrick Tracy, 29, Roman Catholic, assault, bail to appear, can read and write, 12th September.

54, John Bryson, 62, Established Church, assault, imprisoned 1 month, can read, 14th September.

55, James Cherry, 20, Presbyterian, assault, not tried, can read, write and cipher, 26th September.

56, William Wiley, 67, Presbyterian, assault, imprisoned 1 month, can read and write, 18th October.

57, John Gilmour, 19, Presbyterian, assault,

imprisoned 6 months and pay 5 pounds, can read and write, 18th October.

58, John Walker, 24, Presbyterian, assault, pay 3 pounds or imprisoned 3 months, alphabet, 18th October.

59, John Spence, 22, Roman Catholic, assault, pay 11s or imprisoned 1 fortnight in House of Correction, can read and write, 18th October.

60, James Shaw, 48, Presbyterian, assault, keep peace for 3 years, no bail, can read, write and cipher, 18th October.

61, John McCully, 30, Roman Catholic, assault, recommitted twice, keep peace for 3 years, no bail, can read, 18th October.

62, John Rea, 26, Roman Catholic, assault, imprisoned 3 weeks, can spell, 18th October.

63, Robert McKay, 20, Established Church, assault, pay 1 pound or imprisoned 1 month, can read, 18th October.

64, John O'Neill, 18, Presbyterian, assault, pay 1 pound or imprisoned 1 month, can read and write, 18th October.

65, Edward McVey, 19, Roman Catholic, assault, recommitted once, imprisoned 2 months, can read, write and cipher, 28th October.

66, William Peake, 45, Established Church, assault, recommitted twice, pay 1 pound or imprisoned 1 month, can read and write, 28th October.

67, Hugh McCann, 30, Roman Catholic, assault, imprisoned 3 months, alphabet, 31st October.

68, Robert Gribben, 23, Established Church, assault, imprisoned 1 month, can read, 31st October.

69, Edward Gribben, 36, Established Church, assault, imprisoned 1 month, can read, 31st October.

70, Thomas Gribben, 27, Established Church, assault, imprisoned 1 month, can read, 31st October.

71, Francis McCloskey, 58, Roman Catholic, assault, recommitted twice, imprisoned 1 month and bail to keep peace, can read and write, 5th November.

72, Margaret Armstrong, 29, Presbyterian, assault, insane, to be discharged, can read, 30th November.

73, Alice McQuade, 27, Roman Catholic, assault, 3 months for assault, 9 months for theft, imprisoned in House of Correction, can read, 30th November.

74, James Fullar, 19, Established Church, assault, imprisoned 6 months in House of Correction, can read, 31st December.

75, Thomas Adams, 18, Established Church, assault, recommitted twice, imprisoned 6 months in House of Correction, can read, 31st December.

76, Owen McCulloch, 36, Roman Catholic, assaulting a constable, 1 month in House of Correction, can read, 4th January.

77, William Ferguson, 27, Established Church, assault with intent to rape, 6 months in House of Correction, alphabet, 29th April.

78, John Ryan, 70, Roman Catholic, assault with intent to rape, not tried, can read and write, 2nd September.

79, Robert Smyth, 37, Established Church, assault and rescue, imprisoned for 3 months, can read and write, 27th June.

80, David McGambly, 40, Established Church, assault and rescue, imprisoned 1 fortnight, can read and write, 5th April.

81, Edward Hughes, 60, Roman Catholic, assault and rescue, no bill found, can read, 19th October.

82, James Lavery, 30, Roman Catholic, assault and rescue, imprisoned 1 month, can read, write and cipher, 31st October.

83, Samuel Dooley, 28, Presbyterian, attempt to poison, acquitted, can read and write, 4th January.

84, Edward Philips, 35, Roman Catholic, bigamy, admitted to bail, can read and write, 19th July.

85, Daniel McAuley, 18, Roman Catholic, breach of fishery laws, imprisoned 2 months, can read and write, 21st June.

86, James McAlea, 21, Established Church, breach of fishery laws, imprisoned 2 months, can spell, 21st June.

87, John Kinney, 19, Roman Catholic, breach of fishery laws, imprisoned 2 months, can read, 21st June.

88, Robert Magowan, 66, Presbyterian, breach of excise laws, fined 25 pounds, can read, write and cipher, 3rd January.

89, John Reid, 56, Roman Catholic, breach of excise laws, fined 12 pounds 10s, can read and write, 18th January.

90, Margaret McIlvennon, 37, Presbyterian, breach of excise laws, fined 12 pounds 10s, can read, 26th January.

91, Mary Taylor, 31, Roman Catholic, breach of excise laws, fined 50 pounds, ignorant, 10th February.

92, Samuel Milligan, 28, Presbyterian, breach of excise laws, fined 50 pounds, can read, write and cipher, 16th March.

93, John Kennedy, 76, Presbyterian, breach of

excise laws, fined 12 pounds 10s, can read, write and cipher, 18th March.

94, John Lynd, 38, Presbyterian, breach of excise laws, fined 5 pounds, can read, write and cipher, 4th April.

95, John Diamond, 33, Roman Catholic, breach of excise laws, fined 5 pounds, can read and write, 25th April.

96, John Bingham, 34, Established Church, breach of excise laws, fined 10 pounds, can read, write and cipher, 30th April.

97, Alexander W. Brown, 43, Presbyterian, breach of excise laws, recommitted once, fined 30 pounds, can read, write and cipher, 15th May.

98, Alexander W. Brown, 43, Presbyterian, breach of excise laws, recommitted twice, fined 25 pounds, can read, write and cipher, 10th June.

99, John McNeice, 48, Presbyterian, breach of excise laws, fined 5 pounds, can read, write and cipher, 21st June.

100, Charles McIlvennon, 43, Roman Catholic, breach of excise laws, fined 12 pounds 10s, can read, write and cipher, 27th June.

101, Mary Sweeny, 28, Roman Catholic, breach of excise laws, fined 2 pounds or imprisoned 4 days, can read, 10th August.

102, Hugh Watson, 34, Presbyterian, breach of excise laws, fined 50 pounds, can read, write and cipher, 2nd September.

103, Robert Friar, 25, Established Church, breach of excise laws, fined 5 pounds, can read, write and cipher, 18th September.

104, Richardson Taylor, 40, Roman Catholic, breach of excise laws, fined 5 pounds, can read, write and cipher, 26th September.

105, William Mullan, 37, Roman Catholic, breach of excise laws, fined 6 pounds or imprisoned 3 months, can read, 4th October.

106, John Mote, 42, Presbyterian, breach of excise laws, recommitted once, fined 6 pounds or imprisoned 3 months, ignorant, 24th October.

107, Eliza McKillop, 55, Established Church, breach of excise laws, fined 12 pounds 10s, can spell, 21st December.

108, Edward Heron, 40, Presbyterian, breach of excise laws, recommitted once, fined 25 pounds, can read and write, 25th December.

109, Patrick Magill, 42, Roman Catholic, breach of game laws, recommitted once, pay 20 pounds or imprisoned 1 month, can read and write, 22nd September.

110, John McDonald, 28, Roman Catholic, breach of game laws, pay 20 pounds or imprisoned 3 months, can read and write, 14th November.

111, James Griffin, 37, Roman Catholic, breach of revenue laws, imprisoned 3 months, can read and write, 1st February.

112, George Williamson, 20, Roman Catholic, breach of revenue laws, imprisoned 3 months, can read, write and cipher, 1st February.

113, John Cummings, 19, Established Church, breach of revenue laws, pay 100 pounds or imprisoned 6 months, can read, write and cipher, 1st February.

114, Edward Howel, 20, Established Church, breach of revenue laws, pay 100 pounds or imprisoned 6 months, ignorant, 27th July.

115, Charles Douglass, 16, Presbyterian, breach of revenue laws, pay 100 pounds or imprisoned 6 months, ignorant, 27th July.

116, Colin Greer, 49, Presbyterian, breach of revenue laws, can read, write and cipher, 30th August.

117, Andrew O'Neill, 50, Established Church, breach of revenue laws, pay 100 pounds or imprisoned 6 months, can read, 13th September.

118, Peter Barker, 40, Roman Catholic, breach of revenue laws, pay 25 pounds or imprisoned 6 months, 2nd November.

119, Lucy Wiley, 23, Presbyterian, breaking windows, recommitted once, no bill found, can read, 2nd August.

120, Adam Moore, 19, Established Church, burglary, transported for 7 years, can read, write and cipher, 17th July.

121, John McGarrety, 15, Established Church, burglary, transported for 7 years, can spell, 17th July.

122, William Mullan, 50, Established Church, burglary, not tried, can read, write and cipher, 6th December.

123, John Doherty, 29, Roman Catholic, burglary, not tried, can spell, 6th December.

124, Denis McKay, 45, Established Church, burglary, not tried, can read and write, 6th December.

125, James Darragh, 19, Roman Catholic, burglary, not tried, alphabet, 6th December.

126, Bridget McKavanagh, 22, Roman Catholic, Queen's evidence, committed as a Queen's evidence, alphabet, 6th December.

127, James Lees, 18, Established Church, conspiring to rob, not tried, can spell, 16th September.

128, Edward McIlroy, 22, Roman Catholic, conspiring to rob, not tried, can read, 16th September.

129, Richard Fleming, 66, Presbyterian, cow-stealing, recommitted once, not tried, can read and write, 9th November.

130, James Irwin Davis, 32, Presbyterian, cutting timber, recommitted 3 times, no bill found, can read, write and cipher, 3rd May.

131, Michael Kelly, 74, Established Church, cutting timber, recommitted once, pay 12s 6d or imprisoned 1 month, can read and write, 22nd November.

132, William Gresham, 21, Presbyterian, deserter, can read and write, 8th January.

133, James Ramsay, 21, Established Church, deserter, can read, 15th January.

134, John Mooney, 20, Presbyterian, deserter, can read and write, 16th January.

135, Edward McCreevy, 28, Presbyterian, deserter, can read, write and cipher, 9th February.

136, George Saunders alias Elliott, 20, Established Church, deserter, can read, 14th February.

137, Anthony McGinty, 25, Roman Catholic, deserter, can read and write, 12th March.

138, Robert Dunlop, 22, Presbyterian, deserter, can read and write, 23rd March.

139, James Weir, 20, Presbyterian, deserter, can read and write, 9th July.

140, Charles Doherty, 21, Roman Catholic, deserter, recommitted once, can read and write, 13th July.

141, Robert Darragh, 22, Roman Catholic, deserter, can read and write, 18th June.

142, George Dennis, 18, Established Church, deserter, can read and write, 23rd July.

143, Charles Connor, 19, Established Church, deserter, can read and write, 29th July.

144, Robert McQuillan, 21, Roman Catholic, deserter, can read and write, 1st August.

145, James Magill, 18, Established Church, deserter, can spell, 7th August.

146, Patrick Griffith, 29, Roman Catholic, deserter, can read, 14th September.

147, James Boyd, 24, Established Church, deserter, can read, 7th October.

148, William Watson, 17, Presbyterian, deserter, can read and write, 19th October.

149, John McIlvennon, 26, Roman Catholic, deserter, can read, write and cipher, 31st October.

150, Mathew Taylor, 19, Roman Catholic, deserter, can read and write, 17th November.

151, William Jones, 21, Roman Catholic, deserter, can read, write and cipher, 16th December.

152, Nancy Agnew, 22, Presbyterian, deserting infants, convicted, discharged, alphabet, 21st April.

153, Maryanne Paterson, 24, Presbyterian, deserting infants, acquitted, ignorant, 24th September.

154, Jane Connolly, 23, Presbyterian, deserting infants, imprisoned 2 months, ignorant, 7th October.

155, John McFall, 26, Roman Catholic, drunkenness, pay 5s or imprisoned 48 hours, can read, 24th January.

156, Michael Mooney, 63, Roman Catholic, drunkenness, recommitted twice, pay 5s or imprisoned 48 hours, can read and write, 14th May.

157, Michael Mooney, 63, Roman Catholic, drunkenness, recommitted 3 times, pay 10s or imprisoned 96 hours, can read and write, 9th July.

158, Samuel Brown, 34, Presbyterian, drunkenness, imprisoned 48 hours, can spell, 5th November.

159, William Cunningham, 34, Presbyterian, drunkenness, imprisoned 48 hours, can spell, 5th November.

160, John McClure, 45, Established Church, embezzlement, fined 3 pounds 12s or imprisoned 1 month, can read and write, 23rd February.

161, Ellen Corrigan, 20, Roman Catholic, embezzlement, no bill found, ignorant, 18th March.

162, James Harbison, 37, Presbyterian, embezzlement, fined 3 pounds 2s or imprisoned 1 month, can read and write, 19th April.

163, Samuel Crean, 33, Established Church, embezzlement, fined 5 pounds or imprisoned 2 months, can read and write, 17th May.

164, Hugh Martin, 40, Established Church, embezzlement, fined 5 pounds or imprisoned 1 month, can read, 14th June.

165, Samuel McFarland, 18, Presbyterian, embezzlement, imprisoned 1 month, can read, write and cipher, 7th August.

166, John McCann, 40, Roman Catholic, embezzlement, fined 3 pounds or imprisoned 1 month, alphabet, 20th September.

167, Silas Gill, 60, Established Church, embezzlement, acquitted, can read, write and cipher, 2nd November.

168, William McAuley, 30, Roman Catholic, forfeited recognizances, to be discharged on being 3 months in gaol, can read, write and cipher, 21st June.

169, Samuel Ash, 50, Presbyterian, forfeited recognizances, to be discharged on paying 5 pounds, can read and write, 14th January.

170, John Shiels, 24, Presbyterian, frauds in obtaining money under false pretences, recommitted once, imprisoned 1 month in House of Correction, can spell, 23rd February.

171, James Paterson, 20, Presbyterian, obtaining money under false pretences, no bill found, can read, write and cipher, 4th April.

172, Edward Boyd, 47, Established Church, obtaining money under false pretences, imprisoned 3 months, can read, 3rd August.

173, John Skeffington, 40, Roman Catholic, obtaining money under false pretences, acquitted, can read, 6th August.

174, Mary Blackwood, 21, Established Church, obtaining money under false pretences, imprisoned 2 months, alphabet, 15th August.

175, Mary Morton, 20, Presbyterian, obtaining money under false pretences, imprisoned 3 months in House of Correction, can read, 22nd August.

176, Hugh Nixon, 37, Established Church, obtaining money under false pretences, imprisoned 2 months in House of Correction, can read, 22nd August.

177, William Minnis, 21, Presbyterian, obtaining money under false pretences, imprisoned 1 month in gaol, can spell, 30th August.

178, John McDonnell, 26, Roman Catholic, obtaining money under false pretences, no bill found, can read, write and cipher, 16th November.

179, John MacArtney, 25, Roman Catholic, obtaining money under false pretences, no bill found, can read, write and cipher, 6th December.

180, James Longwood, 21, Established Church, obtaining money under false pretences, acquitted, can read, write and cipher, 28th December.

181, Francis McCloskey, 58, Roman Catholic, taking forcible possession, imprisoned 1 month, can read and write, 5th April.

182, Archibald Mooney, 71, Roman Catholic, taking forcible possession, imprisoned 1 month, alphabet, 27th June.

183, Patrick McMullin, 60, Roman Catholic, taking forcible possession, imprisoned 5 months, alphabet, 27th June.

184, Samuel Falloon, 18, Roman Catholic, forgery, imprisoned 4 months, can read and write, 24th May.

185, Charles McCormick, 33, Roman Catholic, forgery, imprisoned 6 months in House of Correction, can read and write, 28th May.

186, Thomas Rainey, 62, Presbyterian, forgery, held to bail, can read and write, 6th September.

187, Edward Grant, 33, Roman Catholic,

forgery, not tried, can read, write and cipher, 20th September.

188, John Stewart, 27, Roman Catholic, forgery, not tried, can read, write and cipher, 29th September.

189, William R. Gooldy, 41, Presbyterian, horse-stealing, imprisoned 1 year in House of Correction, can read and write, 8th March.

190, David Milliken, 20, Presbyterian, horse-stealing, no prosecution, can read and write, 23rd August.

191, Esther Irwin, 48, Presbyterian, house of ill-fame, imprisoned 1 month, can read, 31st October.

192, Alexander McNichol, 41, Presbyterian, illegal procession, to pay 4 pounds or be imprisoned for 3 months, can read, write and cipher, 15th March.

193, William McKinney, 21, Presbyterian, illegal procession, to pay 4 pounds or be imprisoned for 3 months, can read, write and cipher, 15th March.

194, William Cunningham, 30, Presbyterian, illegal procession, to pay 4 pounds or be imprisoned for 3 months, can read, write and cipher, 15th March.

195, James Paul, 27, Presbyterian, illegal procession, to pay 4 pounds or be imprisoned for 3 months, can read, write and cipher, 15th March.

196, James McCormick, 21, Presbyterian, illegal procession, to pay 4 pounds or be imprisoned for 3 months, can read, write and cipher, 15th March.

197, Robert Lesly, 46, Established Church, illegal procession, to pay 4 pounds or be imprisoned for 3 months, can read, write and cipher, 15th March.

198, Alexander Twaddle, 33, Established Church, illegal procession, to pay 4 pounds or be imprisoned for 3 months, can read, write and cipher, 15th March.

199, Robert Smyth, 30, Established Church, illegal procession, to pay 4 pounds or be imprisoned for 3 months, can read, write and cipher, 15th March.

200, Robert McCook, 25, Presbyterian, illegal procession, to pay 4 pounds or be imprisoned for 3 months, can read, write and cipher, 15th March.

201, Chesnut Morrison, 24, Presbyterian, illegal procession, to pay 4 pounds or be imprisoned for 3 months, can read, write and cipher, 15th March.

202, John Lawson, 22, Presbyterian, illegal procession, to pay 4 pounds or be imprisoned for 3 months, can read, write and cipher, 15th March.

203, John McKinney, 18, Established Church, illegal procession, to pay 4 pounds or be imprisoned for 3 months, can read, write and cipher, 15th March.

204, Hugh McQueston, 21, Presbyterian, illegal procession, to pay 4 pounds or be imprisoned for 3 months, can read, write and cipher, 15th March.

205, Samuel Magill, 40, Presbyterian, illegal procession, to pay 4 pounds or be imprisoned for 3 months, can read, write and cipher, 15th March.

206, Robert Hamill, 24, Presbyterian, illegal procession, to pay 4 pounds or be imprisoned for 3 months, can read, write and cipher, 15th March.

207, Samuel Poague, 26, Presbyterian, illegal procession, to pay 4 pounds or be imprisoned for 3 months, can read, write and cipher, 15th March.

208, William McKinstry, 25, Presbyterian, illegal procession, to pay 4 pounds or be imprisoned for 3 months, can read, write and cipher, 15th March.

209, James Houston, 22, Established Church, illegal procession, to pay 4 pounds or be imprisoned for 3 months, can read, write and cipher, 15th March.

210, John Campbell, 55, Presbyterian, illegal procession, to pay 4 pounds or be imprisoned for 3 months, can read, write and cipher, 15th March.

211, Charles Kane, 20, Established Church, illegal procession, to pay 4 pounds or be imprisoned for 3 months, can read, write and cipher, 15th March.

212, George McClelland, 23, Presbyterian, illegal procession, to pay 4 pounds or be imprisoned for 3 months, can read, write and cipher, 15th March.

213, James Forrester, 25, Presbyterian, illegal procession, to pay 4 pounds or be imprisoned for 3 months, can read, write and cipher, 15th March.

214, Samuel Lafferty, 25, Established Church, illegal procession, to pay 4 pounds or be imprisoned for 3 months, can read, write and cipher, 15th March.

215, Robert Fullerton, 36, Presbyterian, illegal procession, to pay 4 pounds or be imprisoned for 3 months, can read, write and cipher, 15th March.

216, Daniel McKeever, 45, Established Church, illegal procession, to pay 4 pounds or be imprisoned for 3 months, can read, write and cipher, 15th March.

217, William Morton, 26, Presbyterian, illegal procession, to pay 4 pounds or be imprisoned for 3 months, can read, write and cipher, 15th March.

218, William Semple, 20, Presbyterian, illegal procession, to pay 4 pounds or be imprisoned for 3 months, can read, write and cipher, 15th March.

219, James Fleming, 23, Established Church, illegal procession, to pay 4 pounds or be imprisoned for 3 months, can read, write and cipher, 15th March.

220, Patrick McIlrath, 35, Established Church, illegal procession, to pay 4 pounds or be imprisoned for 3 months, can read, write and cipher, 15th March.

221, Robert McConaghy, 18, Established Church, illegal procession, to pay 2 pounds or be imprisoned for 2 months, can read, write and cipher, 15th March.

222, Major Smyth, 20, Presbyterian, illegal procession, to pay 2 pounds or be imprisoned for 2 months, can read, write and cipher, 15th March.

223, James McCleery, 26, Presbyterian, illegal procession, to pay 2 pounds or be imprisoned for 2 months, can read, write and cipher, 15th March.

224, William Alexander, 26, Presbyterian, illegal procession, to pay 2 pounds or be imprisoned for 2 months, can read, write and cipher, 15th March

225, Alexander Irwin, 23, Presbyterian, illegal procession, to pay 2 pounds or be imprisoned for 2 months, can read, write and cipher, 15th March.

226, John Magill, 19, Presbyterian, illegal procession, to pay 2 pounds or be imprisoned for 2 months, can read, write and cipher, 15th March.

227, Robert McVeagh, 19, Established illegal procession, to pay 2 pounds or be imprisoned for 2 months, can read, write and cipher, 15th March.

228, Archibald McCleery, 20, Presbyterian, illegal procession, to pay 2 pounds or be imprisoned for 2 months, can read, write and cipher, 15th March.

229, Hugh McCleery, 18, Established Church, illegal procession, to pay 2 pounds or be imprisoned for 2 months, can read, write and cipher, 15th March.

230, James McCart, 28, Presbyterian, illegal procession, to pay 2 pounds or be imprisoned for 2 months, can read, write and cipher, 15th March.

231, Robert Patton, 20, Presbyterian, illegal procession, to pay 4 pounds or be imprisoned for 3 months, can read, write and cipher, 15th March.

232, George O'Neill, 18, Established Church, to pay 2 pounds or be imprisoned for 4 months, can read, write and cipher, 15th March.

233, James Taggart, 20, Presbyterian, felony, imprisoned 6 months in House of Correction, can read, write and cipher, 19th January.

234, James Smyth, 15, Roman Catholic, felony, imprisoned 9 months in House of Correction and whipped 3 times, can spell, 6th May.

235, Hugh McMurray, 16, Established Church, felony, recommitted twice, imprisoned 9 months in House of Correction and whipped 3 times, can read and write, 6th May.

236, Thomas Gilland, 15, Roman Catholic, felony, recommitted 3 times, imprisoned 9 months in House of Correction and whipped 3 times, can read, 6th May.

237, William Short, 16, Roman Catholic, felony, recommitted once, transported for 7 years, imprisoned 18 months, 1 week solitary confinement and hard labour in each month, can read.

238, James McClenaghan, 11, Roman Catholic, felony, transported for 7 years, can read, 1st July.

239, Betty McKillop, 16, Established Church, felony, convicted, discharged by the court, can read, 26th July.

240, Mary McKillop, 20, Established Church, felony, convicted, discharged by the court, ignorant, 26th July.

241, Robert Campbell, 50, Established Church, felony, not tried, can read and write, 1st August.

242, Henry Kerr, 30, Roman Catholic, felony, no prosecution, can read, write and cipher, 15th August.

243, Jane Clark, 13, Roman Catholic, felony, recommitted 3 times, acquitted, can spell, 3rd September.

244, Mary Boyle, 14, Roman Catholic, felony, acquitted, ignorant, 3rd September.

245, William Kidd, 42, Established Church, felony, imprisoned 6 weeks in House of Correction, can read, 16th December.

246, Rachel McBride, 19, Established Church, felony, recommitted 4 times, imprisoned 9 months in gaol, alphabet, 16th December.

247, Mary Doherty, 20, Roman Catholic, felony, 2 months in House of Correction, alphabet, 16th December.

248, Ellen McCollum, 26, Presbyterian, felony, recommitted once, no bill found, alphabet, 17th December.

249, Isabella Chapman, 40, Established Church, felony, acquitted, can read, 17th December.

250, John Savage, 21, Roman Catholic, felony, recommitted once, transported for 7 years, can read, 18th December.

251, Hannah Stuart, 38, Established Church, felony, recommitted twice, transported for 7 years, can read, 19th December.

252, Hugh Nixon, 37, Established Church, felony, recommitted once, acquitted, can read and write, 19th December.

253, John Stevenson, 24, Established Church, felony, imprisoned 3 months in House of Correction, can read and write, 19th December.

254, John Hardy, 32, Roman Catholic, felony, recommitted 4 times, acquitted, can spell, 21st December.

255, Andrew McClure, 17, Presbyterian, felony, imprisoned 9 months, can read, write and cipher, 21st December.

256, John Weir, 17, Presbyterian, felony, imprisoned 9 months, can read, 21st December.

257, William Branagan, 21, Presbyterian, felony, recommitted once, imprisoned 12 months, can spell, 21st December.

258, Robert Robinson, 16, Roman Catholic, felony, imprisoned 9 months, can read, write and cipher, 21st December.

259, John Miller, 16, Established Church, felony, recommitted twice, imprisoned 9 months, can read, write and cipher, 21st December.

260, Jane O'Neill, 35, Presbyterian, felony, recommitted 3 times, acquitted, can read, 21st December.

261, William Henry, 30, Roman Catholic, felony, recommitted once, acquitted, can read and write, 21st December.

262, Abigail Christy, 24, Roman Catholic, felony, imprisoned 3 months in House of Correction, ignorant, 23rd December.

263, John McClelland, 18, Established Church, felony, imprisoned 3 months in House of Correction, alphabet, 23rd December.

264, Anne-Jane Campbell, 22, Established Church, felony, recommitted 5 times, transported for 7 years, can read, 23rd December.

265, Mary McKay, 22, Established Church, felony, recommitted twice, no bill found, can spell, 23rd December.

266, Edward Boyle, 44, Roman Catholic, felony, imprisoned 3 months in House of Correction, can read, 28th December.

267, William Morley, 23, Established Church, larceny from house or shop, imprisoned 12 months in House of Correction, can read, write and cipher, 3rd January.

268, Alexander McLaughlin, 25, Established Church, larceny from house or shop, imprisoned 10 months in House of Correction, can read and write, 4th January.

269, Kitty-Anne Linn, 17, Roman Catholic,

larceny from house or shop, recommitted once, imprisoned 9 months in House of Correction, 4th January.

270, John Fleming, 47, Presbyterian, larceny from house or shop, imprisoned 2 months in House of Correction, 4th January.

271, Thomas McIlroy, 19, Roman Catholic, larceny from house or shop, recommitted once, imprisoned 2 months in House of Correction, 4th January.

272, Richard Connolly, 39, Roman Catholic, larceny from house or shop, imprisoned 3 months in House of Correction, 4th January.

273, Mary Linton, 40, Established Church, larceny from house or shop, imprisoned 3 months in House of Correction, 4th January.

274, Jane Quinn, 18, Roman Catholic, larceny from house or shop, imprisoned 4 months in gaol, can spell, 12th January.

275, Mary Daly, 50, Roman Catholic, larceny from house or shop, imprisoned 2 months in gaol, ignorant, 12th January.

276, Patrick Devlin, 45, larceny from house or shop, imprisoned 1 month in gaol, ignorant, 12th January.

277, John Kelly, 29, Roman Catholic, larceny from house or shop, recommitted 3 times, imprisoned 4 months in gaol, can read, 12th January.

278, Bernard McMannus, 16, Roman Catholic, larceny from house or shop, recommitted twice, transported for 7 years, can read and write, 12th January.

279, John Gallagher, 47, Roman Catholic, larceny from house or shop, recommitted once, no bill found, ignorant, 14th January.

280, Robert Sheals, 14, Roman Catholic, larceny from house or shop, acquitted, can read, write and cipher, 15th January.

281, John Leathem, 26, Established Church, larceny from house or shop, recommitted 5 times, no bill found, ignorant, 16th January.

282, William Miller, 21, Established Church, larceny from house or shop, recommitted once, no bill found, ignorant, 16th January.

283, Roger McKinley, 39, Roman Catholic, larceny from house or shop, imprisoned 3 months in House of Correction, can read and write, 19th January.

284, Hugh Gilmore, 15, Roman Catholic, larceny from house or shop, imprisoned 4 months' hard labour in gaol, can read and write, 21st January.

285, John Clark, 16, Roman Catholic, larceny from house or shop, recommitted 7 times, acquitted, can read, write and cipher, 21st January.

286, Bridget McFadden, 28, Roman Catholic, larceny from house or shop, imprisoned 3 months in House of Correction, ignorant, 24th January.

287, John Hutchinson, 14, Established Church, larceny from house or shop, 3 months' hard labour in gaol, can read and write, 9th February.

288, Susan Ram, 37, Roman Catholic, larceny from house or shop, imprisoned 4 months' hard labour in gaol, can read, 11th February.

289, John Johnson, 28, Roman Catholic, larceny from house or shop, imprisoned 6 months in House of Correction, can read, write and cipher, 11th February.

290, Anne Butler, 24, Roman Catholic, larceny from house or shop, no bill found, ignorant, 11th February.

291, Hugh Riddel, 31, Roman Catholic, larceny not otherwise described, recommitted 3 times, acquitted, can read and write, 13th February.

292, Barbara Davis, 26, Established Church, larceny, recommitted twice, acquitted, can read, 13th February.

293, Jane Burnside, 17, Established Church, larceny, recommitted 3 times, imprisoned 6 months' hard labour in gaol, can read, write and cipher, 14th February.

294, Robert Curry, 17, Roman Catholic, larceny, transported for 7 years, can read, 16th February.

295, Mary Jane [Iles?], 21, Established Church, larceny, imprisoned 3 months' hard labour in gaol, can read, 16th February.

296, Charlotte Hutchinson, 25, Established Church, larceny, died suddenly in gaol, can read, 16th February.

297, William Rainey, 14, Roman Catholic, larceny, imprisoned 2 months in House of Correction, can read and write, 18th February.

298, John Hagan, 15, Roman Catholic, larceny, imprisoned 2 months in House of Correction, can read and write, 18th February.

299, Rose Forsyth, 34, Presbyterian, larceny, imprisoned 2 months in House of Correction, can read, 20th February.

300, Mary Wilson, 31, Established Church, larceny, recommitted once, no bill found, can read, 21st February.

301, Agnes Robinson, 38, Presbyterian, larceny, imprisoned 10 weeks in House of Correction, can read, 23rd February.

302, John Robinson, 8, Presbyterian, larceny, imprisoned 10 weeks in House of Correction, can read, 23rd February.

303, Mary Scullion, 17, Roman Catholic, larceny, no bill found, can read, 25th February.

304, Christina Benson, 45, Presbyterian, larceny, recommitted twice, imprisoned 3 months' hard labour in gaol, can read, 25th February.

305, Margaret Thomson, 45, Presbyterian, larceny, recommitted once, imprisoned 12 months' hard labour in gaol, can read, 25th February.

306, Eliza Fowler, 17, Roman Catholic, larceny, imprisoned 3 months' hard labour in gaol, can read, 25th February.

307, Mary Hamil, 18, Roman Catholic, larceny, no bill found, can read, 28th February.

308, Jane Dalzell, 18, Established Church, larceny, no bill found, can read, 28th February.

309, Mary Anne Hamilton, 20, Presbyterian, larceny, recommitted once, imprisoned 6 months in House of Correction, can read, 28th February.

310, Mary Kelly, 28, Roman Catholic, larceny, recommitted 3 times, transported for 10 years, ignorant, 1st March.

311, Mary Simpson, 30, Roman Catholic, larceny, imprisoned 12 months, can read, 1st March.

312, Bella Stuart, 23, Established Church, larceny, transported for 10 years, can read, 1st March.

313, Catherine Ritchy, 18, Roman Catholic, larceny, recommitted twice, no prosecution, can spell, 1st March.

314, John Crow, 65, Established Church, larceny, recommitted once, acquitted, can read and write, 14th March.

315, James David, 32, Presbyterian, larceny, recommitted 3 times, acquitted, can read, 14th March.

316, Daniel Magee, 36, Established Church, larceny, acquitted, can read and write, 14th March.

317, James Ewing, 15, Presbyterian, larceny, recommitted 4 times, transported for 7 years, can read and write, 19th March.

318, James Greer, 16, Established Church, larceny, imprisoned 2 months' hard labour in gaol, can read and write, 23rd March.

319, Margaret McBirnie, 22, Established Church, larceny, recommitted once, transported for 7 years, can read, 26th March.

320, Mathew McAteer, 30, Established Church, larceny, imprisoned 5 months' hard labour in gaol, can spell, 27th March.

321, Philip Larkin, 50, Established Church, larceny, no bill found, can read and write, 27th March.

322, John Larkin, 21, Established Church, larceny, no bill found, can read and write, 27th March.

323, Robert McCrea, 36, Presbyterian, larceny, acquitted, can read and write, 2nd April.

324, John McCrea, 36, Presbyterian, larceny, acquitted, can read, 2nd April.

325, Bridget O'Neill, 31, Roman Catholic, larceny, recommitted 4 times, acquitted, ignorant, 2nd April.

326, John Hagan, 16, Roman Catholic, larceny, imprisoned 3 months in House of Correction, can read, 2nd April.

327, Henry Mulholland, 22, Roman Catholic, larceny, recommitted twice, transported for 7 years, can read, write and cipher, 3rd April.

328, Archibald McCook, 55, Established Church, larceny, imprisoned 3 weeks in House of Correction, 5th April.

329, Charles Neilly, 32, Roman Catholic, larceny, imprisoned 1 month in House of Correction, 5th April.

330, George Murdock, 25, Presbyterian, larceny, imprisoned 6 months in House of Correction.

331, Mary Stuart, 19, Roman Catholic, larceny, imprisoned 3 weeks in House of Correction, can spell, 5th April.

332, John Bradley, 17, Roman Catholic, larceny, imprisoned 3 weeks in House of Correction, 5th April.

333, John Nowlan, 25, Roman Catholic, larceny, imprisoned 4 months in House of Correction, can read, write and cipher, 16th April.

334, George Neill, 11, Established Church, larceny, imprisoned 3 months in gaol, can spell, 16th April.

335, William Holmes, 15, Roman Catholic, larceny, imprisoned 6 months' hard labour in gaol, can spell, 16th April.

336, Charles Lennox, 22, Roman Catholic, larceny, transported for 7 years, can read, write and cipher, 16th April.

337, Stuart Park, 29, Presbyterian, larceny, recommitted once, imprisoned 6 months' hard labour in gaol, can read and write, 19th April.

338, Robert Burns, 18, Roman Catholic, larceny, imprisoned 8 months in House of Correction, can read, 19th April.

339, Robert Shiels, 14, Roman Catholic, recommitted 4 times, imprisoned 8 months in House of Correction and to be whipped, can read and write, 20th April.

340, John Jordan, 15, Roman Catholic, larceny, imprisoned 8 months in House of Correction and to be whipped, can read, 20th April.

341, James Turbitt, 28, Presbyterian, larceny, acquitted, can read and write, 14th June.

342, Jane Suffern, 29, Presbyterian, larceny, acquitted, can read, 2nd July.

343, James Smyth, 44, Presbyterian, larceny, recommitted once, transported for 10 years, 2nd July.

344, Samuel Thompson, 38, Presbyterian, larceny, imprisoned for 3 months in House of Correction, 2nd July.

345, John Charters, 48, Presbyterian, larceny, imprisoned 8 months in House of Correction, 2nd July.

346, William Blair, 19, Presbyterian, larceny, imprisoned 1 month in gaol, can read and write, 11th July.

347, Susan Smyth, 24, Established Church, larceny, 2 months in gaol, can read and write, 11th July.

348, Jane Magee, 40, Established Church, larceny, imprisoned 1 month in House of Correction, ignorant, 11th July.

349, John Gilmour, 27, Roman Catholic, larceny, recommitted once, imprisoned 6 months in gaol, alphabet, 11th July.

350, Isabella McLaughlin, 20, Roman Catholic, larceny, recommitted once, imprisoned 2 months, can spell, 11th July.

351, Eliza Dunlop, 48, Established Church, larceny, imprisoned 1 month, can spell, 11th July.

352, Mary Farrel, 42, Roman Catholic, larceny, imprisoned 4 months in House of Correction, can read, 27th June.

353, Alexander Smyth, 43, Presbyterian, larceny, imprisoned 8 months in House of Correction, can read and write, 27th June.

354, Thomas Johnson, 18, Roman Catholic, larceny, recommitted once, transported for 7 years, commuted to 18 months' imprisonment in gaol, 1 week's hard labour and solitary in every 3 months, 11th July.

355, Margaret Robinson, 27, Presbyterian, larceny, imprisoned 1 month in gaol, alphabet, 11th July.

356, Penelope McIlroy, 60, Roman Catholic, larceny, imprisoned 1 month in gaol, alphabet, 18th October.

357, Mary McIlroy, 17, Roman Catholic, larceny, 3 months in House of Correction, can read, 18th October.

358, Mary Mahon, 17, Presbyterian, larceny, to pay 2 pounds or 2 months in House of Correction, can read, 18th October.

359, Rachel Mahon, 20, Presbyterian, larceny, to pay 2 pounds or 2 months in House of Correction, can read, 18th October.

360, Anne Mahon, 14, Presbyterian, larceny, to pay 2 pounds or 2 months in House of Correction, alphabet, 18th october.

361, William Telford, 14, Roman Catholic, larceny, recommitted 4 times, transported for 7 years, can read, write and cipher, 25th October.

362, Patrick Hare, 31, Established Church, larceny, transported for 7 years, can read, write and cipher, 25th October.

363, James McArtney, 46, Established Church, larceny, imprisoned 1 month in gaol, can read and write, 30th October.

364, Robert Watt, 16, Roman Catholic, larceny, recommitted 3 times, transported for 7 years, 30th October.

365, Ellen King, 24, Established Church, larceny, recommitted 4 times, can spell, 30th October.

366, Owen Scott, 56, Roman Catholic, larceny, imprisoned 1 month in gaol, alphabet, 30th October.

367, Mary Anne Johnson, 19, Roman Catholic, larceny, imprisoned 3 months in gaol, can spell, 30th October.

368, William McAllister, 18, Presbyterian, larceny, imprisoned 6 weeks in House of Correction, can read, 15th November.

369, Anne Gallagher, 15, Roman Catholic, larceny from the person, recommitted 3 times, 12 months in gaol, can spell, 1st January.

370, Mary Macay, 19, Established Church, larceny from the person, to pay 5 pounds 8s 6d or 14 days in gaol, can read, 1st January.

371, Margaret McIlroy, 45, Presbyterian, larceny from the person, recommitted once, imprisoned 6 months in House of Correction, can read, 1st January.

372, Ellen Cooper, 19, Roman Catholic, larceny from the person, recommitted once, imprisoned 8 months in House of Correction, alphabet, 31st January.

373, James Hagan, 9, Roman Catholic, larceny from the person, recommitted once, imprisoned 4 months' hard labour in gaol, alphabet, 2nd February.

374, Margaret O'Brien, 26, Roman Catholic, larceny from the person, recommitted twice, no bill found, can spell, 6th February.

375, Mary Liddy, 13, Roman Catholic, larceny from the person, acquitted, ignorant, 15th February.

376, James Turbit, 28, Presbyterian, larceny

from the person, acquitted, can read and write, 14th June.

377, Charles Magennis, 18, Roman Catholic, larceny from the person, not tried, can read, 7th December.

378, Thomas Hunter, 18, Roman Catholic, petty larceny, recommitted once, imprisoned 4 months in House of Correction, can spell, 19th January.

379, William Fleming, 18, Established Church, petty larceny, recommitted once, transported for 7 years, can read, write and cipher, 25th January.

381, Maria Magennis, 39, Established Church, petty larceny, recommitted once, imprisoned 2 months in House of Correction, ignorant, 31st January.

382, Phoebe Morrell, 20, Established Church, petty larceny, recommitted once, no bill found, can spell, 7th February.

383, Jane Montgomery, 28, Presbyterian, petty larceny, no bill found, can read, 7th February.

384, James Morrell, 19, Established Church, petty larceny, imprisoned 3 months in House of Correction, alphabet, 8th March.

385, Mary McDowell, 20, Established Church, petty larceny, acquitted, can read, 8th March.

386, Isabella McLoughlin, 20, Roman Catholic, petty larceny, imprisoned 3 months' hard labour in gaol, can spell, 11th March.

387, Catherine Hogan, 21, Roman Catholic, petty larceny, acquitted,
ignorant, 11th March.

388, Hugh McCarnaghan, 22, Roman Catholic, petty larceny, recommitted once, acquitted, 11th March.

389, John McVey, 24, Roman Catholic, petty larceny, acquitted, 11th March.

390, John Carson, 38, Presbyterian, petty larceny, acquitted, can read and write, 14th March.

391, Jane Miller, 26, Established Church, petty larceny, acquitted, can read, write and cipher, 18th March.

392, James Greenlees, 28, Roman Catholic, petty larceny, acquitted, can read, 18th March.

393, Margaret Magee, 71, Presbyterian, petty larceny, no prosecution, can read, 25th March.

394, Patrick O'Hare, 24, Roman Catholic, petty larceny, imprisoned 3 months in goal, can read and write, 3rd April.

395, Thomas Bradley, 13, Roman Catholic, petty larceny, recommitted 3 times, transported for 7 years, can read and write, 3rd April.

396, Margaret Wade, 33, Presbyterian, petty larceny, imprisoned 3 months, can read, 3rd April.

397, David Devlin, 25, Roman Catholic, petty larceny, recommitted twice, 4 months in House of Correction, can read and write, 4th April.

398, James Stuart, 24, Presbyterian, petty larceny, acquitted, can read, 12th April.

399, John McGahy, 23, Established Church, petty larceny, no bill found, can read, write and cipher, 16th April.

400, Patrick Burn, 15, Roman Catholic, petty larceny, imprisoned 2 months, can spell, 21st April.

401, Jane Cullen, 15, Roman Catholic, petty larceny, recommitted once, acquitted, can spell, 21st April.

402, Denis Griffin, 14, Roman Catholic, petty larceny, imprisoned 4 months in House of Correction, can spell, 24th April.

403, Ellen Duffin, 20, Established Church, petty larceny, acquitted, can spell, 26th April.

404, Thomas Devlin, 56, Roman Catholic, petty larceny, no bill found, alphabet, 26th April.

405, John Bell, 37, Presbyterian, petty larceny, transported 14 years, can read, write and cipher, 26th April.

406, Margaret Matear, 25, Established Church, petty larceny, imprisoned 3 months in House of Correction, alphabet, 29th April.

407, Susan Sandes, 17, Established Church, petty larceny, imprisoned 5 months in House of Correction, can spell, 29th April.

408, Catherine McCormick, 19, Roman Catholic, petty larceny, imprisoned 3 months in House of Correction, ignorant, 29th April.

409, Margaret McLoughlin, 30, Established Church, petty larceny, imprisoned 3 months in gaol, alphabet, 30th April.

410, Martha Creggan, 21, Established Church, petty larceny, no bill found, can read, 1st May.

411, Joseph Grey, 16, Established Church, petty larceny, recommitted twice, imprisoned 8 months in House of Correction and whipped, can read, 1st May.

412, Martha Madden, 35, Established Church, petty larceny, recommitted 7 times, 1 month in gaol, can spell, 3rd May.

413, Robert Magee, 14, Presbyterian, petty larceny, recommitted once, transported for 7 years, can read and write, 3rd May.

414, Sarah Cassidy, 50, Roman Catholic, petty larceny, imprisoned 1 month in gaol, alphabet, 6th May.

415, Margaret Scullion, 17, Roman Catholic, petty larceny, 5 months in House of Correction, can read, 6th May.

416, Samuel Quinn, 18, Roman Catholic, petty

larceny, 5 months in House of Correction, can spell, 6th May.

417, Eliza Hamill, 19, Roman Catholic, petty larceny, no bill found, can read, 6th May.

418, Anne Jane Alexander, 30, Presbyterian, petty larceny, 2 months in gaol, can spell, 7th May.

419, Martha Carrol, 21, Established Church, petty larceny, recommitted twice, acquitted, can read, 7th May.

420, Margaret Gibson, 19, Established Church, petty larceny, imprisoned 3 months in House of Correction, can spell, 7th May.

421, Betty Hunter, 18, Established Church, petty larceny, imprisoned 12 months in House of Correction, ignorant, 10th May.

422, William Hunter, 21, Presbyterian, petty larceny, imprisoned 12 months in gaol, can read and write, 10th May.

423, Alexander Nelson, 56, Established Church, petty larceny, acquitted, can read and write, 10th May.

424, Robert Osborne, 62, Established Church, petty larceny, acquitted, alphabet, 10th May.

425, James McAghron, 40, Roman Catholic, petty larceny, no bill found, can read and write, 10th May.

426, William Gamble, 18, Presbyterian, petty larceny, imprisoned 3 months in House of Correction, can read and write, 10th May.

427, Alice McQuade, 27, Roman Catholic, petty larceny, discharged by proclamation, alphabet, 11th May.

428, Jane Patton, 59, Presbyterian, petty larceny, imprisoned 6 months in House of Correction, can spell, 13th May.

429, William Morrison, 21, Roman Catholic, petty larceny, recommitted once, imprisoned 6 months in House of Correction, alphabet, 13th May.

430, James Murray, 19, Roman Catholic, petty larceny, imprisoned 9 months in House of Correction, can spell, 13th May.

431, Francis Thompson, 12, Roman Catholic, petty larceny, imprisoned 2 months in gaol, can read, 13th May.

432, James Harkness, 27, Established Church, petty larceny, transported for 14 years, can read, write and cipher, 14th May.

433, Michael Haughey, 22, Roman Catholic, petty larceny, imprisoned 3 months in House of Correction, can read and write, 17th May.

434, John Rodgers, 18, Established Church, petty larceny, imprisoned 3 months in House of Correction, can read and write, 17th May.

435, Francis King, 32, Roman Catholic, petty larceny, acquitted, can read, 17th May.

436, Hugh Murray, 28, Roman Catholic, petty larceny, no bill found, can read, write and cipher, 7th May.

437, Betty Kelly, 48, Established Church, petty larceny, recommitted 3 times, transported for 7 years, ignorant, 8th May.

438, Mary McDonald, 23, Roman Catholic, petty larceny, no bill found, can read, 20th May.

439, Sarah Moore, 18, Presbyterian, petty larceny, no bill found, can spell, 20th May.

440, Mary Young, 22, Roman Catholic, petty larceny, no bill found, 24th May.

441, Biddy O'Neill, 31, Roman Catholic, petty larceny, recommitted 5 times, no bill found, can read, 24th May.

442, Samuel Hawthorne, 40, Presbyterian, petty larceny, recommitted once, imprisoned 6 months, can read, 25th May.

443, Edward Bute, 35, Roman Catholic, petty larceny, acquitted, can read, 25th May.

444, Anne Jane Burrows, 32, Presbyterian, petty larceny, no bill found, can read, 25th May.

445, Ellen King, 24, Established Church, petty larceny, recommitted 3 times, acquitted, can spell, 27th May.

446, Bella Hunter, 27, Established Church, petty larceny, recommitted twice, no bill found, alphabet, 27th May.

447, Thomas Monagh, 15, Presbyterian, petty larceny, imprisoned 9 months in House of Correction, can read, 28th May.

448, Mary Logan, 40, Roman Catholic, petty larceny, imprisoned 6 weeks in House of Correction, ignorant, 29th May.

449, Jane Lavery, 54, Roman Catholic, petty larceny, recommitted once, transported for 7 years, ignorant, 30th May.

450, Eliza Mullen, 25, Presbyterian, petty larceny, imprisoned 1 month in gaol, can read, 1st June.

451, Patrick McCormick, 18, Roman Catholic, petty larceny, recommitted 3 times, no bill found, can spell, 1st June.

452, Daniel McClean, 14, Established Church, petty larceny, no bill found, can read, write and cipher, 3rd June.

453, John Crone, 26, Roman Catholic, petty larceny, imprisoned 3 months in House of Correction, can read, 3rd June.

454, Sarah Kane, 10, Established Church, petty larceny, acquitted, can read, 3rd June.

455, James Donaldson, 29, Established Church, petty larceny, imprisoned 4 months in

House of Correction, can read and write, 3rd June.

456, Barbara Davis, 24, Presbyterian, petty larceny, recommitted twice, 9 months in House of Correction, can read, 3rd June.

457, Anne Cosgrave, 26, Established Church, petty larceny, no prosecution, ignorant, 3rd June.

458, John McBride, 18, Roman Catholic, petty larceny, imprisoned 6 weeks in gaol, can spell, 7th June.

459, John Hardy, 32, Roman Catholic, petty larceny, recommitted 3 times, imprisoned 4 months in House of Correction, can spell, 10th June.

461, Catherine Crilly, 25, Roman Catholic, petty larceny, recommitted once, no bill found, can spell, 10th June.

462, Thomas Hunter, 18, Roman Catholic, petty larceny, recommitted twice, transported for 7 years, can read, 10th June.

463, Jane McLoughlin, 40, Roman Catholic, petty larceny, imprisoned 4 months in House of Correction, can spell, 11th June.

464, Margaret McKowen, 53, Established Church, petty larceny, recommitted once, imprisoned 2 months in House of Correction, alphabet, 14th June.

465, Charles Magennis, 18, Roman Catholic, petty larceny, imprisoned 4 months in House of Correction, can read, write and cipher, 14th May.

466, William Neal, 51, Established Church, petty larceny, imprisoned 4 months in House of Correction, can read, write and cipher, 14th June.

467, Robert Neal, 15, Established Church, petty larceny, acquitted, can read and write, 14th June.

468, Samuel Fisher, 18, Roman Catholic, petty larceny, acquitted, alphabet, 14th June.

469, Peggy Reilly, 18, Roman Catholic, petty larceny, imprisoned 6 months in House of Correction, ignorant, 14th June.

470, John McGrath, 11, Established Church, petty larceny, no prosecution, alphabet, 15th June.

471, Francis McKenna, 22, Roman Catholic, petty larceny, recommitted once, imprisoned 2 months in House of Correction, can read and write, 15th June.

472, Edward Loughran, 31, Roman Catholic, petty larceny, no bill found, can spell, 15th June.

473, Catherine Colgan, 34, Roman Catholic, petty larceny, imprisoned 4 months in House of Correction, can read, 15th June.

474, John Latham, 26, Established Church, petty larceny, recommitted 6 times, no bill found, can read and write, 17th June.

475, Edward Kelly, 21, Roman Catholic, petty larceny, no bill found, can read and write, 17th June.

476, Thomas Barret, 22, Roman Catholic, petty larceny, recommitted once, no bill found, 17th June.

477, Mary Headly, 30, Presbyterian, petty larceny, recommitted twice, no bill found, 17th June.

478, John McCavock, 38, Roman Catholic, petty larceny, acquitted, can read, write and cipher, 17th June.

479, James McCullogh, 14, Roman Catholic, petty larceny, imprisoned 1 month in gaol, can read and write, 18th June.

480, Eliza Rice, 29, Roman Catholic, petty larceny, recommitted twice, acquitted, ignorant, 18th June.

481, Patrick McCleery, 23, Roman Catholic, petty larceny, recommitted once, imprisoned 3 months in House of Correction, can read, 25th June.

482, Sarah Green, 12, Roman Catholic, petty larceny, imprisoned 3 months in House of Correction, can read, 25th June.

483, John Mulholland, 23, Roman Catholic, petty larceny, imprisoned 2 months in goal, can spell, 25th June.

484, Ellen McDonnell, 14, Established Church, petty larceny, acquitted, can read, 25th June.

485, Thomas Kane, 15, Established Church, petty larceny, imprisoned 3 months in gaol, can read and write, 25th June.

486, John Ward, 28, Roman Catholic, petty larceny, imprisoned 6 months in House of Correction, can read, 25th June.

487, Robert Hawton, 42, Presbyterian, petty larceny, imprisoned 2 months in gaol, can read, 29th June.

488, James Doorish, 17, Established Church, petty larceny, acquitted, can spell, 29th June.

489, Bridget McKenna, 23, Roman Catholic, petty larceny, no prosecution, can read, 29th June.

490, Andrew McAleavy, 16, Roman Catholic, petty larceny, recommitted 4 times, transported for 7 years, can read and write, 29th June.

491, Margaret McDonnell, 42, Presbyterian, petty larceny, imprisoned 2 months in gaol, can read, 1st July.

492, Edward Davison, 16, Established Church, petty larceny, imprisoned 6 months in House of Correction, can read, 1st July.

493, John Crossan, 54, Roman Catholic, petty larceny, recommitted 6 times, imprisoned 9 months' hard labour in gaol, can read, 13th July.

494, Anne Devine, 27, Established Church, petty larceny, recommitted twice, no bill found, can spell, 13th July.

495, Thomas Quinn, 13, Presbyterian, petty larceny, imprisoned 3 months in gaol, can read, write and cipher, 13th July.

496, Susan Sheppard, 23, Established Church, petty larceny, imprisoned 6 months in House of Correction, ignorant, 13th July.

497, Marianne Morrison, 21, Established Church, petty larceny, imprisoned 6 months in House of Correction, ignorant, 13th July.

498, William Tully, 50, Presbyterian, petty larceny, recommitted 4 times, acquitted, can read, 13th July.

499, Edward Boyd, 45, Established Church, petty larceny, imprisoned 2 months in House of Correction, ignorant, 13th July.

500, Andrew Bell, 43, Established Church, petty larceny, imprisoned 1 month in House of Correction, can read, write and cipher, 13th July.

501, Eliza Kerr, 39, Established Church, petty larceny, recommitted once, imprisoned 1 month in House of Correction, can read, 16th July.

502, Margaret Watt, 12, Roman Catholic, petty larceny, imprisoned 2 months in House of Correction, ignorant, 17th July.

503, Mary Maxwell, 53, Presbyterian, petty larceny, imprisoned 1 month in House of Correction, ignorant, 17th July.

504, Mary O'Neill, 19, Roman Catholic, petty larceny, no bill found, ignorant, 17th July.

505, James Glenn, 35, Presbyterian, petty larceny, no bill found, can read, 19th July.

506, William Bowdell, 18, Established Church, petty larceny, acquitted, can read and write, 20th July.

507, Anne Craig, 40, Established Church, petty larceny, imprisoned 4 months in House of Correction, ignorant, 20th July.

508, Thomas Hamil, 12, Roman Catholic, petty larceny, acquitted, alphabet, 23rd July.

509, Alexander Paterson, 15, Established Church, petty larceny, acquitted, can spell, 23rd July.

510, Edward Donaghy, 13, Roman Catholic, petty larceny, acquitted, can read, 23rd July.

511, William Frame, 48, Presbyterian, petty larceny, imprisoned 1 month's hard labour in gaol, can read, write and cipher, 23rd July.

512, Mary McCarrol, 27, Established Church, petty larceny, recommitted once, convicted, discharged by the court, ignorant, 1st August.

513, Mary Johnston, 23, Roman Catholic, petty larceny, recommitted once, imprisoned 2 months in House of Correction, can spell, 3rd August.

514, Jane Cullen, 15, Roman Catholic, petty larceny, recommitted twice, no bill found, can spell, 3rd August.

515, Sarah Jordan, 16, Roman Catholic, petty larceny, no bill found, can read, 3rd August.

516, Biddy Craig, 14, Roman Catholic, petty larceny, recommitted once, no bill found, ignorant, 3rd August.

517, Samuel Cochran, 23, Established Church, petty larceny, recommitted twice, acquitted, can spell, 3rd August.

518, John Gregory, 13, Established Church, petty larceny, recommitted twice, imprisoned 6 months in House of Correction, can read and write, 5th August.

519, William Gamble, 18, Established Church, petty larceny, recommitted once, acquitted, can spell, 5th August.

520, Henry Gribben, 18, Roman Catholic, petty larceny, imprisoned 6 months in gaol, can read and write, 8th August.

521, John Hagan, 16, Roman Catholic, petty larceny, recommitted once, acquitted, can read, 8th August.

522, Robert Watt, 16, Roman Catholic, petty larceny, acquitted, can read, write and cipher, 8th August.

523, Daniel Higgins, 16, Roman Catholic, petty larceny, imprisoned 6 months in House of Correction, can read, write and cipher, 9th August.

524, Rose Blair, 41, Presbyterian, petty larceny, recommitted once, imprisoned 14 days, can read, 9th August.

525, Eliza Scott, 39, Roman Catholic, petty larceny, recommitted 3 times, no bill found, can read, 13th August.

526, Andrew Greenwell, 20, Roman Catholic, petty larceny, imprisoned 1 month's hard labour in gaol, can read, 13th August.

527, Ann Kearns, 25, Roman Catholic, petty larceny, recommitted once, imprisoned 4 months in House of Correction, alphabet, 13th August.

528, Edward Cullen, 17, Roman Catholic, petty larceny, recommitted 6 times, transported for 7 years, can read, 13th August.

529, Nancy Wright, 23, Roman Catholic, petty larceny, recommitted 3 times, no bill found, can read, 13th August.

530, Robert Wilson, 36, Presbyterian, petty larceny, imprisoned 6 months in House of

Correction, can read, write and cipher, 13th August.

531, Margaret Frazer, 40, Roman Catholic, petty larceny, recommitted once, imprisoned 3 months in House of Correction, can spell, 13th August.

532, William Neill, 20, Established Church, petty larceny, imprisoned 9 months in House of Correction, can read and write, 15th August.

533, Margaret O'Brien, 26, Roman Catholic, petty larceny, recommitted 3 times, transported for 7 years, ignorant, 15th August.

534, Maryann Smyth, 65, Roman Catholic, petty larceny, imprisoned 3 months in House of Correction, can read, 15th August.

535, John Connor, 21, Roman Catholic, petty larceny, recommitted once, imprisoned 4 months in gaol, can read, write and cipher, 17th August.

536, Henry McCann, 16, Roman Catholic, petty larceny, imprisoned 1 month in House of Correction, can read, write and cipher, 17th August.

537, William Riddle, 43, Presbyterian, petty larceny, no bill found, alphabet, 17th August.

538, Catherine Mulholland, 18, Roman Catholic, petty larceny, no bill found, alphabet, 19th August.

539, John Hughes, 26, Roman Catholic, petty larceny, imprisoned 9 months in House of Correction, can read, 19th August.

540, Sarah Hunter, 39, Roman Catholic, petty larceny, imprisoned 9 months in House of Correction, alphabet, 19th August.

541, James Adams, 18, Presbyterian, petty larceny, no bill found, can read, write and cipher, 20th August.

542, Margaret Goodwin, 22, Presbyterian, petty larceny, no bill found, can read, 20th August.

543, Eliza Rice, 29, Roman Catholic, petty larceny, recommitted twice, transported for 7 years, alphabet, 21st August.

544, Hugh Rooney, 16, Roman Catholic, petty larceny, imprisoned 6 weeks' hard labour in gaol, can read, 26th August.

545, Sarah Perry, 39, Presbyterian, petty larceny, imprisoned 4 months in House of Correction, alphabet, 26th August.

546, William Forsyth, 40, Established Church, petty larceny, convicted, discharged by the court, can read, write and cipher, 26th August.

547, Mary McDowell, 24, Presbyterian, petty larceny, imprisoned 6 weeks in gaol, can read, 28th August.

548, John McDonnell, 13, Established Church,

petty larceny, imprisoned 1 month in gaol, can read, 29th August.

549, Henry McDermott, 13, Roman Catholic, petty larceny, recommitted once, no bill found, can read and write, 29th August.

550, Margaret Morrison, 77, Presbyterian, petty larceny, imprisoned 1 month, can read, 3rd September.

551, James Kearns, 21, Established Church, petty larceny, acquitted, can read, 6th September.

552, Martha Boyd, 48, Roman Catholic, petty larceny, imprisoned 1 month, can read, 6th September.

553, Mary Boyd, 27, Roman Catholic, petty larceny, recommitted once, imprisoned 2 months, alphabet, 6th September.

554, Susan Butler, 25, Established Church, petty larceny, imprisoned 3 months, alphabet, 6th September.

555, Eliza Ponsonby, 19, Established Church, petty larceny, acquitted, can read, 6th September.

556, Maryann McClelland, 31, Presbyterian, petty larceny, recommitted 3 times, imprisoned 8 months in House of Correction, alphabet, 10th September.

557, Margaret Smyth, 19, Established Church, petty larceny, recommitted once, imprisoned 12 months in gaol, can spell, 11th September.

558, Betty McGregor, 40, Roman Catholic, petty larceny, acquitted, ignorant, 11th September.

559, William Davis, 35, Roman Catholic, petty larceny, imprisoned 1 month, can read and write, 14th September.

560, Mary Davis, 25, Roman Catholic, petty larceny, imprisoned 1 month, can read, 14th September.

561, Anne Doherty, 50, Roman Catholic, petty larceny, imprisoned 2 months, ignorant, 16th September.

562, James Morrow, 46, Presbyterian, petty larceny, recommitted 4 times, no bill found, can read and write, 16th September.

563, Jane Devlin, 17, Established Church, petty larceny, no bill found, ignorant, 17th September.

564, Catherine McVea, 38, Roman Catholic, petty larceny, imprisoned 2 months in House of Correction, ignorant, 17th September.

565, Catherine McGarrity, 21, Roman Catholic, petty larceny, imprisoned 6 months in gaol, ignorant, 17th September.

566, Daniel McNeill, 53, Presbyterian, petty larceny, acquitted, can read, write and cipher, 17th September.

567, Francis Scott, 16, Presbyterian, petty larceny, imprisoned 3 months, can read, 19th September.

568, Thomas McBlaine, 20, Presbyterian, petty larceny, imprisoned 6 months, can read, write and cipher, 19th September.

569, John McWilliams, 24, Presbyterian, petty larceny, recommitted once, transported for 7 years, can read, 20th September.

570, Anne Dunstan, 23, Established Church, petty larceny, transported for 7 years, alphabet, 20th September.

571, James McDonald, 32, Roman Catholic, petty larceny, recommitted 3 times, imprisoned 12 months in House of Correction, can read, write and cipher, 20th September.

572, Eliza McCartney, 30, Presbyterian, petty larceny, imprisoned 6 months in House of Correction, ignorant, 20th September.

573, Patrick Loughran, 21, Roman Catholic, petty larceny, acquitted, can read, write and cipher, 26th September.

574, Charles McAteer, 50, Roman Catholic, petty larceny, imprisoned 3 months, can spell, 26th September.

575, Mary McAteer, 28, Roman Catholic, petty larceny, acquitted, can spell, 26th September.

576, James Black, 32, Presbyterian, petty larceny, acquitted, can read and write, 27th September.

577, Agnes McConkey, 36, Established Church, petty larceny, imprisoned 4 months, alphabet, 2nd October.

578, Eliza Neill, 18, Established Church, petty larceny, imprisoned 6 months, can spell, 2nd October.

579, Christina Neill, 33, Established Church, petty larceny, imprisoned 6 months, can read and write, 2nd October.

580, Henry Connor, 14, Established Church, petty larceny, recommitted twice, imprisoned 2 months, can read, 3rd October.

581, James Noon, 17, Roman Catholic, petty larceny, recommitted 3 times, no bill found, can read, 3rd October.

582, James Loughran, 12, Roman Catholic, petty larceny, recommitted once, no bill found, can read, 3rd October.

583, Biddy O'Neill, 31, Roman Catholic, petty larceny, recommitted 6 times, no bill found, alphabet, 3rd October.

584, Mary Morrow, 56, Roman Catholic, petty larceny, recommitted twice, no bill found, ignorant, 3rd October.

585, Mary Ross, 20, Established Church, petty larceny, recommitted 4 times, imprisoned 12 months in House of Correction, can spell, 7th October.

586, Sarah McGeough, 19, Roman Catholic, petty larceny, imprisoned 3 months in gaol, alphabet, 7th October.

587, John Jefferson, 12, Established Church, petty larceny, imprisoned 2 months in House of Correction, can read and write, 8th October.

588, James Morgan, 23, Roman Catholic, petty larceny, no bill found, alphabet, 8th October.

589, John Farrel, 8, Roman Catholic, petty larceny, imprisoned 1 fortnight in House of Correction, 8th October.

590, Archibald Finlay, 10, Presbyterian, petty larceny, imprisoned 1 fortnight in House of Correction, 8th October.

591, Anne Moore, 31, Presbyterian, petty larceny, pay 1 pound 3s 6d or be imprisoned 1 month in House of Correction, can spell, 8th October.

592, Eliza Moore, 40, Presbyterian, petty larceny, pay 1 pound 3s 6d or be imprisoned 1 month in House of Correction, can spell, 8th October.

593, Samuel Jordan, 12, Presbyterian, petty larceny, no bill found, can spell, 9th October.

594, Charles Donaghy, 37, Roman Catholic, petty larceny, imprisoned 2 months in gaol, 9th October.

595, John McCann, 14, Roman Catholic, petty larceny, no bill found, alphabet, 11th October.

596, Jane Brennan, 21, Established Church, petty larceny, imprisoned 9 months in House of Correction, can read, 14th October.

597, Bessy Cowan, 38, Roman Catholic, petty larceny, acquitted, ignorant, 14th October.

598, Martha Cassidy, 20, Roman Catholic, petty larceny, no bill found, can spell, 14th October.

599, Jane McMahon, 21, Roman Catholic, petty larceny, no bill found, can spell, 14th October.

600, Mary McIlvena, 47, Presbyterian, petty larceny, recommitted 3 times, no bill found, ignorant, 14th October.

601, Eliza Anne Watt, 14, Roman Catholic, petty larceny, recommitted twice, transported 7 years, can read, 17th October.

602, Robert Ward, 38, Roman Catholic, petty larceny, imprisoned 3 months in House of Correction, alphabet, 17th October.

603, Ally Anne Watson, 17, Established Church, petty larceny, recommitted twice, 6 months' hard labour in gaol, can spell, 19th October.

604, Mary Mathews, 29, Presbyterian, petty larceny, acquitted, can spell, 19th October.

605, Esther Benn, 44, Presbyterian, petty larceny, acquitted, can read, 19th October.

606, Charles Stuart, 15, Roman Catholic, petty larceny, recommitted 5 times, imprisoned 18 months, can read, write and cipher, 31st October.

607, Margaret Jane Horner, 19, Established Church, petty larceny, acquitted, can read, 1st November.

608, Eliza Darragh, 16, Established Church, petty larceny, imprisoned 3 months' hard labour in gaol, can read, 1st November.

609, William Montgomery, 43, Presbyterian, petty larceny, recommitted 4 times, transported for 7 years, can read, 1st November.

610, Charles Connor, 36, Roman Catholic, petty larceny, acquitted, can spell, 1st November.

611, Catherine Malone, 22, Roman Catholic, petty larceny, recommitted once, acquitted, ignorant, 5th November.

612, Eliza Cowan, 38, Roman Catholic, petty larceny, recommitted once, acquitted, ignorant, 5th November.

613, John Clark, 13, Roman Catholic, petty larceny, recommitted 4 times, imprisoned 12 months in House of Correction, can spell, 8th November.

614, Biddy Craig, 14, Roman Catholic, petty larceny, recommitted twice, imprisoned 12 months in House of Correction, can spell, 8th November.

615, William Bell, 46, Roman Catholic, petty larceny, imprisoned 1 month in House of Correction, can read and write, 9th November.

616, David Patterson, 23, Presbyterian, petty larceny, recommitted twice, acquitted, can read and write, 11th November.

617, James Rafferty, 57, Roman Catholic, petty larceny, acquitted, alphabet, 11th November.

618, Mary Jane Isles, 22, Established Church, petty larceny, recommitted once, imprisoned 12 months, can read, 11th November.

619, John McKenna, 14, Roman Catholic, petty larceny, recommitted once, imprisoned 9 months, 11th November.

620, James Loughran, 14, Roman Catholic, petty larceny, recommitted twice, imprisoned 12 months, can read, 11th November.

621, William Davis, 35, Roman Catholic, petty larceny, recommitted once, imprisoned 9 months, can read and write, 12th November.

622, John Hutchinson, 15, Established Church, petty larceny, recommitted once, imprisoned 12 months, can read, write and cipher, 14th November.

623, William Loughran, 14, Roman Catholic, petty larceny, recommitted twice, imprisoned 12 months, can read, 14th November.

624, Mary McArdle, 27, Established Church, petty larceny, recommitted twice, imprisoned 9 months in House of Correction, alphabet, 15th November.

625, Joseph Kane, 22, Roman Catholic, petty larceny, imprisoned 3 months in House of Correction, can read, write and cipher, 15th November.

626, Jane Wilson, 61, Presbyterian, petty larceny, recommitted 3 times, transported for 7 years, can read, 16th November.

627, Anne Kelly, 19, Established Church, petty larceny, imprisoned 6 weeks, alphabet, 16th November.

628, Thomas Grant, 19, Established Church, petty larceny, imprisoned 6 months in House of Correction, can read, write and cipher, 17th November.

629, Bernard Kearns, 14, Roman Catholic, petty larceny, imprisoned 1 month in gaol, can spell, 18th November.

630, Hana Ker Rowney, 31, Roman Catholic, petty larceny, recommitted once, imprisoned 6 weeks in gaol, can read, 19th November.

631, Mary Anne Barry, 19, Roman Catholic, petty larceny, imprisoned 6 months in House of Correction, can spell, 20th November.

632, Mary McEnarry, 20, Established Church, petty larceny, imprisoned 6 months in House of Correction, can spell, 20th November.

633, Mary McIlree, 30, Presbyterian, petty larceny, imprisoned 6 months in House of Correction, ignorant, 22nd November.

634, Rebecca Doherty, 40, Presbyterian, petty larceny, imprisoned 3 months in goal, can spell, 22nd November.

635, Edward Gilliland, 16, Roman Catholic, petty larceny, imprisoned 6 months in House of Correction, can read and write, 22nd November.

636, Jane McAreevy, 47, Roman Catholic, petty larceny, no bill found, can read, 23rd November.

637, Henry McDermott, 13, Roman Catholic, petty larceny, imprisoned 2 months in gaol, can read, write and cipher, 23rd November.

638, William McClernon, 16, Roman Catholic, petty larceny, no bill found, can read, 25th November.

639, James Drennan, 50, Established Church, petty larceny, imprisoned 1 fortnight in House of

Correction, can read and write, 27th November.

640, Barbara Davis, 27, Established Church, petty larceny, recommitted 5 times, transported for 7 years, can read, 27th November.

641, William Gamble, 18, Presbyterian, petty larceny, recommitted twice, imprisoned 9 months in House of Correction, can read and write, 28th November.

642, Bernard McCloskey, 19, Roman Catholic, petty larceny, imprisoned 3 months in House of Correction, can spell, 4th December.

643, Sarah Irwin, 19, Established Church, petty larceny, imprisoned 1 week in gaol, can spell, 4th December.

644, Maria Cole, 32, Roman Catholic, petty larceny, acquitted, ignorant, 6th December.

645, George Stuart, 18, Roman Catholic, petty larceny, imprisoned 6 weeks in House of Correction, can read, write and cipher, 10th December.

646, Donald McCudden, 19, Roman Catholic, petty larceny, recommitted once, not tried, can read, 10th December.

647, George Parker, 13, Established Church, petty larceny, recommitted 3 times, no bill found, can read, write and cipher, 14th December.

648, Thomas Crawford, 51, Presbyterian, misdemeanour, imprisoned 3 months, can read and write, 12th March.

649, Patrick McCann, 43, Roman Catholic, misdemeanour, recommitted once, to find bail to keep the peace, can read and write, 28th September.

650, Anne Cromie, 40, Roman Catholic, misdemeanour, imprisoned 1 week, can spell, 18th December.

651, Mary McAreevy, 53, Roman Catholic, misdemeanour, imprisoned 7 days, can spell, 24th December.

652, James O'Brien, 26, Roman Catholic, misdemeanour, to pay 4 pounds 16s 5d, can spell, 27th December.

653, John Connor, 21, Roman Catholic, perjury, admitted to bail, can read, write and cipher, 20th July.

654, William Cuff, 16, Roman Catholic, rape and accessory to it, acquitted, can read and write, 8th May.

655, William Ferguson, 27, Established Church, rape and accessory to it, imprisoned 6 months in House of Correction, alphabet, 29th April.

656, John Morris, 27, Roman Catholic, rape and accessory to it, to appear at next assizes, can spell, 16th April.

657, Andrew Irwin, 18, Presbyterian, rape and accessory to it, to appear at next assizes, can read, write and cipher, 16th April.

658, James Morris, 18, Established Church, rape and accessory to it, to appear at next assizes, can read, 18th April.

659, John Logan, 28, Roman Catholic, rescue, imprisoned 1 month, can read and write, 2nd July.

660, James Logan, 19, Roman Catholic, rescue, imprisoned 1 month, can spell, 2nd July.

661, Hugh Logan, 21, Roman Catholic, rescue, imprisoned 1 month, can read, 2nd July.

662, Bernard Heney, 26, Roman Catholic, rescue, imprisoned 1 month, can read, 2nd July.

663, Thomas Patterson, 24, Established Church, rescue, imprisoned 3 months, can read and write, 31st October.

664, Thomas Smyth, 43, Established Church, receiving and having stolen goods, imprisoned 6 months in House of Correction, can read and write, 4th January.

665, Patrick McCormick, 18, Roman Catholic, receiving and having stolen goods, recommitted 3 times, transferred to petty sessions, discharged, spelling, 12th January.

666, Michael Hughes, 23, Roman Catholic, receiving and having stolen goods, acquitted, can read, 19th January.

667, Patrick Short, 65, Roman Catholic, receiving and having stolen goods, imprisoned 3 months' hard labour in gaol, can read, 25th January.

668, Susanna Coulter, 36, Presbyterian, receiving and having stolen goods, recommitted twice, transported for 7 years, can spell, 25th January.

669, John McDowell, 48, Presbyterian, receiving and having stolen goods, recommitted once, acquitted, can read, write and cipher, 28th January.

670, William John McDowell, 22, Presbyterian, receiving and having stolen goods, imprisoned 12 months in House of Correction, can read, write and cipher, 28th January.

671, Samuel McDowell, 20, Presbyterian, receiving and having stolen goods, imprisoned 12 months in House of Correction, can read, write and cipher, 28th January.

672, James McGivern, 11, Presbyterian, receiving and having stolen goods, acquitted, can read, 28th January.

673, Robert Brownlee, 15, Presbyterian, receiving and having stolen goods, an appearance in the above case, discharged, can read and write, 28th January.

674, Mary Johnston, 40, Roman Catholic, receiving and having stolen goods, recommitted once, imprisoned 3 months in gaol, can read, 5th February.

675, John McClure, 16, Presbyterian, receiving and having stolen goods, imprisoned 4 months' hard labour in gaol, ignorant, 6th February.

676, John Keatings, 15, Roman Catholic, receiving and having stolen goods, imprisoned 4 months in House of Correction, can read, 7th February.

677, James Carrothers, 23, Roman Catholic, receiving and having stolen goods, acquitted, can read, write and cipher, 11th February.

678, Michael Dyer, 14, Roman Catholic, receiving and having stolen goods, imprisoned 3 months' hard labour in gaol, can read, 11th February.

679, Michael Loughran, 25, Roman Catholic, receiving and having stolen goods, imprisoned 4 months' hard labour in gaol, can read and write, 14th February.

680, James Carrothers, 72, Presbyterian, receiving and having stolen goods, acquitted, can read, 16th February.

681, Arthur Beatty, 27, Presbyterian, receiving and having stolen goods, imprisoned 6 months in House of Correction, can read and write, 18th February.

682, Susan Beatty, 35, Presbyterian, receiving and having stolen goods, acquitted, can read, 18th February.

683, Eliza Beatty, 33, Presbyterian, receiving and having stolen goods, acquitted, can read, 18th February.

684, John McKay, 62, Established Church, receiving and having stolen goods, imprisoned 1 year in House of Correction, can read, write and cipher, 23rd February.

685, Nancy Esler, 32, Presbyterian, receiving and having stolen goods, imprisoned 2 months in gaol, can read, 23rd February.

686, Eliza McIlvena, 23, Established Church, receiving and having stolen goods, recommitted 3 times, no bill found, can read, 23rd February.

687, John Martin, 23, Established Church, receiving and having stolen goods, recommitted once, imprisoned 9 months in House of Correction, can read, 14th March.

688, Robert Blair, 38, Established Church, receiving and having stolen goods, recommitted once, imprisoned 2 months' hard labour in gaol, can read, 14th March.

689, James Loughran, 12, Roman Catholic, receiving and having stolen goods, imprisoned 3 months in gaol, alphabet, 14th March.

690, Owen Loughran, 14, Roman Catholic, receiving and having stolen goods, imprisoned 3 months in gaol, alphabet, 14th March.

691, James Johnson, 20, Established Church, receiving and having stolen goods, imprisoned 12 months in House of Correction, can read, write and cipher, 18th March.

692, Ellen Hutchinson, 50, Presbyterian, receiving and having stolen goods, imprisoned 2 months' hard labour in gaol, can spell, 22nd March.

693, Margaret Bailly, 42, Established Church, receiving and having stolen goods, acquitted, ignorant, 25th March.

694, Mary Anne Johnson, 17, Established Church, receiving and having stolen goods, recommitted once, imprisoned 6 months in House of Correction, 26th March.

695, Henry Donaldson, 11, Established Church, receiving and having stolen goods, imprisoned 1 month's hard labour in gaol, can read, 27th March.

696, Mary McKay, 20, Established Church, receiving and having stolen goods, imprisoned 3 months in House of Correction, ignorant, 29th March.

697, Sarah Hagan, 56, Presbyterian, receiving and having stolen goods, imprisoned 3 months in House of Correction, ignorant, 29th March.

698, Robert Morrell, 23, Roman Catholic, receiving and having stolen goods, transported for 7 years, spelling, 29th March.

699, Andrew Wilson, 16, Presbyterian, receiving and having stolen goods, transported for 7 years, can read, 2nd April.

700, Margaret Carmichael, 24, Roman Catholic, receiving and having stolen goods, recommitted 3 times, transported for 7 years, ignorant, 3rd April.

701, Charles Holland, 19, Roman Catholic, receiving and having stolen goods, recommitted twice, transported for 7 years, can read, 3rd April.

702, Owen O'Hara, 32, Roman Catholic, receiving and having stolen goods, recommitted once, imprisoned 12 months in House of Correction, can read and write, 12th April.

703, Charles Magennis, 33, Established Church, receiving and having stolen goods, imprisoned 6 weeks in gaol, can read, write and cipher, 16th April.

704, Margaret Best, 12, Established Church, receiving and having stolen goods, imprisoned 6 weeks in gaol, can read, 16th April.

705, Catherine Gilligan, 28, Roman Catholic, receiving and having stolen goods, imprisoned 6 months in House of Correction, ignorant, 18th April.

706, Ellen Crone, 15, Roman Catholic, receiving and having stolen goods, imprisoned 4 months in House of Correction, ignorant, 18th April.

707, Anne Kearns, 25, Roman Catholic, receiving and having stolen goods, imprisoned 4 months in House of Correction, ignorant, 18th April.

708, Arthur Simpson, 14, Established Church, receiving and having stolen goods, imprisoned 4 months in House of Correction, can read and write, 18th April.

709, William Hull, 16, Established Church, receiving and having stolen goods, no bill found, can read, write and cipher, 20th April.

710, James Cullen, 45, Roman Catholic, receiving and having stolen goods, acquitted, can read, 24th April.

711, Sarah Cullen, 51, Roman Catholic, receiving and having stolen goods, recommitted once, imprisoned 9 months in House of Correction, ignorant, 24th April.

712, William Shorter, 22, Presbyterian, receiving and having stolen goods, imprisoned 6 months in House of Correction, 24th April.

713, Anne Cullen, 12, Roman Catholic, receiving and having stolen goods, recommitted twice, acquitted, ignorant, 24th April.

714, Margaret Frazer, 40, Roman Catholic, receiving and having stolen goods, imprisoned 1 month in gaol, ignorant, 29th April.

715, Eliza Ferguson, 35, Presbyterian, receiving and having stolen goods, imprisoned 2 months in gaol, alphabet, 29th April.

716, Douglas Walsh, 11, Established Church, receiving and having stolen goods, acquitted, can read, 8th May.

717, Hannah Stewart, 28, Established Church, receiving and having stolen goods, recommitted once, imprisoned 6 months in House of Correction, can read, 16th May.

718, Margaret McMullen, 18, Presbyterian, receiving and having stolen goods, imprisoned 1 month in gaol, ignorant, 16th May.

719, Jane McShane, 49, Established Church, receiving and having stolen goods, recommitted once, imprisoned 4 months in House of Correction, ignorant, 16th May.

720, James Bell, 31, Presbyterian, receiving and having stolen goods, imprisoned 2 months in goal, can read, 20th May.

721, Henry McDermot, 13, Roman Catholic, receiving and having stolen goods, imprisoned 1 month in gaol, 24th May.

722, Catherine Scott, 44, Roman Catholic, receiving and having stolen goods, imprisoned 4 months in House of Correction, can read and write, 24th May.

723, Jane Kidd, 41, Established Church, receiving and having stolen goods, recommitted twice, imprisoned 2 months in House of Correction, ignorant, 27th May.

724, John Dougall, 17, Established Church, receiving and having stolen goods, acquitted, can read and write, 28th May.

725, James Boyle, 16, Roman Catholic, receiving and having stolen goods, acquitted, can spell, 28th May.

726, Michael Dyer, 15, Roman Catholic, receiving and having stolen goods, recommitted once, transported for 7 years, can read and write, 30th May.

727, May Eustace, Roman Catholic, receiving and having stolen goods, imprisoned 6 weeks, ignorant, 6th June.

728, Robert Read, Roman Catholic, receiving and having stolen goods, imprisoned 2 months in House of Correction, can read and write, 7th June.

729, William Dennis, 21, Established Church, receiving and having stolen goods, imprisoned 6 weeks in gaol, can spell, 7th June.

730, Jane Savage, 28, Established Church, receiving and having stolen goods, acquitted, can read, 1st July.

731, William Smyth, 40, Presbyterian, receiving and having stolen goods, imprisoned 6 months in House of Correction, 2nd July.

732, Anne Stevenson, 21, Established Church, receiving and having stolen goods, imprisoned 3 months in gaol, can read and write, 11th July.

733, Peter McKenna, 36, Roman Catholic, receiving and having stolen goods, imprisoned 6 weeks in gaol, alphabet, 11th July.

734, Mary Scully, 24, Roman Catholic, receiving and having stolen goods, transported for 14 years, can read, 11th July.

735, George Coulter, 15, Presbyterian, receiving and having stolen goods, no prosecution, discharged by the court, can read, write and cipher, 13th July.

736, Edward Boyle, 43, Roman Catholic, receiving and having stolen goods, acquitted, can spell, 20th July.

737, Roseanne Kane, 48, Established Church, receiving and having stolen goods, acquitted, ignorant, 20th July.

738, Margaret Kane, 17, Established Church, receiving and having stolen goods, recommitted twice, acquitted, can read, 20th July.

739, Ellen Kane, 15, Established Church, receiving and having stolen goods, recommitted once, can read, 20th July.

740, Mary Tipping, 23, Roman Catholic, receiving and having stolen goods, imprisoned 6 months in House of Correction, can read, 24th June.

741, Hugh McConaghy, 18, Presbyterian, receiving and having stolen goods, imprisoned 2 months in House of Correction, alphabet, 28th June.

742, James Green, 16, Established Church, receiving and having stolen goods, recommitted once, imprisoned 6 months in gaol, can read, 23rd July.

743, James Young, 16, Presbyterian, receiving and having stolen goods, no bill found, can read and write, 24th July.

744, Catherine Sutton, 26, Established Church, receiving and having stolen goods, recommitted 3 times, transported 7 years, can read, write and cipher, 25th July.

745, Edward McGladigan, 30, Roman Catholic, receiving and having stolen goods, imprisoned 6 weeks in House of Correction, can spell, 25th July.

746, Elizabeth McAlister, 73, Presbyterian, receiving and having stolen goods, recommitted once, acquitted, can spell, 25th July.

747, Anne Lawes, 47, Presbyterian, receiving and having stolen goods, recommitted once, acquitted, can read, write and cipher, 25th July.

748, George Parker, 13, Established Church, receiving and having stolen goods, recommitted 4 times, acquitted, can spell, 25th July.

749, Patrick Hagan, 18, Roman Catholic, receiving and having stolen goods, acquitted, can read, 25th July.

750, John Hepburn, 18, Presbyterian, receiving and having stolen goods, imprisoned 2 months in gaol, can read, write and cipher, 29th July.

751, John Magennis, 25, Roman Catholic, receiving and having stolen goods, imprisoned 4 months' hard labour in gaol, can spell, 1st August.

752, Margaret McCann, 50, Roman Catholic, receiving and having stolen goods, imprisoned 4 months' hard labour in gaol, ignorant, 1st August.

753, John Porter, 30, Established Church, receiving and having stolen goods, acquitted, can read and write, 3rd August.

754, Edward Doherty, 21, Roman Catholic, receiving and having stolen goods, imprisoned 4 months, can spell, 5th August.

755, Margaret McCully, 30, Presbyterian, receiving and having stolen goods, imprisoned 2 months in House of Correction, ignorant, 7th August.

756, James Harper, 31, Presbyterian, receiving and having stolen goods, recommitted once, imprisoned 2 months in gaol, can read, write and cipher, 7th August.

757, John Mahon, 38, Presbyterian, receiving and having stolen goods, recommitted once, imprisoned 2 months in gaol, can read, write and cipher, 9th August.

758, Andrew Connery, 30, Roman Catholic, receiving and having stolen goods, imprisoned 4 months in House of Correction, can read, 10th August.

759, Mary Ward, 11, Roman Catholic, receiving and having stolen goods, acquitted, ignorant, 10th August.

760, James Ward, 8, Roman Catholic, receiving and having stolen goods, imprisoned 2 months in gaol, alphabet, 10th August.

761, Thomas Eustace, 18, Roman Catholic, receiving and having stolen goods, imprisoned 1 month's hard labour in gaol, can read and write, 13th August.

762, Christy Eustace, 16, Roman Catholic, receiving and having stolen goods, imprisoned 1 month's hard labour in gaol, can read, 13th August.

763, Thomas Russel, 14, Presbyterian, receiving and having stolen goods, imprisoned 3 months' hard labour in gaol, can read, 15th August.

764, Isabella Weir, 50, Roman Catholic, receiving and having stolen goods, imprisoned 1 month in House of Correction, ignorant, 17th August.

765, Bernard Mooney, 31, Roman Catholic, receiving and having stolen goods, imprisoned 1 fortnight in House of Correction, can read, 17th August.

766, George Mill, 11, Established Church, receiving and having stolen goods, recommitted once, imprisoned 6 months' hard labour in gaol, can read, 17th August.

767, Sarah Holden, 19, Roman Catholic, receiving and having stolen goods, imprisoned 1 month in House of Correction, can read, 17th August.

768, Martha Madden, 35, Established Church, receiving and having stolen goods, recommitted 7 times, imprisoned 2 months in House of Correction, can spell, 23rd August.

769, William Hurst, 21, Established Church, receiving and having stolen goods, imprisoned 6 months in gaol, can read and write, 23rd August.

770, Bernard Campbell, 30, Roman Catholic, receiving and having stolen goods, acquitted, can read, 23rd August.

771, Ellen McLean, 19, Roman Catholic, receiving and having stolen goods, imprisoned 2 months in House of Correction, ignorant, 24th August.

772, Rachel Black, 19, Roman Catholic, receiving and having stolen goods, imprisoned 4 days in gaol, can read, 24th August.

773, Daniel Hughes, 27, Roman Catholic, receiving and having stolen goods, imprisoned 12 months' hard labour in gaol, can read and write, 24th August.

774, Mary McKissock, 29, Roman Catholic, receiving and having stolen goods, imprisoned 2 months in House of Correction, ignorant, 27th August.

775, Hugh Blair, 14, Established Church, receiving and having stolen goods, acquitted, can read, 27th August.

776, Joseph Patterson, 17, Established Church, receiving and having stolen goods, acquitted, can read and write, 27th August.

777, Charles Delany, 18, Roman Catholic, receiving and having stolen goods, acquitted, can spell, 27th August.

778, Anne Brennan, 14, Presbyterian, receiving and having stolen goods, imprisoned 1 month's hard labour, can read, 29th August.

779, Richard Martin, 21, Established Church, receiving and having stolen goods, imprisoned 2 months' hard labour, can spell, 29th August.

780, Jane O'Neill, 28, Roman Catholic, receiving and having stolen goods, imprisoned 3 months in gaol, can spell, 30th August.

781, Eliza McCullough, 27, Presbyterian, receiving and having stolen goods, recommitted once, imprisoned 3 months in gaol, ignorant, 30th August.

782, Mary Harkness, 28, Roman Catholic, receiving and having stolen goods, imprisoned 3 months in House of Correction, ignorant, 30th August.

783, John Kane, 18, Roman Catholic, receiving and having stolen goods, recommitted 3 times, transported 7 years, can read and write, 31st August.

784, Susanna McCall, 19, Established Church, receiving and having stolen goods, imprisoned 3 days, can read, 2nd September.

785, Catherine Ritchies, 18, Roman Catholic, receiving and having stolen goods, recommitted once, imprisoned 6 months in House of Correction, can spell, 2nd September.

786, Jane Clark, 13, Roman Catholic, receiving and having stolen goods, recommitted 3 times, acquitted, can spell, 2nd September.

787, Mary Boyle, 14, Roman Catholic, receiving and having stolen goods, acquitted, ignorant, 2nd September.

788, Rose Connell, 61, Roman Catholic, receiving and having stolen goods, imprisoned 6 months in House of Correction, ignorant, 6th September.

789, Patrick McCormick, 18, Roman Catholic, receiving and having stolen goods, imprisoned 6 months in gaol, can read, 7th September.

790, James Thompson, 13, Presbyterian, receiving and having stolen goods, imprisoned 3 months in gaol, can spell, 7th September.

791, Hugh Gilmour, 15, Roman Catholic, receiving and having stolen goods, recommitted once, transported for 7 years, can read and write, 7th September.

792, Westley Miller, 15, Established Church, receiving and having stolen goods, transported for 7 years, can spell, 7th September.

793, Hugh Murray, 28, Roman Catholic, receiving and having stolen goods, recommitted once, imprisoned 6 months, 7th September.

794, Eliza O'Neill, 35, Roman Catholic, receiving and having stolen goods, recommitted once, no bill found, ignorant, 11th September.

795, John Ward, 17, Roman Catholic, receiving and having stolen goods, recommitted once, transported for 7 years, can read and write, 12th September.

796, James Hendron, 14, Roman Catholic, receiving and having stolen goods, imprisoned 6 months, can read, 12th September.

797, Robert Houston, 42, Presbyterian, receiving and having stolen goods, recommitted once, imprisoned 6 months, can read, 15th September.

798, Alexander Ritchie, 13, Presbyterian, receiving and having stolen goods, imprisoned 2 months' hard labour, can read and write, 18th September.

799, Henry Piggott, 14, Presbyterian, receiving and having stolen goods, imprisoned 2 months' hard labour, can spell, 18th September.

800, William Montgomery, 43, Presbyterian, receiving and having stolen goods, recommitted 3 times, acquitted, can read, 19th September.

801, Patrick Robinson, 15, Roman Catholic, receiving and having stolen goods, recommitted once, acquitted, can read, 20th September.

802, James McGann, 15, Established Church, receiving and having stolen goods, imprisoned 6 weeks, can read, 20th September.

803, Mary Ann McStay, 22, Established Church, receiving and having stolen goods, recommitted once, acquitted, can spell, 28th September.

804, James Carson, 33, Established Church, receiving and having stolen goods, imprisoned 2 months, can read and write, 2nd October.

805, John Tate, 28, Established Church, receiving and having stolen goods, imprisoned 3 months, can read, write and cipher, 2nd October.

806, James Guinness, 27, Established Church, receiving and having stolen goods, recommitted twice, acquitted, can read, 2nd October.

807, Robert Bates, 23, Established Church, receiving and having stolen goods, imprisoned 6 months, can read, write and cipher, 7th October.

808, Grace Quigley, 38, Established Church, receiving and having stolen goods, imprisoned 2 months, ignorant, 9th October.

809, James Dornan, 24, Roman Catholic, receiving and having stolen goods, imprisoned 4 months' hard labour, can read and write, 10th October.

810, Martha Moorehead, 37, Presbyterian, receiving and having stolen goods, acquitted, can read, 10th October.

811, Margaret McAuley, 34, Roman Catholic, receiving and having stolen goods, recommitted once, imprisoned 6 months in House of Correction, can spell, 18th October.

812, William Kearns, 32, Presbyterian, receiving and having stolen goods, recommitted once, imprisoned 6 months in House of Correction, 18th October.

813, Mary Brown, 28, Established Church, receiving and having stolen goods, recommitted twice, imprisoned 3 months, can read, 18th October.

814, James Stewart, 27, Presbyterian, receiving and having stolen goods, recommitted twice, transported for 7 years, can read, write and cipher, 7th November.

815, Eliza McMullen Junior, 25, Presbyterian, receiving and having stolen goods, recommitted once, transported for 7 years, can read, 7th November.

816, Margaret McMullen, 18, Presbyterian, receiving and having stolen goods, recommitted once, transported for 7 years, can read, 7th November.

817, Eliza McMullen Senior, 44, Presbyterian, receiving and having stolen goods, transported for 7 years, can read, 7th November.

818, Henry Butler, 16, Roman Catholic, receiving and having stolen goods, imprisoned 6 months in House of Correction, can spell, 9th November.

819, Samuel Heron, 17, Established Church, receiving and having stolen goods, admitted to bail, can read, write and cipher, 16th November.

820, Mary Anne Hamilton, 21, Presbyterian, receiving and having stolen goods, recommitted twice, transported for 7 years, can read, 23rd November.

821, Eliza Ritchie, 30, Established Church, receiving and having stolen goods, imprisoned 3 months, 29th November.

822, Patrick Harvey, 18, Roman Catholic, receiving and having stolen goods, not tried, 9th November.

823, Mary Elliott, 20, Established Church, receiving and having stolen goods, imprisoned 3 months in House of Correction, can spell, 30th November.

824, John Vance, 30, Presbyterian, receiving and having stolen goods, recommitted once, imprisoned 9 months in gaol, can read, 5th December.

825, Edward Cornwall, 21, Established Church, receiving and having stolen goods, imprisoned 12 months in gaol, can spell, 7th December.

826, Ellen Cornwall, 25, Established Church, receiving and having stolen goods, recommitted twice, acquitted, can read, 7th December.

827, John Wilkinson, 50, Established Church, receiving and having stolen goods, transported for 7 years, can read, 7th December.

828, Eliza Dyer, 23, Established Church, receiving and having stolen goods, imprisoned 9 months in House of Correction, can read, 7th December.

829, William King, 39, Roman Catholic, receiving and having stolen goods, recommitted once, transported for 7 years, can read, 7th December.

830, Mary McIlhenny, 48, Roman Catholic, receiving and having stolen goods, imprisoned 6 weeks in House of Correction, can spell, 10th December.

831, Mary McManus, 19, Roman Catholic, receiving and having stolen goods, imprisoned 6 weeks in House of Correction, can spell, 11th December.

832, John Armstrong, 59, Roman Catholic, receiving and having stolen goods, imprisoned 3 months in House of Correction, can read, 16th December.

833, Thomas Laverty, 27, Roman Catholic, receiving and having stolen goods, recommitted once, imprisoned 9 months in gaol, can read and write, 20th December.

834, Eliza O'Neill, 35, Roman Catholic, receiving and having stolen goods, recommitted twice, imprisoned 9 months in gaol, can spell, 20th December.

835, Jane Ragsbottom, 28, Presbyterian, receiving and having stolen goods, imprisoned 9 months in gaol, can spell, 21st December.

836, Sarah Hepburn, 38, Roman Catholic, receiving and having stolen goods, imprisoned 3 months in House of Correction, can read, 23rd December.

837, Maria Skelton, 37, Established Church, receiving and having stolen goods, imprisoned 3 months in House of Correction, can read, 27th December.

838, Martha Madden, 35, Presbyterian, receiving and having stolen goods, recommitted 9 times, transported for 7 years, can spell, 28th December.

839, Mary McKibben, 28, Established Church, receiving and having stolen goods, imprisoned 3 months in House of Correction, can read, 28th December.

840, Isabella McLaughlin, 21, Presbyterian, receiving and having stolen goods, recommitted once, sick, untried, can spell, 28th December.

841, Bessy Dunn, 17, Roman Catholic, receiving and having stolen goods, recommitted twice, imprisoned 3 months in House of Correction, can read, 28th December.

842, Jane Quinn, 19, Roman Catholic, receiving and having stolen goods, recommitted twice, transported for 7 years, can spell, 30th December.

843, Martha Abbott, 33, Established Church, receiving and having stolen goods, imprisoned 1 month in House of Correction, can spell, 31st December.

844, Charles Cassidy, 29, Roman Catholic, riot and assault, imprisoned 4 months in House of Correction, can read, 4th January.

845, John O'Neill, 23, Roman Catholic, riot and assault, imprisoned 6 weeks in House of Correction, can read, 4th January.

846, James O'Raw, 20, Roman Catholic, riot and assault, imprisoned 6 weeks in House of Correction, 4th January.

847, William Davison, 28, Established Church, riot and assault, bail to keep peace and 6 months in House of Correction, 4th January.

848, John Cunningham, 41, Presbyterian, riot and assault, recommitted twice, imprisoned 3 months in House of Correction, 5th April.

849, Andrew McKenna, 42, Established Church, riot and assault, imprisoned 2 months in House of Correction, 5th April.

850, Peggy Stuart, 34, Established Church, riot and assault, recommitted once, imprisoned 1 month in House of Correction, ignorant, 5th April.

851, Mary McKee, 21, Established Church, riot and assault, imprisoned 1 month in House of Correction, ignorant, 5th April.

852, John Burns, 26, Established Church, riot and assault, imprisoned 3 months in House of Correction, 5th April.

853, Laughlin Burns, 17, Established Church, riot and assault, imprisoned 3 months in House of Correction, 5th April.

854, Daniel Frizzle, 18, Established Church, riot and assault, imprisoned 3 months in House of Correction, 5th April.

855, Duncan Burns, 21, Established Church, riot and assault, imprisoned 2 months in House of Correction, 5th April.

856, John McMullans, 17, Established Church, riot and assault, imprisoned 2 months in House of Correction, 5th April.

857, John Smyth, 39, Presbyterian, riot and assault, imprisoned 1 month in House of Correction, can read and write, 5th April.

858, Thomas Goodwin, 22, Roman Catholic, riot and assault, imprisoned 4 months' hard labour in gaol, can read, write and cipher, 16th April.

859, William McCool, 23, Roman Catholic, riot and assault, imprisoned 2 months' hard labour in gaol, can read, write and cipher, 16h April.

860, Hugh Drene, 28, Roman Catholic, riot and assault, imprisoned 2 months in gaol, can read, 28th June.

861, Michael McIntyre, 20, Roman Catholic, riot and assault, imprisoned 2 months in gaol, can read and write, 28th June.

862, Neill McAlees, 24, Roman Catholic, riot and assault, imprisoned 2 months in gaol, can read, 28th June.

863, Hugh Dillon, 22, Roman Catholic, riot and assault, imprisoned 3 months in gaol, can read, 28th June.

864, Charles Sheals, 20, Roman Catholic, riot and assault, pay 10s or imprisoned 3 weeks in gaol, can read, write and cipher, 28th June.

865, Andrew Fulton, 24, Presbyterian, removing goods, acquitted, can read, write and cipher, 30th April.

866, Patrick McKillop, 19, Established

Church, sheep-stealing, imprisoned 12 months in gaol, can read, 14th September.

867, Charles Downey, 20, Roman Catholic, sheep-stealing, not tried, can read, 19th September.

868, Charles Gillespie, 19, Roman Catholic, stabbing, recommitted 4 times, not tried, can read, 22nd November.

869, Rose Thomson, 28, Roman Catholic, stealing children, not tried, can read, 7th September.

870, Francis McNeill, 42, Roman Catholic, stealing linen, recommitted once, transported for 7 years, can read, 5th February.

871, John Kirkpatrick, 53, Established Church, throwing stones, recommitted once, in custody, can read, 15th August.

872, Thomas Entwistle, 40, Established Church, trespass, fined 10s and to find bail to keep the peace, can read, write and cipher, 27th September.

873, John Hamilton, 37, Presbyterian, uttering and having base coin, acquitted, can read, write and cipher, 29th April.

874, Samuel Boyd, 23, Presbyterian, uttering and having base coin, imprisoned 18 months in House of Correction, can read, write and cipher, 22nd May.

875, Michael Hughes, 23, Roman Catholic, uttering and having base coin, recommitted once, imprisoned 6 months in House of Correction, can spell, 13th July.

876, Jane Morris, 61, Established Church, uttering and having base coin, recommitted twice, not tried, can spell, 10th August.

877, Margaret Doherty, 28, Roman Catholic, uttering and having base coin, recommitted twice, not tried, can spell, 10th August.

878, Anne McGenny, 37, Established Church, uttering and having base coin, imprisoned 6 months in gaol, ignorant, 19th October.

879, Jane Stuart, 70, Established Church, vagrancy, acquitted, can read, 19th February.

880, Wilson Gillespie, 18, Established Church, waylaying, acquitted, 12th March.

Drawings by James Boyle

ANCIENT AND MODERN TOPOGRAPHY

Illustrations

A plan of Carrickfergus taken in 1550 from a copy of Carrickfergus from the original drawing in the Lambeth Library, scale 160 feet to an inch.

Town of Carrickfergus within the walls, copied from a map in the possession of D. Ker Esquire, made by John Handcock, apparently very old but without date; scale 280 feet to an inch; time employed 15 hours.

Ancient drawing of the town of Carrickfergus by John Dunstall, 1612, copied from the engraving, published by the Society of Antiquaries, 23rd April 1838; time employed 18 hours.

Carrickfergus Castle from the Scotch Quarter, view showing houses on shoreline north of castle; time employed 20 hours.

Detail drawings of Carrickfergus Castle: window (closed up) in the east side; entrance to the sally-port (closed up); ornamental stone east half-moon; window in the magazine yard, 2 arrow-slits in the tower; window in the tower, north side; the stones are drawn to scale, 1 inch to 4 feet; time employed 5 hours.

Detail drawing of window in the eastern half-moon of the castle, scale 1 inch to 4 feet; time employed 4 hours.

View of interior of the gateway at Carrickfergus Castle.

Detail drawings of 2 windows in Carrickfergus church, scale 1 inch to 4 feet; time employed 3 hours.

Stone face in the east gable of Carrickfergus church, dimensions 9 by 6 inches; time employed 2 hours.

Stone cross in Carrickfergus church with date inscribed, scale 1 inch to 4 inches; time employed 8 hours.

Ancient seal of the mayor of Carrickfergus; time employed 6 hours.

The common seal of Carrickfergus; time employed 13 hours.

Official seal of the port of Carrickfergus; time employed 7 hours.

Specimen of the masonry of Duncrue church, scale 1 inch to 40 feet; time employed 2 hours.

Druidical altar; time employed 10 hours.

Second druidical altar, showing figure of man with stick; time employed 11 hours.

Druidical altar; time employed 8 hours.

Forts: plans with section drawings of a square fort, 2 round forts, scale 1 inch to 80 feet; time employed 2 hours.

Plans with section drawings of an oval-shaped fort with foundations of a castle in centre, a double-banked fort and 5 other forts.

Plans with section drawings of 7 tumuli.

Fort and cove, plan and section drawing, scale 1 inch to 20 feet; time employed 2 hours.

Enclosures near the Friar's Glen, scale 1 inch to 40 feet; time employed 3 hours.

Iron spear, iron instrument, iron blade found in Troopers Land drawn to size; time employed 5 hours.

Mould for casting celts found in Troopers Land (half size of original), with key and dimensions of hollows, stone 2 inches thick.

Stone amulet (half size of original); time employed 4 hours.

2 wooden methers with dimensions: height 8 inches, width 4 and a quarter inches; height 7 and a quarter inches, width 3 and three-quarter inches; time employed 7 hours.

Wooden vessel 11 inches by 7 inches and 9 and a half inches deep, found in a bog; time employed 3 hours.

Brazen cup drawn full-size; brazen pin drawn full-size; rings of armour, iron ring and 2 brazen rings found in an ancient burial ground in Troopers Land; time employed 5 hours.

Brazen instrument with decoration found near Great Patrick; brazen cup found in Troopers Land; time employed 6 hours.

Fair Sheets by J. Bleakly, with Queries and Corrections by J. Boyle, May 1839 to June 1840

MODERN TOPOGRAPHY

Presbyterian Meeting House

The Presbyterian meeting house is situated in North Street. The date of its erection is MDC-CXXVII, in raised characters on stone on the front of the house. It was built by subscription and cost 2,000 pounds. Its external dimensions is 77 and a half by 53 feet. It contains 116 single pews; 78 of these are in the lower part, 64 of which measure each 9 feet 9 inches by 2 feet 9 inches and 14 each 8 and a half by 2 feet 9, making accommodation in the lower part for 635, at 14 inches to each person. The gallery contains 38 single pews, 4 of which are each 12 feet by 2 feet 9 inches, 20 are each 9 feet 9 by 2 feet 9 and 14 each 11 feet by 2 feet 9; total accommodation for 363 sitters on the gallery, allowing 14 inches for each person. There is ample accommodation in the meeting house for 1,000 persons.

The 2 alleys in the lower part are each 4 feet wide, all boarded and matted. The alley under the pulpit for the communicants is 7 feet 9 inches wide. The gallery is supported by 8 metal pillars; 2 alleys on the gallery each 3 feet 3 wide. Entrance

to the gallery is by 2 doors with stairs leading to each, of wood. Entrance to the lower part is by 2 doors also. Committee room is on the gallery floor and measures 28 by 10 and a half feet. Hall below measures 39 and a half by 10 feet. The house is well lit by 27 windows, 13 of which are arched, circular segment, and 14 are oblong. There is a water closet and minister's room in the lower part. The house is in excellent repair. Paling is of iron in front with an iron gate. Meeting house stands east and west. From John Coates and Rev. James White.

Independent Meeting House

The Independent meeting house is situated in Castle Street. It was built by subscription in 1820 and cost about 480 pounds. It is intended to improve the exterior very shortly by stone finish, and placing pillars and paling and gate in front.

It contains 55 single pews, 44 of which are each 6 by 2 and a half feet, and 10 pews 8 and a half feet by 2 and a half feet, with 1 which is 9 by 2 and a half feet; ample accommodation for 299, allowing 14 inches for each sitter. Meeting house measures interiorly 40 by 32 and a half feet; 2 alleys each 4 feet wide and one 3 and a half feet wide; well lit with 4 large, circular-segment, arch windows, 5 chandeliers; all in good repair and stands north east by south west with 1 door on end. Built of stone and lime, slated. From Alexander Johns Esquire and the minister. 28th May 1839.

Roman Catholic Chapel

The Roman Catholic chapel stand on a hill locally called the Barley hill, in the Western Division of the town. It was substantially built of stone and slated. On a stone on the north end is the following inscription: "1826 W. Crolly B.D., A. O'Neill P.P." It was built by subscription and cost 325 pounds, with 30 guineas for the altar and pulpit; total cost 356 pounds. Only 1 pew, built by Mrs Bruce for her own occupation. The floor is of earth and occupied by forms. The chapel alone measures in the clear 45 by 24 feet and is lit with 4 [blank] windows, 2 large doors with a window over each. Priest resides under the same roof of the chapel. House built same time as the chapel. [Insert query: From what funds was the erection of the priest's house defrayed; from the same funds with the chapel?].

Wall round chapel yard, which is the graveyard, is 5 feet high, enclosing half a rood of ground. Purchased by subscription and cost 100 pounds. There are only a few modern gravestones in it. The only ornament is a plain stone cross on the north gable. There are nothing but temporary seats (forms). Chapel is substantially built of stone and lime, slated. From the priest, Rev. Arthur O'Neill.

Wesleyan Methodist Chapel

The Wesleyan Methodist chapel is situated in West Street. It was built by subscription in 1810 and cost 600 pounds. Its total dimensions is 51 by 29 in the clear. It contains 25 single pews, 15 of which are each 14 by 2 and a half feet, 6 each 11 by 2 and a half feet, 2 each 9 by 2 and a half and 2 each 6 and a half by 2 and a half feet, with 51 feet of a space occupied by forms, equal to 22 single seats, each 6 feet by 2 and a half; total accommodation for 376 sitters, allowing 14 inches to each person. 2 alleys each 2 feet 8 wide, well lit by 7 circular-segment arch windows and 5 square windows. Door is on the south end and pulpit on the north end. Paling in front, of iron, and a good gate of iron; 4 chandeliers. House is well furnished and in good repair. All boarded floor, a good 8-day clock inside, given to the congregation by Mr Samuel Hay. Built of stone and lime, and slated.

Unitarian Meeting House

The Unitarian meeting house is situated in the Scotch Quarter, on Joymount Bank. House is all of brick and slated but not yet finished. It was commenced last year, 1838, by subscription. The front is supported by 2 brick pillars. It stands north and south and measures externally 50 by 41 feet; the porch measures 14 feet in length. House is lit by 8 circular-segment arch windows and 1 square window; door is on the south end. Probable cost when finished will be 1,000 pounds; at present 879 pounds 13s 9d is expended on it; no gallery. It contains 44 pews, of which 40 are single and 4 are double pews. 20 of the single pews measure each 6 feet 4 inches by 3 feet and 20 more measure 8 by 3 feet, and 2 of the double pews measure each 6 feet 4 inches by 5 feet 8 inches, with 2 alleys each 4 feet 4 wide, all boarded and in good repair. There is ample accommodation for about 300, at 14 inches to each sitter.

Original clergy: the first minister was the Rev. James Malcom in 1835, who continued 1 year. Until the end of 1838 the congregation was supplied by the Rev. William Glendie of Ballycarry. The present minister, the Rev. James Nixon Porter, came at the end of 1838.

Methodist Chapel

The Wesleyan Association Methodist chapel in North Street is the upper storey of a 2-storey house, rented at 4 guineas per annum. Established in 1837, a room fitted up for the purpose and well lit with 7 square windows; no pews but forms. The house or room measures 53 by 17 feet in the clear. Preaching is held twice on each Sunday and once on Tuesday evening.

Ranters' Chapel

The Ranters' or Primitive Methodist chapel is a small, stone and lime, slated house in the Scotch Quarter, built AD 1838 by subscription and cost about 60 pounds. It has no other furniture than a few temporary forms and measures 31 by 18 feet 3 inches in the clear, but is not yet finished; 1-storey high and is lit by 4 square windows; there is only 1 door. From James Sloan and others, 30th May 1839.

Covenanting Meeting House

Covenanting meeting house at Loughmourne is substantially built of stone and lime, slated; was built in 1805 by subscription. It measures 40 by 26 feet in the clear and contains 29 single pews and 1 double pew; each single pew measures 8 feet 9 inches by 2 feet 4 inches. Each pew will accommodate 7 and a half persons, and the double one 16; total accommodation for 186 persons. All in tolerable repair and well lit with 6 square windows. Floor is all of earth, not boarded; no gallery. Aisle is 5 and a half feet wide. Entrance is by a small vestry room door. About 1 rood of ground for a graveyard attached, all fenced round with a ditch of stones and earth, quicked and planted round with fir trees, 12 years planted; property of the corporation. There are only 8 tombstones; oldest stone 1808. Stuart is the most prevalent name: 5 Stuarts are on tombstones.

Gentlemen's Seats in 1821

At that time 21 gentlemen's seats in the county of the town. The following are their names: Thomas Pottinger Esquire, town, left the country; John Gregg Esquire, Ballynascreen, died; Richard Brice Esquire, now Bruice, Ballynascreen; Thomas Ludford Stewart Esquire, Sea Park; James Craig Esquire, Scoutbush; Thomas Millar Esquire, Mount Cottage; Rev. John Gwynn, Woodford, now in parish Kilroot; Rev. John Savage, Farm Hill, dead, now Stuart Dunn Esquire; William Burleigh Esquire, St Catherine's, now town; Henry Clements Ellis Esquire, Prospect, dead, now [blank] Nicholy Esquire; Peter Kirk Esquire, Thornhill; Hill Wilson Esquire, Thornhill; George Porteous Price Esquire, North Lodge, dead, now Mrs Craig.

Rocklands is the residence of John Bowie Esquire, Lieutenant R.N. and inspecting commander of the coastguards. Situated on the shore a few perches west of Carrickfergus, a good 2-storey house, plain, built 12 years ago by Alexander Wilson, architect, who resided in it, but only occupied by Lieutenant Bowie since 1836, who purchased it; 2 acres of ornamental ground attached.

Sea View is the 2-storey built house at Ballynascreen House on the Belfast line, 7 years ago built by Mr Robb Simpson, a farmer, West Division of Carrickfergus; no ornamental ground or planting worth notice.

The cottage occupied by Captain Harrison is a short distance from Sea Park and on the shore and Belfast line. It is called Green Island. The cottage is 1-storey and slated, 9 years built and is let yearly to tenants, chiefly sea bathers; no ornamental ground or planting attached. The proprietor is Mr Thomas Mairs.

The other cottage is a few yards distant and is occupied by Mr Thomas Mairs, and was built same time and is a 1-storey cottage, slated. The third is a few perches distant and is 2-storey, slated and plain, and is let to sea bathers, and was built same time by the same proprietor, Mr Thomas Mairs.

A few perches distant from the above, on the same side of the Belfast line and on the shore, is a 2-storey house, slated, called Raven Hill Lodge. It is also for the accommodation of sea bathers and was built about 12 years ago by James Magill of Belfast, who is still the proprietor and has it let to Councillor Gilmour. No ornamental ground or planting worth notice attached.

The next house worth notice is Ballynaverin House. It is a plain 2-storey house, slated and situated on the shore. It was built by John Gregg Esquire about 35 years ago. It is also for the accommodation of sea bathers and occupied by Mr Goddart; Miss Jane Gregg is the proprietor.

Joshua Rice Esquire, Glynn Park, dead now; John Legg Esquire; William Finlay Esquire, Glenfield, dead; Rev. John Dobbs, Oakfield, dead; Wilson Boyde Esquire, Eden House; Rev. Snowden Cupples, Eden Cottage, dead; Captain Thompson, dead.

Sea Park is the residence of the Very Rev. John Chaine, Dean of Connor. The house is 2-storey high, slated, situated about 1 and a half miles west of Carrickfergus, on the shore and near the mail coach road from Belfast. It was built by Thomas Stuart Esquire, Belfast, about the year 1804. His son, William Stuart Esquire, occupied it. Dean Chaine is only 4 years in it. He rents it from William Stuart Esquire. It contains 16 acres of ornamental grounds and planting.

Scoutbush is the seat of Edward Bruce Esquire. It is situated about 1 mile from Carrickfergus, on the same road. The house is a plain 2-storey house, slated, and was built about 33 years ago by [blank], and was rebuilt in [blank] by the present proprietor. The ornamental ground and planting consists of about 5 acres of all sorts of forest trees; the oldest is 33 years planted, the latest 3 years ago. In 1821 it was occupied by James Craig.

The Mount Cottage was built by Mr Thomas Millar about 20 years ago; 1-storey high, slated, situated near the Belfast line and about half a mile from Carrickfergus; ornamental ground and planting consist of about 2 acres. Mr Richard Thompson is its proprietor, who resides in it.

The next house worth notice is Silverstream House. It is a plain 2-storey house, slated, situated at the boundary of the corporation and on the Belfast line. It was built by Miss Ellen Fulton about 30 years ago. After Miss Fulton it was let yearly till, about 20 years ago, Thomas Pottinger Esquire let it to tenants. Colonel Walshe purchased it and afterwards Mr Edward Pennal purchased it. The present proprietor is Captain Manley, who purchased it. There is no ornamental planting attached.

Glynn Park is the residence of John Legg Esquire. The house is situated 1 mile from Carrickfergus. The house is 3-storeys high, slated, with wings in front and was built about 40 years ago by James Craig Esquire. It was improved 14 years ago. The planting and ornamental ground consist of 4 acres.

Rose Brook is situated a few perches from Carrickfergus, on the North Road. It is a plain 2-storey house, slated, built 30 years ago by Richard Dobbs Esquire. In 1821 Mr Hill Wilson resided in it, afterwards John Thompson; after him Dr Forsyth; Peter Kirk Esquire, M.P. is the proprietor; no ornamental ground or plantings.

Thornfield is the seat of Peter Kirk Esquire, M.P. It is a short distance from Rose Brook. It was built 45 years ago by Sir William Kirk. It is a plain 2-storey house of stone, slated; 3

acres of ornamental ground and planting attached.

Prospect was built about 40 years ago by Henry Clements Ellis Esquire. He continued till his death about 14 years ago, when he was succeeded by his daughter, and [it] is now occupied by Christian William Nicolly Esquire. It is a 2-storey house with 2 sexagonals in front. The ornamental ground and planting consists of 14 acres.

Farm Hill is of the cottage form and is situated near the Knockagh, on the Woodburn Road. Part of it is a 2-storey house and part 1-storey. It was built about 45 years ago by the Rev. John Savage, a Presbyterian minister. 10 years ago the present proprietor, Stuart Dunn Esquire, purchased it; 6 acres of ornamental ground and planting attached.

Barn Cottage is situated near the Scotch Quarter, above the maypole. It is a plain 1-storey house, slated, and was built by Mr John Moore about 50 years ago. Mr James Cowan, its present proprietor, is 12 years in it. There is about 2 acres of ornamental ground and planting attached.

Woodford is situated near Mount Cottage and is a very plain 2-storey house, slated, and very old. It was the residence of the Rev. John Gwynn, Established Church minister, until 1838; it is now a farmhouse; ornamental ground and planting about 3 acres; originally was a farmhouse.

Oakfield is a plain 2-storey house situated near the North Road. It was built about 35 years ago by William Dobbs Esquire, who lived in it about 10 years and was succeeded by his brother, the Rev. John Dobbs. He lived in it 12 years and was succeeded by Rev. John Chaine (now dean). He lived 3 years in it and Dr Duncan lived in it till last year, 1838; now vacant.

North Lodge is near Rose Brook on the North Road. A plain 2-storey house, slated, built 60 years ago by Major Edmondstone. It is now a farmhouse occupied by a widow Craig; no ornamental ground or planting attached.

St Catherine's is situated on the North Road and is a plain 2-storey house, slated. It was built about 35 years ago by William Burleigh Esquire. He was succeeded by William Stuart Esquire, 14 years ago; Colonel Walsh is now 4 years in it. About 12 acres of ornamental ground and planting attached; now to be let.

Burleigh Hill House is also a plain 2-storey house, with wings. It was built by George Burleigh Esquire about 45 years ago. John Robbinson, his nephew, succeeded him 16 years ago and still resides in it; 36 acres of land attached, greater part is planting.

Old Market House

The town hall or old market house is a plain building situated in the centre of the town. It contains an assembly room on the second storey, where all public meetings are held and petty sessions. Its dimensions are 39 by 21 feet 8 inches. Room under this was the market shed; it is same dimensions but the arched doors are closed up, and is in contemplation to be turned into a petty sessions room; news room is on the second storey. A small weigh-house is under the news room and is the same dimensions. Total dimensions 62 by 27 feet in the outside. House is 2-storeys high, slated.

[Insert note: The market house was built about 80 years ago by the corporation, and about 10 years ago the last roof was put on it at the expense of the corporation. The corporation arms was on a stone over the middle arch, but is long since defaced and covered with roughcast. It is 2-storeys high and contains 4 arches, but are all closed up; one was also on the North Street end of the house but is also closed up].

Harbour

The cost of the quay near the castle in Carrickfergus is 2,000 pounds. The ballast office was established in 1834; rates of ballast is 8d per ton. The tonnage is about 3,000 register tonnage. The annual amount of harbour dues is 150 pounds. The goods imported are as follows: coal, grain, oak bark, provisions, stone, brick, black cattle and horses, slates, iron, tiles and salt. The quantity imported annually of each is: of coal about 9,000 tons; grain 140 tons; oak bark 120 tons; freestone 200 tons; slates 200 tons; salt 150 tons; fire-brick 10,000; tiles 6,000. Exports: grain 280 tons; bricks 250,000; black cattle from 1,800 to 2,500; horses 20; potatoes 180 to 200 tons; hay 60 tons; beans 150 tons. Income of the harbourmaster is 25 pounds per annum, with 8s per pound for collecting the harbour dues.

The description of vessels is chiefly schooners. About 3 are annually employed in the foreign trade and about 36 in the coasting trade. There are no licensed pilots employed in this port; jobbing pilots or harbour boatmen are employed. The business of the harbour-master is [to] regulate the ships in the port. From James Stannus, harbour-master. 28th May 1839.

Brickyards

There are 2 brickyards in Carrickfergus corporation, 1 in the Irish Quarter South, at the end of the town near the Roman Catholic chapel. It can burn from 3 to 4 kilns per annum, but only 1 kiln is burned at a time. The yard contains about three-quarters of an acre. 13 hands are daily employed for the present, sometimes more. Established in 1833; James Stannus is the proprietor. About 325,000 bricks are made annually. Information from Mr James Stannus.

The brickyard at the north east end of the town can burn from 5 to 6 kilns per annum or 1 kiln at a time. It contains about 1 and a half acres of land; at present 10 men, 2 women and 4 boys are employed daily, sometimes more and less. Paul Logan rents it from Mr James Wilson, who rents it from the Marquis of Downshire. Upwards of 25 years established. Information from James Stannus and the workmen at the yard, 8th May 1839.

Tanyard

The only tanyard in the town at present occupied is that in the Scotch Quarter, the property of John Legg Esquire, established about 63 years ago. There are 4 houses occupied in the establishment. No.1 tan house is 2-storeys high, slated, and measures externally 130 by 22 feet. Tan house no.2 is 1-storey, slated, and is 56 by 22. No.3 tan house, 1-storey, slated, and is 77 by 28 feet; all in good repair. There are 64 tan holes and 4 lime holes in the yard. There are 15 men daily employed; produce of the tanyard about 1,500 hides annually for sole leather and 1,800 of kipp for upper leather per annum, and from 300 to 400 dozen per annum of calf skins, besides horse hides etc.

Sales are chiefly in Belfast and the country Antrim at large, with occasional exports to Dublin and the Scotch markets. Sometimes hides are imported from Russia, Hamburg, Petersburg; this is only when hides are scarce and markets higher. The quantity of bark which is ground in the tanyard for use is 150 tons per annum, imported chiefly from North Wales, besides Valencia and other foreign bark. Bark is ground by horsepower.

There was another tanyard in the town but is idle since last year, 1838, in West Street.

The tanyard formerly occupied by Mr William Stephenson in West Street ceased to work in 1838; one house is 2-storey high and 50 by 25 feet; the second is 1-storey high, 50 by 25 feet; third is 1-storey, 50 by 25 feet, in middling repair.

Cotton Manufactory

Woodburn cotton spinning manufactory: John

Vance Esquire of Belfast is the proprietor; it was established 35 years ago. The house, which is situated about three-quarters of an English mile north west of Carrickfergus, is a good house, built of stone and lime, 4-storeys high with a garret, and slated. The machinery is propelled by 1 overshot water wheel 34 feet in diameter by 5 and a half feet at the buckets or face, is of iron and 24 horsepower; fall of water is 34 feet, on the Woodburn stream. The engine is 24 horsepower; total power of both 48 horsepower. Idle in summer from want of water, when steam power supplies its place. The house measures externally 110 by 40 feet, including an additional part of 40 feet which was built in 18[blank] by Mr Vance; all in good repair. The chimney is of brick, 7 years built and is 80 feet high.

Total hands employed 106, of whom 24 are males and 82 females. There are 2,520 thistle spindles and 2,664 mule spindles. The latter is worked by men only, the thistle spinning by females. Cotton spinning by mules (anciently jenny spinning) was first introduced into England by Hargraves, and in 1792; by operative hands, by Arkwright. Cotton spinning was first introduced in the reign of Henry VIII.

The following are the rooms: preparation room, cording engines, 3 drawing frames, 4 tube frames, a scutcher and spreading machine. Establishment all insured. Dr Hannah of Belfast was the first who commenced cotton spinning in this establishment. Mr Vance is only 3 years proprietor and who built the additional part to it. Mr Vance purchased the mill and 19 acres of good land attached for 3,500 pounds.

Cotton Factory

There is also ruins of a cotton factory on a small scale at Loughmorne. Nothing but part of the walls are standing. It was established about 50 years ago and ceased to work 21 years ago in consequence of a failure in the trade. It was originally the property of Mr Shaw of Celbridge near Dublin, who is said to have carried the raw material on his back from Belfast while his wife managed the business in his absence.

Paper-Printing

There is a paper-printing establishment on a small scale on the Belfast line from Carrickfergus by Thomas Mairs, and in an upper room of his house called Green Island, near Sea Park; it is 3 years established. Copies of the Scriptures and advertisements are printed here.

Machinery

Mill of James Barnett Esquire is situated in the town of Carrickfergus, Irish Quarter. It was built 25 years ago for the sole purpose of grinding malt, barley and oats for the distillery. It is double-geared, propelled by 1 water wheel, a breast, 14 feet in diameter by 7 feet at face, fall of water is 17 feet, water wheel of wood and iron. House measures 76 by 26 [feet] in the clear, substantially built of stone and lime, 3-storeys high, slated, in good repair, can work all seasons of the year, on the Woodburn stream; corn kiln is included in the dimensions.

Millmount corn and flour mill: Mr James Wilson is the proprietor. 2-storeys high, of stone and thatched, double-geared; 2 water wheels, each a breast: 1 is 17 and a half by 1 foot 6 inches, the other is 17 and a half by 4 and a half feet face; fall on each 17 feet. Buckets of one wheel is of iron and the other of wood. 2 pairs of stones for flour and 2 pair for oats. Can work all seasons of the year, situated on the Woodburn stream, situated in Carrickfergus. Houses are in very bad repair. From Mr James Wilson, proprietor, 13th March 1839. Mr Wilson's corn and flour mill measures externally 38 and a half by 90 feet.

There is a cotton-banding and twisting manufactory, also for preparing wadding and candlewick, established in the old cotton-print manufactory before described at Woodburn as a flax mill in 1839. 2 scutchers, 2 small carding engines, 1 stretcher, 1 drawing frame, 6 hands employed daily, all preparing cotton bands for the flax spinning mills, and all for home consumption; Hill Wood, proprietor, all done by water. This is the only establishment of this sort in this district or county. The cotton is purchased in Belfast. From the proprietor Hill Wood.

Distillery

Mr Barnett's distillery was established in 1824 by Mr John Thompson, a Scotsman, now deceased. It was idle in 1826 and 1827, and was re-established by Mr Barnett in 1828; situated at the Irish Quarter; on the same stream with the corn mill and can work all seasons; built of stone and lime. Total power, full 32 horsepower. It has only 1 water wheel, a breast, of iron, 12 feet in diameter by 5 broad at the face; wooden buckets with iron segments. Fall of water is only 6 feet and is propelled by a stream called the Woodburn stream, and can work all seasons of the year. It has 2 steam engines: one is 8 horsepower and the other 2 horsepower. Malt house is 3-storeys high, slated, and measures 88 by 33 and a half feet externally and is 20 feet high.

Kiln is 2-storeys high, 33 by 33 feet and 20 feet high. Weigh-house, carpenter's shop and car house is 1-storey high and measures 51 feet 3 inches by 20 feet, and is 11 feet high. Cistern and coach is 2-storeys high, 33 by 19 feet and 11 feet high. Coalshed is 1-storey high and measures 24 by 19, and is 11 feet high. Queen's warehouse, nos 1 and 2, is 2-storeys high and is 96 by 24 and 20 feet high; containing a cowhouse and stable with 2 lofts. Back house is 3-storeys high and 73 by 27 feet 8 inches, and 20 feet high. Still-house 1-storey and is 40 by 40 feet and 15 high. Cooler is 40 by 30 and 25 high, supported by pillars of brick and arches. Copper's house is 1-storey and is 35 by 26 feet, and 10 feet high.

Mash house is 2-storeys high, with 2 lofts, and 25 by 30 feet and 20 feet high. Steam mill is 3-storeys high and is 44 and a half by 21 and a half and 20 feet high, all of stone and brick and all in good repair. Chimney is of brick and is 80 feet high, 7 years built. Mixed grain whiskey is made, and all for home consumption. Average produce is 15,000 gallons per annum. Cost of the establishment, mill and kiln included, 10,000 pounds. All the establishment is insured. The grains are sold for feeding for cows and pigs at 6d per bushel, and the pottail at 2d per 16 gallons.

Spinning Mills

Joymount Bank flax spinning mill was established 1834; 1-storey high, slated, in good repair and measures 121 by 40 and a half feet; 1 water wheel, breast, 28 by 8 feet at face, of iron; fall of water 26 feet. Can work all seasons on a stream proceeding from Lough Mourne and a spring called Cillytober. 2,500 spindles employed and 130 hands; 75 females and 65 males. Storehouse measures 56 by 44 and is 4-storeys high, slated; Mr Samuel Walker, proprietor.

The new flax spinning mill of Mr James Cowan, a little above the town of Carrickfergus, about 2 furlongs above the new quay and near Barn Cottage, which is his residence. The part intended for the spinning room measures 40 feet 8 inches by 127 feet in the clear; built of brick and stone, part of the walls only up. The wheel house is all of stone and measures 60 by 40 feet in the clear. Breast wheel will take the water near the top. Situated on a stream which proceeds from Loughmorne and Cillytober.

Mills and Print-Works

About three-quarters of an English mile north east of Carrickfergus there stands, almost in ruins, an establishment which was formerly occupied as a linen bleach mill upwards of 50 years ago and about 30 years ago it became a cotton print mill. It ceased to work in 1833, from failure in trade; Jones Brothers of London, proprietors.

None of the machinery remains but an old decayed water wheel and 2 small old wash wheels, all of wood. Water wheel is 13 by 2 feet 4 inches, fall of water 13 feet; 2 small wash wheels each 6 by 1 and a half feet; overshot all. One of the houses, a 2-storey one, is 46 by 24 feet in the clear; second is also a 2-storey house 60 by 24 feet; and the third is a 1-storey house 33 by 24 feet; all slated. On the Loughmorne and Cillytober stream; called the Glenfield print-works. The place is occupied by a caretaker.

About 3 fields above the Glenfield print-works, in Oakfield, Conway Dobbs Esquire, proprietor, there is another old bleach mill in middling repair, on the same stream and in disuse for many years past. Part of the house is 3-storeys high and 21 by 36 feet. The other house is 2-storey, 39 by 21 feet, all of stone; slated.

Also a cotton factory about 3 fields above the former, now in complete ruins, on same stream. Supposed to have been maliciously burned 5 years ago by Mr Lamb, a foreman in the works, now in America; Mr Burleigh, proprietor at present.

Woodburn print-works: the erection of this establishment in 1805 by Stewart Dunn Esquire, who occupied it as print-works till 1834, and since 1836 it was a flax spinning mill, thread-dying manufactory under the firm of Brown, Warnock and Company until 1838. Since that time it is idle. It is situated about 1 English mile north west of Carrickfergus, on the Woodburn stream, and road leading from Carrick to Straid. From 1834 till 1836 it was idle.

The machinery is propelled by an overshot water wheel of metal (with arms of wood) 30 feet in diameter by 4 and a half face. The dam is situated a little above the mill and was made in 1833 by Warnock and Company. It contains about 280 feet by 60 feet and is 12 feet deep. Fall of water on the wheel is about 13 feet.

There are 7 houses. One of the houses, a 2-storey house of stone and brick, slated, built in 1833, and contains 2 spinning rooms, a preparation room, a twisting room, an engine house and a mechanics' workshop. [Insert footnote: This was the flax spinning mill only; rest of the house was print-works]. The first spinning room measures internally 40 and a half by 24 feet; second spinning room 44 feet 9 inches by 24 feet. Preparation room is on the second floor and measures 40 and a half feet by 24 feet. Twisting room on the same floor and is 40 and a half by 24 feet. Engine house is 34 and a half by 10 feet, on 1st floor. Boiling house on same floor is 16 and a half by 34 and a half feet. Mechanical workshop is underneath the house (cellar-like); is 12 feet 9 inches by 24 feet.

The second house is of stone and lime and slated, and is 4-storeys high. This was the original print-house. First room is on ground floor, is 48 by 24 feet, was lastly used as a hackling shop. Third storey is 48 by 24 feet; fourth storey contains 4 small rooms each 16 by 14 feet. The pin shop is 41 by 24; second pin shop is 22 and a half by 24 feet, on same storey. Lapping house is 2-storeys high, of stone and lime, slated.

First reeling room is 24 by 16 and a half feet; second reeling room is 19 and a half by 16 and a half feet; third reeling room is 14 and a half by 16 and a half feet. Blue house is 1-storey high, thatched and is 41 and a half by 16 and a half in the clear. Press room is 1-storey high, slated, and measures 30 and a half by 11 feet. All in good repair except the dye house, and all substantially built of stone and lime, slated; and all insured.

Cotton and Flax Mills

Duncrue cotton mill, James Cowan Esquire, proprietor, is situated a short distance from the Woodburn print-works and on the same stream. The house, which is 5-storeys high with a garret, was established 16 years ago by Mr Cowan. The machinery is propelled by 1 water wheel, breast, and 50 feet in diameter by 4 and a half at the face; fall of water 50 feet. House measures 164 by 41 feet in the clear, substantially built of stone and brick, slated, and insured. Water wheel is of iron; can work all seasons.

The house contains a carding room with 24 cards, 8 drawing frames, 3 fly frames, 3 tube frames, 2 roving frames, 1 pickling room, 1 willow room, 1 reeling room containing 15 reels, 1 spreading machine and 3 scutchers; all in good repair. The machinery is 45 horsepower; total hands employed 159, of whom 55 are males and 104 females. Total spindles employed 18,000, all mules.

The new spinning mill for flax, a little above the town of Carrick: a part of the walls are only up, is of stone and brick. The water wheel stands inside the walls and is of metal, 32 and a half feet in diameter by 8 feet at the face; James Cowan Esquire, proprietor. [Insert query: What is meant by above; and why is not the stream mentioned and why is its situation not properly described?].

About half a mile north west of Carrickfergus, on the Woodburn stream, there are 8 houses, now almost in ruins, which was about 50 years ago a linen bleach green and was then the property of Lindon and Company. About 20 years ago it was a calico print-works, then occupied by Mr Samuel Hay. It ceased to work about 9 years ago. Shortly after that the roof was taken off some of the houses by Mr James Wilson, the present proprietor.

About 4 years ago Mr Wilson built a flax mill at these ruins, 1-storey high, of stone and lime and slated; in good repair. Measures 26 feet by 23 feet outside, propelled by 1 water wheel, breast, of wood, 13 feet in diameter by 6 at the face, fall 10 feet; 1 large metal roller, 6 feet 8 inches in diameter by 3 feet at the face, with 7 smaller ones acting on the large one.

One of the old houses of this establishment (i.e. the calico print-works) is 3-storeys high, slated, in very bad repair; it measures 77 by 25 feet. The other is 1-storey high, slated; it measures 33 by 21 feet, in middling repair. Chimney is 40 feet high, of brick. Blue house 64 by 22, in good repair. Large house is 3-storey high, 77 by 25 feet. Other houses all in ruins; one is 2-storeys high and measures 120 by 21 feet; other is 2-storey and 18 by 42 feet; and the other 1-storey, is 57 by 18 feet, in ruins also.

Machinery

The Woodburn mill before described as being vacant is now working as a linen thread manufactory. It was established as such on the 1st July 1839 by Mr Robert Gamble, the proprietor. It gives employment at present to 50 hands. The machinery consists of 1,500 spindles, and about 100 of them are at present at work. The machinery is 16 horsepower. The flax is put through all the process, from hackling to spinning, in this mill.

Corn Mill

A corn and threshing mill, about 1 mile north east of Carrickfergus, on a small stream proceeding from springs in the mountain or hilly part of the corporation: it is of stone and lime, thatched, 2 years built, and for the proprietor's own use.

House measures 30 by 15 feet, 1-storey high; breast wheel 18 by 3 feet and of wood, single-geared, fall 15 feet. Idle 3 parts of the year from want of water; wheel of wood in good repair; James Berry, proprietor.

Bridges

Bridge at Cowan cotton mill is locally called Duncrue bridge; is 3 years built by contract. It has 1 large circular-segment arch 42 feet in the span by 20 feet high, with a ring-course of cut stone and a capstone of cut stone on top of the wall. Wall measures 42 feet in length and 4 feet high by 18 inches thick, with 4 butments with cut stone on top, all ashlar masonry and most permanently built, on the Woodburn river. The top is 22 and a half feet broad. Road leading to this bridge is 21 feet broad clear of drains and fences. Made same time as the bridge and by contract.

[Insert note: The bridge at Cowan's cotton mill is on the road leading from the Carrickfergus road and the Knockagh road to Bellahill, across the North Road].

Also the Woodburn bridge at Vance's cotton mill has 3 arches, circular segment. 2 of these are each 21 feet in the span by 4 feet high; the other is 23 feet in the span by 6 feet high. The range wall is 100 feet long and 5 feet high, and very crooked and 18 inches thick on the top; is 18 feet broad; very old but in tolerable repair. Road leading to this bridge is 25 feet clear of drains and fences. The footpath is 5 feet on the Carrickfergus side of the bridge. All made by presentment and now kept in repair by presentment, and is in good repair; on the road leading from Carrickfergus to Straid.

Roads

The mail coach road leading from Carrickfergus to Larne near Carrickfergus is 21 feet clear of drains and fences, with 5 feet of a footpath for a short distance, and in good repair; kept in repair by contract. Also the road leading from Carrickfergus, called the North Road, is 24 feet broad with 6 feet of a footpath, in good repair; kept in repair by presentment of grand jury. Also the mail coach road from Belfast to Carrickfergus near Carrick is 30 feet, with 5 [feet] footpath; by contract, good repair. 21st June 1839.

The new line of road leading from the Straid and Carrickfergus road to Slieveatrew is not finished. It was commenced summer 1838 and runs across part of the Commons, only through the Marquis of Downshire's estate for the accommodation of his tenants and made at his expense. It is 21 feet clear of drains and fences.

Troopers Road, leading across the Knockagh to the mountain from Woodburn, was for the accommodation of the troops to draw fuel, turf for the garrison at Carrickfergus in ancient times; it is 45 feet broad, only furrowed not stoned. 22nd June 1839.

PRODUCTIVE ECONOMY

Spirit Sales and Distillery

There are 66 retailers of spirits in the corporation of Carrickfergus; 50 of these are in the town and 16 in the country, and about 20 shebeen <sheban> houses and 16 petty hucksters. There are 4 officers of excise in the town of Carrickfergus.

There was a distillery in North Street which was the first ever in Carrickfergus; after it ceased, Barnett's commenced. This distillery closed 20 years ago. Previous to that there was only 1 excise officer in the town.

Market

Chiefly owing to the favourable state of the weather and the backwardness of agriculture, the market on this day (May 25th, 1839) was very small. The following are the articles and commodities exposed for sale: 50 carts of potatoes, average price 2s 8d per cwt; 6 carts of young pigs; 2 stands of delph; 2 stands of soft goods; 2 stands of fish; 2 carts of oats; 1 stand of crocks; 1 stand of hardware; 1 stand of old or second-hand clothes; 2 [of] baskets; and 5 stalls of meat, mutton and beef.

Wages

The average wages of a male farm servant is about 4 pounds 4s per half-year in the house; outdoor labourers' wages on a farm is 5s per week with food and 7s without food. Average wages of a female servant in a farmhouse is 3 pounds per annum; average wages of a female to work on a farm or in a farmhouse, in spring and winter, 4d per day with meat and 8d per day without meat, and during the harvest season as much wages as the men.

Cottiers

A cottier pays for a house and garden throughout the corporation 4 pounds per annum; cow's grass will be 4 pounds per annum; cost of a horse and cart and man is 3s per day.

SOCIAL ECONOMY

Population

It appears by an actual survey in 1821 by James O'Kane, that the population of the town and suburbs was males 1,547, females 1,798; of the county and parish, males 2,361, females 2,316; total males 3,908, females 4,114.

Gentlemen

The following are the names of those gentlemen residing within the corporation to whose names the title of Esquire may be attached: Peter Kirk Esquire, M.P., Thornfield; John B. Gilmour Esquire, councillor, Raven Hill Lodge; Edward Bruce Esquire, J.P. for county Antrim, Scoutbush; William Burleigh Esquire, J.P., [for] town, Carrickfergus; James Wills Esquire, J.P. for county of town, residing in Carrickfergus; Alexander Dawson Esquire, Lieutenant R.N., Carrickfergus; John Bowie Esquire, Lieutenant R.N., Rock Lands; Noah Dalway Esquire, Lieutenant R.N., Carrickfergus; Edward Rowan Esquire, Lieutenant R.N. and inspector of gaol, Carrickfergus; Henry Mouley Esquire and late Captain Foot, Silverstream; Christian William Nicolly Esquire, Prospect; George Forsythe Esquire, M.D. and first sheriff for county of town; John Legg Esquire, second sheriff, Glynn Park; John Robinson Esquire, Burleigh Hill; Stephen Rice Esquire, town of Carrickfergus; Daniel Legg Esquire, clerk of peace, Carrickfergus; Hill Wilson Esquire, Lough View; George Spear Esquire, treasurer for the county of the town; John Wright Esquire, chief constable of police, Glynfield Cottage; Alexander Johns Esquire, manager of bank, Carrickfergus; Godfrey Wills Esquire, barrister, Carrickfergus; Charles Wellington Stewart Esquire, barrister-at-law, Carrickfergus; Valentine Boyd Esquire, Carrickfergus.

[Insert note: The following names have been added: William Molony Esquire A.M., T.C.D., Carrickfergus; James Forsythe Esquire, surgeon, Carrickfergus; Robert Wills Esquire, Carrickfergus; Mr John Smith, clerk of petty sessions, and others. 17th August 1839].

Freeholders

There are 60 freeholders in the corporation, 2 rent-chargers, 20 leaseholders and 1,045 freemen; this is the gross number. What constitutes a freeman is marriage to a freeman's daughter or son, or by birth a freeman, or by serving 7 years by indenture to a freeman. 1st August 1839.

Proprietors' Names

The following persons are head proprietors (holding in fee) of the county of the town of Carrickfergus: Lord Donegall; Lord Downshire; Peter Kirk Esquire, M.P.; Miss Crymble; the corporation; William Burleigh Esquire; Mrs Cupples, Lisburn; John Legg Esquire; David Legg Esquire; Gill's trustees; Alexander Gunning Esquire; Lord Blaney; John Bowie Esquire; Mrs John Dobbs; total 14. From Mr John Smyth, agent, North Street.

Value of Commons

About 30 years ago the late James Craig Esquire offered the Corporation of Carrickfergus 700 pounds per annum for the 1,700 acres of the commonable lands, which no person has benefitted by but those who reside on the skirts of the Commons, who up to the present date have let their farms at double their value, in consequence of those tenants having the Commons to run their cattle on. Notwithstanding there is a penalty of 5 pounds for every square yard skinned or carried away off the Commons, there is a great quantity of it both skinned and carried away to all parts of the district when fuel is scarce.

County Cess

Lent assizes 1839, 588 pounds 17s 9d; summer assizes 1839, 675 pounds 12s 11d.

Petty Sessions

The petty sessions for the county of Antrim was established on the 4th April 1837 and held in Carrickfergus court house on the first Saturday of each month. It includes the parish[es] of Kilroot, Templecorran, part of Island Magee parish, part of the parish of Raloo and part of the parish of Ballynure. The magistrates who attend is Edward Bruce Esquire of Scoutbush and the mayor for the time being.

Previous to the establishment of the above petty sessions the above district was in the Larne district of petty sessions. The disputes are settled between the parties at home, which is the cause of so few adjudications in comparison with the number of summonses issued.

There are 2 courts of petty sessions held in the town of Carrickfergus, one for the county of the town of Carrickfergus, established 11th June 1827, and held on every Wednesday in the old market house, and the other for the county of Antrim, established 4th April 1837 and held in the court house on the first Saturday of each month. The mayor for the time being is the presiding magistrate for the petty sessions of the county of the town, assisted by William Burleigh Esquire and James Wills Esquire.

In 1824 a pair of white gloves have been presented by the high sheriff to the judge at the assizes, in consequence of his having no criminal case to try or pass sentence upon.

Quarter Sessions

Trials of criminal business arising within the county of the town are held by the mayor, recorder and magistrates, and their courts are in all respects similar to the quarter sessions for criminal business of counties. But at these quarter sessions no civil bill business can be done, the county of the town being, by the civil bill acts, part of the county of Antrim for the purposes of these acts, so that parties, either plaintiff or defendant, residing in Carrickfergus have their cases disposed of before the assistant barrister for the county of Antrim, at the sessions held for that division of the county Antrim called "the division of Carrickfergus."

The assistant barrister of Antrim holds courts for this division (which embraces a considerable part of the county of Antrim, as well as the county of the town of Carrickfergus) twice a year in the court house in the town of Carrickfergus, viz. in April and October, at which he disposes of all civil bill processes brought before him by parties resident in Carrickfergus, as the defendant cannot be taken to any town except Carrickfergus. But the assistant barrister for Antrim has no jurisdiction as to criminal business occurring within the county of the town.

The Mayor of Carrickfergus has, under the charter 14th December 10th year of James I (which is the charter now regulating the corporation), power to hold courts twice a week, Monday and Friday, which is a court of record. At this court any sum can be recovered when the cause of action has arisen within the county of town. The mode of proceeding is by attachment, judgement and execution. Information obtained from David Legg Esquire, clerk of peace for county of the town of Carrickfergus.

[Insert addition: At the January sessions the magistrates are appointed for 12 months].

Mayor's Court and Clerk

The mayor's court is supposed to be held twice a

week, but is only held when business is to be done, which is very seldom, as the parties generally agree to make up the cases among themselves. There is little or no business transacted in this court.

The clerk of peace fees are the same as those of any other county: he receives 24 pounds per annum, paid by presentment of the grand jury, under the act of parliament.

Constabulary

Carrickfergus became a station for constabulary on the 25th July 1837; previous to that date it was connected with the Belfast district; consists at present of 6 constables and an officer or chief.

Members of Parliament and Candidates

The following are the members of parliament and candidates, with the number polled at each election, petitions and their results within the constituency of Carrickfergus.

In December 1832 the candidates were Sir Arthur Chichester, Conway Richard Dobbs Esquire, James Wills Esquire, Sir Stephen May. The numbers polled for each are as follows: for Sir Arthur Chichester 447, Conway Richard Dobbs Esquire 495, James Wills Esquire 6, Sir Stephen May 0; total number polled 948; Conway Richard Dobbs Esquire returned.

A petition was forwarded against Dobbs in 1832, by which he was de-seated. No writ was issued until the next general election, which was in 1835. In that year the candidates were Peter Kirk Esquire and Thomas Verner Esquire; Verner withdrew, no poll, Peter Kirk was returned.

In 1837, July, at the election the candidates were Peter Kirk Esquire and Matthew Bolton Rennie Esquire. Polled for Kirk 446, polled for Rennie 418, majority for Kirk 28; Kirk was elected. There was a petition but not prosecuted. Peter Kirk Esquire is the present member.

Constituency

The whole constituency appearing on the face of the clerk of the peace's books is 1,623, but as this number includes all persons or registered voters dead since registry, and also duplicate registries, it cannot be taken as the actual existing constituency.

Wesleyans

The Wesleyan Methodist congregation were established in 1835, but no stationed minister till 1838. Income of the Methodist minister of the Wesleyan Association, the Rev. Joseph Thompson, is 60 pounds per annum, paid by the association. Congregation consists of 20 regular members; total hearers about 70 and about 6 poor persons attached to it. From the preacher and Mr Samuel Hay.

Primitive Wesleyans

The Primitive Wesleyan Methodist congregation was established about 18 years ago. At present it consists of about 40 members; about 20 is the number of members in society. Meetings are held once a fortnight in the Lancasterian national schoolroom in the town, in Lancasterian Street. This congregation has no stationed minister but is supplied from Antrim. The collection in the poor box is about 1s per Sunday.

Primitive Methodists

The Primitive or Church Methodist congregation was established 18 years ago in Carrickfergus. It consists of about 20 members, who all attend; average collection is about 6d per Sunday. There is no stationed minister, as it is a branch mission of Belfast and is supplied with a minister from Belfast.

Religious Worship

The Wesleyan Methodist service is performed at 11.30 a.m. and at 7 p.m. on Sunday, and at 7 p.m. on Tuesdays and Thursdays. It was established in Carrickfergus upwards of 60 years ago and is now rather stationary. It was the first established here; yard measures 45 by 13 yards.

The Primitive Methodist or Ranters are only 2 years established in Carrickfergus. Worship is performed at 11.30 a.m. and at 7 p.m. on Sundays, and sometimes on Thursdays at 7 p.m. The congregation is rather diminishing. Their chapel is 10 feet high.

Remonstrant Synod congregation or Unitarian congregation perform their service at 12 o'clock at noon and at 7 p.m. on Sunday only, in summer and winter; they are increasing. Their house measures 26 feet in height.

The Independents' worship is performed at 11.30 a.m. and at 7 p.m. on Sundays only. Their meeting house is now a stone finish in front and roughcast on all the other parts; it is 20 feet high.

Covenanters' service is performed at Loughmourne at 12 o'clock at noon on Sunday only.

Orthodox meeting house yard is 36 by 26 yards; house stone finish and 32 feet high.

The Wesleyan Association Methodists perform their service in a rented house at the North Gate. They separated from the Wesleyan Methodists in 1835. Their worship is performed at 11.30 a.m. and at 7 p.m. on Sundays. They are increasing a little. The room in which their service is performed was formerly occupied by the Unitarians until their house was built.

The worship of the Primitive Wesleyan Methodists is held in the Lancasterian schoolroom at 4 p.m. on every second Sunday; no stationed minister.

Episcopalians and Poor

There are about 2,000 Episcopalians in the corporation, and about 500 is the average attendance on each Sunday at church in the morning and about 200 at evening service. From the curate and the clerk. Average collection on each Sunday amounts to about 1 pound; there are 144 poor persons' names on the church books for the year 1838.

There were 39 poor persons buried by the parish, and at their expense, during the year 1838. From William Burleigh, churchwarden.

Income of the Clergy

Income of the Rev. James White, Presbyterian [insert note: Trinitarian] minister of Carrickfergus, amounts to 75 pounds regium donum and 60 pounds stipend per annum, with 12 pounds per annum arising from the rent of a house attached to the congregation, which was intended for the minister's residence but not sufficiently comfortable to reside in. The minister resides at private lodgings in the town. Total income 147 pounds per annum.

Total number of hearers about 6,000; total average attending worship about 600; average collection on each Sunday 16s, which sum goes to the Mendicity Association. [Insert query: Number of poor?]. From the minister.

Income of the Independent minister, Rev. John McAssey, is 70 pounds per annum, viz. 40 pounds from the congregation, which sum is forwarded to the Irish Evangelical Society and is paid with the donation to the minister. His residence is in private lodgings in the town.

Average attendance at worship 60 persons; total hearers about 100; collection on each Sunday 3s 6d, which goes to defray the incidental expenses of the congregational affairs; no poor

attached to the congregation. Congregation was established in 1816.

Original clergy: 1st was the Rev. George Hamilton, continued 1 year; 2nd was the Rev. William Flinter, from 1817 till 1836; 3rd was the Rev. John Murphy, the present; he came in 1838; no stationed minister from 1837 till 1838. From the minister.

Income of the Rev. James Nixon Porter, minister of the Unitarian congregation of Carrickfergus, is 75 pounds Irish regium donum and 30 pounds stipend per annum. His residence is also in private lodgings in the town. Congregation consists of about 150 persons, of which 90 is the average attendance at worship. Collection on Sunday amounts to 5s 6d per Sunday. [Insert query: Why is not this clergyman styled a Presbyterian? How many poor]? [Answer] None.

Income of the Covenanting minister, Rev. John Paul, 52 pounds, all paid by the congregation. Congregation consists of about 160 persons, that is the average attendance at worship; total hearers about 300. Collection 3s 6d per Sunday; total poor: 6 poor householders. The present minister, Dr Paul, was the first minister. Congregation was established in 1805; at that time it separated from the Kellswater congregation, to which it was united. His residence is in a rented house in the town.

Income of the parish priest, the Rev. Arthur O'Neill, is 56 pounds 18s per annum, of which 20 pounds per annum is paid by him to the curate, with board and lodging. His residence is under the same roof with the chapel.

Income of the parish priest, according to his own statement, is 36 pounds 18s 6d from the county for chaplaincy of the gaol and 20 pounds per annum stipend. Congregation is composed of coastguards, cotton spinners, daily labourers and servants, with about 30 permanent householders in the town and about 20 families in the country parts. Average attendance at mass on Sunday 300, congregation is fluctuating. Collection averages about 3s 4d per Sunday; total poor about 6, all paupers; collection goes to the Mendicity. From the priest, 13th May 1839.

The income of the Protestant curate, Rev. Henry Carter, is 100 pounds per annum, paid by the dean. There is another curate just come to Carrickfergus, whose income is 75 pounds per annum, paid also by the dean. His name is the Rev. Bennett Johns. From the dean.

Income of the Methodist preacher (connected with the Wesleyan Association Methodists), Rev.

Joseph Thompson, is 60 pounds per annum, paid by the congregation.

Income of George Spear, treasurer for the county of the town of Carrickfergus, for that office is 45 pounds per annum. 2nd August 1839.

Congregations

Wesleyan Methodist congregation consists of about 60 individuals; average attendance 50, collections on each Sunday 4s. Chapel is in West Street. Income of the preacher is 60 pounds for this year; Robert Beauchamp is preacher. Their salary is fluctuating. 13th May 1839.

Dispensary

The dispensary was established in Carrickfergus on the 1st January 1832. It is supported from voluntary contributions and an annual county grant equivalent to the amount of subscription. Dispensary days are Tuesday, Thursday and Saturday in each week from 10 till 2 o'clock p.m. It was first held in Dr Eakin's old shop in the main street for 2 years. Dr Phillips was the medical attendant. It was discontinued for some time, say [blank] years. It was afterwards held in a rented house at 4 pounds per annum in the same street and re-established through the instrumentality of Mr Johns and a few others, Peter Kirk Esquire M.P. and Captain King, but met with great opposition in consequence of the electioneering spirit which was at that time so prevalent, and fever being prevalent at that time.

In 1816 and 1817 [insert query by Boyle: 1832 or 1837?], fever being prevalent, a fever hospital was got up or rented; a small house in 1817 [insert alternative: 1832] in a field above Clipperstown, half a mile north east of Carrickfergus, from Mr Hilditch; only held for 1 year. No rent is charged since the dispensary was removed to Dr Forsythe's shop in 1837 in the main street. From a spirit of opposition in 1835 and 1836, the county grant was withdrawn. Dispensary is confined to the corporation. Managed by a committee but do not meet. In 1837 and 1838 fever was also prevalent.

[Table] Subscribers of 5 pounds each: 2 in 1832, 1 in 1833; subscribers of 3 guineas each: 2 in 1837; subscribers of 2 guineas each: 3 in 1833; subscribers of 1 guinea each: 20 in 1832, 15 in 1833, 12 in 1834, 11 in 1835, 9 in 1836, 7 in 1837; subscribers of under 1 guinea: 3 in 1832, 7 in 1833, 6 in 1834, 6 in 1835, 5 in 1836, 3 in 1837; total: 25 in 1832, 26 in 1833, 188 in 1834, 17 in 1835, 14 in 1836, 12 in 1837.

Mendicity

The Mendicity is in Cheston Street; 2 houses are occupied, each 2-storeys high and each measures 27 by 21 feet in the outside. One of the houses contains 11 inmates, all poor women, and the other contains 5; and a small house near the church contains 5 inmates. As accommodation cannot be afforded in the houses, lodgings are taken for the poor. [Insert marginal note: Other particulars cannot be ascertained until Mr Coates returns].

The Mendicity Society was established on the 1st May 1827. It is supported from voluntary subscription and donations, and governed by a committee which varies in number and is annually renewed. Its object was the employment and support of the resident poor within the corporation. Relief is also extended to the labouring poor in seasons of distress, the aged and infirm. The diet consists chiefly of oatmeal, potatoes and milk. The paupers are [crossed out: chiefly] females, who are employed in spinning.

The committee have frequently had occasion to complain of a decrease not only in the number, but in the liberality of the subscribers; and yet the utility of the society has been fully substantiated. It appears from the report of the society for the year ending 1st May 1832 that above 8,000 hanks of yarn were manufactured, and that, during the spring months of that year, many of the poor were afflicted with fever. The subscription for that year fell short of those of former years to the amount of 43 pounds. This deficiency was partly covered by an increase in the donations presented to the society by the Marquis of Downshire, Earl of Belfast and the Honourable Major-General O'Neill, Miss Jane Dobbs and Captain Bryce, 64th Regiment.

In the above year, 1832, above 420 cases, including more than 1,000 individuals, have received either temporary relief, when sick or in distress, or have been entirely supported out of its funds. Since its commencement in 1827 to 1832 upwards of 50,000 hanks of yarn have been spun by the poor (with scarcely 1 case of fraud). For this work nearly 1,000 pounds have been paid them.

Mendicity Society

Report of the Carrickfergus Mendicity Society for the year ending 30th April 1839.

They commenced the year under very unfavourable and discouraging circumstances, having but a trifling balance in the treasurer's hands and the prospect before them of a considerable reduction being made in the subscriptions and donation lists. Their worst anticipations have been too fully realised as respects these items, which alone exhibit a deficiency of 44 pounds 4s 3d. The whole income of the year would have been upwards of 100 pounds less than that of the former years, had it not been for the well-timed collection taken on behalf of the society in the Establishment church, in March last, amounting to 63 pounds 10s, and which with a few small items reduced the entire deficiency in the year's receipts to about 38 pounds; add this, however, to the increased expenditure of nearly 40 pounds, occasioned by the high price of oatmeal, and about 12 pounds additional cash paid away in the weekly distributions, and there appears to have been a decrease in the means of the society equal to about 90 pounds.

Number on the book 1st May 1838, 158, number admitted during the year 47, total 205; died since May 1st 1838, 20, struck off 39, total 59; on books April 30th 1839, 146; of this number, receiving rations and work when able 138, receiving work only 8; total subscribers 225; highest subscription is 10 pounds, lowest is 2s.

Church Missionary Society

This society was established in Carrickfergus in 1820; Alexander Johns Esquire, secretary, Mrs Stuart, collector. The following is the amount of subscriptions for 18 years.

In 1820 subscription 5 pounds 14s; in 1821 10 pounds 10d; in 1822 12 pounds 19s 2d; in 1823 11 pounds 4s 3d; in 1824 9 pounds 9s 6d; in 1825 10 pounds 13s 4d; in 1826 10 pounds 17s 8d; in 1827 6 pounds; in 1828 6 pounds 15s 4d; in 1829 9 pounds 13s 8d; in 1830 10 pounds 4d; in 1831 8 pounds 14s; in 1832 6 pounds 6s 10d; in 1834 17 pounds 6s 4d; in 1835 6 pounds 7s 4d; in 1836 7 pounds 19s 4d; in 1837 5 pounds 8d; total amount of subscription for 18 years 161 pounds 3s 2d; number of subscribers are fluctuating. From Mr Johns, secretary.

Clothing Society

The Carrickfergus Clothing Society was established in 1819. There was no memo kept of it previous to 1829. In that year the amount of subscription was 14 pounds 13s; in 1830 14 pounds 11s 5d; in 1832 17 pounds 14s 4d; in 1833 17 pounds 19s 10d; in 1834 14 pounds 18s, donations that year 5 pounds 8s 8d, sermon in the church 13 pounds 2s 6d; in 1835 amount of subscription was 15 pounds 11s; in 1836 it was 16 pounds 10s 6d, in treasurer's hands that year 12s; in 1837 subscription amounted to 17 pounds 12s 2d; in 1838 16 pounds 9s 6d.

The society is managed by a committee composed of a manager, secretary, a treasurer and 4 collectors. The clothing consists of wearing apparel and blankets, distributed once a year (generally before Christmas) at the discretion of the committee. Subscription is generally 1d per week; established May 1st 1825.

[Insert note: Mr Bleakly will state on the other side the number who annually receive clothing]: [answer] cannot be ascertained at present.

90 is the average number of articles given out annually to the poor, chiefly in petticoats. Each subscriber of 4s 4d per annum recommends 1 individual for clothing, and each subscriber of 10s recommends 2 individuals; those of a pound recommend 5 individuals.

Bible Society

The Carrickfergus Auxiliary Bible Society was established in 1810. In 1820 a deputation from the parent society came to re-establish it, being inactive. A ladies' association, however, was actively engaged. In 1835 another deputation visited Carrickfergus, when the society was reorganized, Peter Kirk Esquire, M.P. in the chair, when the committee was enlarged and additional members also placed on the ladies' society, the members of which visited their respective districts weekly and met together on the first Thursday of each month.

Since the formation of the society in 1810 to the 23rd April 1839, when the public anniversary was held in the market house, 582 bibles and 453 testaments have been issued. To those who can afford to pay the full price, it is charged; to others a reduction is made of one-third of the cost price; and to those who are too poor to purchase, the Scriptures are gratuitously given. Patron the Very Rev. Dean Chaine, Dean of Connor; committee, Rev. Henry Carter, curate, Rev. John Paul D.D., Rev. James White, Presbyterian, Rev. John McAssey, Independent; John Coates Esquire, Alexander Johns Esquire, treasurer and secretary.

Temperance Society

The Temperance Society was established in September 1829 but discontinued since 1837, in consequence of the influential persons not being interested in it. At that time (1837) it consisted of about 120 members. Meetings were held in the places of worship.

Friendly Society Fines

Any member absenting himself without just cause 15 minutes late pays 6d; a president 1s 6d; vice-president 1s and secretary 1s 6d. Any member not attending a member's funeral, a distance not exceeding 3 miles, 6d. Any member making scandalous reflections on the society 2s 6d. Any member disclosing the vote of another given on any occasion in the society 2s 6d. Disorderly members 6d. President neglecting to call a meeting 2s 6d. Collectors not warning the members within 1 mile of the town 3d each. Refusing to act as a president 2s 6d; secretary or visiting members 2s. When any alteration of the rules etc., shall be submitted to the barrister appointed by the attorney-general in Ireland to certify rules of friendly societies for his certificate upon the same. Annual meetings are held on the first Monday in March. Since the commencement only 4 members have died; some have left the country.

Farming Society

This is locally called the Kilroot and North East Division of Carrickfergus Farming Society; it was established in 1837. At its commencement it consisted of 49 members. The subscriptions amounted in that year to only 7 pounds 11s. The first ploughing match was held on Mr William Hogset's farm, Kilroot parish, on the 21st February 1837. 10 premiums were awarded, amounting to 4 pounds 12s 6d, for which 18 ploughs started. The second year, 1838, there were 59 members attached. Subscription amounted 9 pounds 19s, expenditure that year was 6 pounds 16s 3d ha'penny; balance in hand 4 pounds 2s 8d ha'penny; total amount 10 pounds 19s. Ploughing match that year was in Mr Samuel Davy's farm, North East Division, on 1st February 1838. 10 premiums amounting to 5 pounds 5s; 20 ploughs attended. There was a visible improvement in the ploughing from the preceding year.

Annual amount of subscription of each member is 2s 6d. Object is to improve the state of agriculture; managed by a committee chosen annually. Annual meetings are held in the town hall, and all dine together in some house in the town. The society is prospering. It was suggested in 1838 the formation of an agricultural library for the dissemination of agricultural knowledge amongst its members, and also to offer premiums for green crops, seeds, and best fenced and cultivated farms and cleanliness of cottages, and an improved description of horses, cows, sheep and pigs.

Harmonic Society

The Carrickfergus Harmonic Society was originally established about the year 1803, but was several times dissolved, in consequence of the death of members and others leaving the country. It was re-established last year, 1838, and at present consists of 16 members and 3 honorary members; conducted by a president, vice-president and secretary. The nights of meeting are Monday and Thursday in each week, from 7 till 10 o'clock, in the market house or town hall. Each member pays 5s entrance and from 1s to 1s 3d per week, which sum goes to pay a doorkeeper and purchase fuel, and to purchase instruments and to keep them in repair.

The band is composed of 17 instruments, viz. 5 clarinets, 1 Kent bugle, 1 trumpet, 2 French horns, 1 bass horn, 2 bassoons, 1 serpent, 3 flutes and 1 big drum; 215 tunes arranged for each instrument, with sacred music. Previous to erection of the organ in the church, the band used to accompany the singers in psalmody in the church. The instruments of the Harmonic Society, at its first dissolution, were deposited in the hands of the mayor, until new members were elected to fill the place of those deceased and gone out of the neighbourhood; members chosen by ballot. 27th May 1839.

Guilds or Trades

There are 9 guilds or, as they are commonly called, trades in the town of Carrickfergus, and the following are the names: the Gentlemen Hammermen, Mechanical Hammermen, Weavers' Guild, Shoemakers, Fishers, Trawlers, Butchers, Carmen or Carters and the Guild of Tailors.

In 1670, on the 3rd day of December and in the 22nd year of the reign of Charles II, King of England, Scotland, France and Ireland, the charter was granted by the mayor, sheriffs, burgesses and commonality of the town of Carrickfergus: full liberty and authority to incorporate bodies etc.

Guild of Carmen

The guild of carmen was incorporated as one body by charter on the 27th day of June 1812, according to the charter granted by the late Queen Elizabeth and King James I. Lord Donegall was then (in 1812) mayor, John Campbell and Thomas Millar, sheriffs, Samuel Murray then master, William Simm and Alexander Hamilton, wardens. The master and wardens of each guild are generally sworn in for the year ensuing, before the council or magistrates assembled, on the first court day before the feast of St Stephen, and on which day the guild all meet and dine. There appears to have been no regular registry kept of members' names etc. until 1814, when there appears to have been 21 names on the face of the books; James Davison, master, Edward McCann and William Simm, wardens. From 1831 till 1836 11 names of new members were admitted; no new members made since 1836. In 1836 John McCann, master, James Close and William Simm, wardens. This year, 1839, James Simm, master, James Campbell and Samuel Ferguson, wardens.

Annual meetings are always held, and quarterly meetings when business is to be transacted. Each member on admission pays 1 pound. No other expenses are incurred, except the cost of the dinner and drink. The mayor for the time being always presents 1 pound to each guild, and some guilds more according to the number who dine, but this is discretional with the mayor. There is no provision made for any member, except 3 pounds which is given to defray the funeral expenses of a member; nor is there any fund connected with this guild.

This guild is rather stationary; their charter, oaths and rules are the same as other guilds. Information obtained from the books and from James Simm, master.

Gentlemen Hammermen

The Guild of Gentlemen Hammermen was established by charter granted in 1748, Edward Bruce Esquire then mayor, Edward Jones and William McCartney, sheriffs, William Jamfrey, master, and Thomas Godfrey and William Thompson, wardens. In 1768 there appears 32 names of members on the books. At present, 1839, 50 members' names appear on the books. On the 1st January annual meetings are held, and quarterly meetings when business is to be transacted.

Butchers' Guild

This guild was established by charter 1809, and at present, 1839, consists of 40 members' names in the book, some of which are dead and others left the country, so that about 35 names are at present the actual number existing. It is rather decreasing, and do not hold their meetings as regular as the tailors or other guilds, as they are poorer and have not means to support their guild. Their oaths, rules etc. are the same as other guilds; Nathaniel Moore, master, Thomas Robinson, warden.

Cordwainers or Shoemakers

The Guild of Cordwainers or Shoemakers was established by charter in 1674. From upwards of 60 years ago down to the present date there appears on the face of the books 147 members' names. The number at present existing is about 100 members; this guild is rather stationary.

Trawlers' and Dredgers' Guild

The Guild of Trawlers and Dredgers was established by charter of Elizabeth and James I in 1812; Noah Dalway Esquire, mayor, Thomas Kirk and Robert McGowan, sheriffs, James Campbell, master, James Wheeler and John Johnston, wardens. Their charter bears date 1812. From 1812 down to 1839 there appears on the books 134 names. There is at present about 30 names of members in connection with the guild; John McHafferty, master, William Mulholland and Robert Wills, wardens.

Fishers' Guild

The Guild of Fishers was created by the mayor and sheriffs of the Corporation of Carrickfergus on the 28th day of September 1790, in the 30th year of the reign of George III; Ezekiel Davys Wilson Esquire, mayor, Robert Clements and Thomas Legg Esquire, sheriffs. Their annual meetings are held on the feast of St Peter; William Craig Esquire, master, Robert Donald and Robert Shearer, fishermen, wardens. Ezekiel Davys Wilson Esquire, then mayor, presented the guild at its commencement with a silver oar, which the master has suspended with a blue riband round his neck at their meetings and dinners.

Their last meeting was held in Sinnott's Hotel on the 22nd December 1838, when 20 members were present. From the commencement down to that date there appears on the books 224 names; 20 is the total number at present of regular members. The guild is rather decreasing, chiefly owing to the want of zeal in the influential members and the death of others, and removals. They have no funds; James Conway Esquire, master, William

Jack and Charles McFerran, wardens for the present year. The master's oath is the same as the master's oath of the Guild of Tailors. Freemen not residing within the corporation are bound to give every information where fish may be caught. Information obtained from the Charter of Fishermen.

Weavers' Guild

The fund in connection with the Guild of Weavers at present amounts to 2 pounds 5d ha'penny, chiefly arising from the rent of a house in Lancasterian Street, where all the warping materials are deposited; now, 1839, 100 members' names on books. This guild was established in 1751 by charter. Since 1751 to the year 1812, 486 names of members appear on the books; in 1812 80 names were admitted.

Annual meetings are held by all the guilds. Quarterly meetings are held generally on the 17th March, 24th June and 29th September, and on St Stephen's Day by the weavers. The Weavers', Hammermen and Tailors' Guilds all walked in procession on the occasion of the passing of the Reform Bill. Master's name of the weavers in 1756 was James McIlwaine and John McDonald and John Black, wardens.

News Room

The news room is held in the town hall, in a small room measuring 16 by 11 feet, on the second floor. It was established on the 1st January 1835 and consists of 30 subscribers of 1 pound each per annum. Managed by a committee consisting of a chairman, a secretary and treasurer.

Papers and periodicals are all sold after reading, at half-price. The following papers are received, London: *Morning chronicle, Standard, Bell's Life, United service gazette, Christian advocat*, and the *Spectator*; Dublin: *Evening mail, Evening post, General advertiser*; Belfast: *Newsletter, Commercial chronicle, Ulster Times* and *Northern Whig*. Scotch papers are the *North British advertiser* and the *Scotsman*. Periodicals are *Dublin University magazine, New monthly magazine, Edinburgh Magazine, Quarterly review, Bentley's Miscellany*, with the *Army* and *Navy lists*. Annual meetings are held. From the secretary, Samuel Stewart.

Libraries

The circulating library in Church Street is upwards of 20 years established and contains upwards of 500 volumes, chiefly novels and romances. Each subscriber pays 6s per quarter; no limited number of subscribers, no rules. Books are all very old and in bad repair; the private property of Miss Thompson.

There is a circulating library held in the minister's room in the Orthodox Presbyterian meeting house in Carrickfergus. It is called the Congregational Library, as it was got up by subscriptions of the congregation and for their use, some paying at the commencement, towards its advance, 1 guinea each and all pay 1s per annum. It was established 5 years ago. It consists of 80 subscribers and 300 volumes of religious, historical and travels. It is managed by the session. Each member or subscriber receives 1 book each sabbath day.

There is also a circulating library for the use of the children of the Sunday school of the same congregation. It is also held in the meeting house and was got up 6 years ago by local subscription. It consists of 300 volumes of religious, historical and travels. Books are exchanged every Sunday. From Mr John Coates.

Ball Alley

There is a ball alley on Joymount Bank, in the rear of Percival Ingram's public house, Scotch Quarter. It was established in 1830 at his expense. Its dimensions are 64 by 24 feet. Walls are all of brick and is 24 feet high all round; floor is flagged. 2d per game is given to the proprietor. Ball playing and the Ring are the chief amusements. 4th June 1839.

Clock Clubs

There are only 2 watch or clock clubs in the town; upwards of 30 years since first established. In almost every farmhouse there is a clock and in every respectable householder in the town.

Minor Officers

Town clerk and clerk of the peace, David Legge Esquire; coroner, Mr Samuel Parkhill; only one, a vacancy for another.

John Mulholland, Andrew Stewart and James Burns, sergeants-at-mace, the eldest of whom to wit is John Mulholland, who is mace-bearer; water-bailiff to the mayor for making arrests on the sea, James Burns; magistrates for the county of the town are William Burleigh Esquire, James Wills Esquire and the mayor for the time being. From Mr John Smyth, sword-bearer.

Gaol Conspiracy

At the Lent assizes, March 1838, a conspiracy to murder the governor, deputy governor and turnkeys: this conspiracy was formed by John Lynn of Belfast, who was convicted for the murder of his father and was sentenced to 7 years' transportation; and in order to effect his escape and effect the murder, he swore all the male prisoners in the criminal ward to assist him in the murder. The instruments which was found on his person was an iron bar with a sharp chisel edge and about 18 inches long, with 2 sharp-pointed knives. One of the party discovered the plot. From Mr Erskine, governor, and many others. 18th May 1839.

Gaol

The following are the names of the various officers connected with the gaol of Carrickfergus, with the salary of each per annum: local inspector Edward Rowan Esquire, 96 pounds 6s 2d; physician John McGowan Esquire, M.D., 74 pounds; Episcopalian chaplain Rev. Henry Carter, 36 pounds 18s 6d; Presbyterian chaplain Rev. James White, 36 pounds 18s 6d; Roman Catholic chaplain Rev. Arthur O'Neill, 36 pounds 18d 6d; governor Mr James Erskine, 276 pounds 18s 6d; deputy governor, which is also the clerk, Mr Robert Forbes, 45 pounds; first turnkey, 35 pounds; 7 other turnkeys, 30 pounds each; matron Mrs Orr, 55 pounds; deputy matron Margaret Morgan, 18 pounds; hospital nurse Mary McMaster, 22 pounds; lamp-lighter, 16 pounds 17s; schoolmaster William Larmour, 27 pounds 13s 10d; total 960 pounds 11s.

The governor, deputy, 8 turnkeys, matron, deputy matron, hospital nurse and lamp-lighter all [live] inside the gaol and all receive rations, except the governor. Total expenditure of the gaol for 1838, 2,670 pounds 8s 9d.

Total number of visits of the outdoor officers during the last year, 1838: local inspector 168, physician 362, Established Church clergy 152, Presbyterian clergy 170, Roman Catholic clergy 249.

Each prisoner receives one-half lb. of oatmeal stirabout with 1 pint of new milk for breakfast and 4 lbs of potatoes with 1 pint of buttermilk in summer, and 1 pint of new milk in winter, for dinner; breakfast at 9 o'clock in summer and dinner at 3 o'clock p.m., and breakfast at 10 in winter and dinner at 3 p.m.

The prisoners receive one-third of their earning: stones are supplied at 1s per ton and sold broken at 14d per ton. There are 218 prisoners in the gaol at present; 48 of these are for debt.

Each class of the male felons consists of 40 pupils at school hours. Total male classes 3, total males 118, total females 52. Males are taught spelling, reading, writing and arithmetic. Females are taught spelling and reading only, with plain needlework, knitting and washing. The juvenile class today consists of 24 boys. The clothing of the prisoners is all made in the gaol by the prisoners.

In 1832 there were 293 debtors; in 1833, 230 debtors; 1834, 187; 1835, 171; 1836, 229; 1837, 334; 1838, 392 debtors. From Mr Erskine, 17th May 1839.

Defence

In 1681 men fit to bear arms in Carrickfergus between the ages of 16 and 20 years: Protestants and Dissenters 398, Roman Catholics 71, total 469; in 1765 Protestants, Established Church, 809, Presbyterians 2,004, other Dissenters 30, Roman Catholics 209, total 3,052; in 1813 Protestants, Established Church, 915, Presbyterians 4,667, Roman Catholics 554, total 6,136; in 1821 Protestants, Established Church, and Presbyterians 6,767, Roman Catholics 917, total 7,684; in 1831 Protestants, Established Church, 1,353, Presbyterians 5,995, other Dissenters 345, Roman Catholics 950, religion not known 63, total 8,706. From the dispensary book cover of Dr Forsythe.

Executions

The last execution took place on the 31st March 1830. Since 1817 to that date, 1830, only 4 executions took place.

Stamp Office

Total sum of receipts in the stamp office in Carrickfergus for the year ending 1838 was 385 pounds 6s 8d.

Secret Societies and Party Spirit

There were 3 Orange lodges in the corporation and 4 Masonic lodges; the latter is still in existence.

Party spirit is more exhibited at elections in Carrickfergus than at any other time.

Early Marriage

Mrs Thompson of North Street was married at 14 years of age in 1831 and has 4 children living.

Nathaniel Montgomery's daughter Mary [married] in 1837 at 15 and three-quarters and has 1 child. Mrs Anne Lattimor was married 20 years ago at 14 years of age and has 5 children, Irish Quarter West. Mrs McClure of Carrickfergus married at 13 years of age and has 8 children.

Longevity

The oldest freeman now living in Carrickfergus is Philip McKinley of Scotch Quarter; he is 76 years of age. Alexander Boyde is still living at 80 years, and healthy. Samuel McMaster is alive and is 75 years. Andrew McDowell of Straidnahanna is 10 years dead and lived to be 100 years old. 7th May 1839.

John Herdman of the Knockagh, farmer, is still living at 98 years of age and retains almost all of his faculties. Robert Hall, late of Carrickfergus, died 3 years ago at the age of 104 years. Jane Black, a mendicant, died in the poor house at 104 years of age.

Samuel Baxter, West Division, is 80 years of age, his wife 77; had 6 children, 5 are living. Jane McMaster, Scotch Quarter, is 89 years of age; was twice married and had 3 children. John Herdman, West Division, is now 100 years of age and very healthy, and had 4 children; 2 are living. He can play cards till this day.

Illegitimacy

The following is the total number of oaths and declarations of illegitimate children which came before the magistrates at petty sessions in Carrickfergus, from the 16th August 1834 till 9th April 1839: for the county of the town, including the town, 35; for the town alone 5; for the parish [sic] of Magheramorne 1; for the parish of Raloo 5; for the parish of Island Magee 3; for the parish of Templecorran 3; for the parish of Ballynure and Mount Hill 4; total 56, of whom 50 are spinsters; bachelors are of the labouring class chiefly, with a few servants and tradesmen. From Mr John Smith, clerk of petty sessions.

Education: Private Schools

Carrickfergus Day and Boarding School, for young gentlemen only, is situated in the town of Carrickfergus, at Governors Place, and held in a house fitted up for the purpose, built at the expense of the master who, with his family, resides in the house. The house is substantially built of brick, 3-storeys high and slated. The schoolroom is on the second floor, suitably fitted up with desks and forms, and well lit with 4 square windows. It measures internally 34 by 17 feet and is 10 feet high.

The school was established in 1837. The income of the master is 500 pounds per annum, paid by the pupils. The physical education is gymnastics, with the attendance of a drill-sergeant on every day of the week, Saturday and Sunday excepted. The intellectual education is a regular Trinity College course. The books used are all sorts of classical and scientific works. The moral education consists of the Authorized Version of Scripture and catechisms of the Established and Presbyterian Churches on Saturday, with the Authorized Version of Scripture. There are 40 pupils, all males, 12 of whom are boarders. There are 10 pupils above 15 years of age, 26 from 10 to 15 and 4 under 10 years of age. There are 24 of the Established Church, 13 Presbyterians and 3 Unitarians. Hours of attendance from 10 till 3 p.m. and from 9 till 12 on Saturday. Gymnasium is 24 by 9 feet. William Molony Esquire M.A. (TCD), and of the Established Church, is the principal.

[Insert note: Ascertain how many assistants and, if you can, their salary, the rent paid, the names and persuasions of the assistants]? [Answer] There are 2 assistants in the Carrickfergus Day and Boarding School: one is Issac Powell of Trinity College, Established Church; the other is a temporary teacher. From a matter of delicacy their income cannot be ascertained. Neither can the assistants in the Ladies' Boarding and Day School be ascertained, nor their names published. Mistress Stuart of the Established Church is the mistress of the Ladies' Day and Boarding School.

Carrickfergus Boarding and Day School for young ladies is held in the main street, in a good private house fitted up for the purpose and well lit. The school was established in 1814. The income of the mistress is 1,024 guineas for the last year, 1838, all paid by the pupils. The physical education consists of gymnastics, skip-rope, dancing, swinging and battledore. The intellectual education comprises the general course of books used in other similar schools, with drawing, music, dancing, writing, arithmetic, mathematics, history etc. The moral education includes the Authorized Version of Scripture, with catechisms of the Established Church; visited by Dean Chaine on Saturdays.

Total pupils 25, of whom 12 are boarders and 13 day pupils; there are 12 above 15 years of age, 7 from 10 to 15 and 5 under 10 years of age. Terms for boarders: 70 guineas per annum for board and tuition in English, writing and arithmetic, geography, use of the globes, astronomy, and history, ancient and modern, plain and ornamental [needle]work included, music, use of pianoforte, tuning, French, dancing and drawing; no charge for entrance or for stationery. Summer and winter vacation 1 month each; no other holidays given. The pupils are allowed 3 hours exercise each day in the open air, when the weather admits of it. At present there are 12 boarders at 70 guineas per annum, and 8 day pupils at 18 guineas per annum each, and 5 minor pupils at 8 guineas per annum.

The pupils have the use of the whole house, consisting of a dining-room, a drawing-room and a very comfortable dormitory. The chief schoolroom is in the rear of the dwelling house, held in the second storey of a good slated house, and measures internally 23 and a half by 15 feet. Total cost of the whole establishment between 600 and 700 pounds; built at the expense of the mistress. A French and English governess, a French governess, a drawing master and a writing master; Madam Kennedy attends also. Information communicated by Mrs Stuart, mistress. [Insert note: There are 10 of Mrs Stuart's pupils of the Established Church and 15 Presbyterians].

Church Street private school for females only is situated near the church and held in a good room on the upper storey of a rented house, 2-storeys high. The schoolroom measures internally 21 by 10 feet, well lit, and suitably fitted up with desks and forms; established in 1834. Income of the mistress is 55 pounds per annum, paid by the children. Books used are *Manson's Primer and spelling book, Pinnock's Works, Murray's English grammar, Thompson's Geography, Knowles' Elocutionist*, with plain and fancy needlework, music, with Thompson's Arithmetic. The Authorized Version of Scripture and catechisms on Friday of the Established Church and Presbyterian Church.

There is no school held on Saturday. Total pupils 28 (all females), 5 of whom are of the Established Church, 19 are Presbyterians and 4 Methodists; there are 4 above 15 years of age, 16 from 10 to 15 and 8 under 10. Miss Anne Jane Hays, a Wesleyan Association Methodist, is the mistress.

High Street private school is situated near the court house and held in the upper storey of a good 3-storey house, free. The schoolroom measures internally 18 and a half feet by 11 feet, well lit and comfortably fitted up with forms and tables; established in 1832. Income of the mistress is

about 40 pounds per annum, paid by the pupils. There are 30 pupils, of whom 4 are males and 26 females; the males are all under 10 years of age; 4 females above 15 and 7 from 10 to 15, and 15 are under 10; 6 Established Church, 13 Presbyterians, 6 Roman Catholics, 5 Methodists; Authorized Version of Scripture and catechism of Established Church and Presbyterian Church are taught on Saturdays.

The books used are *Manson's Primer and spelling books, Pinnock's Catechism of English grammar and geography, Thompson's Geography, Lennie's English grammar*; with plain and fancy needlework; Miss Catherine Anna Gunning Cunningham and Miss Margaret Jane Cunningham of the Established Church are the teachers. Terms for English grammar, geography, history, writing and arithmetic, and plain and ornamental work, 16s per quarter; plain work and English 8s per quarters.

Carrickfergus private day school is situated on Joymount Bank, Scotch Quarter, and held in a good room on the second storey of a private house 2-storeys high, slated, rented by the master at 7 pounds per annum. The schoolroom measures internally 21 feet 9 by 14 feet 9. Well lit and suitably fitted up with desks and forms, established in 1814. Income of the teacher is 60 pounds per annum, paid by the pupils. Books used: *Knowles' Elocutionist, Parley's Tales, Thompson's Geography and atlas, Thompson's Arithmetic* and *Gough's [Arithmetic], Murray's English grammar, Jackson's Book-keeping*, with *Manson's Primer and spelling book*. Authorized Version of Scripture and catechisms of Established Church and Presbyterian Church on Saturday.

Average attendance for last quarter 60, of whom 47 are males and 13 females; of the males, 1 above 15, 25 from 10 to 15 and 22 under 10; of the females, there are 7 from 10 to 15 and 6 under 10; Established Church 12, Presbyterians 30, Roman Catholic 8 and 10 Methodists. William Larmor, a Presbyterian, is the teacher; not visited by any of the clergy. Visited 6th March 1839.

Private school held in a small room on the upper storey of a 2-storey house, slated, in Irish Quarter West, rented at 1s per week, paid by the master. The schoolroom measures internally 16 by 12 feet, tolerably well lighted and fitted up with forms and desks. Income of the master is 10 pounds per annum, paid by the children; established in 1836. Total scholars for last quarter 40, of whom 25 are males and 15 are females; 5 males from 10 to 15 and 20 under 10; 5 girls from 10 to

15 and 10 under 10; 10 Established Church, 17 Presbyterians and 13 Roman Catholics. Books in use are *Manson's Primer and spelling book, Gough's Arithmetic*, Authorized Version of Scripture and catechism on Saturday of Established and Presbyterian Churches. William Hanley, a Presbyterian, is the master.

North Street private school is held in a small room in a private house, rented at 8 pounds per annum, paid by the master. Schoolroom measures 18 feet 4 inches by 15 feet 3 inches in the clear, tolerably well lit and fitted up with forms and desks; established 1838. Income of the master for last year 6 pounds 6s per annum, paid by the children. Books used are *Knowles' Elocutionist, Thompson's Arithmetic and geography, Murray's English grammar, Morrison and Jackson's Book-keeping, Manson's Primer and spelling book;* Authorized Version of Scripture and catechism of Presbyterian Church on Saturday by the master. Total pupils 20, all boys; 8 from 10 to 15 and 12 under 10; 2 Established Church, 18 Presbyterians. Robert Martin, a Methodist, is the master.

Private school, situated in Back Lane, and held in a small room in a 1-storey house, rented at 1s 4d per week; established 1825. Income of the mistress 5 pounds per annum, paid by the children. *Manson's Primer and spelling book*, with the Authorized Version of Scripture are the only books used, with catechisms on Saturday by the mistress, of Established and Presbyterian Churches. Total scholars for last quarter 16, 2 of whom are boys and 14 are girls; all the boys are under 10, 2 of the girls are from 10 to 15 and 12 under 10; 2 Established Church, 13 Presbyterians and 1 Roman Catholic. Mary Anne Agnew, a Methodist, is the teacher.

Private school for small children and very poor, held in a room in a small house, 1-storey high, in Scotch Quarter, rented at 2 pounds per annum; nothing but forms; established in 1821, but only 6 years in this house. Income of the mistress is 6 pounds per annum, paid by the children. Books are *Manson's Primer and spelling book*, with the Sunday school books. Only spelling and reading is taught. Authorized Version and catechism on Saturday by mistress, of Presbyterian Church. Total scholars last quarter 24, of whom 12 are boys and 12 are girls, all under 10 years of age, Established Church, Presbyterian, Roman Catholic; Margaret Robertson, a Presbyterian, [mistress].

Bonnybefore private school is a small private school for young children only. Held in the kitchen of a small thatched house rented by the teacher at 2 pounds per annum; established about 19 years. Income of the mistress is 3 pounds per annum, paid by the children. Not visited by any of the clergy, Authorized Version of the Scriptures and catechism of the Presbyterian Church is taught on Saturday by the mistress. Books used are Manson's Primer and Spelling Books chiefly. Total pupils 15 for last quarter, viz. 10 boys and 5 girls, all under 10 years of age, 14 all Presbyterians, only 1 of the Established Church. Mary Magee, a Presbyterian, is the mistress.

There is a small private school held in Ellis Street, in the suburbs of the town, in a good slated house and well lit with 2 square windows, boarded floor. Schoolroom measures 22 and a half by 10 feet in the clear; no desks but forms; established 4 months. Income of the master for last quarter is about 2 pounds 5s, all paid by the pupils; house built at the master's expense and cost about 50 pounds. Books used are Manson's books with Authorized Version of Scripture, and catechism on Saturday by the master to all the children of all denominations. Total pupils 30, viz. 18 boys and 12 girls; 6 boys from 10 to 15 and 12 under 10; 2 girls from 10 to 15 and 10 under 10 years of age; 2 Established Church, 7 Roman Catholic and 21 Presbyterians. Not visited by any [clergy]; William Donnelly, a Presbyterian, master. 8th August 1839.

Public Schools

Carrickfergus Lancasterian national male school, situated in a street of the same name and held on the ground floor (which is of earth) of a 2-storey house, slated, which was originally a cotton mill but was given by the Marquis of Donegall in 1811 for a Sunday school house. The schoolroom measures internally 46 by 16 feet, tolerably well fitted up with desks and forms, and tolerably well lighted; established as a national school in 1834, but was formerly a Lancasterian school. Income of the master is 25 pounds per annum, 10 of which is paid by the National Board and 15 is paid by the pupils.

Books used are those published by the National Board exclusively. The Authorized Version of Scripture is taught, but no catechism, visited by the Presbyterian minister. Total scholars for last quarter 41, all males, 5 Established Church, 33 Presbyterians and 3 Roman Catholics; 8 above 15, 10 from 10 to 15 and 23 under 10; John Hood, a Presbyterian, is the master.

Female Lancasterian national school is held in the upper storey of the male school. The room measures 41 by 16 feet internally, and tolerably well lighted and fitted up with forms and desks; established in 1834. Income of the mistress of 13 pounds per annum, 8 pounds of which is paid by the board and 5 pounds is paid by the children. Books published by the board only are used, with plain and fancy needlework. Visited by the Presbyterian clergy; Authorized Version is taught; no catechism. Total scholars 30, all under 10 and all Presbyterian. Miss Jane Wiley, a Presbyterian, is the mistress.

Wilson's Endowed School is situated in Lancasterian Street and held on the second floor of a good 2-storey house, slated and rented by the teacher at 3 pounds per annum. The schoolroom measures internally 24 and a half feet by 20 and a half feet, suitably fitted up with desks and forms, and well lit with 5 oblong windows. The school was established in May 1822, agreeable to the will of the late Ezekiel Davys Wilson Esquire, who bequeathed 40 guineas per annum forever to the rector of the parish, to instruct 40 boys and 20 girls in reading, writing and arithmetic. Books used at present are those published by the Kildare Place Society, with *Thompson's Arithmetic*, provided by the master and at his expense; visited by the Established Church and Presbyterian clergy; Authorized Version of Scripture and catechism on Saturday by the master.

Total pupils for last quarter 75, of whom 40 are males and 35 are females; 15 males from 10 to 15 and 25 are under 10; there are 20 of the females from 10 to 15 and 15 under 10; 42 Established Church, 25 Presbyterians, 5 Roman Catholics and 3 are Methodists. 15 of the females have been taken into the school (above the number mentioned in the bequest) at the request of the ladies of the town. In 1834 a mistress was employed to teach the 35 females plain needlework in the male schoolroom, assisted by the ladies of the town, and in 1835 they were removed (part of each day for 5 days in each week) to the vestry room of the church for convenience sake, and there instructed in plain needlework and knitting, chiefly by Mrs Carter, the curate's wife, assisted by a few of the ladies of town. They are taught the other branches of intellectual education by the master in the male schoolroom.

[Insert query: What is the female teacher's salary? When did Mr Wilson die? Where is the school situated? What is the master's salary; and what is his name and persuasion]? [Answer] Mr Wilson died 27th January 1821, at 83 years of age. Master's salary is 50 guineas per annum; his name is John Morrison Eccleston, Established Church. School is situated in Lancasterian Street. Master pays the rent of the schoolhouse out of his salary. Rent is 3 pounds per annum. The annual income of the mistress is 4 pounds, paid by Mrs Carter, by subscription of the respectable inhabitants of the town; Mary Girvin, Established Church, is the mistress.

Corporation school, situated nearly 2 miles north west [of] Carrickfergus, on the road leading from the Belfast road to the Knockagh. The house measures internally 22 by 16 feet, is built of stone and lime and is slated, 1-storey high, is well lit and suitably fitted up with forms and desks. It was erected by subscription in 1838 and cost about 50 pounds. The income of the teacher is 30 pounds per annum, including 5 pounds from Dean Chaine. Kildare Place Society books are used, with the London Hibernian Society, *Thompson's Arithmetic and geography, Gough's Arithmetic, Murray's English grammar*; visited on Saturday by the master. Total pupils for last quarter 45, of whom 23 are females and 22 males; 3 of the males above 15 and 3 from 10 to 15, and 16 under 10; of the females, 7 from 10 to 15 and 16 under 10; 7 Established Church, 30 are Presbyterians and 8 Roman Catholics; Robert Lennox, Established Church, teacher. 26th March 1839.

[Insert query: Does the teacher derive 25 pounds per annum from scholars]? [Answer] The teacher of the corporation public school, Robert Lennox, receives 25 pounds per annum from the pupils and 5 pounds per annum from the Dean Chaine.

Woodburn national school is situated 2 miles north west of Carrickfergus. The house is 2-storeys high, substantially built of stone and lime, slated. The schoolroom measures internally 27 and a half by 16 and a half feet, well lit and suitably fitted up with forms and desks on the upper storey.

It was erected by subscription [in] 1831 and cost 90 pounds. The National Board gave 23 pounds 13s 4d towards clearing off the debt. Kildare Place Society gave 12 pounds towards furnishing the schoolroom. Mr Cowan gave 10 pounds, as the workers in his cotton spinning mill occasionally attend. Master's apartments are below stairs. The school is 4 years connected with the board and was originally connected with the Kildare Place Society. Income of the master is 24 pounds per annum, 8 pounds of which is paid by the board and 16 pounds by the scholars. House rent is 2 pounds per annum, paid by the committee of the school.

The books used are those published by the board only. Visited by Dr McGowan, patron, and occasionally by the Presbyterian clergy. Authorized Version is taught but no catechism. Total pupils for last quarter 28, of whom 18 are males and 10 females, 3 from 10 to 15 and 7 under 10, 6 Established Church, 13 Presbyterians, 4 Roman Catholics and 5 Methodists. William Todd, a Methodist, is the teacher. The school was much larger before the last quarter, previous to the master going to Dublin to be trained. The mistress teaches an unlimited number of girls plain and fancy needlework, and to knit, for 2 hours each day for 5 days in each week, for which the board gives her 4 pounds per annum. Mrs Todd, a Methodist, master's wife, [teacher].

Aldoo national school, situated about 3 miles [crossed out: north] of Carrickfergus, in the West Division. The house measures internally 22 by 16 feet, and is substantially built of stone and lime and is slated; is well lit and suitably fitted up with forms and desks. It was erected by subscription in 1836 and cost 70 pounds, of which the board gave 35 pounds 5s 4d. Mr Robert Mearns, a farmer, gave the ground, for which he receives 5s per annum rent, paid by the committee of the school. 5 years before it became connected with the board (which was in 1837), the school was held in a small thatched house on opposite side of the road.

Income of the master is 16 pounds, 8 pounds of which is paid by the board and 8 pounds by the pupils. Books published by the board only. Visited by Dr Magowan; Authorized Version and catechism on Saturday by the master, chiefly the *Shorter Presbyterian catechism.* Total pupils 30, of whom 20 are males and 10 are females; 1 of the males above 15 and 9 from 10 to 15, and 10 under 10; 6 of the females are from 10 to 15 and 4 under 10; 22 Presbyterians and 8 Roman Catholics; Samuel Irwin, a Presbyterian, [master].

Carrickfergus national school no.2 is held in a room in a private house in the Irish Quarter West. The schoolroom measures internally 18 by 14 feet; established 48 years ago, but only 1 year in the present house. It was formerly held in North Street. Income of the master is 13 pounds per annum, 8 of which is paid by the board and 5 pounds by the pupils; total pupils for last quarter 40, of whom 30 are males and 10 females; above 15 (of the males) 2, 12 from 10 to 15 and 16 under 10; 20 girls under 10; 28 Presbyterians and 2

Roman Catholics. No catechism, Authorized Version; books published by the board only are used; upper storey of a 2-storey house; Thomas Hagan, a Presbyterian, [master].

Loughmorne national school is situated on the shore of Loughmorne and held in a good house substantially built of stone and lime, slated, and measures 18 by 14 feet in the clear, well lit with 5 square windows and well fitted up with desks and forms. It was built by local subscription about 50 years ago and was thatched until 1830, when the roof was taken off and it slated by subscription. The annual income of the master is about 15 pounds, of which the National Board pay 8 pounds and the children 7 pounds per annum. The books used are those published by the National Board only.

Not visited by any of the clergy, as the school is situated in so remote a part of the district. Presbyterian catechism on Saturday by the master, Authorized Version of Scripture on the days and hours appointed by the Board. Total scholars for the last quarter 26, of whom 21 are males and 5 are females. Of the males, there are 4 above 15 years of age, 11 from 10 to 15 and 6 under 10 years of age; of the females, only 1 above 15 years of age and 4 from 10 to 15 years of age. Of the Established Church 1 and 25 Presbyterians. Matthew Davison, a Presbyterian, is the master.

Straidnahanna national school is situated near the extremity of the West Division of the county of the town of Carrickfergus, on the road leading from Straid to Belfast. The house is substantially built of stone and lime, slated, well lit and comfortably fitted up with desks and forms. Its dimensions are 24 by 16 feet in the clear. Erected in 1834 by local subscription and cost 50 pounds. Income of the master is 18 pounds per annum, 8 pounds of which is paid by the board and 10 paid by the children.

Books published by the Board only are used, with *Thompson and Gough's Arithmetic*; visited by the Rev. William Heron, Unitarian minister, Authorized Version of Scripture and catechism of the Presbyterian Church on Saturday by the master. Total average for the last half-year 46 pupils, 27 of whom are males and 19 females; 4 of the males are above 15, 8 from 10 to 15 and 15 under 10; of the females, 7 are from 10 to 15 and 12 under 10; 43 Presbyterians and Seceders. David John McCune, Unitarian, master; visited 1st and 2nd May 1839.

Duncrue national school is situated in the Middle Division of the corporation of Carrickfergus and held in a small stone house, slated and fitted up with desks and forms, and lit with 6 small windows. It was established in 1829 by subscription and cost about 15 pounds. The present teacher is only 4 years in it. Income of the teacher is 14 pounds per annum, viz. 8 pounds from the board and 6 pounds from the pupils. Books published by the board only are used. Not visited by any [clergy]; catechism on Saturday by the mistress, of both churches.

Average attendance for the last quarter 15, viz. 8 boys and 7 females; boys are all under 10 years of age and all the girls are also under 10 years of age; 1 Established Church, 2 Roman Catholics and 12 Presbyterians; Sarah Nugent, a Roman Catholic, [mistress]. A Sunday school was held in this schoolhouse until the summer. Information obtained from the mistress, Sarah Nugent, 27th May 1839.

Adult Schools

Adult class is held in the schoolhouse of the corporation public school; established June 1838. 36 scholars, 10 boys and 26 girls, all above 15 years of age, 3 Established Church, 30 Presbyterians, 3 Roman Catholics. Day school books used, writing and arithmetic. Hours from 6 till 8 p.m. during summer, and through the houses in winter; Robert Lennox, Established Church, [master].

Adult class is held in the schoolroom of the Woodburn national school; established 1831. Only held during the summer evenings for 4 evenings in each week. Income of the master is 1 pound 16s per quarter, paid by the pupils; only held for 4 months. 12 pupils, all boys and all above 15, 1 Established Church and 11 Presbyterians; William Todd, a Methodist, [master]. Chiefly for the use of those employed in the cotton factory.

Adult class for the benefit of the teachers of the Presbyterian Congregational Sunday school is held in the meeting house on every Sunday evening after worship. 100 attend, all above 15; 22 are male and 78 are female. Religious instruction is given by the minister; catechism only is taught.

Adult female class held in the Wesleyan Methodist Association chapel at North Gate; 9 months established, on Sunday evening from 5 till 6 p.m. Religious instruction only is imparted by the preacher's wife, Mrs Thompson. 16 girls, all above 15 years of age, 4 Methodists. Sunday School Society give books; 12 are Presbyterians. Commences with singing and prayer and concludes with the same.

Flowering Schools

Held in Ellis Row, in a room in a private house rented at 8d per week, and is 12 by 12 feet; established 30 years; 7 pupils at 4d per week; 3 are above 15 and 3 from 10 to 15, and 1 under 10, 4 Established Church and 3 Presbyterians; Sarah McCormick, Established Church, mistress. There are upwards of 300 flowerers within the county of the town of Carrickfergus.

There is a flowering school held in the upper storey of a 2-storey house in Back Lane; established in 1833. Income of the mistress is 5s per week, paid by the pupils. Room measures 11 feet 3 by 10 feet 10; a private house. Total pupils 30, all girls; 2 are above 15 and 4 under 10, and 24 from 10 to 15; 8 Established Church, 13 Presbyterians, 8 Roman Catholic and 1 Methodist. Collars, frills, caps, gowns and cuffs are flowered, all brought from Scotland; Margaret McDowell, Presbyterian, [teacher].

Singing School

There is a singing school held in the Aldoo national schoolhouse, but only 1 quarter established and will, in all probability, continue no longer, as it is mainly to teach a class to sing sacred music, chiefly Presbyterian. It contains 32 pupils, chiefly adults; each pay 1s per quarter for 1 lesson in each week. From Andrew Bruce, teacher, a Presbyterian.

Sunday Schools

The Presbyterian Congregational Sunday school is held in the meeting house of that congregation; established 4 years ago, superintended by the minister. 30 teachers viz. 15 males and 15 females. Total scholars 300, of whom 140 are males and 160 female, all Presbyterian. Hours of attendance from 9 till 11 a.m. Sunday School Society for Ireland give books; catechism is taught and Authorized Version; closes with singing and prayer. [Insert note: The minister is the Rev. James White, meeting house is North Street].

Sunday school is held in the corporation public day schoolhouse, 2 miles north west of Carrickfergus; established 1838. Superintended by the master of the day school; 8 teachers, 4 males and 4 females. Hours of attendance from 5 till 7 p.m. in summer and from 3.30 till 5.30 in winter. Sunday School Society give books. Total scholars 54, 26 boys and 28 girls; 121 Established Church, 30 Presbyterians and 12 Roman

Catholics; 30 exclusively Sunday school scholars; concludes with prayer only.

Wesleyan Methodist Association Sunday school is held in the North Street chapel; established in 1837. Superintended by Mr Samuel Hay, a Methodist; 6 teachers, 3 males and 3 females. Hours of attendance from 8 till 11 a.m. and from 3 till 5 p.m. Books published by the Sunday School Society. 100 pupils, 40 males and 60 females; 10 Established Church, 90 Presbyterians, Commences with singing and prayer and concludes with the same. [Insert note: Wesleyan Methodist Association chapel is in North Street].

Sunday school of the Independent congregation is held in the Independent meeting house and was established in 1838. Superintended by the Rev. John McAssey, minister; 3 teachers, 2 males and 1 female. 36 total scholars, 15 males and 21 females, 36 Independents. Sunday School Society give books. Hours of attendance from 1.30 till 3 p.m. Commences with prayer and closes with singing and prayer. [Insert note: The Independent meeting house is situated at Governor's Place, near the quay].

Established Church Sunday school is held in the church; established 1828. Superintended by the curate, Rev. Henry Carter; 10 teachers, viz. 4 males and 6 females. Hours from 9 till 11 a.m. and from 3 till 4 p.m. Sunday School Society give books. Total scholars 55, viz. 20 males and 35 females, all of the Established Church; exclusively Sunday school scholars, none. [Insert query: How many are exclusively Sunday scholars]? [Answer] Exclusively Sunday school scholars 47, chiefly those who attend mills all the week.

Singing school in connection with the Presbyterian congregation, for sacred music only, was established 5 weeks ago. Held in the meeting house and consists of 75 pupils, 24 males and 51 females. Terms 1s 6d per quarter for 1 evening in each week; pupils from 8 years of age to 24. Andrew Bruce and [blank] Brown, masters.

There was a Sunday school held in the day schoolhouse at Woodburn until 1837, when the children were taken to the different schools of the different congregations in the town.

Carrickfergus Sunday school no.2 and held at present in the assembly room in the market house. It was established on the 23rd April 1811; contained then 118 boys and 107 girls, total 225; in the following year 164 girls and 185 boys, total 349. For many years it was the only Sunday school in the town of Carrickfergus and for a long period nearly 400 scholars attended.

At the establishment of another school, in connection with the Methodist congregation, many children were withdrawn. Then followed a school in connection with the Established Church, which consequently reduced the number; but when one was established by the Presbyterian body, the largest number was withdrawn. It was held in the Lancasterian schoolroom until this year, 1839.

Report for the year ending 30th September 1838: total teachers 8, viz. 2 males and 6 females; total scholars 71, of whom 10 are males and 61 females. Annual average attendance 50, of whom 8 are males and 42 females, 35 Established Church, 23 Presbyterians, 2 Roman Catholics, 11 other denominations, total 71; superintendent Alexander Johns Esquire. Hours of attendance from 9.30 till 11 a.m. Sunday School Society for Ireland gives books; concludes with prayer only by the superintendent. Exclusively Sunday school scholars in the town are those who work all week in the spinning mills. Communicated by Alex Johns Esquire, 6th May 1839.

Wesleyan Methodist Sunday school is held in the Wesleyan Methodist chapel in West Street and was established about 18 years ago, and is superintended by Mr James Sloan, a Methodist. There are 8 teachers, 4 males and 4 females. Sunday School Society for Ireland gives books. Hours of attendance from 9 till 11 a.m. and 4 till 5 p.m. Total scholars 70, of whom 30 are males and 40 females, 35 Presbyterians and 35 are Methodists; 12 are exclusively Sunday school scholars. Commences with singing and prayer and concludes with the same, by the Methodist preacher or the superintendent.

A library is attached to the Sunday school and was established by subscription in 1839 of the funds of the Methodist Society. It contains about 106 volumes of religious work, chiefly biography, for the use of Sunday school only.

Emigration in 1836

[Table contains the following headings: name, age, trade, religion, residence, capital, port emigrated to].

Ezekiel McCann, 66, Established Church, weaver, Carrickfergus to Quebec.

James McDowell, 70, labourer, Presbyterian, Carrickfergus to Baltimore.

Bridget Burgoine, 36, Roman Catholic, Carrickfergus to Quebec.

Thomas Murray, 21, blacksmith, Nancy Murray, 55, Nancy Murray Junior, 14, Samuel Murray, 19, tailor, John Murray, 17, tailor, Sarah

Murray, 15, Presbyterians, Carrickfergus to New York.

William Connor, 20, labourer, Roman Catholic, Carrickfergus to Quebec.

William Moffit, 55, Ellen Moffit, 53, Eliza Moffit, 23, Sarah Moffit, 18, Nancy Moffit, 16, Presbyterians, Carrickfergus to New York.

Richard Erskine, 66, Anne Erskine, 66, Betty Erskine, 20, Margaret Erskine, 25, Richard Erskine, 18, William Erskine, 16, Robert Erskine, 14, Henry Erskine, 12, Jane Erskine, 10, Isabella Erskine, 8, Anne Erskine, 6, Presbyterians, Carrickfergus to New York.

William Connor Junior, 16, labourer, Presbyterian, Carrickfergus to New York.

Henry McCullen, 24, labourer, Presbyterian, 18 pounds capital, Loughmourne to New York.

Agnes Stuart, 20, chequer weaver, Covenanter, Loughmourne to New York.

Jane Junkin, 18, Betty Junkin, 20, Covenanters, Loughmourne to New York.

William Connor Senior, 65, labourer, Presbyterian, Middle Division to New York.

Susana Connor, 60, Roman Catholic, Middle Division to New York.

Mary Millar, 30, James Millar, 32, carpenter, Presbyterians, West Division to New York.

Robert Connor, 20, cotton printer, Archibald Connor, 18, labourer, Presbyterians, West Division to New York.

William McDowell, 35, labourer, Presbyterian, West Division to New York.

Thomas Jamison, 35, Anne Jamison, 35, Jane Jamison, 4, Janet Jamison, 1 and a half, Presbyterians, West Division to New York.

8th, 10th, 11th and 12th June 1839.

Emigration in 1837

Arthur Cahey, 20, Presbyterian, labourer, North East Division to Quebec.

Thomas Lattimor, 21, labourer, Presbyterian, 21 pounds capital, Middle Division to Quebec; returned 1838.

Robert Moffit, 23, Presbyterian, blacksmith, Woodburn to New York.

Susana Connor, 15, Presbyterian, Middle Division to New York.

Agnes Moffit, 3 weeks, Presbyterian, Middle Division to New York.

Edward McQuillan, 27, labourer, Presbyterian, Carrickfergus to New York.

Eliza McDowell, 21, Margaret McDowell, 40, Jane McDowell, 26, Ellen McDowell, 16, Presbyterians, Carrickfergus to New York. 14th June 1839.

Emigration in 1838

Samuel Kell, 60, farmer, Presbyterian, 30 pounds capital, Knockagh to Quebec.

James Shearer, 21, carman, Presbyterian, Carrickfergus to New York.

Ephraim McDowell, 32, Jane McDowell, 26, Matilda McDowell, 7, Margaret McDowell, 5, Mary Eliza McDowell, 3, Jane McDowell, 1, Presbyterians, Knockagh to Quebec.

John Wilson, 40, cotton spinner, Nancy Wilson, 30, cotton spinner, Presbyterians, Middle Division to Charleston.

William McCormick, 50, cotton spinner, Jane McCormick, 18, cotton spinner, James McCormick, 14, clerk in mill, 30 pounds capital, Nancy McCormick, 12, dressmaker, Presbyterians, Middle Division to New York.

John Gordon, 23, blacksmith, Presbyterian, Middle Division to New York.

James McDowell, 66, farmer, Presbyterian, Carrickfergus to New York.

John McKeen, 22, shoemaker, Presbyterian, Carrickfergus to Quebec.

Migration

Hugh Mulholland, 30, labourer, Roman Catholic, Torrytown to Glasgow.

William Macauley, 35, dyer, Established Church, Torrytown to Glasgow.

William Gilland, 35, printer, Presbyterian, Torrytown to Glasgow.

Andrew Baird, 25, labourer, Roman Catholic, Torrytown to Glasgow.

Joseph Keenan, 30, printer, William Keenan, 24, labourer, Roman Catholics, Torrytown to Glasgow.

Patrick Mulholland, 28, weaver, Roman Catholic, Loughmourne to Glasgow.

Alexander Neill, 18, weaver, Roman Catholic, Loughmourne to Glasgow.

William Killigan, 20, weaver, Roman Catholic, Loughmourne to Glasgow.

George Pullan, 24, weaver, Presbyterian, Loughmourne to Glasgow.

William Magill, 34, Anne Magill, 26, weavers, Presbyterians, Loughmourne to Glasgow.

James Close, 50, labourer, Roman Catholic, Carrickfergus to Liverpool.

George Creighton, 30, labourer, Presbyterian, Knockagh to Glasgow.

Peter Mulholland, 26, labourer, Roman Catholic, West Division to Glasgow.

Edward Hall, 20, carman, Presbyterian, West Division to Whitehaven.

John Moffit, 40, blacksmith. Established Church, West Division to Glasgow.

Extracts from Fair Sheets by Thomas Fagan, February to November 1839

NATURAL FEATURES

Rivers

The above county is the seat of sundry streams and small rivers, most of which have their source from the mountainous districts. But the principal one within the county is the Woodburn river, which forms 2 sections or branches in the north west side of the county and unite into 1 nearly about its centre, near Mr Dunne's threadworks, about 2 and a half miles north west of the lough or sea. From the above place to the lough it has a gradual fall through a nearly flat district of ground, and during the heavy rains and occasional floods that occur from time to time, it inundates to some extent the low grounds on its route from the aforesaid union of its 2 branches, and in some instances not only injures the growing crops but also removes, by the force of its current, any light crop that chance to be pulled or cut down on its way to the lough.

Of the latter's removal of crops, however, there have been but few instances within memory. Many of the other streams are also said to inundate their borders during heavy rains or occasional floods, but do no material injury to the crops on their route, save that of retarding their management either as regards sowing, cutting or drying or removal, as the case may be.

Spring Waters

The depth at which spring water is found in sinking pumps in the town of Carrickfergus vary from 20 to 40 feet. The mains or pipes for supply the town with water were laid at the expense of the county of the town of Carrickfergus, but those laid for the use of the county of Antrim jail were laid at the expense of the latter county. The town is about to be, in a few weeks, supplied generally with spring waters. The expense of the works is to be borne partly by the assembly and partly by presentment of the grand jury for the county of the town.

Caves

The principal of the 2 caves situate over the cascade at Woodburn river, West Division, stands between 50 and 60 feet above the bend of the river and about 15 feet beneath the surface of the rocky eminence in which it is situate. It was explored about a distance of 7 or 8 yards, but not to the extremity. It is supposed to be artificially hewn out in the rock and to be of considerable length, also to contain different apartments (which, from fear, have not been entered). The part explored vary from 2 to 5 feet wide and 2 to 5 feet high.

The smaller cave is situate about 8 feet north west of the latter and in the same pile of rock, and more immediately overhanging the cascade. It is about 40 feet above the bottom of the river and about 20 feet beneath the surface of the rock. This cave is but limited in size. The fall of the water here is at least 30 feet.

Contiguous, on the north side of the pool and issuing from the face of the north bank of the river, stands a spring of good quality. The scenery here is sublime and much frequented during the summer seasons. Informants Samuel Watson and others, 1st August 1839.

Woods and Bogs

A considerable portion of the grounds along the south side of the Knockagh hills, and now partly reclaimed and under cultivation, was within memory studded with scrag of native wood and supplied with quantities of nuts in the season. The banks of Woodburn river, as well as that of other ravines within the corporation, were also covered with scrag of native wood within the memory of some of the local inhabitants.

Detached patches of bogs were also pretty numerous within the corporation and in common use for fuel within memory, and some still to be seen. The timber found in these bogs consisted in oak, hazel, sallow and alder. Informants John McCombs and Samuel Watson, 2nd August 1839.

It would appear, from the situation in which the copper antique described [later] was found, embedded in a peat or moss subsoil, coupled with many discoveries of similar subsoil being made in sinking foundations in the town of Carrickfergus from time to time, and also along the water mark of the adjoining sea, that the ground on which the town and suburbs are situate was at some former period a tract of bog. Many other vestiges of fallen wood or of mossy nature have also been found beneath the surface in the town and its immediate vicinity, all which to some extent proves the place to have been the seat of ancient bog.

Modern Topography

Roman Catholic Chapel

The Roman Catholic chapel of Carrickfergus is situate on a handsome site at the west end of the town; to it is attached a chapel house for the accommodation of the parish priest. Both were erected by public subscriptions from liberal persons of every religious denomination, in the above and other counties. The cost of the chapel was 326 pounds and that of the pulpit and altar 31 pounds 10s. The cost of the chapel house was between 70 and 75 pounds, not including interior fixtures, done at the Rev. Mr O'Neill's expense.

The site of the above buildings and attached graveyard, containing in the whole 1 and a half roods of ground, was purchased or obtained from Edward Smyth Esquire of Dublin, at 105 pounds fine and 1 pound 11s 6d annual rent, for a term of 999 years.

Divine service is held in this chapel on Sundays throughout the year at 12 o'clock noon, and on Mondays at 9 o'clock morning during summer and during winter at 10 o'clock morning same days. The Roman Catholic congregation at Carrickfergus is fluctuating: the attendance on Sundays depend much on seasons and circumstances, but average from 200 to 300 persons.

The Rev. Arthur O'Neill is parish priest of Carrickfergus. His charge annexed to the latter comprise the parishes of Kilroot, Templecorran, Raloo, Island Magee, Kilwaughter <Kilwalter>, Maybush, Glen and Larne. The inhabitants of these parishes, (except Carrickfergus, Glen and Larne) are chiefly Protestants and Presbyterians. Informant Rev. Arthur O'Neill.

Church

The Donegall Aisle have been opened and added to Carrickfergus church in 1832.

The organs were erected in Carrickfergus church in 1830.

Andrew Gardener's monument is situate in the south aisle of the above church, commonly called Wills' Aisle.

The Donegall monument in the above church was constructed in Florence, Italy, and imported here from that country. Informants James Stannus and William Laverty. 3rd October 1839.

Buildings

The following tables will show the number and height of houses in the principal streets and other parts of the town and suburbs of Carrickfergus,

distinguishing the numbers slated and thatched, occupied and unoccupied, together with the derivations of the names in the various streets. They will also shew the numbers and descriptions of houses built for the 5 to 10 or more years past, and the parts in which they were built.

High Street: 22 3-storey houses, 7 2-storey, 1 1-storey, total 30, all slated, 29 occupied, 1 waste. This street derived its name from being originally the seat of the highest houses in the town.

Old Market Place: 3 3-storey houses, 6 2-storey, total 9, 7 slated, 2 thatched, 9 occupied. This street or place derived its name from the market being originally held there. 3 streets now form a sort of diamond or square.

Castle Street, Parade and Governor's Walk: 10 3-storey houses, 17 2-storey, total 27, 17 slated, 24 occupied, 3 waste. This street derives its names from the castle, military parade and the governor's walk, all which were situate in that place.

North Street: 3 3-storey houses, 30 2-storey, 17 1-storey, total 50, 37 slated, 13 thatched, 47 occupied, 3 waste. This street derives its name from its situation, leading north of High Street, the latter being the main street of the town.

West Street: 18 3-storey houses, 33 2-storey, 2 1-storey, total 53, 47 slated, 6 thatched, 52 occupied, 1 waste. This street also derives its name from its situation, leading west of the High Street.

Church Street or Lane: 8 2-storey houses, total 8, all slated and occupied. This, being the street leading to the church, derives its name from the latter.

Jail Lane or Antrim Street: 1 3-storey house, 6 2-storey, 1 1-storey, total 8, all slated. This lane derives its name from the county Antrim jail adjoining it.

Pogue's Court: 8 2-storey houses, total 8, 6 occupied, 2 waste. This court derives its name from the founder, Captain Pogue.

Cheston Street or Butcher's Row: 11 2-storey houses, 6 1-storey, total 17, 8 slated, 9 thatched, 15 occupied, 2 waste. This street derives its original name of Butcher's Row from being the original residence of the town butchers.

Essex Street: 6 2-storey houses, 5 1-storey, total 11, 10 slated, 1 thatched, 9 occupied, 2 waste. This street derives its name from the Earl of Essex having his house there when he was Governor of Carrickfergus.

Lancasterian Street: 11 2-storey houses, 22 1-storey, total 33 houses, 21 slated, 12 thatched, 31 occupied, 2 waste. This street derives its name from a Lancasterian school situated there.

Cork Hill: 3 2-storey houses, 16 1-storey, total 19, 15 slated, 4 thatched, 16 occupied, 3 waste. This place derives its present name from some cause now unknown.

Bachelor's Walk: 3 2-storey houses, 3 1-storey, total 6, 3 slated, 3 thatched, all occupied. This place took its name merely from fancy.

Back Lane: 2 3-storey houses, 7 2-storey, 7 1-storey, total 16, 12 slated, 4 thatched, 14 occupied houses, 2 waste. This lane took its name from its backward situation.

Pound Lane: 2 2-storey houses, 2 1-storey, total 4, 2 slated, 2 thatched, 3 occupied, 1 waste. This lane derives its name from being the seat of the old castle pound.

Irish Quarter South: 3 3-storey houses, 29 2-storey, 51 1-storey, total 83, 44 slated, 39 thatched, 76 occupied, 7 waste. This quarter derives its name from being exclusively the seat of Roman Catholics about 200 years back.

Irish Quarter West: 38 2-storey houses, 71 1-storey, total 109, 43 slated, 66 thatched, 100 occupied, 9 waste. This quarter derives its name as above, as well from its more western situation.

Ellis's Row: 16 2-storey houses, 20 1-storey, total 36, 29 slated, 7 thatched, 26 occupied, 3 waste. This row took its name from a Mr Ellis, the owner of the ground.

Davys Street or Brewing Lane: 27 2-storey houses, 19 1-storey, total 44, 41 slated, 3 thatched, 3 waste. This street derived its present name from the owners of the ground, and its former name from the old brewery which stood there.

North Gate Out: 1 3-storey house, 10 2-storey, 11 1-storey, total 22, all slated, 18 occupied, 4 waste. This place derives its name from the North Gate of the town wall, situate at that place.

Scotch Quarter: 1 4-storey houses, 7 3-storey, 19 2-storey, 73 1-storey, total 100, 49 slated, 51 thatched, 97 occupied, 3 waste. This quarter derived its name from a colony of Scotch fishermen who settled there about 180 [years] back.

Green Street: 5 2-storey houses, 48 1-storey, total 53, 20 slated, 33 thatched, 50 occupied, 3 waste. This street derives its name from a green situate there for the purpose of drying the fishermen's nets.

Total number of houses in the town and suburbs, not including the church, castle, mills, factories, manufactories or distillery buildings 746: 4-storey houses 1, 3-storey 70, 2-storey 302, 1-storey 373, slated 491, thatched 255, occupied 692, waste 54.

Modern Buildings

The following is a list of the number, height and description of houses built, rebuilt and raised in the town and suburbs of Carrickfergus during a series of time, particularly within the last 15 years; also the names of many of the persons by whom they were built and the different parts of the town in which these improvements were made, together with other observations.

High Street: 1838, 1 house, by Samuel Eskin, rebuilt and raised 1 storey, a large brick house, 3-storeys high and slated.

1800-1824: several other houses have been rebuilt and raised a storey by different persons within memory. In the south end of this street stands a house on an old plan, with the garret winds raised perpendicular in the roof. The oldest house in the town is that in which the public bakery is kept, opposite the Corporation Arms Hotel, and is said to be part of an ancient castle belonging to the Dobbin family. Portions of the projecting turrets are still visible in the front of the house. This is the main street of the town and averages 65 to 80 feet wide, and the majority of the houses neat and 3-storeys high.

Castle Street, Parade and Governor's Walk: 1836-1839, by Samuel D. Stewart, timber merchant, built on the site of the old jail and court house of county Carrickfergus, 3 large brick houses, 3-storeys high and slated, also a timber yard.

1829: by the Rev. Mr Folan, Presbyterian minister, rebuilt and raised 2 storeys, 1 brick house, 3-storeys high, slated.

1829-1834: by Davis Bowman, grocer, built 3 brick houses, 3-storeys high, slated.

1836: by Mr McKee, bombadeer, rebuilt and raised 1 storey, 2 brick houses, 2-storeys high, slated. Other houses were rebuilt and raised 1 storey within memory.

Here stand a 2-storey house on an old plan, with the windows of the upper storey projecting out in front. This line of streets averages 30 feet wide and the majority of the houses 2-storeys high.

Cheston Street: 1828, by Marriet Shannon, rebuilt and raised 1 storey, 2 brick and stone houses, 2-storeys high, slated.

1836: by the late James Wills, rebuilt and raised 1 storey, a stone and brick house, 2-storeys high, slated. This line of streets averages 30 feet wide and the majority of the houses 2-storeys high.

Old Market Place: 1837, by Russel Bowman, grocer, rebuilt and raised 1 storey, a stone and brick house, 2-storeys high, slated. The market house and Mrs Dobbs' house adjoining it stands on the site of 2 ancient castles, one of which belonged to the O'Neills and the other to the Davys family. Other houses in the Market Place was rebuilt and raised a storey within memory. This place is 55 to 100 feet wide and about 130 feet in length.

Church Street or Lane: 1829 and 1830, by the late James Millican, farmer, rebuilt 4 brick houses, 2-storeys high, slated. This street is an average of 17 feet wide and the houses 2-storeys high.

North Street: 1829-1837, by different persons, rebuilt and raised 1 storey, 10 brick and stone houses, 2-storeys high, slated; (before 1832, 6 of these houses). This street average 25 feet wide and the majority of the houses 2-storeys high.

West Street: 1827-1829, by William Pogue, shipmaster, rebuilt and raised 1 storey, 3 brick houses, 3-storeys high, slated. Also in the rear of the above and in a court called, after himself, Pogue's Court, 8 new brick houses, 2-storeys high, slated.

1829: by William Stephenson, farmer, rebuilt and raised 1 storey, a brick house, 3-storeys high, slated.

1829-1834: by Samuel McSkimin, historian, rebuilt 2 brick houses, 2-storeys high, slated. By others, 2 brick houses, 2-storeys high, slated.

1836: by Russel Bowman, grocer, 1 new brick house, 3-storeys high, slated. The latter stands on the site of an ancient castle belonging to the Dobbin family. In this street stands a house on an old plan, with the garret winds raised perpendicular above the thatch.

1839: building by Daniel Magey, 2 brick houses. Several other houses have been rebuilt and raised a storey within memory. This street is 16 to 28 feet wide and the majority of the houses 2-storeys high.

Jail Lane or Antrim Street: 1825, by James Askin, jailor, built on the site of an old cotton factory, a stone and brick house, 3-storeys high, slated. The majority of the houses here are 2-storeys high.

Back Lane: 1827, by John McDowell, a carpenter, rebuilt and raised 1 storey, 1 stone and brick house, 2-storeys high, slated.

1832: by the Rev. Duncan Wilson, Established Church, rebuilt and raised 1 storey, a brick house, 2-storeys high, slated. Other houses have been rebuilt and raised a storey within memory. This lane averages 23 feet wide.

North Gate Out: 1829-1835, by Daniel Blair,

merchant, built 5 stone and brick houses, 1-storey high, slated.

Essex Street: 1829, by Mrs Gunning; rebuilt and raised 1 storey, 2 brick houses, 2 storeys high, slated.

Lancasterian Street: 1832, by George Harrison, rebuilt and raised 1 storey, 1 brick house, 2-storeys high, slated.

1836: by Mr McCurly, pawnbroker, rebuilt and raised 1 storey, a brick house, 2-storeys high, slated.

Irish Quarter South: 1827, by John Kelly, shipmaster, rebuilt and raised 1 storey, 2 brick houses, 2-storeys high, slated.

1834: by James Barnet, distiller; rebuilt and raised 1 storey, 2 brick houses, 2 storeys high, slated.

1838: by Samuel D. Stewart, merchant, a new timber yard. This quarter average 30 feet wide and the majority of the houses 1-storey high, thatched.

Irish Quarter West: 1827, by Con Logan, shipmaster, rebuilt and raised 1 storey, 6 brick houses, 2-storeys high, slated.

1839: 2 brick houses built, 2-storeys high and slated.

1833-1835: by George Harrison and Patt McGuckan, rebuilt and raised 1 storey, 2 brick houses, 2-storeys high, slated. Other houses have been rebuilt and raised a storey in this place within memory. The street average 30 feet wide, the majority of the houses 1-storey high, thatched.

Scotch Quarter: 1833, by John Eccles, schoolmaster, built 2 brick and stone houses, 2 storeys high, slated.

1829: by Mr Wilson, architect, rebuilt and raised 1 storey, 1 stone and brick house, 2-storeys high, slated.

1822: by Mr Ingram, publican, rebuilt and raised 1 storey, 1 stone and brick house, 2-storeys high, slated.

1834-1838: by James Cope and others, rebuilt and slated 4 brick and stone houses, 1 storey high.

1838: by William Burleigh Esquire, J.P., built 1 brick and stone house, 3-storeys high, slated.

1838: by that class of Methodists called Ranters, a small meeting house of brick and stone, 1-storey high, slated.

1837-1838: by the Unitarians, a large brick meeting house, 1-storey high, slated. The west end of the above quarter, on which this meeting house is situated, is locally called Joymount Bank, and took that name from a splendid palace erected there at some former period by the 1st Viscount Chichester, and which palace he dedicated by name to his then patron, a late Lord Mountjoy.

Green Street: 1828-1833, by different persons, rebuilt and slated, 4 stone and brick houses, 1-storey high.

1823: by Samuel Hill, built and slated 4 stone and brick houses, 2-storeys high.

1838: by Mrs McFarren, rebuilt and raised 1 storey, 1 stone and brick house, 2-storeys high, slated.

New dwelling houses built in the town and sub-urbs: 1820-1835, 3-storey houses built 4, rebuilt and raised from 2 to 3 storeys 6; 2-storey houses built 11, rebuilt and raised from 1 to 2 storeys 38; 1-storey houses built 5, rebuilt and not raised 6; total built 20, total improved 50, total raised a storey higher 44.

1835-1839: 3-storey houses built 5, rebuilt and raised from 2 to 3 storeys 1, 2-storey houses built 3, rebuilt and raised from 1 to 2 storeys 10, rebuilt and not raised 1; 1-storey houses built nil, rebuilt and not raised 2; total built 8, total improved 14, total raised a storey 11.

1820-1839: houses built 28, rebuilt and improved 64.

Above three-quarter of these houses are built of brick, and the entire of them slated and the majority of them built or rebuilt by merchants, grocers and shipmasters residing in the town. The streets are chiefly paved and rather uncleanly kept. The majority of the houses of the town, and suburbs too, are much neglected as to external neatness or cleanliness, save High Street.

The latter constitutes the main street of the town. It is wide and healthy, and the houses pretty regular, lofty and neat. There are some large and handsome houses in various other parts of the town and suburbs, but their external appearance much overcast by the houses of inferior kind immediately adjoining them. High Street, Old Market Place, Castle Street, West Street and North Street are said to be the oldest parts of the town.

Buildings of every description have greatly improved here within the last 30 or 40 years, both as to number, size and appearance, though the annual rent or value of dwelling houses, in pro-portion to the modern improvement, is much less now than 20 years ago, and the demand for houses fast sinking, in consequence of the decline of trade and business in the town. Information obtained from Samuel McSkimin, Samuel Eskin, John McDowel, Charles Reid and many others, and collected between the 12th and 30th March 1839.

Market Place

The new market place of Carrickfergus is situ-ated in the north west side of the town and was opened for business 1836. It stands 122 by 97 feet inside, and enclosed partly by high stone and lime walls topped with cut stone and partly by iron railing gates and piers of cut stone. On the front, adjoining North Street, stands the entrance, con-sisting of 1 large and 2 small iron gates; the remainder of the front (except a small piece at each end) is enclosed by iron railing over a low wall. Adjoining Lancasterian Street also stands another entrance, by a large close wooden gate which, together with a range of 1-storey and slated sheds, enclose the south east side of the market.

This range consists of 10 meat shops or stalls, divided and supported in front on timber columns and neatly enclosed by timber and brickwork. On the north west side is also an undivided range of 1-storey and slated sheds, for the accommodation of the cranes and sale of different commodities, and in the west end a small enclosure or office for the accommodation of the weigh-master. On the south west it is enclosed by a high stone and lime wall, and towards the south west and mid-dle of the area stands a good weighbridge. It is, for its extent, a neat market place and well arranged.

As regard public accommodation, the expense of its erection is stated at about 700 pounds, including all appendages and purchase of the site on which it stands. The latter cost about 300 pounds and was purchased by the assembly from Mrs Kirk, for the above purpose. The cost of erecting the market place was raised as follows: Peter Kirk Esquire, M.P., who was mayor of the town in 1836, gave towards its erection 100 pounds; also, for the site of the old jail and court house of Carrickfergus, sold by the assembly to Samuel D. Stewart, general merchant, Carrickfergus, about 300 pounds. The remainder, up to 700 pounds, was defrayed by the assembly, under whose control the affairs of the market is conducted. The benefits now deriving from the market go partly to defray the weigh-master's salary and partly to raise funds for the further improvement and enlargement of the market place.

The shelter and other advantages afforded here, since opened 1836, brought an influx of dif-ferent commodities to market and seem annually to increase. This place was formerly the site of a tanyard and also of the first Presbyterian meeting house erected in Carrickfergus, and which was a small thatched house. These were superseded by a brewery, and the latter by a distillery which ceased about 16 years back. Information obtained from Samuel McSkimin, Samuel Hay and others. 2nd April 1839.

Before the opening of the new market place 1836, the markets were held in front of the old market house, in that area or sort of square formed by the junction of 4 different streets in that part of the town, and which place was found to be insufficient, either as regard extent or comfortable accommodation, for a market. After the change of the market from this place, the understorey of the old market house was closed up and the upper storey continues to be the town court house.

Court House

The county of Antrim court house, adjoining the county jail, measures in the front, opposite High Street, 100 feet in length and the south east wing 64 feet in length, all on the outside. The interior consists in 31 apartments, namely 1 hall, 1 crown court, 1 record court, 2 judges' rooms, 3 jury rooms, 1 dining-room, 1 treasurer's room, 2 secretaries' offices, 2 dressing-rooms, 1 wine store, 1 kitchen, 3 bedrooms, 2 pantries, 1 sitting-room, 1 barristers' room, 1 treasurer's office, 2 card rooms, 5 water closets. There are also different small enclosures for depositing papers and sundry other articles in, as well as for the porter's accommodation.

The hall of the court house measures 43 by 28 and a half feet, the record court 34 by 30 feet and the crown court 33 by 31 feet, all in the clear. 11th May 1839.

Harbour

Average depth of Carrickfergus harbour at neap and spring tides: at the Ship Quay, at neap tide, 6 to 8 feet, but chiefly 7 and a half feet deep; and at spring tides 8 to 11 feet, but chiefly 10 and a half feet deep. Fishers Quay: average depth at neap tide 6 feet and at spring tide 8 feet.

Friends' Graveyard

In the Middle Division, and suburbs of Carrickfergus, there stands in the corner of a kitchen garden the burial ground of a Quaker and family, consisting of himself, his wife and 3 children, all who are interred in this place of modern selection. As yet there are no headstone erected, though one has been lately cut for the purpose.

The family name is Reilly; they at one period possessed considerable property within the corporation.

The last male of the family, Lazarus Reilly, opened the above burial ground for himself and family about 50 years back, but no other branch of the family have condescended to join him in his new sepulture, though it is sheltered and carefully preserved from trespass. Informants James Stannus, Luke Reilly, Samuel McSkimin, 16th September 1839.

Village of Eden

Eadengreene (the sunny bank), now called Eden <Eaden>, is a small village on the Larne road and situated 1 mile east of Carrickfergus. It contains 43 houses, 23 of which are slated and 20 thatched; 7 are 2-storeys high and 36 1-storey high; 37 are occupied and 6 unoccupied. The first house erected here was a small thatched house by David Craig, a cotton weaver, in 1807; the last house erected is a 2-storey and slated house, built 1838 by Richard Hill, shipmaster. The grounds of the village is chiefly the property of the Wilson family, who let the building ground to different persons.

The following are trades and occupations in the village: carpenters 2, troopers 1, flowerers 3, fiddlers 1, grocers 2, hucksters 1, publicans 3, labourers 15, schoolmasters 1, smiths 1, shoemakers 2, weavers (cotton) 2, work women (poor) 7, pensioners 1, total 42.

A religious society vulgarly called Ranters hold religious meetings in this village, but have no settled house of worship in the place, though meetings are held twice a week. Information from James Marshal and Samuel McSkimin. 27th May 1839.

The street of Eden village is 46 to 76 feet wide. The Wilson family are the proprietors of the latter village and other tracts of land within the corporation of Carrickfergus. The tenures given by them of building ground and small tenements in the above village are leases forever; and of larger farms, 31 years leases. The present proprietor, William Duncan Davys Wilson Esquire, M.D., Carrickfergus, continue to give similar tenures. Informants John Smyth, Alexander Johns and Samuel McSkimin. 10th and 11th September 1839.

Village of Bonybefore

It contains 25 houses, 23 of which are thatched and 2 slated; 2 are 2-storeys high and 23 1-storey.

It contained more houses before the changing of the road from that place. The following are the trades and occupations in the village: carters 2, dressmakers 1, flowerers 12, farmers 1, schoolmistresses 1, weavers (cotton) 5, labourers 8, total 30.

This village is said to be of long standing and to have derived its name from a neat flower garden that formerly stood before a lady's dwelling in that place. Informants Samuel Smyth and others.

PRODUCTIVE ECONOMY

Markets

The following are amongst the commodities exposed for sale in the market of Carrickfergus on Saturday 9th February 1839, also from whence supplied and the prices brought by many of the articles as registered on the above date.

Beef: moderate supply by town's butchers, per lb. 4d to 5d; mutton: moderate supply by town's butchers, per lb. 5d to 6d; fresh butter: surrounding district and Island Magee, per lb. 9d to 10d; eggs: surrounding district and Island Magee, per dozen 6d; potatoes: surrounding district and Island Magee, per cwt 2s 6d; fruit and vegetables: by town's hucksters, sundry prices; hardware: limited, and sundry prices; sucking pigs: limited, and 10s each; shots or feeding pigs: few, and sundry prices; second-hand farming utensils and household furniture: sold by auction; forest trees and thorn quicks from Ballyclare, distance of 7 miles: the trees per 100 2s; thorn quicks per 1,000, according to age, 3s to 7s; stable brooms per dozen 1s 6d and supplied from King's moss.

This market was smaller than usual. Grain, oatmeal, pork, hay and straw is purchased by the town merchants and hucksters at their own places. Fresh fish is also sold through the different streets and houses. Information obtained from William McIlroy, Jacob Culbert and others. 9th February 1839.

Commodities at Market

The following commodities were exposed for sale in the market of Carrickfergus on Saturday 23rd February 1839. The prices brought by different articles, and from whence these articles were supplied, is also enumerated, as well as the number of stalls or loads of each kind.

Oats, 1 load, from Island Magee, per cwt 8s 6d to 9s; potatoes, 45 loads, from the above, per cwt 2s 6d; forest trees and thorn quicks, 1 load, from Ballyclare; trees per 100 2d, per 1,000 3d to 7d; fresh butter, 63 parcels, from Island Magee, per lb. 11d; eggs, 31 parcels, from Island Magee, per dozen 6d; fowls, 9 parcels, from Island Magee, each fowl 10d to 12d; turkeys, 2 parcels, from Island Magee, each turkey 1s 6d to 2s 6d; beef and mutton, 5 stalls, by the town's butchers, beef per lb. 4d to 5d, mutton per lb. 5d ha'penny to 6d ha'penny, veal per lb. 6d; of these a good supply; vegetables, 3 stalls, by the town hucksters, sundry prices; dairy vessels, 1 stall, from Crumlin, sundry prices; farm riddles, 1 stall, from Belfast, each 1s 3d; white hampers, 1 stall, from Belfast, each 1s; potato baskets, 1 stall, local manufacture, each 8d; hardware, 1 stall, [origin] uncertain, sundry prices; shot or small pigs, total 18, from the neighbouring districts, sundry prices.

This market was small but the different commodities all sufficient for the demand, though much less in the quantity and quality of different commodities than other markets usually are. Meal, grain, hay and straw etc., as before mentioned, are purchased by the merchants and other dealers of the town, at their respective stores, where they are supplied from the above county as well as from various districts of the county of Antrim, more particularly from the district of Island Magee, as regards grain, meal, potatoes, butter, eggs, fowl and sundry other commodities, the latter district being their chief market for the sale of the above articles. Fresh fish is supplied chiefly from the inhabitants of the Scotch Quarter, who to a large extent are fishermen.

The following articles were exposed for sale in the aforesaid market on Saturday 2nd March 1839: potatoes, 19 loads, per cwt 2s 6d; fresh butter, 81 parcels, per lb. 11d; eggs, 53 parcels, per dozen 5d; fowl, 13 parcels, hens each 8d, ducks each 10d, turkeys each 1s 6d; beef in good supply, per lb. 4d ha'penny to 5d ha'penny; mutton, in good supply, per lb. 5d ha'penny to 6d ha'penny; vegetables, 2 stalls, sundry prices; hardware, 2 stalls, sundry prices; pedlars, 2 stalls, sundry prices; riddles, 1 stall, each riddle 1s 3d; stable brooms per dozen 1s 6d; sucking pigs each 10d, and larger ones sundry prices. Informants John Shaw, Malcolm McMickan, James Moore and others, 23rd February and 2nd March 1839.

The following commodities were sold at the market of Carrickfergus held on Saturday 9th March 1839. It will show the quantity of each kind and prices brought by different articles: potatoes, 33 loads, per cwt 2s 6d; fresh butter, 94 parcels, per lb. 11d; eggs, 134 parcels, per dozen 5d ha'penny; fowl, 29 parcels, hens each 8d to

10d, ducks each 8d to 10d, turkeys each 18d to 30d; beef, in good supply, per lb. 4d to 5d ha'penny; mutton, in good supply, per lb. 5d ha'penny to 6d ha'penny; veal, per lb. 6d; potato baskets each 8d; hardware, 3 stalls, sundry prices; pedlars, 1 stall, sundry prices; brooms, 2 stalls, per dozen 1s 3d; thorn quicks, 1 stall, per 1,000 3s to 7s; live sheep, 2 only, prices uncertain; live pigs, 13 only, prices uncertain. Except butter, eggs, fowl and meat, all other commodities and attendance was unusually small at this market. Informants John Vints and others, 9th March 1839.

The following is a list of the commodities exposed for sale at the market of Carrickfergus on Saturday 16th March 1839, as also the prices brought by many of the articles sold: potatoes, 33 loads, per cwt 2s 6d; butter, 76 articles, per lb. 10d to 11d; eggs, 86 parcels, per dozen 4d to 5d; beef in good supply, per lb. 4d ha'penny to 5d ha'penny; mutton in good supply, per lb. 5d ha'penny to 6d ha'penny; cabbage plants, 2 stalls, per 100 6d; corn riddles, 1 stall, per riddle 1s 3d; hosiery, 1 stall, sundry prices; hardware, 2 stalls, sundry prices; vegetables, 2 stalls, sundry prices; brooms, 2 stalls, per dozen 1s 3d; live sheep, 2 only at market; sheepskins, unfleeced, sold at sundry prices; grains, meal and fish is sold through the different streets of the town where the merchants and other buyers hold their stores and shops. Information obtained from James Moore and others, 16th March 1839.

Market

The following is a list of commodities exposed for sale in Carrickfergus market on 8th June 1839, also the prices brought by sundry articles: potatoes, 47 loads, per cwt 2s 10d to 3s; butter, 83 parcels, per lb. 9d to 10d; eggs, 67 parcels, per dozen 5d to 6d; fowl, 23 parcels, per dozen 6s to 10s; fish, 13 parcels, sundry prices; pedlars, 2 stalls, sundry prices; hardware, 2 stalls, sundry prices; brooms, 4 stalls, per dozen 1s 3d; vegetables, 2 stalls, sundry prices; delf, 2 stalls, sundry prices; beef, per lb. 6d; mutton, per lb. 6d ha'penny; veal (fed), per lb. 6d.

The meat stalls were well supplied in the 3 latter articles of meat. Every article in the provision way met ready sale and prices advancing. 8th June 1839.

List and prices of commodities offered for sale in Carrickfergus market on 29th June, 1839: potatoes, 21 loads, per cwt 3s 4d; sucking pigs, 5 loads, per pair 16s to 21s; butter, 93 parcels, per

lb. 9d; eggs, 81 parcels, per dozen (hen's) 4d, duck's 5d ha'penny, turkey's 10d; fowl, 19 parcels, hens 1s each, ducks 8d each, chickens 8d each; Meat: beef per lb. 6d, mutton per lb. 6d ha'penny, lamb per lb. 6d ha'penny; vegetables, 14 stalls, sundry prices; pigs, 26 head, sundry prices; pedlars, 3 stalls, sundry prices; hardware, 3 stalls, sundry prices; delf, 1 stall, sundry prices; dulse, 3 stalls, sundry prices. Potatoes were limited and in great demand, as was also other provisions. 29th June 1839.

Market

The following is a list of the quantity and prices of different commodities exposed for sale in the market of Carrickfergus on Saturday 27th July 1839: potatoes (old), 1 load, per cwt 4s; potatoes (new), 13 stalls, per stone 9d; vegetables, 19 stalls, sundry prices; fruit, 12 stalls, sundry prices; butter, 81 parcels, per lb. 9d to 10d; eggs, 61 parcels, per dozen 5d to 6d; fowl, 23 parcels, per couple 12d to 20d; meat, 7 stalls, beef per lb. 5d to 6d, mutton per lb. 5d ha'penny to 6d ha'penny, veal per lb. 6d, lamb per lb. 5d to 6d; brooms, 8 stalls, per dozen 12d to 15d; turf, 17 loads, per load 14d to 18d; hardware, 5 stalls, sundry prices; pedlars, 4 stalls, sundry prices.

Fresh fish was also in abundance and sold or carried through the different streets. The quantity of the above and other commodities exposed for sale through the different parts of the town were all sufficient for the demand, particularly meat, the latter being abundantly provided by butchers for the assizes, which occurred here in the early part of the week.

The following is a list of the quantity and prices of different commodities exposed for sale at Carrickfergus market on 17th August 1839: potatoes (new), 4 loads, per stone 5d; butter, 83 parcels, per lb. 10d; eggs, 98 parcels, per dozen 6d; hens, 17 parcels, each 11d; ducks, 13 parcels, each 6d; vegetables, 13 stalls, sundry prices; dulse, 4 stalls, sundry prices; fruit, 9 stalls, sundry prices; meat, 8 stalls, beef per lb. 5d, mutton per lb. 6d, veal per lb. 6d, lamb per lb. 6d; hardware, 4 stalls, sundry prices; pedlars, 3 stalls, sundry prices; delf, 1 stall, sundry prices; toys, 2 stalls, sundry prices; brooms, 5 stalls, per dozen 12d; turf, 7 loads, per load 18d.

Fresh fish was sold in abundance through the different streets, as was also new potatoes. The market was rather thin, but the marketable commodities all sufficient for the demand. 17th August 1839.

The following is a list of the quantity and prices of different commodities exposed for sale in Carrickfergus market on 7th September 1839: potatoes, 13 loads, per stone 3d ha'penny; meat, 8 stalls, beef per lb. 5d, mutton per lb. 6d ha'penny, veal per lb. 6d, lamb per lb. 5d ha'penny; butter, 67 parcels, per lb. 10d; eggs, 73 parcels, per dozen 6d; hens, 17 parcels, per brace 22d; ducks, 14 parcels, per brace 14d; pedlars, 2 stalls, sundry prices; hardware, 2 stalls, sundry prices; fruit, 7 stalls, sundry prices; gingerbread, 4 stalls, sundry prices; vegetables, 9 stalls, sundry prices; hosiery, 2 stalls, sundry prices; turner's work, 2 stalls, sundry prices; brooms, 6 stalls, per dozen 15d; fresh fish, 12 stalls, sundry prices.

All commodities were in abundance for the demand; particularly everything in the way of food or provision were amply supplied from the neighbouring districts. Salt butter, grain and meal was as usual sold to the merchants at their respective stores.

Market Dues

Schedule of rents, tolls, fees and duties payable and to be paid by all persons resorting to the market in Carrickfergus, and for and on goods and merchandise to be weighed at the crane.

1. For each shop or booth by way of rent per week, 1s 6d.
2. For each carcase of beef exposed for sale by any person not renting a shop or booth by the week, 1s.
3. For each dead sheep, lamb, calf or pig exposed for sale by any person not renting a shop or booth by the week, 11d.
4. For each sack of meal and grain weighing 1 cwt or upwards, 1d ha'penny.
5. For each sack of meal and grain weighing under 1 cwt, 1d.
6. For each cart of potatoes to be weighed by the owner, 2d.
7. For each car of potatoes to be weighed by the owner, 1d ha'penny.
8. For each sack of potatoes to be weighed at the crane, and being upwards of 1 cwt, 1d.
9. For each sack of potatoes to be weighed at the crane, and weighing 1 cwt or less, a ha'penny.
10. For each load of fish, oysters or other shell-fish 4d.
11. For each barrel of herrings 2d.
12. For each load of crockeryware 2d.
13. For each cart or car-load of vegetables 2d.
14. For each cart or car of fruit 4d.

15. For each cart or car of plants, trees or shrubs 3d.
16. For each cart or car of any article exposed for sale, not herein particularly specified, 4d.
17. For each sack of fruit 2d.
18. For each hamper or other vessel, not being a sack or basket of fruit, 1d.
19. For each hamper or other vessel (not being a basket) containing any article for sale, except eggs, butter, poultry, fish and yarn, 1d.
20. For each basket containing any article for sale, except eggs, butter, poultry, fish and yarn, a ha'penny.
21. For each firkin of butter (large or small) 1d ha'penny.
22. For each crock or tub of butter, weighing under 50 lbs, 1d.
23. For each crock or tub, weighing 50 lbs or upwards, 1d ha'penny.
24. For each draught of cheese under 1 cwt, 1d.
25. For each draught of cheese, 1 cwt or upwards, 1d ha'penny.
26. For each dead pig, weighed at crane and not exposed for sale, 3d.
27. For each hide 1d.
28. For each calfskin a ha'penny.
29. For each cake of tallow 1d.
30. For each cow or horse offered for sale 6d.
31. For each live sheep, lamb and calf offered for sale 3d.
32. For live pigs not exceeding 6 in number, the property of 1 person and exposed for sale, 1d.
33. For each pig where upwards of 6 in number, the property of the same person, shall be exposed for sale, a ha'penny.
34. For each large flat stall or ground or otherwise (except for meat) 4d.
35. For each small flat stall or ground or otherwise (except for meat) 2d.
36. For each covered stall 8d.
37. For each draught on weighbridge 4d.
38. For weighing any article not herein before specified, for each draught 1 cwt or less, 1d.
39. For each draught of upwards of 1 cwt, 1d ha'penny.
40. For each advertisement or notice pasted 2d.
41. Butter (not in firkin, crock or tub), eggs, poultry, and fish in creels and baskets and yarn, exempt for the present.

Tares: 1. On each draught of meal and grain, 1 lb. under 1 cwt; on each draught from 1 cwt to 3 cwt, both inclusive, 2 lbs; on each draught upwards of 3 cwt, 3 lbs.
2. On potatoes, 7 lbs on each bag, including the bag, and 14 lbs on a sack.

3. On pork, to be the same as allowed in the Belfast market and to be ascertained by the weigh-master from time to time.

Dated at Carrickfergus 15th December 1836, P. Kirk, mayor.

The foregoing item is a copy of the market schedule pasted up in the new market place of Carrickfergus; the schedule contains a long list of other regulations observed in the market place, but seem to be unnecessary to be taken down here as they relate to nuisances etc. punishable by the market committee.

Weigh-Master

The weigh-master, Carrickfergus, gets as annual salary 35 pounds and a free house or office in the market place; the above sum is paid him from the proceeds of the market dues.

Grain Market

Grain, pork and firkin butter are purchased by the merchants and other buyers on Saturdays in Carrickfergus. These commodities not being offered for sale in the market place, there is no possibility of ascertaining the quantity annually purchased, as the different commodities are bought by the respective buyers at their own private stores or shops. However, the quantity of grain is considerable, but that of pork or butter very limited. Information obtained from Samuel McSkimin and [blank] Stannus, harbour-master. 8th July 1839.

Carrickfergus Fair

A table showing the quantities of the different commodities exposed for sale in the fair of Carrickfergus held on 13th May 1839, and also the districts from which supplied.

Black cattle, 107 head, from the neighbouring districts; books, old and new, 4 stalls, from Belfast and Antrim; butter (Irish), 46 parcels, from the neighbouring districts; ballad singers 5, travellers. Clothes, old and new, 6 stalls, from Belfast; cheese, 4 stalls, from Belfast and Carrickfergus; cabbage plants, 4 stalls, from county Down chiefly. Delph, 2 stalls, from Belfast; dishes (wooden), 4 stalls, from Belfast. Gingerbreads etc., 27 stalls, from Belfast and other places; hardware, 13 stalls, travellers; hosiery, 4 stalls, procured chiefly in Donegal.

Kelp, 1 load, from Island Magee. Pigs 89, from the neighbouring districts; pigs (sucking), 25 loads, from the neighbouring districts; potatoes,

9 loads, from the neighbouring districts; pedlars, 9 stalls, travellers; pictures, 1 stall, from Belfast. Toys, 5 stalls, from Belfast; toys or earthen images, 4 stalls, from Belfast; tinware, 3 stalls, from Carrickfergus and Belfast. Whips and canes, 5 stalls, from Belfast. Vegetables, 3 stalls, from suburbs of Carrickfergus.

There were no meats exposed for sale, but fresh fish was in abundance, at the prices stated on the general table of fish qualities and prices.

A table showing the prices of sundry commodities exposed for sale at the fair of Carrickfergus held on 13th May 1839: butter (fresh), from 9d to 10d per lb.; ballads a ha'penny each; books, old and new, sundry prices. Clothes, old and new, sundry prices; cheese 5d per lb.; cabbage plants from 2d to 4d per 120. Delph, sundry prices; dishes (wooden), sundry prices. Eggs from 4d to 5d per dozen. Gingerbreads, sundry prices. Hardware, sundry prices; hosiery (stockings) from 1s to 1s 8d per pair; hosiery (socks) from 6d to 10d per pair. Kelp 3s per cwt. Pigs, shot, sundry prices; pigs (sucking) from 12s to 18s per pair; potatoes 2s 8d per cwt. The prices of many of the articles were fluctuating.

First and second quality of springers brought from 7 pounds to 11 pounds each and were in great demand, but few in number. Dry cows and strippers, first and second quality, brought from 4 pounds to 7 pounds each and was, as to number and demand, in proportion to the springers. On the whole, every description of black cattle were in good demand, but limited as to number or good quality. The cattle, both young and old, were held by their respective owners or leaders on hay, straw or hemp halters. No horses or sheep appeared for sale in the fair.

The attendance as regards people or commodities was very limited, more limited it is said than on former similar occasions. Decrease in the quantity and quality of black cattle at this fair, compared with that of former fairs, is ascribed to the cattle jobbers having, during the present season, purchased them on the grass throughout the country and shipped them off to the English markets.

2 fairs are annually held in Carrickfergus, the first on 12th May and second on 1st November. There is neither sheep or horses exposed for sale at these fairs; neither is tolls or customs charged for any commodities offered for sale at the fairs, save such articles as are exposed for sale in the new market place. The charge in the latter place is the same as charged on common market days.

The quantity of black cattle brought to these fairs are on the decrease within latter years; much of such stock is now bought by cattle jobbers on the grass. Besides, the fairs in neighbouring towns are increasing in size and are consequently visited by cattle sellers in preference to Carrickfergus. However, the November fair here is much larger, as regards cattle, than the May fair. Information obtained from John and Hugh Laferty, Samuel McSkimin, 13th May 1839.

Carriage of Goods

Carriage per ton, for drawing goods between Carrickfergus and Belfast, distance 8 miles, vary from 5s to 6s; the average is 5s per ton. Informants William Gurley, a carrier, and others. 30th April 1839.

Employment

Shoemakers and tailors are 2 classes of tradespeople who are said to suffer some privation in consequence of a slackness in their trade during the 2 or 3 first months of the summer half-year. Most of other trades have average employment throughout the year, labourers included.

Trades and Callings

Trades, callings and occupations of Carrickfergus: apothecary shops and surgeons 2, attorneys 1, architects 0, armourers 0, auctioneers 1; bankers 1, bakers 6, butchers 11, boot and shoemakers 6, bonnetmakers 8, brewers 1, bellowmakers 1, barbers 1, brick moulders 2, brickyards 2.

Church 1, chapel (Roman Catholic) 1, chapel (Wesleyan Methodist) 1, clergy (Established Church) 1, clergy (Roman Catholic) 2, clergy (Presbyterian) 2, clergy (Unitarian) 1, clergy (Independents) 1, clergy (Wesleyan Methodists) 1, clergy (New Light Methodists) 1, clergy (Ranters) 1, circulating libraries 1, chandlers and soap boilers 1, chandlers and journeymen 1, castle 1, coastguard 7, coopers 5, carpenters (house) 14, carpenters (mill) 2, carpenters (ship) 3, carpenters (hedge) 2, cabinetmakers 1, clerks (office) 2, clerks (church) 1, clerks (mendicity) 1, clerks (town) 1, clerks (petty session) 1, carters 4, curriers 5, captains (coastguard) 1, captains (revenue) 1, captains (ship's) or masters 6, (old) clothes shops 1, cartmakers 2, copper and tinsmith and plumber 1, copper and tinsmith 1, coal stores 2, crane-master 1, custom house (old) 1.

Doctors (M.D.) 5, distillers 1, distillery 1, dressmakers 13, dyers (silk) 2, delph shops (small) 5, dairies (small) 2; farmers 6, flowerers (muslin) 55, fishermen 57, flax dressers 12, flax stores 1, flax or yarn factory 1, flax or yarn manufacturers 1, fishing boats 25; excise office 1; gaugers 2, gentlemen (private) 2, gentlemen (agents) 1, grain merchants 2, grain stores 2, gardeners 2, gunners (chief) 1, grocers, wine and spirit (general) 5, grocers (general) and woollen drapers 52, grocers and publicans 10, grocers (small) 14, grocers (green) 1.

Hotels 3, haberdashers and grocers 6, haberdashers 2, hucksters 23, huntsmen 1, hunt 1, harbour-master 1; iron shops 1, iron shops (old) 1; jail 1, jailors and governor 1; kennel 1; ladies (widow) 15, ladies (spinster) 9, literary men 1, lodging houses (common) 17, labourers 93, lamp-lighters to jail 1, letter carriers to post office 1; magistrates 2, meeting house (Presbyterian) 1, meeting house (Unitarian) 1, meeting house (Independent) 1, meeting house (New Light Methodist) 1, meeting house (Ranters) 1, milliners 3, masons and bricklayers 12, mariners 45, market place 1, maltsters 1, mendicity 1, mill (flour) 1, mill (corn) 1, mill (malt) 1, mill (spinning) 1, miller (flour) 1, miller (corn) 1.

News room 1, nailers 8, naval (officers) 1; post office 1, postmaster 1, publican or common spirit shops 33, printers (calico) 3, painters and glaziers 2, process servers 1, post chaises 5, post cars (daily) 7, post horses 42, peace officer 1, peace police 6, pawnbrokers 1, plasterers (stucco) 1, poor families getting of Gill's legacy 6, pensioners 5, poor meal and coal store 1, prostitutes 10, poor widows in the mendicity 17, poor working women 14, porters (session house) 1, police (chief constable of) 1, posting cars 6; quay (ship) 1, quay (fishers) 1.

Surgeons 2, schools 15, schoolmasters 7, schoolmistresses 8, secretary (grand jury) 1, saddlers and harnessmakers 4, session house (county Carrickfergus) 1, session house (county Antrim) 1, sessions (petty) 1, sessions (quarter) 1, stamp office 1, stamp master 1, blacksmiths 6, whitesmiths 0, tinsmiths 2, slaters 2, seamsters 6, stoneyard (cut) 1, stone cutters 2, scriveners 1, servants (gentlemen) 5, shoemakers 17, salt and coal stores 1, supervisor of excise 1, sextons (church) 1, sawyers 2, sergeant (town) 1, slate and timber yards 2.

Tanyards at work 1, tanyards now idle 1, tanyards in ruins 1, tanners 6, timber merchants 2, timber yards 1, tailors 8, thatchers 2, tide waiters 0, turnkeys (jail) 8; upholsterers (female) 1; watch and clockmakers 3, weavers (cotton) 35, washwomen 14, wheelwrights and turners 2, wine and spirit stores [blank], work women (poor) [blank], windmill (old) 1, widows (old) [blank].

Building Materials

Building stones, quarried or raised at Woodburn river and other parts within 2 miles of the town, are supplied at the town buildings, per ton 1s to 1s 3d; bricks, made in the suburbs, are sold at the kilns, per 1,000 18s, and if left at the buildings, per 1,000 1 pound.

Lime, partly supplied from the limeworks at Duffs hill, about 1 mile north east of the town, at the rate of 1s per barrel, and from Carnmoney, distance 5 to 6 miles, at 1s 4d per barrel, but at the kilns 1s per barrel; the latter lime is preferable for building. Sand supplied from the shore and other parts within half a mile of town at 8d per ton.

Cut stone: in North Street stands a stone yard where cut stone is supplied at sundry prices, according to the size and description of the stones required. Some of the freestone cut here is procured from Scrabo, county Down, but chief part brought from Scotland.

Slates and timber: slates have been procured partly from Bangor, county Down and partly from Belfast, but both slates and timber are now landed and supplied in town by Samuel D. Stewart, general merchant, who established 2 timber and slate-yards here in 1838-9. One of these yards are situate in Castle Street and the other in Irish Quarter South.

Prices of timber and slates 1838-9: American red pine, per ton 4 pounds; American white pine, per ton 3 pounds 6s 8d; 12 feet deals, per 120 20 pounds; smaller deals in proportion to the latter; and an average of 500 tons of timber annually sold. Slates: countesses, per 1,000 4 pounds 17s 6d; lady, per 1,000 2 pounds 10s; princes and quernstones, per ton 2 pounds 15s; ridge tiles, per dozen 5s; fire-brick, per 100 10s.

The above is the quality of timber and slates chiefly used in building here at present. Information obtained from Mr Stewart, merchant, 15th April 1839.

Wages

Average rates of wages of artisans and labourers, daily and weekly: masons and bricklayers, per day 2s 9d; slaters 3s; stucco plasterers 3s 4d; house carpenters 3s; labourers 1s 2d; stone cutters, per week 18s to 21s; saddlers 15s to 21s; curriers 20s to 25s; tanners: foreman 10s to 13s, common 7s; flax dressers: foreman 25s to 30s, common 10s; watch and clockmakers 20s; coopers 15s; boot and shoemakers 15s; bakers, with diet, 7s.

Grazing and Provisions

Grazing for milch cows is sufficiently got within 1 mile of the town, at the rate of 4 pounds to 4 pounds 4s each, during the summer half-year; and for younger cattle in proportion to the above. Milch cows are grazed in the mountain parts of the parish during the summer half-year at 3 pounds each, and younger cattle in proportion to the latter sum; very few instances of fattening or stall feeding of cattle within the parish.

Gardening: none large or public to supply the markets; the latter is moderately supplied from private gentlemen.

Potatoe ground is sufficiently got in the vicinity of the town and commonly let by the square perch from 10d to 1s 6d, but the applicant get but the first crop of his manure.

Milk and fresh butter is at all seasons of the year in sufficient supply, partly in the town and suburbs, partly brought from the neighbouring mountains and from Island Magee etc. Fresh butter vary from 8d to 12d per lb., but average 10d per lb. throughout the year; new milk is 2d per quart at all seasons.

Buttermilk, supplied in the town and suburbs and partly sent in from the neighbouring mountains and Island Magee etc. in large wooden casks, is sold during the summer at 3 quarts for 1d and in the winter at 2 quarts for 1d.

New milk cheese, which is made in great abundance in the town and its vicinity, and little inferior in quality to foreign cheese, is sold from 4d ha'penny to 7d per lb. and purchased for different other districts.

Eggs and poultry is at all seasons sufficiently supplied from the interior parts of the parish, as well as from Island Magee and other neighbouring districts.

The town is also supplied with fish by the local fishers, who regulate their prices according to quality and seasons.

Fruit is also in good supply, and is partly reared in the vicinity of the town and partly brought from Belfast.

Water Supply

The town has a sufficiency of stream or river water, and some pump water also, and metal spouts or cisterns erected in various streets and other parts of the town, for the more immediate or local accommodation of the inhabitants, and the water conveyed from the fountains into these cisterns by pipes laid beneath the surface; but spring water is limited. The only good spring in the town or suburbs is Bride Well, situated about a quarter of a mile north of the town and from which the jail is supplied.

For the supply of the latter, a reservoir adjoining the well is enclosed by a wall of stone and roofed or covered with a brick arch to prevent nuisance of any kind getting into the water; the latter is conveyed from thence to the jail by metal pipes laid beneath the surface.

St Bride's Well

The main well (which, as regard to spring water, is the chief support of the town) is 2 and a half feet square and a like depth, and enclosed by a wall of well-dressed stone and lime, and seem to have been at some former period enclosed within a house of small size; some traces of the foundation walls of the latter is still to be seen round the well and are cemented by grouted mortar of a superior quality.

This well is said to be dedicated to a St Bride, but more probable to St Bridget; its site is also said to be the site of an ancient religious edifice with which it was connected, perhaps for religious purposes too. Information obtained from Samuel McSkimin, John McCollough and others. 16th April 1839.

Fuel

Coal and turf are the fuel used in Carrickfergus, but coal is the chief fuel and is landed at the quay. English coal is mostly looked for, and rate according to circumstances from 11s to 16s per ton; average price for the year 12s 6d per ton. Scotch coal 1s 6d to 2s less than the former prices.

Turf, which is brought from the Commons and from Ardboley, distance 3 to 4 miles, are sold during the summer from 1s 3d to 2s 2d per load, which is little more than a statute gage or gauge, and are used merely for kindling coal fires.

Improvement in Buildings

The town is increasing in size, but more particularly in rebuilding and raising of old houses. The only reason for those modern improvements is a growing taste and enhancing of the ground rent on the fall of old tenures.

Decline in Trade

The town is decreasing in trade. This decline in business is ascribed to falling off within the last 20 years of cotton factories, print greens, breweries and tanyards which formerly gave constant employment to hundreds of different descriptions of the working classes, caused a large circulation of money and consumption of various commodities now seldom used or called for in Carrickfergus.

Mail Coach

The Royal Mail between Larne and Belfast was established 1833. Arrives from Belfast at the Queens Arms Hotel, Carrickfergus, at 8.30 a.m. and from Larne at 5 p.m. during the summer, and in winter arrives at the above arms from Belfast at 9 a.m. and from Larne at 4.15 p.m. Runs every day in the week and stop to change horses at Carrickfergus, as above stated. Fare from Carrickfergus to Belfast, outside 1s, inside 2s; fare from Carrickfergus to Larne, outside 1s 3d, inside [blank]; distance 9 miles. Proprietors of the coaches, Messrs Anderson Magee and Company. 17th April 1839.

Conveyances

John Anderson, proprietor of the Queens Arms Hotel, Carrickfergus, has in his posting establishment 4 chaises, 4 cars and 40 post horses.

Mrs Sinnott, Corporation Arms Hotel, has for posting 2 cars, 1 chaise and 2 horses.

There are 7 common post cars, belonging to different persons in the town, which run daily between Carrickfergus and Belfast, and start for Belfast from 8 to 10 o'clock morning and arrive back at Carrickfergus from 3 to 5 o'clock in the evening; fares vary from 9d to 1s. Several of the Belfast cars also drive occasionally to this town, so that on the whole, travellers are seldom disappointed or long detained for want of conveyances between Carrickfergus and Belfast. Information obtained from John Anderson, Samuel McSkimin and others.

Stone Quarries

North East Division, and about 14 mile from the town, there is a good quarry of whinstone, and a second in the West Division and a like distance from the town. In the Commons also are several others of the same description. But brick is now chiefly preferred, as the cheapest and also as the speediest material to be wrought in building.

Prison Labour

The quantity of stones annually broken here average 2,000 to 2,500 tons. They are taken in at 1s per ton and sold out broken at 1s 2d per ton; but when brought in by roadmakers to be broken, they are charged 4d per ton for breaking them. About 6 tons of oakum is annually picked. This is brought in at 12 pounds per ton and, when picked, is sold out again at an average of 18 pounds per ton.

The female prisoners are employed in sewing, quilting, knitting and washing. The annual profit on their work average 40 to 50 pounds. All prison apparel for male and female, and shoes also, are made up within the jail; also bed ticks and other necessaries. Information from the governor.

Building Ground and Tenures

The rent for building ground in the town and suburbs of Carrickfergus vary according to the situation for business and also according to extent of rear. However, it rates from 1s 6d to 10s per foot of front; 6s per foot would be about the average. Tenures from 61 to 91 years or forever, according to fines and other circumstances. Very little building ground to let or have been let for a series of past years, other than by purchasing out of interests in tenements. Information obtained from Samuel D. Stuart Esquire, Dr Forsyth, James Stannus, Samuel McSkimin and others. 15th July 1839.

Tenures

The tenures commonly given by landed proprietors within the county of the town of Carrickfergus are as follows: Marquis of Donegall 61 years; Lord Blaney 99 years; Lord Downshire 31 years and 3 lives; and others 31 or 21 [years] without any lives. Informants Samuel and William Catherwood.

Size of Farms

The holding or farms within the county of the town of Carrickfergus vary from 5 to 60 acres, but the majority of them are 10 to 30 Irish acres. Few tenures have been given under the corporation for a series of past years; those latterly given were 61 years. Information obtained from Dr Forsyth and Samuel McSkimin, 26th July 1839.

Tithes

The rectorial tithe of Carrickfergus is 400 pounds per annum. The Very Rev. John Chaine is rector and Dean of Connor also. His income from the deanery is [blank] per annum. He was installed to both the rectory and deanery within the present year (1839). Information from the Very Rev. Dean of Connor.

Mills

A cut or stream from Woodburn river supply Millmount mills at Carrickfergus with water.

Quays

There are 39 vessels belonging to or frequenting this harbour, not including boats. 8 years ago there were not more than one-third of the above number belonging to this harbour; increase seems to continue in this respect but the harbour is much too small even for the present trade. The dues raised from vessels amount to about 140 pounds per annum, all which go to improvement of the harbour, except the salaries of the ballast and harbour-master and water-bailiff. The latter gets 10 pounds per annum and former 25 pounds per annum, besides 1s in the pound for keeping boats and collecting of the harbour dues etc.; he acts as harbour and ballast-master.

Strange vessels coming to this harbour have the same privilege as those belonging to the place. The shipping amount at present to about 3,000 tons register, capable of taking in or putting out above 5,000 tons. About 300,000 brick, 200 to 300 tons of grain, 200 tons of potatoes and 100 tons of hay are annually exported. From 11th April to 30th June last, there was 1,114 black cattle and 13 horses exported. 3 vessels trade foreign: 150 tons of bark and 200 tons of salt have been imported here within the past year.

The ancient corporation have the control and management of the harbour, through a committee by them appointed for that purpose, consisting of 13 members, the mayor for the time being being their head. The present committee consist of the following persons: Marriott Dalway, mayor; George Forsythe, John Legg, William Burleigh, Daniel Blair, James Barnett, John Coates, James Wilson, Samuel D. Stuart, John McGowan M.D., Alexander Johns, William Pogue, Paul Logan; and 5 of whom form a quorum. James Wilson acts as secretary and Alexander Johns as treasurer.

This committee was embodied in January 1839, since which the regulations and improvement of the harbour is conducted and attended to with more regularity than for many previous years.

Harbour Surveys

Sir John Rennie, in 1832, made a survey for a contemplated new harbour at Carrickfergus. Mr Bald, a civil engineer, made in 1834 at the same place a similar survey for the above and other purposes.

SOCIAL ECONOMY

Population

The population of the parish of St Nicholas, or county of the town of Carrickfergus, in 1834 stood as follows: Episcopalian Protestants 1,353, Protestant Dissenters 5,995, other Protestant Dissenters 345, Roman Catholics 950, others not known what they are 63, total population of the parish 8,706. Taken from the parliamentary census made in the above year.

Character of the Inhabitants

The majority of the working classes in the town and suburbs, as well as a number of the lower classes in business, are tolerably partial to drinking of spirituous and other liquors. Such practice prevail in a more or less degree among almost all classes, save those whose station in society or religious considerations take precedence of the former.

Notwithstanding the attachment of the lower classes of the people to tippling, there are rarely any instances of party quarrels prevail[ing] amongst them: the majority of the inhabitants are rather of a quiet disposition, pretty attentive to their occupations and trades or other avocations, and, with few exceptions, strictly observant as regard their sabbath or religious duties. They are also, with a few exceptions, or that of modern settlers, said to be of an honest, inoffensive and neighbourly disposition towards each other.

Their dress on Sundays is tolerably fair, but in this latter respect the majority of them are far behind other towns and districts, not only as regard dress but also as regard general taste in either their habitations and other appendages.

Increase of spirit shops in the town and suburbs, and a growing disposition of tippling in those places, contribute much to retard here the increasing growth of general taste and refinement that is generally prevailing in many other towns and districts of comparatively modern rearing.

It may be also added that many of the female portion of the humbler classes here are somewhat disposed to tippling, which practice does not only retard taste for improvement in their deportment, but also encourage an indulgence on the part of the male portion of families in this evil destructive practice of tippling in the ale houses, thereby not only wasting the means left for their family's natural support but also wasting the leisure hours, spared from their ordinary or daily avocations, which are, in different other towns and districts, turned to employment profitable to the growing generations, as well as contributing to the further comforts of that portion of the present race now on the decline. Information obtained from Samuel McSkimin, John McDowel and many others.

Jurisdiction

No ancient customs or jurisdiction at present prevail within the county of the town of Carrickfergus, save such as in their official capacity are occasionally observed by the corporation.

Manor Courts

Carrickfergus is situate in the manor of Joymount, and the corporation the lord of the manor. No manor courts held now, or for a series of past years; extent of its jurisdiction not at present known.

No tongues of slaughtered cattle demanded now, or for a series of past years, by the Mayors of Carrickfergus.

Derivation of Townlands

Names and derivations of tracts of ground and places situate in the West, Middle and North East Divisions of the county of the town of Carrickfergus.

West Division: Slieve True or Thirui "the mountain of wail or lamentation," its summit being the seat of sepulture; Knockagh "a long ridge of hills or a number of neighbouring hills;" Troopers Land, grounds anciently given for the use of the troops at Carrickfergus; Straidnahana or Straidnahania "a flat plain mantled with herbs called coltfoot;" Ballynascreen, derived from a shady wood or other shelter on the ground; Ballylagan "town of valleys or flat grounds."

Middle Division: Mairnstown, derived from a family name; Ardboley "a lofty milking-place" (where cow cattle were collected together); Duncrue, intimating "a fort [the] shape of a horseshoe;" the fort here alluded to, and which gave name to the place in which it is situate, was anciently called Duinn Crum or "the stooped fort;" it certainly inclines over a deep precipice nearly a horseshoe shape. Sulla Tober derived that name from the fountain or source of the spring constituting the river or stream called by that name. Its source issues from a limestone rock in the mountain and was anciently called Suill-a-thobbar or "the well eye," but subsequently changed to Cillatober.

Townlands

The following are the names of [additional] townlands, subdivisions of townlands and other localities within the county of town of Carrickfergus, and many of the derivations also.

East Division. Marshaltown: being formerly the residence of a provost-marshal of the corporation; Cairnkeela: derived from some ancient cairn and burial ground now unknown; Downshires Land: derived from the lord of the soil, Lord Downshire; Duffshill: derived either from the black moory surface of the hill or from Duff, a family surname; Bonnybefore: derived from a front improvement, see census of Bonnybefore on Fair Sheets; Barrys Land: derived from a family surname; Black Park: derived from the blackness of the surface; Legnetomack: "the valley of hillocks, tufts or small banks;" Porters Land: derived from a family surname; Bray Land: derived from a brae or hill; North Lodge: derived from a seat or mansion; Barnfarm: derived from a barn; Oakfield: derived from old oaks; Kain's Hill: derived from a family surname; Top Land: derived from a height or summit; Youngers: derived from a family surname; Lyndons Park: derived from a family surname; Wolf Moss: derived from a bog, the supposed habitations or haunt of wolves; Town: part of Carrickfergus.

Middle Division. Cauldhame: derived from the cold spewy nature of the soil; Thornfield: derived from ancient thorns; Byrtts Land: derived from a family surname; Killycrott: derived from some ancient burial ground now unknown; Burleigh Hill: derived from a family surname, a gentleman's seat; Cross Green: derived from some old cross now unknown; Prospect: the name of a gentleman's seat; Cairnrassy: "the cairn of the roses;" Cairnamrock: "the badgers' cairn;" Duncrew: "the horseshoe fort;" Briantange: derived from the junction of 2 sections of the Woodburn, at the face of a brae.

West Division. Windmill Hill: derived from an old windmill on the place; Rahanbwee: derived from "yellow" and "a fort," or "the yellow fort;" Chapel: derived from a Roman Catholic chapel on the place; Knockagh: "a combination of hills;" Troopers Land: derived from being set apart for grazing horses belonging to the garrison troops; Sea Park: derived from its vicinity to the sea and is a gentleman's seat; Scoutbush: a gentleman's seat and derived its name from an entrenchment and scout party formerly at the place, and also a large bush; Little Knockagh: the smaller hills; My Lords Mountain: derived from the lord of the soil, Lord Donegall; Ree (or Reagh) Hill: derived from the rough grey colour of the surface of the hill.

These names copied from a register in the hands of Mr John Smyth, clerk of the petty sessions, Carrickfergus, and derivations subsequently affixed opposite many of the places. 25th September 1839.

Roman Catholic Clergy

The following is a list of the Roman Catholic clergy of Carrickfergus since the institution of the Penal Code: Cavner was the first registered, Grant, McClarnon, Lees, Fitzpatrick, Scullion, McCarry, Cassidy, Boyle, McMullan, O'Neill, the present parish priest. Information obtained from John McCombs, Samuel Watson and others. 3rd August 1839.

Elections

Peter Kirk Esquire, M.P. was in 1834, without opposition, elected to represent the borough of Carrickfergus in parliament, and in July 1837, contested the representation of the same borough, against Mathew B. Rainie, an English gentleman. In this contest also he was the successful candidate.

Military Force

The largest force remembered to be in the castle of Carrickfergus was 600 persons, and that in the year 1800. The arms were in 1834 removed from the above castle to Charlemont. In 1834 the military (except a sergeant's party) were withdrawn from the above castle. The latter party remained till June 1839, when they were also withdrawn. The tower or keep of the castle was in [blank] converted into a magazine for arms.

Mendicity

The 3 houses occupied by the Mendicity at Carrickfergus accommodate in the whole 20 persons. The remainder, to the number of about 180 persons, get weekly sums to pay their lodgings.

Bank

The Northern Branch Bank was established in High Street, Carrickfergus, in April 1836; Alexander Johns, manager.

Guilds

List of the names of the masters and wardens of the under-mentioned guilds, 1839. Weavers: John Legg Esquire, master, James Penny and Thomas Donnell, wardens; Gentlemen Hammermen: David Legg Esquire, master, Robert Lockhart and Issac Baxter, wardens; Cordwainers: William Hay, master, William Williamson and William Hanna, wardens; Tailors: Percival Ingram, master, William Larmer and James Stannus, wardens; Dredgers: John Mahaffy, master, Robert Willis and William Mulholland, wardens. Information obtained from members, 13th September 1839.

Newspapers

The following are amongst numbers of periodicals and newspapers got in the town and county of Carrickfergus. Periodicals: *Quarterly review* 2, *Gentleman's magazine* 1. An average of newspapers coming daily through the post office, including English, Scotch and Irish papers, is calculated at 70, or 490 in the week. Average number sent weekly from Belfast by hand or by carriers employed for that purpose 100, brought down 490, total newspapers believed to be read weekly within the corporation of Carrickfergus 590.

The demand for periodicals in this town and corporation of Carrickfergus was much more limited within the last 10 years than at preceding periods. The reasons assigned for decrease in the demand for periodicals is that not only is the taste of the present inhabitants for such publications fast declining, but that many who formerly got them have either died or removed to other districts. Information from the postmaster and Samuel McSkimin, 10th June 1839.

Amusements

Horse-races, bull-baiting and bullet-playing etc., which were annually practised within the above district or parish, time immemorial, ceased almost altogether about 20 years ago. Up to about 1760 the horse-races were held on the Gallows Green adjoining the sea-shore, West Division, and about half a mile west of the town. They were subsequently held on the Commons, but ultimately ceased about 20 years back. The attendance at these races was so numerous that from 15,000 to 20,000 persons was often congregated together on the occasion.

However, the only amusements at present prevailing are cock-fighting at Loughmourne on May Eve, ball-playing at a ball court in the Scotch Quarter. Dancing and other trivial practices among the youth of both sexes are held Easter Monday and May Eve at Fairy Mount, a handsome fort situate about half a mile north east of the town. Informants Samuel McSkimin and Samuel Barclay, 20th July 1839.

Fairs and Races

Of the origin of the races and horse fair, usually or annually held on Christmas Day, on the Reagh or Ree hill, West Division, there is no local detail to be had at present, but it continued for a series of past years, and ceased about 9 years ago, the cause attributed partly to drinking quarrels and latterly to the reclaiming and cultivation of a large portion of the racegrounds by the Stewart family, who are the occupants of the farm.

The assemblages here on Christmas Days were considerable and a large quantity of horses exposed for sale on the occasion, as well as several heats being run for saddles etc. Horses and whiskey were the chief articles for sale: the latter article met a speedy and extensive consumption. Informants John McCombs, Samuel McSkimin and others. 31st July 1839.

On that part of the commonable lands locally called Kirkshall horse-races and a horse fair etc. was established between 35 and 40 years back. It commenced annually on 2nd July and continued from 2 to 4 days each time, but ultimately ceased about 15 years ago. The assemblages at this place was usually very large. Horses, cows, sheep and pigs were exposed for sale; also confectionery and liquors of the ordinary kinds. The only imposts raised on the occasion were subscriptions, from the owners of whiskey tents, to produce saddles, bridles and money prizes to be contested for by horse-racing; also to procure pigs, wearing apparel and other articles to be contested for by men and women racing.

These sports were vigorously held up for several years, until the death or removal from the neighbourhood of many of their best supporters operated in their utter decline. The most interesting portion of the sports consisted in the human racing, which usually commenced by dressing with ribbons of various colours the head and neck of a middle-sized pig which, after its tail being shaved and well soaped, was then set at large on an extensive plain, where it was pursued by hundreds of the assembled multitude, each eagerly endeavouring to secure the prize, which was only to be won by catching and holding it fast by the shaved and soaped tail. The wearing apparel and other prizes were subsequently run for by persons of both sexes. Gambling of various kinds, and drinking to profusion, was also practised on the occasion.

For several years subsequent to the 1641 war and during a period of perhaps of some centuries before that event, there were 2 fairs annually held on the Commons for the sale of every description of cattle and other articles also. These fairs, which is said to be some of the largest known in the neighbourhood in their days, was held on the south side of Commons. The first of them was held on the 4th September and second held on the 2nd October.

These fairs were relinquished here some time near the end of the 17th century, in consequence of one of the Dobbs family, then proprietor of Straid, having succeeded in changing them to a hill or eminence in Straid locally called Straid hill. The fairs are still held on the aforesaid dates, but have been changed from Straid hill and are now held [blank].

Longevity

John Herdman, a farmer in West Division, is now in the 98th year of his age; his health, memory and sight is tolerably good, but weak in the limbs and his teeth gone. Thomas Herdman, brother to the former, and residing in the West Division also, is now in the 86th year of his age, and to a reasonable extent possessed of his natural faculties and still able to conduct the business of his farm.

Robbers

About 120 years back there was occasionally residing at the Knockagh a batch of noted robbers, the chief leaders of which was a family of the O'Haghins consisting of 4 brothers; the principal of the latter was Eneas.

However, they and their confederates were the terror for many years, not only of the peaceful inhabitants of the above county but also of different parts of the county of Antrim and such other counties as they thought proper to visit on their plundering excursions. Their object was always the robbing of the wealthy and in some instances the relieving (by share of their booty) the distressed wherever they found occasion. Their chief

abode while at the Knockagh was with a Widow Jacques, who resided at the south base of the above hill and contiguous to the 2 most western of the 4 caves situate in the face of the cliffs. These caves are also said to have been frequently their places of retreat in times of peril or when they dreaded attacks or pursuit from any quarters, and are likewise thought to be their favourite depository for money and such other booty as they thought proper to lodge there during their stay in the place.

Some of the old inhabitants in the neighbourhood of the Knockagh are still of opinion that a quantity of the O'Haghins' money still remain in the aforesaid 2 caves, which they occasionally call, after the name of their former inhabitants, O'Haghins Caves; but the critical and dangerous situation of the caves, standing in the face of an almost perpendicular cliff, and considerably above its base, still retard the anxious design of many who, under other circumstances, would make a diligent search for the aforesaid supposed hidden treasure.

The O'Haghins are also thought to have another depository, contiguous to their abode, in a thicket called to the present day Archy's Bushes. This latter place is said to have been explored by some persons unknown; however, it is familiarly pointed out by the local inhabitants by the above name and as one of the O'Haghin's depositories.

The O'Haghins and their confederates are said to have undergone the extreme penalty of the law: Eneas, the principal of the 4 brothers, together with 6 of his brother robbers, were executed at Carrickfergus about the aforesaid period and their heads subsequently exhibited over the county jail.

One rather singular Christian act is recorded of the O'Haghins and their confederates, as follows. At some period previous to their arrest they, on a Sunday night, designated on robbing different persons in their neighbouring parish (Raloo). The first of the designed victims' houses they entered, they found the owner of the house reading his Bible; struck by the piety of the man and their own wicked design, they desisted and departed in peace.

The very same circumstance occurred in the second house they entered, but on entering a third house they found the owner, a man named Fullerton, and his family at some enjoyment not of such piety as the 2 former. They at once commenced and ransacked his house, more enraged perhaps at the piety of the former and their own disappointment than at the impiety of the latter, on whom they revenged their own affected reverence to the Bible.

A number of caves in different parts of the county Antrim (being sometimes the abode of the aforesaid robbers) are still known as the O'Haghins Caves. It appears that up to about the middle of the 18th century the neighbourhood of the Knockagh, as well as other parts of the above county, was a receptacle for local and remote robbers of the most barbarous description; but of all who from time to time took up their abode in this district, the O'Haghins were the most notorious and most dreaded by all peaceable inhabitants in this and neighbouring districts.

Their caves, or places of refuge in the Knockagh, they ascended by steps cut in the face of the cliff for that purpose, but which are now nearly destroyed. It is also said that wood was so thick and so lofty along the south base of the Knockagh that the aforesaid robbers readily entered the above caves by stepping from the top of one to another of the neighbouring trees. In the place are still to be seen some of their dwelling house. Information obtained from John McCombs, Hugh Catherwood, Samuel McSkimin and others, 8th August 1838.

Remarkable Circumstance

A family bewitched: in the Commons of Carrickfergus, or adjoining thereto, a very singular circumstance occurred about 1764. John Ross, a small farmer in that district, who had 8 in family, all young and, by some mysterious conjuration, was rendered distressing to themselves, grievous to their parents and surprising to the inhabitants of the district that gave them birth. This unhappy family laboured under the following circumstances.

The majority of the children fell into occasional fits of a distressing nature and confusion of mind and body. They, after those convulsive fits, exhibited the greatest agility in leaping and jumping about the floor, and climbing up the walls and along the roof, even to the very top of the house, with as much seeming ease as monkeys. These unprecedented circumstances attracted the notice of the neighbouring inhabitants, who flocked in numbers to the scene of the distress and supposed conjuration. Those of distant districts also, on hearing of the circumstances, repaired to the place and, after viewing with surprise the facts above stated, exhibited some generosity by subscribing some small sums

of money towards the support of the family in question.

At length the father, the aforesaid John Ross, obtained from the Mayor of Carrickfergus a certificate stating his locality and unaccountable distress of his large and young family. After obtaining the certificate, he brought several of his afflicted children to many towns in the county Antrim and other counties, for the purpose of exhibiting their melancholy situation and thereby obtaining, from a generous public, subscriptions towards their support.

The only cause that could be conjectured for the aforesaid sudden and distressing affliction in a large family was the drinking of a cow's milk supposed to have been affected by sorcery or witchcraft. One of the male portion of the Ross family, who in youth laboured under the aforesaid circumstances, is residing within the county of Carrickfergus at the present time. Information obtained from John Stewart, Samuel McSkimin and others. 22nd June 1839.

MODERN TOPOGRAPHY

New Line of Road

In 1838 there was a piece of new line of road opened between the distillery and old custom house, south west end of Carrickfergus, and now forming a new and improved communication in that part of the town between High Street and Irish Quarter South, or Belfast Road. This piece of new road averages 30 feet wide, leads through Governor's Place, along the shore or quay into Castle Street, and is now the route for carriages etc. travelling to or from Belfast to pass by; and thereby not only affords the travellers a full view of the quay, but also of the castle.

Previous to this road being opened, 1838, all conveyances passing between Belfast and Carrickfergus and Larne had to pass through West Street, Carrickfergus; consequently the travellers had not the pleasing view of the quay and the castle that the new arrangement now afford[s].

ANCIENT TOPOGRAPHY

Town Wall and Discoveries

In opening the new line of road alluded to, a considerable portion of the town wall, together with some projecting bastions, were torn down to make way for the road. In razing the foundations of these old erections, there was discovered, at the base of the wall, and about 3 feet beneath the surface, the remains of a human skeleton, an ancient urn, above 2 dozen of Dane's pipes and some ancient silver and copper coins; some of the silver coin was that of Charles and Elizabeth. There was also found in the same place a small piece of supposed gold coin. The Rev. Mr [blank], curate of the Established Church, Carrickfergus, has some of the coin, and Mr Coates, secretary to the grand jury, has the earthen urn.

North of and adjoining the above new road stands 35 feet in length of the town wall, together with the ruins of a bastion. The wall stands about 10 feet high and nearly 5 feet thick, built of hard rough stones and cemented by grouted mortar like other ancient erections. Between the road and the sea, and forming a portion of the parapet on that side of the road between the distillery and the castle, also stands 88 yards of the town wall, but reduced from its original size, both in height and thickness.

In the rear of High Street, and intervening between the castle and site of East or Water Gate, adjoining the Unitarian meeting house, Joymount Bank, there stands a considerable portion of town wall and now partly serving as a parapet wall between the sea and the land, but, like the former, greatly disfigured and perforated by small gates and doors being opened through it to accommodate the inhabitants in the east side of High Street, whose gardens and yards intervene between their houses and the sea.

This portion of the town wall contains a large quantity of hard brick and freestone, and is said to be built in Elizabeth's reign and to be much older than any other part of the wall. Over it are raised the gables of sundry office houses.

A large portion of the bastion that formerly adjoined the East or Water Gate on Joymount Bank is still extant, but much disfigured by dilapidation. This was called the east bastion, and seems to have projected 26 feet outside the wall and to be 33 feet long in both fronts or sides. The wall from the east bastion now described to the north east bastion measures 130 yards in length, about 18 feet high and 5 to 5 and a half feet on the top; coarse but strongly built and still almost entire, with the embrasures or loopholes at arranged distances. Along the top the north east bastion above mentioned project 27 feet outside the wall, 81 and a half feet in length on one angle or square and 80 and a half feet on the other; corners of cut freestone, each from 8 to 13 inches high and 2 to 2 and a half feet in length.

This bastion is entire. The distance from the latter to the north west bastion is 108 yards. The wall here is nearly in its original state. The bas-

tion project 27 feet outside the wall, from 2 angles, each 75 feet long; the corners are disfigured but the centre between the 2 angles is of cut stone. The distance from the latter to North Gate, as near as can now be judged, is about 45 yards; the wall here is somewhat disfigured by modern buildings.

Windmill and Encampment

The old windmill is situated on a commanding eminence at the west end of the town and contiguous to the west end of the Irish Quarter; but about one-half of the building on the north east and east side is now nearly razed to the ground; the door stood on the north east side, but disfigured long since. The existing part of the building is the west side and stands 20 to 24 feet high and 3 feet thick, built chiefly of whinstone and grouted by mortar of good quality. It seems to have stood about 60 feet in circumference on the outside and between 13 and 14 feet in diameter inside. However, from its present disfigured state its original dimensions is difficult to be judged.

The site, which has a bold command of the town, was selected by Duke Schomberg as a fitting place for one of his battery stations during his siege of Carrickfergus. Some of the ruins of the batteries were razed within memory, as late as 1837. Some of their old coins and also a small disordered brass cannon were found beneath the surface in labouring the ground round the windmill; the cannon was subsequently sold in Belfast. Of the foundation or destruction of the mill, there is no local detail.

Ancient History: Abbey

The Franciscan Abbey of Carrickfergus, which stood where the jail of the county of Antrim now stands, was, in the reign of James I, commonly called and known by the name of the King's Palace and was at that period a separate governorship from that of the castle. 4th September, 1st James I, John Dalway was appointed constable of the palace, at a salary of 4s per diem, and had under him 20 warders at 8d per day each. The last constable was George Wood who, in the same monarch's reign, was granted a sum for his loss of that office, which was then abolished. Records Rolls Office, Dublin.

The above edifice is said to have been of considerable extent; in sinking the foundations and labouring about the place from time [to time], sundry religious relics have been discovered. One of these, a large and neatly engraved stone cross, was discovered 1815 in sinking a foundation for the south east wing of the prison, built at that period. There were also raised several oak coffins of square form, also a large quantity of human bones. The cross, coffins and bones were reburied on the site. These, together with preceding discoveries of a chiefly similar nature, prove that there was a burial ground attached to the abbey in that place.

Gold Ring

Adam Cunningham of Carrickfergus, in labouring a potato garden outside the jail wall, a site of the ancient building above mentioned, found, at some depth beneath the surface, a gold ring, on the outside of which was a Latin inscription.

Churchyard

The following are amongst the surnames of families who bury and have vaults, tombs and headstones in Carrickfergus churchyard. Those whose vaults and monuments stand in the interior of the church are as follows: Chichester or the noble family of Donegall and friends bury in their family vault in the north aisle of the church; Dobbs, Davys, Dobbin, Williamson, Catherwood, Clements, Couper, Gardiner, Gill, Hill, Lang, O'Brien, Openshawe. The oldest of these monuments is that of Richard Lang, situated in the south side of the church and erected 1620. The greatest age of persons is that of Edmond Davys, alderman, who died 6th July 1696, aged 73 years.

[Additional] family surnames in the churchyard: McBrin, Browne, McBride, McCarn, McClewarty, McCann, McCullough, McConnell, McDowell, McFerran, McGill, McGown, Gyle, Houard, Hendern, Hilditch, Jafrey, McKeen, Ker, McMurtry, McMaster, Murnay, Pogue, Picken, Robertson, McSkimin, Sherer, Stephens.

The oldest stone in the church or churchyard is 1620 and the greatest age of persons on any of them is 101 years. Few graveyards perhaps in the north that the ages of persons between 80 and 90 and between 90 and 10[0] years are so numerous in, or that the ages of men and their wives are so proportionate to each other.

The churchyard is tolerably large and well occupied by tombs and headstones, a few of which display some taste, both as to construction and engravings. The yard is enclosed partly by stone and lime and brick walls, and partly by houses, and sheltered on the north and west by a number of full-grown trees standing along the parapet walls. Entrance from Church Street to the churchyard by a large iron gate, arch and piers of cut stone, and bearing the following inscription: "Erected by this parish, 1831."

There is also a second or back entrance from Lancasterian Street, by a small iron gate. Inside, in one of the church windows, lies the remains of an ancient and very curious constructed stone cross, having date 1164 engraven on one of its shoulders. It is said to have been found in the church wall many years back, as well also at a subsequent period 2 other relics of stone. One of these resembled a circular font, with 2 handles attached but a hole through the bottom. These 2 last-mentioned articles were given to a carpenter in Belfast.

Church

The body or nave of the church is said to be much older than the north or south aisles. This may be conjectured from the walls of the former being strengthened by buttresses on the outside. Behind the communion table, in the inside of the east gable, are still to be seen the ruins of a Gothic door opening into a subterraneous passage, said to lead from the church to the Franciscan abbey that formerly stood where the jail of the county of Antrim is now situate. The roof of this passage have been often discovered in sinking foundations on the line between the church and abbey aforesaid.

Of the founding of the church there is no local detail, save that from the circumstance of the discovery of the above passage leading from the church to the abbey the former is believed to have been attached to the latter as an oratory or chapel for Roman Catholic worship. It is also said to supersede a druidical or pagan temple that stood there before the introduction of Christianity to the kingdom.

Church Bell

15th April, 1832, being the day on which intelligence of the passing of the Reform Bill reached Carrickfergus, the church bell split open, to the great surprise of the inhabitants, some of which attributed the cracking of the bell to the above unexpected enactment. However, the consequence was that the bell had to be taken down, sent to be recast in Belfast, and was again put up on 13th September following. Information obtained from Samuel McSkimin, Henry Laverty and others. 26th April 1839.

Great Patrick

The above drawing [of a cross] is copied from a plan of Carrickfergus taken in 1550 and represent[s] a large stone cross called Great Patrick which then stood in the main street of the town, now called High Street, and immediately opposite the south east end of North Street. Of its design, or period of its foundation, there is no local detail, but it must have been destroyed subsequent to the above original plan of the town [having] been taken, 1550. It also appears to be of a large dimension and designed for religious purposes, the town and suburbs being then the seat of different and extensive religious edifices.

Its base or pedestal, in which it stood, as appears by the original drawing, was of a circular form and of dressed or cut stone, consisting of 6 rows or steps rising one above the other from the base to the foot of the cross. On removing part of the pavement in the south west end of High Street or Old Market Place, and near the south east end of North Street, in 1818, a square foundation of dressed stones (believed to have been that of Great Patrick) was discovered; it was about 6 feet square.

Woodburn Abbey

Woodburn ancient abbey was situated about half a mile west of Carrickfergus, on the west bank of the Woodburn river and contiguous to the sea-shore. Nothing now remains to denote its existence at any period but tradition, save some trifling remnants of ornamental freestone, pieces of old pavement and some of the old foundation walls on the site. Contiguous, on the site of the attached burial ground, are also 3 of the ancient thorn bushes supposed to have formed a portion of the old shelter. The graveyard is now under tillage and the site of the abbey now the seat of houses and gardens.

The ornamental stone above mentioned consist in 2 pieces of cornice, neatly cut, and were discovered in sinking foundations for modern buildings in the place within the present year; here were also found a neat cut freestone having the figure of a large bird or fowl raised on its surface, but this stone was put in the bowels of the new wall. Several foundation walls, about 4 feet thick and cemented by very hard grout, were also discovered.

At the base of one of these walls, and about 4 feet beneath the surface, were also found the remains of a human skeleton. The skull was in moderate shape but the other bones much decayed. In the same place were also found 2 ancient copper coins and a silver coin, all of small size. Sundry other antiques were also found here from time to time, but were subsequently either sold or destroyed. A portion of the wall of the abbey about 6 feet high and of great thickness was razed to the ground within the last few years.

In reclaiming and labouring the attached graveyard from time to time within the last century, a large quantity of every description of human bones, together with pieces of lettered and unlettered headstones, have been raised, all which have been interred again on the site, save some pieces of cut stone which have [been] brought to Woodburn Cottage, now the seat of Richard Thompson Esquire.

The extent of the abbey, including attached buildings, was so great that several of the dwelling houses in the Irish Quarter were built of the stones taken from its ruins; but of its foundation there is no local detail to be had. The situation, contiguous to the sea-shore and town of Carrickfergus, was truly delightful and very fertile. Informants John McQuillen, Samuel McSkimin and others. 1st May 1839.

Mill and Gallows

About 1 furlong west of Woodburn old abbey stood an ancient corn mill supposed to have been attached to the abbey. Some traces of the mill-dam are still to be seen in the holding of Richard Thompson Esquire.

A short distance south west of the abbey also stood an old gallows, composed of masonry, wood and iron. This gallows, which stood adjoining the sea-shore, was sold by auction, 1819, as a second-hand gallows, and as such was purchased at 5s 10d.

Forts

In [Blank] Division and within a few yards of Woodburn Cottage, the seat of Richard Thompson Esquire, and now forming part of the pleasure grounds, stands a fort locally called a mount. It approaches to circular shape, 30 yards in diameter and its summit from 8 to 12 feet above the level of the ground on which situate. It consists of earth and stones and forms a convex shape. It is planted with forest and ornamental trees from the base to the top, and is also the seat of a neat icehouse. The trench on the west and north west sides is 13 feet wide and full of water, and forms an ornamental pond; the south and east sides is closed up and now the seat of shrubs and gravel walks. Adjoining the fort stands a handsome circular fishpond which, together with the improved state of the fort, contributes much to the appearance of the seat.

In Middle Division, and holding of Charles McBrinn, stood a fort of considerable size but destroyed some years back, at which time, in the levelling of it, were discovered brass weapons and other antiques, together with pieces of ornamented freestone. The finder of these articles is now in America; consequently no further detail can be given of them.

In the latter farm stood a second fort destroyed about 20 years back, and in which were found several pieces of ancient silver coin which have been subsequently lost. A third fort in the same farm was locally called the Mad Mount.

Carnrawsie Church

The ruins of Carnrawsie ancient church and graveyard is situated on a handsome elevation about 1 and a half miles north west of Carrickfergus and about 100 yards north of Burleigh Hill mansion house. Of this ancient edifice, which stood east and west, nothing now remains but 13 feet long by 1 to 6 feet high on the east gable. This wall is 3 feet thick, of whinstone, and cemented by grouted mortar of a good kind, and now mantled over with ivy. From the ruined state of the place, no idea can be formed of the width of the edifice, but its length seems to have been about 62 feet.

The body of the church is now the seat of a vault erected 1827 by John Robinson of Burleigh Hill, Esquire, for the place of sepulture of himself and family, and who, at the above period, razed to the ground a large portion of the church walls then standing. The grounds of the church and graveyard are now ornamented and sheltered with a variety of forest trees. Of the foundation or destruction of the church, there is no local detail to be had.

In reclaiming the graveyard, which is said to have been of considerable size and is now under meadow, a large quantity of human bones [was] raised. In labouring an adjoining field in 1830, there was discovered, at some depth beneath the surface, a grave containing the remains of a human skeleton. The grave was paved in the bottom with small stones. Leading from one end of it lay an enclosed pipe, supposed to have been designed for conveying off any water lodged about the grave.

In the graveyard, and within a few yards of the church, stood an ancient spring well which is now closed, and a pipe laid to convey off the water constantly issuing from the site.

Contiguous, on the west side of the graveyard, stands a large ancient thorn; extensive orchards are said to have been formerly attached to the church; from the roses or flowers in those orchards, the church or place probably derived its name of Rawsie or Carn Rawsie, and the latter is an Irish name or term for garden flowers. A cairn also might have stood there at some former period which, if combined with the Irish name for garden flowers, would have constituted the full name by which the place is now designated. However, it may not be the original name, as some say it was dedicated to St Nicholas.

A number of ancient silver and copper coin have been found about the ruins of the church at some former period. The situation was truly delightful, commanding an extensive prospect of the ocean and surrounding scenery, as well as Carrickfergus and other towns. Informants Peter Bolf, Samuel McSkimin and others. 2nd May 1839.

Killyann Church

The ruins of Killyann ancient church is situated on a handsome eminence in the Middle Division and about 2 miles north west of Carrickfergus. Of this edifice, which stood nearly east [and] west, nothing now remains but the foundation walls grown over with soil, and 12 feet in length by about 15 feet high of the west gable. These walls were 3 feet thick and cemented by grout of a coarse kind. The stones are of the grey or whin kind, tolerably large and chiefly in their natural shape, without the marks of a hammer. The edifice seems to have stood 41 by 16 feet in size.

Nearly the whole of the west gable remained up to about the year 1800, at which period a large portion of it was razed to the ground. Of its foundation or destruction, there is no local detail to be had. There was a burial ground attached on the east side, which was reclaimed at some former period and in which were discovered human bones and coffin boards.

Contiguous, on the north side, stands an ancient thorn. On the west and south west, and within a few yards of the church, there is a deep glen or ravine through which passes a stream or rivulet. The situation is truly delightful, being on a rising eminence commanding an extensive prospect of the ocean and other scenery, as well of Carrickfergus and other towns in county Down.

Forts and Castle

Contiguous on the south west of the old church, and overhanging the ravine and rivulet before mentioned, there stands a circular fort called Duncrue Fort. It consists of earth and stones, but chiefly of the former, measures 17 yards in diameter on the top and on a slanting elevation; measures between the base and the top 25 to 66 feet and its summit 60 to 66 feet above the bottom of the glen adjoining the north and north east sides. It still retains much of its original shape, and from its eminent situation commands a bold and delightful prospect of the surrounding scenery.

About 80 yards west of the above fort, and in the Middle Division also, stands the ruins of ancient oblong fortress 110 by 50 yards, enclosed by a fosse or trench 10 to 15 feet wide, entrance by the east end, by a sort of bridge or gate which seems to have been 12 or 13 feet wide. The trench, though now much disfigured, is in some parts 6 feet in depth. The area is now partly under tillage.

Within 40 yards of the east end, in the middle of the area, and situated nearly north and south, stood a castle or other building of stone and lime work. Some traces of the foundation is still perceptible. Its size seems to have been about 34 by 26 feet; the thickness of the walls cannot be judged, but the grout or mortar combining them was of a good quality. One of the corner stones still remains; is of the whin kind and measures 5 feet long, 2 feet broad and is 1 foot above the surface.

In razing the ruins a few years back, there was discovered, in the centre of the building, a circular floor of freestone flags, cut and closely jointed together. They were quite smooth on the top surface. The floor was about 18 feet in diameter and 3 steps of cut freestone ascending it, but when razed and a few days exposed to the air the flags crumbled away to dust. This castle, which stood on an elevated and delightful site, is generally believed to have belonged to a family of the Russells, who formerly held a large landed property in this district of the county but who are extinct about 2 and a half centuries back. The ruins now described are situate in the holding of Charles McBrinn and contiguous to Killyann old church.

Forts and Standing Stones

In the Middle Division, and situated in a field adjoining Mr Vance's cotton factory, stands the ruins of a fort approaching to square shape, 20 by 20 yards. The parapet, which is chiefly of earth, stands from 10 to 15 feet above the bottom of the trench, 4 to 10 feet above the area of the fort and 25 to 30 feet thick at the base, and had on each corner a mound or sort of raised bastion of earth. The north square is now disfigured by a modern fence. This fort was situated on the verge of a deep glen, [on] the side of which is now growing a plantation of forest trees.

In the Middle Division, and holding of Samuel Watson, stands the ruins of a fort composed of earth and stones; is 5 to 10 feet high and 10 yards across on the top. In the centre stands some old pit 11 by 11 feet and 4 feet deep. On the west side and base of the fort is a stone column 2 feet high, 1 and a half feet broad and 1 and a half feet thick. Informants Charles McBrinn and Samuel McSkimin, 4th and 6th May 1839.

Forts and Gentle Bushes

In Middle Division, and holdings of Robert and William McKeen, stands a circular fort composed chiefly of earth and 10 yards in diameter on the top. Its summit is 8 to 10 feet above the bottom of the trench. The latter is now greatly disfigured and seems to have averaged 10 feet wide. The fort retains nearly its original shape. About 400 yards east of it stands a large ancient thorn formerly called a gentle bush.

About 80 yards west of the fort, and in the same farm, also stands a second fort of rather oval shape, 12 by 8 yards on the top, and the latter on a slanting elevation 15 to 30 feet above the bottom of the trench, and the trench 12 to 20 feet wide. The fort is composed of earth and stones. At each end, and 12 feet distant from the fort, stands a small earthen mound, but seems of natural formation and to be reduced to their present shape by the cutting of the above trench through them.

About 100 yards west of the latter, and on the verge of the north branch of Woodburn river, are some traces of another fort, but quite disfigured by cultivation. All these are on a direct line west of Duncrue Fort.

Castle Lugg

The ruins of Castle Lugg ancient castle is situated on a handsome eminence about 3 English miles west of Carrickfergus and contiguous to the mail coach road leading from the latter town to Belfast. Nothing of this old building now remains but 27 feet in length of the north square and about 3 feet in length of the east square. These walls stand from 20 to 25 feet high and 3 and a half feet in thickness, built chiefly of whinstone, the larger of which are laid in their natural and undressed state. The grout combining them is of a very good quality. The sand used in this mortar seems to have been procured from the sea-shore, as it is interspersed with small shells.

The lower part of the walls, particularly the corners, are much disfigured by the surface stones being picked off for modern erections. About the middle of the north square, and reaching from the base near to the top, stands a piece of modern brick and stonework which fills up some ancient breach in the wall, or perhaps where a door and window originally stood.

In the lower part of the modern building stands (now closed up) a small doorway that formerly served as an entrance to a shed built against the south side of the main wall. The breach above mentioned is 4 to 5 feet wide near the base but narrower towards the top. There are some rough pieces of freestone observable in parts of the walls. On the top of the east corner stands a small sloebush in a natural state of growth.

In labouring about the base and ruins of this building at sundry periods within the last century, human bones, old coins and some large keys were discovered beneath the surface, but none of these antiques at present to be seen. Neither is there any detail to be had of the foundation or destruction of the castle, save that it is believed to have derived its present name from a family of the name of Lugg who held some tracts of the neighbouring ground at some former period, and probably inhabited the castle also. This castle was situate in the West Division.

Forts

In the West Division, and holding of Stewart Dunn, stood a fort, but now destroyed and the site under tillage.

In the same division, and holding of Thomas Herdman, stood a fort which is also destroyed. Informants Thomas Herdman and Samuel McSkimin, 7th May 1839.

Fort and Mill

In the Middle Division, and holding of John Smyth, stood a large fort locally called a mount, but now destroyed. The field in which it stood is still called the Mount Park and is situate in the suburbs of Carrickfergus.

Contiguous to this fort and in the same division, and situate on the verge of a small river, stood an ancient walk mill, for the purpose of thickening and scouring woollen cloth of local manufacture. Some traces of the stone and lime work are still to be seen in the place. Informant Samuel McSkimin.

Cairns

In Middle Division, and holding of the late Captain Ellis, there stood, on the summit of hill called Cairn na Neale, a cairn of stones from which the hill derived its present name; but the cairn is now destroyed and its site the seat of a modern wall of stone and lime erected by Mrs Nickles for an ornament. This wall is 14 feet long, 2 feet thick and about 10 feet high, and surrounded by a modern planting. This hill, which stands about 3 and a half miles north west of Carrickfergus, commands a good prospect of the surrounding scenery.

On the summit of Slieve True, a lofty hill in the West Division and about 3 and a half miles north west of Carrickfergus, there stands the ruins of an ancient cairn of stones, now the seat of an old schoolhouse which, when viewed from a distance, gives the place the appearance of some old castellated fortress, the schoolhouse, which was a square building, being now unroofed.

The cairn seems to have been circular, about 25 yards in diameter, and its summit about 5 feet above the surface. It consisted of several hundred cart-loads of large and small stones, a large portion of which have been removed from the place. The largest stone visible now in place lies near the bottom of the cairn and measures on the extreme points 5 and a half feet long, 3 and a half feet broad and 2 feet thick, and of the whin kind, and is supposed to have been one of the supporters of a druid's altar at the place.

The schoolhouse here alluded to stood 1-storey high, 16 and a half feet square inside, stood in the middle of the cairn and was erected many years ago by the late James Craig Esquire, proprietor of the mountain before mentioned; but in consequence of its lofty and cold situation, it soon fell to disuse and consequently a prey to neglect. Few hills perhaps command a wider or more delightful prospect than Slieve True does.

At its west base, and about half a mile from the cairn, lie, forming part of [the] fence, 3 rocks or whinstones of large size, commonly called the Three Brothers. They average 3 feet high and vary [from] 6 to 8 feet in length and 3 to 4 and a half feet in breadth, and the distance between them as follows: a to b 7 feet, and b to c 12 feet. In one corner of the centre of these stones stands a circular hole 4 inches in depth and 1 inch in diameter, and designed perhaps for some gate appendage.

These stones are by some persons thought to have given name to the aforesaid mountain but it has more probably derived its original name of Slieve-a-thirui or "mountain of wail or lamentation" from the circumstance of the cairn and perhaps a place of sepulture being situated on its summit. In exploring the cairn at some former period, there were earthen urns containing calcined bones and ashes discovered.

About 1 English mile west of Slieve True, in the holding of James Stewart and in the West Division, also stood, on the summit of a hill locally called the Reagh hill, an ancient cairn of stones, but the chief part of the stones have been long since removed to modern fences. The cairn was above 20 yards in diameter.

Standing Stone and Fort

In Lord Donegall's mountain, and West Division also, there stands an ancient stone column 4 feet high, 2 feet broad and 1 and a half feet thick. It is situated within a few yards of Thomas Boyd's dwelling house. Informants James Stewart, Thomas Boyd and others, 15th and 16th May 1839.

In West Division and holding of Mathew Anderson, and situated on a lofty eminence, stands a fort of earth and stones. It is oval shape and 10 by 4 yards at the top, and the latter 6 to 7 feet high, and commands a wide and handsome prospect of the surrounding scenery.

Lakes and Habitations

In the mountainous parts of the parish stood several small lakes or sheets of water called the Loughans, but many of them are now dried up.

In these mountains also stands many ancient fences and ruins of ancient habitations, all which prove them to be inhabited and partly cultivated at some period.

Fort and Cave

In West Division and holding of David Fulton, and nearly adjoining the new road leading through Jordanstown, there stands the ruins of a fort approaching circular shape, 30 yards in diameter and its summit about 6 feet above the bottom

of the moat. The existing part of the latter averages 15 feet wide; the parapet is destroyed.

In the north west side of this fort stood 3 sections of caves connected with each other; 2 of these were situated nearly east and west and 1 north and south. One of the former stood about 33 feet long, the other 21 feet and the north and south section 33 feet in length, but all are now destroyed, except 13 and a half feet in length of the south west section which is built with rough landstones and roofed with long flat stones, similar to many other caves before described. It varies from 1 and a half to 2 and a half feet wide and 3 and a half to 4 feet high; the parts now destroyed have averaged perhaps the same dimensions. Herewith is a ground plan of the fort and caves [drawing]. The original entrance was at the west point and base of the fort, as shown on ground plan.

[Insert note by Boyle: The plan you have given is excellent and most satisfactory, but I think the interior of the cave must be more than 1 and a half or 2 and a half feet wide and that this must be the width of the entrance only; [?] try again. [Answer] On a re-examination of the within cave, I find it does not admit of any additional observations than that contained on the other side. 25th July 1839.

Weapon and Forts

Hugh Catherwood has at present in his house in West Division an ancient steel weapon found in same division, but quite corroded by rust. The blade was 12 inches long, 1 inch broad, small in the point and thick in the back like a sword. It has a tang 6 inches long to embrace a handle. Beneath is its shape [drawing].

In the above division, and holding of William Hanley, stood a fort, but now disfigured by modern fences.

In West Division and holding of John Hanley, and situated on the summit of a small hill nearly at the base of Knockagh, there stood an ancient fort or other enclosure 26 by 16 yards, and enclosed by a stone wall, some traces of which are still visible. Traces of other ancient enclosures appear along the base of the above range of hills, but much disfigured at present. 18th May 1839.

Religious Edifice and Discoveries

In West Division and holdings of James Adams and company, and towards the east extremity of the Knockagh, stands a winding glen or valley called the Friar's Glen, and in which glen stood some ancient religious edifice, the foundation walls of which have been dug out about 30 years back. The walls were very thick, contained some freestone and was cemented together by grout of a very hard quality, but of the size of the building no idea can be formed.

Here were found 2 gold rings of large size and supposed to have been worn by some of the ancient clergy, as one of them bears some inscription of a religious nature. It, together with 2 ancient silver coins found in the same place, is now in the possession of Mrs Adams, who resides on the site of the old edifice in question.

In the same place were also found an ancient wooden vessel about the size and shape of a large water glass or tumbler, but having a handle to one side. This vessel was much decayed and subsequently fell down.

On the same site were also found a quantity of decayed bones.

A few yards in the rear of Adams' house, and on the site of the above establishment, stands an ancient circular mound of earth and stones. It is 15 feet in diameter, 3 feet high and faced on the outside with circular courses of stones from the base to the top; the latter form a sort of concave seat.

Within 8 yards of this mound, and in the same garden, also stands an ancient spring well called the Friar's Glen Well, and is considered a valuable spring.

Contiguous also stands on an eminence some ancient thorns commonly called the Fairy Bushes.

The situation of the edifice before mentioned, whether a church or a friary, was very eligible for the purpose, being a retired and fertile glen or valley commanding a fine prospect of the surrounding scenery on the south and sheltered by lofty hills on the east, west and north. It has probably been the seat of some monastic institution, from the circumstance of the glen deriving its name from friars.

Friar's Bush and Enclosures

At the north west end of the same glen, and about 2 furlongs distant from the site of the old edifice above mentioned, stands, situated in a flat valley surrounded by hills on either side, a large ancient thorn called the Friar's Bush, where it is believed that Roman Catholic worship was held during the existence of the Penal Code.

On an eminence north of and contiguous to the above Friar's Bush stands the ruins of some ancient enclosure of oval shape, 27 by 20 yards, and was enclosed by a parapet of earth and stones, some traces of which are still to be seen.

Immediately adjoining the latter stands the ruins of a second ancient enclosure 10 yards in diameter, and in the centre of which is a raised terrace 5 yards in diameter. This enclosure, like the former, was enclosed by a parapet of earth and stones but the latter disfigured. Informants John Boyd, James Adams, Samuel McSkimin, 20th and 21st May 1839.

Standing Stone and Cairn

In West Division and holding of William Gynn, and on the east extremity of the Knockagh hills, near Mr Dunn's plantation, there stands an ancient stone column 3 feet high, 1 and a half feet broad and 1 and a half feet thick.

On the same hill and holding of William Hanley, and contiguous to a valley called Eaken's Glen, there stands the ruins of an ancient cairn which seems to have been about 30 feet in diameter, but now disfigured and much of the stone removed from the place; of those still remaining, several are large. One in particular, which perhaps covered a grave, measures 6 feet long, 4 feet broad and 1 and a half feet thick, and is situate on the bottom of the cairn.

Forts in West Division

In the above division, and holding of George Anderson, stood a fort but now disfigured. In same division, and holding of John Ferriss, stood a fort but now disfigured also. In same division, and in Scoutbush demesne, stands the ruins of a fort approaching to circular shape, 30 yards in diameter. The parapet is of earth, 4 feet high and 11 feet thick in some parts. The trench average 9 feet wide.

In West Division, and demesne of Scoutbush, the seat of [blank] Bruce Esquire, there stood a fortress or entrenchment of large [size], and about the centre of which the mansion house is now situate; but no traces of the fosse or trench now to be seen. In the same demesne also stood a smaller fort, but has been long since destroyed.

On the top of the Knockagh hills, and holdings of William Hanley and others, there stands a circular fort 9 yards in diameter; the parapet, which is of earth, is 1 to 2 feet high and the trench 3 feet wide. The summit of this fort is about 4 feet above the bottom of the trench.

About half a furlong south of the latter, and in the same mountain grazing, stands a second fort of circular shape, 10 yards in diameter and 3 feet high, and a small pit in its centre. The parapet is of earth, 2 to 5 feet high and 6 to 8 feet thick. The trench is 2 to 8 feet wide. These forts, though small, command a fine prospect.

Towards the west end of the above hills, in the holding of Robert Gordon, and near to an old cattle pound, there stands another of these small forts of earth. It is circular shape, 8 yards in diameter and 2 feet high. The parapet is of earth but in a disfigured state and is in some parts 2 feet high and 8 to 12 feet thick; the trench is 10 to 15 feet wide.

Ancient Coin

In West Division, and in the ruins of an old causeway, were found 1833 by Daniel McAlanney a few pieces of ancient silver coin, size of halfcrown pieces. They have been subsequently sold at price of old silver.

Spa Well

In the commons attached to Carrickfergus stands an old spa well, the water of which is of an irony flavour. It was formerly celebrated and much esteemed as an effectual medicine for the cure of sundry bodily diseases and consequently was visited by multitudes of people from different districts, who laboured under different disorders. The water was in some cases applied externally, sometimes drunk, and in other cases boiled before drunk, the multitudes being so large on some occasions that several tents containing eatables and drinkables were brought to that place for their accommodation; but all these practices have long since ceased. Informants Samuel Davys and Samuel McSkimin, 22nd May 1839.

Fort and Gentle Bushes

In North East Division and holding of Samuel Davys, and situate on the verge of a ravine or glen, there stands a fort of oval shape, 60 by 50 yards and enclosed by a trench and parapet. The latter is of earth and its summit 5 to 10 feet above the bottom of the trench, and in some parts 20 feet thick. The trench is 8 to 15 feet wide. It was partly surrounded by a second parapet, some traces of which still appear. The fort commands a fine prospect on the east and south.

Contiguous, on the banks of the above glen, also stands 2 ancient thorns frequently designated gentle bushes.

Forts

In Oakfield, the seat of the Dobbs family, there stood a fort of considerable size but now destroyed. In levelling this fort from time to time there was a quantity of skulls and other human bones found beneath its surface.

In same division, and holding of James Davys, stands the ruins of a circular fort 35 yards in diameter and its summit 5 feet above the level of the field on which [it] stands. It is now the seat of a lime-kiln, but the trench and parapet now destroyed. Informants Samuel Davys and others, 23rd May 1839.

Fort: Fairy Mount

A seat of pleasure: in North East Division, and holding of William Apsley, there stands an oval fort of earth and stones 26 by 20 yards on the top and its summit about 15 feet higher than the level of the field on which it is situate, and commanding a fine prospect of a wide extent of the surrounding scenery. Some traces of a trench is here visible but no vestige of a parapet. This fort is locally called Fairy Mount and has been, during the last 8 years, the seat of some local amusements on certain festivals, such as cock-fighting on Easter Mondays, and assembling of the youth of both sexes on new May Days, for the purpose [of] enjoying themselves at walking, drinking and eating of gingerbread etc., all which are in abundant supply for their accommodation.

In consequence of the immediate vicinity of this place to the town of Carrickfergus, the attendance on the above occasions are pretty large. These pleasure meetings were usually held in a green or sort of commons at the west end of the town, but that place being reclaimed about 8 years ago, Fairy Mount became the new pleasure ground. 24th May 1839.

Craignabrahir

Craignabrahir (the Friar's Rock) is a rocky hill in the Middle Division and situated in the Commons, and on the top of which are still visible the foundations of several small huts of rude erection, but no appearance of grout or any other lime mortar about the place. Some opinions prevail regarding this place being at some period the seat of religious worship.

Commons

In the Commons are said to have formerly stood

ancient stone columns, but none of these at present extant.

It appears from vestiges still to be seen on the face of the Commons, that they were at some period the seat of industry and of numerous habitations, but the latter of limited size and rude construction. The houses were small and their walls chiefly of sod and stone. The grounds were dissected into fields and gardens of various sizes by thick stone walls and wet ditches, the foundations of which is still traceable on the face of the surface. These extensive · tracts afforded turbary, spring and stream waters, and many other natural properties conducive to health and improvement; much of these features now destroyed. 28th May 1839.

Miscellaneous Discoveries

Robert Junkin, in labouring new land in his holding in the Middle Division, 1839, discovered about 3 feet beneath the surface an earthen urn carved on the surface and containing some quantity of calcined bones and ashes. Both the urn and bones were much decayed and subsequently fell to dust. He found in the same place, and beneath a very large stone, a brass pistol but quite corroded by time and rust. Henry Adams got in the above division, and at some depth beneath the surface of a bog, an ancient wooden vessel nearly the shape of a coffin but quite decayed. This vessel is said to have contained some ancient money, which Adams privately sold.

Robert Dunn discovered, at some depth beneath the remains of bog in the above division, 3 wooden vessels nearly the shape and size of noggins but bound by brass or copper hoops and ornamented round the mouth and handles with the same metal. Sam McSkimin has a sketch of these curious vessels. Informants Robert Junkin, Samuel McSkimin and others.

Monastic Ruins

In North East Division, and suburbs of Carrickfergus, adjoining the east end of Green Street, on the road leading from the latter town to Larne, there stood some ancient religious edifice and burial ground, but all now destroyed and the site partly under cultivation and partly occupied by the above road. Strangers and children were interred here within memory. Some portions of the ground walls of the building was dug out within the last 50 years, as well as large quantities of human bones and coffins, nearly in full shape. The grounds are now called the Spittle

Parks, in consequence, it is said, of a hospital that stood in the place and attached to the monastic institutions of the town.

Fort and Gentle Bush

In West Division, and holding of Hugh Catherwood and company, there stood 2 forts but now destroyed.

Contiguous to these stood a gentle bush, the ruins of which is still to be seen in the place. The person who cut down the bush some years ago had one of his eyes nearly destroyed while cutting it down, and this, it is said, in retaliation for destroying the sacred bush. Informants Hugh Catherwood and Samuel McSkimin, 29th May 1839.

Enclosures and Discoveries

In West Division, and holdings of Hugh Catherwood and company, there stands the ruins of some ancient enclosures, the walls or parapets of which were of earth and stones. One of these enclosures approaches to square shape, 23 by 23 feet inside, and some of the stones constituting the walls 1 to 3 feet above the surface and standing perpendicular. Contiguous to the latter stood many others, also an ancient cairn of stones, likewise the foundations of well-shaped houses.

In digging out these ancient erections from time to time within the last 20 years, there were large quantities of decayed bones and earthen urns discovered. On the whole, the place is believed to have been the seat of ancient burial, as well as of ancient but rude buildings, and perhaps of religious worship too.

Here were found several stone rings, also 2 brass or copper brooches, with a circular ring in the head of each; these brooches are still extant. Informants Hugh Catherwood and others. 30th May 1839.

In West Division and contiguous to Mathew Anderson's dwelling house, and situated on an eminence, there stands the ruins of some ancient enclosure 13 by 10 feet, and bound in by a wall of earth and stones. Some of the latter stand 1 to 3 feet above the surface. Contiguous stand the ruins of several other enclosures of a similar construction, but these ancient erections are so numerous along the south base of Knockagh and so lost either as to name or tradition that it would be waste of time, and perhaps useless matter too, to particularise them respectively.

In labouring and digging out some ruins in this place from time to time, decayed bones and broken urns were frequently discovered. Informants William Hanley and others.

Fort and Discoveries

In that part of West Division locally called Troopers Land, and also in the holding of William Hanley and company, there stands the ruins of a fort approaching to circular shape, 40 yards in diameter and 4 to 10 feet above the level of the ground on which it stands. The trench and parapet, if any there were, is now destroyed. The fort is of earth and stones. Its summit commands a wide and sublime prospect of the surrounding scenery. In the same farm stood other forts and mounds but long since disfigured; traces of some still appear.

In this farm also stood an ancient burial ground, together with ancient foundations of stone and lime work, perhaps those of some religious edifice, but have been long since dug out. Several graves are still visible and enclosed at sides and ends with large stones, and in some cases paved on the top.

It frequently occurs, in digging out those graves, that decayed bones, earthen urns and other antiques are discovered beneath their surface. During the present month (May) several pieces of carved urns, decayed bones and other antiques, such as brass and iron articles, curious stones, timber cinders, ashes and fire hearths, have been discovered beneath graves, cairns and large stones.

Contiguous, in an adjoining field, were also discovered from time to time within the last 20 years several vaults and caves of different shapes and sizes, but in all cases built with care and strength. The walls were of dry stonework and roof composed of long stones. Some of these vaults, 4 feet wide at the base, were not more than 1 foot wide at the roof. Some were 5 feet high between roof and floor, but seldom contained any other than ashes or black earth; these caves and vaults are now destroyed.

This place seems on the whole to have been a seat of great antiquity, both for burials and erections of different descriptions, and chiefly of rude construction and perhaps of druidical times. Information obtained from William Hanley, Patt Kerr and others. 31st May 1839.

Mould, Holestone and Arrowhead

The above [drawing] is a sketch of a mould or stone mould for casting battleaxes of 3 different sizes but nearly of equal shape. The stone here shown is of the whin kind and measures in the extreme points 7 by 6 inches and 1 and a half inches thick: "a" is 3 by 2 inches, "b" is 2 and a half by 1 and a half inches and "c" 1 and a half by 1 inch, and all between a half to three-quarters of an inch in depth and all situated in the stone as above shown.

The annexed sketch [drawing] represents an oval stone of the granite kind, with a circular hole 2 inches in diameter through its centre. The stone is 5 by 4 and a half inches and 2 inches thick. The hole is much wider at the entrance than in the centre.

The annexed sketch [drawing] represents the size and shape of an ancient steel arrow or spearhead found deposited with bones and ashes in an earthen urn a considerable depth beneath the surface of a paved grave, June 1st 1839. It is solid but much corroded by rust. Jaw-bones and teeth found with it were of very large and unusual size, and the urn in which they were contained glazed on the outside a greenish yellow, an ornament seldom seen on ancient urns.

These, together with the mould and holestones, were, with sundry other antiques, found in an ancient and supposed Danish or druidical burial ground in that part of the West Division called Troopers Land, and holding of William Hanley and company. Information from William and John Hanley, 1st June 1839.

Pot, Hammer and Weapons

About 6 feet beneath the surface of a bog in North East Division, and holding of George Allen, were discovered about 40 [years] back an ancient and curious shaped pot, seeming to be a compound of brass and copper. It is 9 inches in diameter at the bottom and 5 and a half inches in diameter at the mouth. Round the latter is a margin resembling that of a pewter plate and 1 and a half inches wide.

The pot is 7 inches in depth and supported on 3 feet, each 1 and a half inches broad and 1 and a half inches high, and has 3 cords or raised ribs on the surface of each. Round the middle of the pot, on the outside, are also 3 raised ribs. The lugs or handles are 1 and a half inches long each. This curious pot, which has been in common use since found, is still in tolerable preservation and is at present in Allen's, blacksmith, Carrickfergus.

In the above bog were also found a very well-shaped stone hammer which embraced the handle through the centre, similar to modern iron hammers. It was purchased by Mr Binn, now of Belfast.

Here were also found bronze weapons, flint arrowheads and other antiques of odd construction, but subsequently disposed of.

Boot and Discoveries

In Middle Division and holding of John Millar, and about 4 feet beneath the surface of a bog, were discovered, 1836, the foot of an ancient channel boot. The heel, which was of very neat shape, was studded with wooden pegs. Attached to or on the heel was a most neatly made brass spur, on one of the appendages of which are 2 letters, R.L. The spur was whole when found, but was subsequently broken and still remains in the above Millar's house.

In the above bog were also found 2 brass hatchets and a few other antiques; the hatchets were subsequently sold to a tinker.

Fort

In North East Division, and holding of John McMurtry, there stood a fort which seems to have been circular shape, about 40 yards in diameter. Some traces of the trench and parapet are still vis-ible, but in a disfigured state. Information obtained from George Allen, John Millar and others.

Druid's Altar, Vaults and Mounds

In that part of the West Division called Troopers Land and holding of John Hanley and company, and near the base of Knockagh hill, there stands, supported on other stones and elevated 2 to 4 feet above the surface, a large stone 6 by 5 feet and 1 and a half feet thick, and probably designed for a druid's altar, as in the same holding are the ruins of many rude erections, supposed to be of druidical bearing.

[Insert query by Boyle: By how many stones is this slab supported? Does it stand east and west or how? To which point does it slope or incline? Is there any earth underneath it? Has it ever been covered by small stones? Might it not be a grave? How far is this altar from the burial ground, and how far from the other altar? 5th June 1839].

[Answer] The supposed altar within described is resting over a large collection of large and small stones, but more immediately supported on 6 stones of tolerable large size. These are resting

Druidical altar.

on a number of others beneath and adjoining, but none stand perpendicular like the columns supporting many other altars. The altar stone lies or points south east by north west and inclines rather to the latter point. It does not appear to have been at any period covered by other stones, neither does it bear any appearance of a grave. A considerable quantity of other stones lie between it and the earth beneath. The original base erection has undergone some alterations. It stands on an elevation about 2 furlongs north west of the old burial ground and in the same field, and about 4 furlongs south west of the other altar, 25th July 1839.

In the same farm were frequently discovered circular enclosures or vaults, some of which were 4 feet in diameter at the bottom, 4 to 5 feet high between the roof and floor, and not more perhaps than 1 foot in diameter. At the closing of the roof these vaults were enclosed by rough stone walls and so constructed, projecting inwards from the base, that 1 moderate-sized stone closed them at the top or roof. To some of them were attached tunnels or pipes, in the order of a lime or corn-kiln. But in none of them were discovered matters of any interest other than rich black earth.

In the lowlands of the same farm also stood several raised mounds of earth and some of earth and stones. They were circular, 15 to 10 feet in diameter and 2 to 5 feet high, but are now chiefly destroyed. Informants John and William Hanley and others, 5th June 1839.

Vaults

The vault or subterraneous passage that formerly led between the town church and the old abbey that stood where the jail of the county of Antrim now stands was about 64 years ago opened in 4 different places on the line, and found to be entirely built of cut stone. This vault is stated to stand between 4 and a half feet and 5 feet wide, and a like height, and arch roof.

In the centre of the floor, and extending the whole line, there is sunk in the stone a half-arch channel or gutter, supposed to be designed for conveying off any water lodging in the passage. About midway between the church and jail also stands a sort of chamber or supposed resting place, where the nuns rested while on their passage between the abbey and the church. On either side of this chamber there is a seat of cut stone extending the full length of the chamber; but all access to this curious vault is now closed up. Information obtained from John Millar, who assisted in opening up the vault, 6th June 1839.

Graves and Urn

In that part of the West Division called Troopers Land, and holding of John Hanley and company, were dug out, on the 6th of the present month, several graves in which were discovered pieces of plain and glazed earthen urns and also a quantity of decayed jaw-bones and teeth. At the head of one of these ancient graves stands a headstone nearly 6 feet long, 5 feet broad and 12 to 18 inches thick; about half its length was absorbed in earth.

In the adjoining farm have been found within the last 3 years graves of the above description and containing urns, decayed bones and other antiques, here sketched. [3 drawings]: The annexed seems to be a horn amulet; the annexed is a steel ring believed to be part of a coat of mail; this small ring is of brass and was found with the steel ring. Informants Hugh Catherwood and others. 6th June 1839.

In the last-mentioned farm, and about 2 feet beneath the surface of an ancient grave, were found, the present month, an earthen urn, to one side of which was attached a handle of crockery also. Within this urn appears to have stood a smaller but bottomless urn, perhaps to keep apart the more precious part of the bones and ashes they contained. The latter urn was tastefully carved on the outside, but both were broken in quarrying out a hard pavement which covered them. The handle of the larger urn is now in the possession of Mr Alexander Johns, banker, Carrickfergus, and a piece of the smaller urn is in the possession of Samuel McSkimin.

In the above farm and site of an ancient burial ground are almost daily dug out, in clearing off old graves and parcels of stones, quantities of human bones, broken urns and sundry other antiques. Informants John Hanley and others, 17th June 1839.

Druid's Altar and Cup

In West Division and holding of William Hanley, and near the base of the Knockagh hill, there stands a large stone resting on smaller stones beneath, and supposed to have been a druid's altar. This stone stands perpendicular at the south east side of a rocky hill and stands 5 feet 10 inches high, 4 feet broad and 3 and a half feet thick, and average 3 and a half feet square on the top, but the base or lower end much smaller. It seems to have been artificially placed in its present berth for the above or some other purpose.

[Insert query: How does this altar or grave bear by the other; how far is it from it; and how far is it from the burial ground]? [Answer] The within altar stands about 4 furlongs north east of the former altar and about a like distance north of the old burial ground. The summit or top of this altar has, by its natural shape, a slope or inclination to the west in its present position.

Here were found, 1836, a stone cup much resembling a ladle. It was of whinstone, circular shape, about 5 inches in diameter and 2 and a half inches in depth, and had a handle between 1 and 2 inches long with a hole drilled through the upper end to accommodate a cord by which it might be suspended. The surface of the vessel was carved outside and inside to some extent and is supposed to have been used in some of the druidical rites, but it has been lately lost by children. Informants Robert Boyd, Hugh Catherwood and others. 17th June 1839.

Skeletons

Tradition states that in putting a new roof on the tower or keep of the castle, 1793 or 1803, there was discovered, in a niche or recess at the base of the old roof in one of the main walls, a human skeleton. The cause of its being there deposited is not known, but it has been again closed up in the bowels of the wall.

In removing some nuisance of earth and stones from within the inner yard, commonly called the magazine yard, 1803, there was discovered at some depth beneath the surface a quantity of every description of human bones. Informants Samuel McSkimin, the chief gunner and others, 25th July 1839.

Gallows Loom

One of the ancient gallows condemned and taken down in 1710, and being chiefly of good oak timbers, was purchased by a person who changed it into a linen loom. This loom was for many subsequent years known in Carrickfergus as the gallows loom. The gallows here alluded to stood on the Gallows Green, about half a mile west of the town of Carrickfergus.

West Gate

The West Gate, opening on the Irish Quarter, though destroyed many years back, is still, on every Christmas Eve, closed up by carts, cars and other timbers; this in commemoration of some ancient event unknown to the present generation, but supposed to be a design of obstructing any attempt of ingress to the town by the Roman Catholics who congregate at midnight mass on the above anniversary of the birth of Our Saviour; or perhaps the expulsion of nuns or friars from their ancient abbey in the town. The other 3 gates are said by a few of the inhabitants to have been also closed, but the West Gate seem the principal. Information from Samuel McSkimin, James Stannus and others, 26th July 1839.

Standing Stone

The 3 large stones at present lying at the north east base of Slieve True, and locally called the Three Brothers, were standing perpendicular within memory.

Brass Cup

The brass cup sketched beneath [drawing] was found near the base of the Knockagh, and under a large stone contiguous to one of the supposed druid's altars alluded to on preceding Fair Sheets. It had 2 handles, with a circular hole in each, but one of the handles has been broken subsequent to its being discovered. Its shape is nearly circular, 1 and three-quarter inches in diameter in the extreme and 1 inch in diameter inside, and nearly half an inch in depth. The margin round the edge or mouth of the vessel, is a quarter of an inch broad. The mark in the centre of sketch shows some impression inside the bottom of the cup; in the centre of the bottom on the outside is also a small circular swelling about the size of the head of a small brass nail. The cup was varnished or painted a green colour. It is still extant and in possession of the finder, James Boyd, a farmer at the Knockagh. 5th August 1839.

Copper Antique

The ancient copper article, shown in full size and shape beneath [drawing], was found about 4 feet beneath the surface, near the site of Great Patrick. The latter was a beautiful and large stone cross that formerly stood about the centre of the town. This antique was dug out of a peat subsoil which, as above mentioned, stands about 4 feet beneath a clay and sand surface. Its use can scarcely be conjectured by any of the local inhabitants, but it is thought by some to have been some top appendage of an ecclesiastical vessel. It was on one side ornamented by carving and gilding, but now much defaced. The top strap embraced a handle, which seems to have rotted away. Informants James Stannus and others, 15th August 1839.

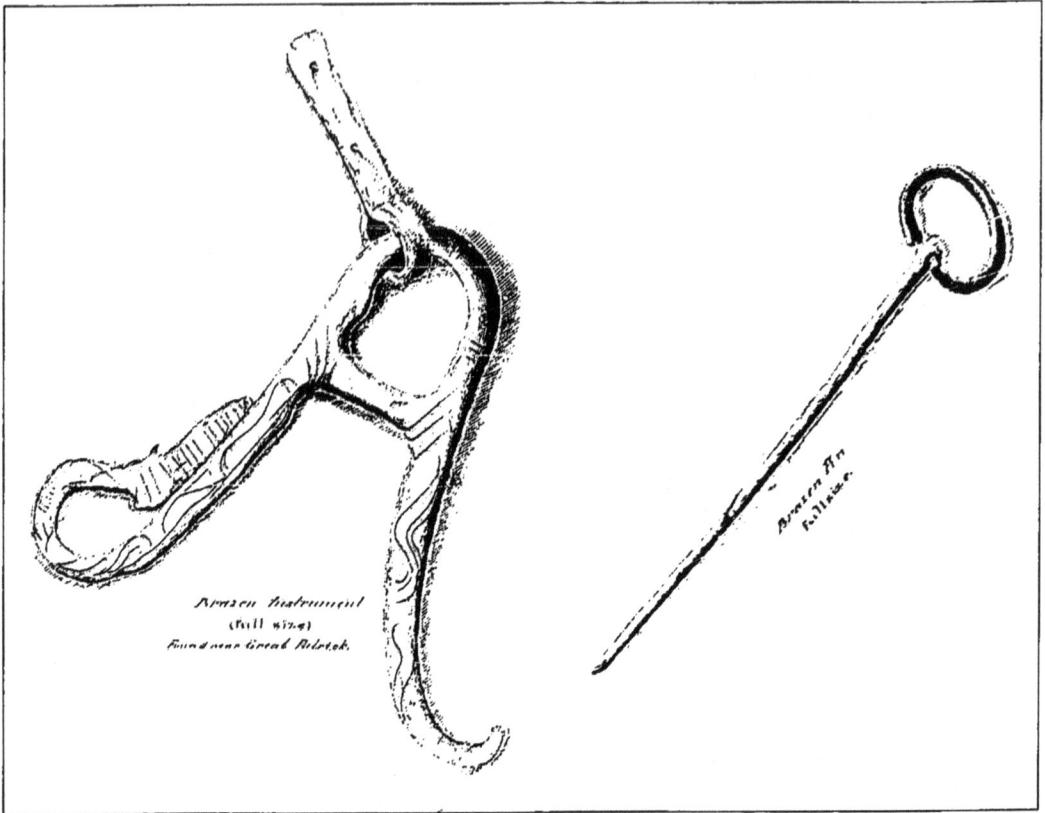

Discoveries from Carrickfergus.

Querns and Spurs

Several quern stones are also found from time to time in sinking foundations in the town. One of these lately found is at present in the possession of John Smyth, North Street, Carrickfergus.

Brass spurs, of rather unusual construction, have been also discovered considerably beneath the surface in the town and suburbs. One of these lately found is at present in the possession of Mr Johns, banker, High Street, Carrickfergus.

Castle

The battery in front of the officers' quarters in the castle yard, town of Carrickfergus, is 150 feet in length by an average of 22 feet in width. The lower storey or bottom of the half-moons in the castle yard is not built but filled up in the interior. The west range of barracks in the castle yard is 119 feet in length by 20 feet in width on the outside; the east barrack, or officers' quarters, 102 feet in length by 19 and a half feet in width on the outside also. These barracks are all 2-storeys high and slated.

SOCIAL ECONOMY

Deserters in Gaol, 1830-1

The following tables will shew the number, names and ages of soldier deserters lodged in the gaol of the county of Antrim, situated at Carrickfergus, from September 1830 to August 1839, specifying the number within each year, the period of imprisonment of each person, together with the sum allowed or drawn for his support, also the date on which each was imprisoned.

1830, 27th September: Sampson Cadman, age 26, confined 14 days, 7s drawn for his support.

27th December: James Thompson, 18, 13 days, 6s 6d drawn;

Total drawn 13s 6d.

1831, 19th February: John Williamson, 24, 29 days, 14s 6d drawn.

10th April: Thomas Harden, 27, 15 days, 7s 6d drawn.

26th April: James Reid, 32, 11 days, 5s 6d drawn.

31st May: James Sterling, 25, 13 days, 6s 6d drawn.

16th June: James Anderson, 27, 18 days, 9s drawn.

28th June: Bernard Coyle, 34, 30 days, 15s drawn.

28th September: William Jones, 26, 24 days, 12s drawn.

11th October: James Jamison, 18, 20 days, 10s drawn.

12th November, William Savage, 20, 20 days, 10s drawn.

19th December, Robert Boyd, 36, 17 days, 8s 6d drawn.

Total drawn 4 pounds 18s 6d.

Deserters in 1832

11th January: Richard Wilkins, 22, 12 days, 6s drawn.

3rd March: Hugh McAuley, 22, 11 days, 5s 6d drawn.

20th March: John Oakly, 28, 13 days, 6s 6d drawn.

25th April: Daniel McClure, 29, 7 days, 3s 6d drawn.

2nd May: Robert Dyes, 20, 10 days, 5s drawn.

24th July: George Williamson, 28, 65 days, 1 pound 12s 6d drawn.

14th August: William Devlin, 26, 13 days, 6s 6d drawn.

14th September: George Walker, 24, 14 days, 7s drawn.

26th October, Thomas Goss, 21, 15 days, 7s 6d drawn.

12th November, Duncan McCaw, 28, 16 days, 8s drawn.

13th December, William McClure, 28, 15 days, 7s 6d drawn.

15th December, Joseph Taylor, 28, 28 days, 14s drawn.

Total drawn 5 pounds 7s 6d.

Deserters in 1833

25th January: James Brander, 25, 10 days, 5s drawn.

6th February: James Anderson, 28, 19 days, 9s 6d drawn.

26th February: Robert Harmon, 27, 18 days, 9s drawn.

16th March: Thomas Fisher, 22, 11 days, 5s 6d drawn; George Evans, 22, 11 days, 5s 6d drawn.

20th March: John Payne, 21, 7 days, 3s 6d drawn; Richard Barber, 27, 7 days, 3s 6d drawn; William Bullers, 26, 7 days, 3s 6d drawn.

30th March: William Ferguson, 33, 33 days, 16s 6d drawn.

25th April: Saunders Gauley, 19, 11 days, 5s 6d drawn.

5th April: John Chickel, 34, 182 days, 1 pound 11s drawn.

5th August: James McNally, 18, 18 days, 9s drawn.

7th August: Alexander Davison, 22, 11 days, 5s 6d drawn.

12th November: James Rafferty, 20, 42 days, 1 pound 1s drawn.

29th November: Malcom McGregor, 20, 36 days, 18s drawn.

7th December: Francis Coldroy, 26, 65 days, 12s 6d drawn.

Total drawn 12 pounds 4s.

Deserters in 1834

1st January: John O'Brien, 27, 9 days, 4s 6d drawn.

4th March: James Gauge, 21, 10 days, 5s drawn.

21st March: Alexander Murphy, 30, 29 days, 14s 6d drawn.

22nd March: Henry Mesterfee, 23, 20 days, 10s drawn.

8th May: Robert McKevell, 22, 86 days, 2 pounds 3s drawn.

19th May: Samuel Anderson, 27, 9 days, 4s 6d drawn.

15th July: Thomas Anderson, 27, 76 days, 1 pound 18s drawn.

18th July: Hugh Whiteside, 27, 17 days, 8s 6d drawn.

19th July: John McCarthy, 36, 59 days, 1 pound 9s 6d drawn.

24th July: Archibald Purvis, 24, 13 days, 6s 6d drawn; Hugh Price, 20, 41 days, 1 pound 6d drawn; Charles McAnulty, 23, 29 days, 14s 6d drawn.

29th July: Peter McLenden, 19, 29 days, 14s 6d drawn; Thomas Forrester, 24, 29 days, 14s 6d drawn.

31st July: John Nowlan, 34, 20 days, 10s drawn.

5th August: Angus McEntosh, 21, 41 days, 1 pound 6d drawn.

6th August: James Greeny, 27, 10 days, 5s drawn.

29th August: William Winn, 22, 26 days, 13s drawn.

18th September: Daniel McGuigan, 9, 11 days, 5s 6d drawn.

4th October: John Connor, 22, 9 days, 4s 6d drawn.

12th November: Peter McGrier, 21, 12 days, 6s drawn.

13th November: Robert Lendray, 21, 16 days, 8s drawn.

5th December: James Neilis, 21, 25 and a half days, 12s 9d drawn.

8th December: William Nichols, 21, 21 and a half days, 10s 9d drawn.

Total drawn 16 pounds 4s.

Deserters in 1835

2nd March: James McLaughlin, 20, 11 days, 5s 6d drawn.

11th March: James McCarthy, 34, 12 days, 6s drawn.

30th March: James Blaney, 19, 8 days, 4s drawn.

23rd April: James Parker, 30, 14 days, 7s drawn.

25th April: Thomas Briggs, 29, 25 days, 12s 6d drawn.

10th June: Richard McCenlas, 20, Roman Catholic, 15 and a half days, 7s 9d drawn 4th July: James Errol, 38, Presbyterian, 14 days, 7s drawn.

8th August: John Dyer, 21, Roman Catholic, 14 days, 7s drawn.

31st August: George Barr, 23, Established Church, 14 and half days, 7s 3d drawn.

1st September: John Kennedy, 19, Presbyterian, 25 days, 12s 6d drawn.

22nd July: Alexander Spence, 30, Presbyterian, 48 days, 1 pound 4s drawn.

7th October: James Cook, 21, Roman Catholic, 12 days, 6s drawn.

12th November: George Lardsay, 18, Established Church, 11 and a half days, 5s 9d drawn.

12th November: Robert Davison, 21, Presbyterian, 18 and a half days, 9s 3d drawn; William Stewart, 24, Presbyterian, 18 and a half days, 9s 3d drawn; Hugh McClean, 27, Presbyterian, 18 and a half days, 9s 3d drawn.

21st November: James Lowe, 18, Presbyterian, 11 and a half days, 5s 9d drawn.

Total drawn 7 pounds 5s 9d.

Deserters in 1836

27th January: Alexander Cameron, 21, Presbyterian, 13 and a half days, 6s 9d drawn.

12th February: John Maginnis, Roman Catholic, 26, 18 and a half days, 6s 9d drawn.

22nd February: James Morrison, Presbyterian, 20, 12 days, 6s drawn.

28th March: John Moran, 34, Roman Catholic, 34 and half days, 17s 3d drawn.

14th July: Bernard Hoy, 17, Roman Catholic, 15 days, 7s 6d drawn; Samuel Armour, 19, Presbyterian, 15 days, 7s 6d drawn.

12th October: James Kaine, 22, Roman Catholic, 14 days, 7s drawn.

10th November: James Wright, 22, Established Church, 19 days, 9s 6d drawn.

5th December: Thomas Baxter, 21, Established Church, 22 days, 11s drawn.

7th December: James Nelson, 22, Presbyterian, 12 days, 6s drawn.

Total drawn 4 pounds 7s 9d.

Deserters in 1837

8th February: William Crick, 28, Established Church, 12 days, 6s drawn.

14th February: Andrew Scott, 16, Established Church, 13 days, 6s 6d drawn; John Ward, 24, Established Church, 13 days, 6s 6d drawn.

15th February: George Ross, 27, Established Church, 23 days, 11s 6d drawn; John Nicholson, 21, Established Church, 23 days, 11s 6d drawn.

23rd February: James White, 27, Established Church, 12 days, 6s drawn.

28th February: Samuel Freeman, 23, Established Church, 13 days, 6s 6d drawn.

13th April: John Bradley, 21, Roman Catholic, 12 days, 6s drawn.

30th May: John Tally, 24, Roman Catholic, 12 days, 6s drawn.

8th June: John McKay, 16, Established Church, 12 days, 6s drawn.

14th July: Peter Bretherton, 20, Roman Catholic, 10 days, 5s drawn.

7th August: Hugh Gilmore, 18, Roman Catholic, 10 days, 5s drawn.

12th August: Thomas Walsh, 34, Presbyterian, 10 days, 5s drawn.

16th August: Charles Edwards, 20, Established Church, 12 days, 6s drawn.

21st August: Jonas Bamborough, 23, Established Church, 12 days, 6s drawn.

28th August: James Wilkins, 28, Established Church, 28 days, 5s drawn.

8th September: John Haughey, 31, Roman Catholic, 10 days, 5s drawn.

21st September: Charles Murray, 23, Roman Catholic, 18 days, 9s drawn.

29th September: William Harley, 24, Established Church, 10 days, 5s drawn.

25th November: William Johnston, 28, Established Church, 9 days, 4s 6d drawn.

23rd December: Samuel Sloan, 23, Presbyterian, 13 days, 6s 6d drawn.

Total drawn 1 pound 10s.

Deserters in 1838

16th February: Mitchell Taylor, 27, Presbyterian, 15 days, 7s 6d drawn; William O'Hara, 22, Presbyterian, 15 days, 7s 6d drawn; Michael Bain, 29, Presbyterian, 15 days, 7s 6d drawn.

21st February: Hugh Jameson, 24, Established Church, 13 days, 6s 6d drawn.

26th April: John Grant, 22, Roman Catholic, 18 days, 9s drawn.

27th March: John Smyth, 24, Established Church, 49 and a half days, 1 pound 4s 9d.

9th May: Thomas Stone, 25, Established Church, 22 days, 11s drawn; Ralph Wirrow, 25, Established Church, 26 days, 13s drawn.

16th May: James Thompson, 19, Presbyterian, 17 days, 8s 6d drawn.

6th June: William Anderson, 22, Established Church, 10 days, 5s drawn; John Howe, 22, Established Church, 10 days, 5s drawn.

3rd July: James Stevens, 21, Established Church, 14 days, 7s drawn; William Burke, 24, Roman Catholic, 20 days, 10s drawn.

21st July: John Vann, 19, Established Church, 20 days, 10s drawn.

31st July: Samuel Baxter, 20, Established Church, 20 days, 10s drawn.

9th August: Thomas Phillips, 19, Presbyterian, 11 days, 5s 6d drawn.

15th August: William Walsh, 21, Roman Catholic, 13 days, 6s 6d drawn.

17th August: Hugh Moore, 23, Established Church, 11 days, 5s 6d drawn.

4th September: Richard Hickson, 30, Established Church, 10 days, 5s drawn.

12th December: Daniel Scullion, 19, Roman Catholic, 15 days, 7s 6d drawn.

19th December: James Johnston, 21, Established Church, 19 days, 9s 6d drawn.

20th December: Thomas Forde, 28, Established Church, 26 days, 13s drawn.

25th December: Thomas Campbell, 25, Roman Catholic, 13 days, 6s 6d drawn.

Total drawn 10 pounds 1s 3d.

Deserters in 1839

8th January: William Graham, 21, Presbyterian, 13 days, 6s 6d drawn.

15th January: James Ramsay, 21, Established Church, 20 days, 10s drawn.

From 19th December 1838 to 11th February 1839: William McChesney, 19, Roman Catholic, 54 days, 1 pound 7s drawn.

16th January: John Mooney, 20, Presbyterian, 27 days, 13s 6d drawn.

9th February: Edward McCreavey, 28, Presbyterian, 13 days, 6s 6d drawn.

14th February: George Saunders, 20, Established Church, 11 days, 5s 6d drawn.

12th March: Anthony McGinty, 25, Roman Catholic, 13 days, 6s 6d drawn.

23rd March: Robert Dunlop, 22, Presbyterian, 16 days, 8s drawn.

18th June: Robert Darragh, 22, Roman Catholic, 14 days, 7s drawn.

9th July: James Weir, 20, Presbyterian, 15 days, 7s 6d drawn.

13th July: Charles Dougherty, 21, Roman Catholic, 11 days, 5s 6d drawn.

23rd July: George Dennis, 18, Established Church, 14 days, 7s drawn.

29th July: Charles Connor, 19, Established Church, 19 days, 9s 6d drawn.

1st August: Robert McQuillan, 21, Roman Catholic, 11 days, 5s 6d drawn.

7th August: James Magill, 18, Established Church, 10 days, 5s drawn.

Total drawn 6 pounds 10s 6d.

The soldier deserters imprisoned have access to the gaol course of education that other prisoners have, but there is no goal register kept of their state of education, like that of the other prisoners.

Total number imprisoned, for which subsistence was drawn, 150; total sum drawn for the subsistence of the above 74 pounds 7s 3d; imprisoned at different periods during the above years and subsequently discharged by government, and during their confinement were supported at the expense of the county, 8 deserters.

Information obtained from the governor and deputy governor of the gaol and also extracted from the gaol register. [Signed] Thomas Fagan, 21st to 24th October 1839.

www.ingramcontent.com/pod-product-compliance
Lightning Source LLC
Chambersburg PA
CBHW080249030426
42334CB00023BA/2748